"Psychological warfare methods were deployed to manage public responses to the assassinations of my uncle and father. In the modern digital world, PsyWar is becoming more and more sophisticated and successful in manipulating populations, groups, and individuals, and is now being widely deployed on Western nation citizens by their governments. This book is a manual on how to recognize and fight the effects of these methods and technologies that strive to control all information, thought, feelings, and speech."

—**Robert F. Kennedy Jr.**

"Very few people have learned more in the past five years than Robert and Jill Malone—or been braver in telling the rest of us about it. The result is this remarkable book."

—**Tucker Carlson**

"Dr. Robert Malone went from being a respected scientist to a pariah in the eyes of the establishment. All he did was to question the international COVID consensus. If we believe in liberty and freedom, then this book matters."

—**Nigel Farage, Member of Parliament and Leader of the Reform UK Party**

"A compelling must-read! Warfare, power, and free speech converge in the covert battlegrounds of *PsyWar*. Robert and Jill masterfully tell the story at the heart of America's decline, starkly warning of a future where our hard-fought freedoms and democratic values hang in the balance. The book sheds light on a global PsyWar strategy involving seen and unseen digital warriors and forces at play amidst the complexity and nonlinearity of the digital battleground. It exposes how our own government engages in PsyWar against its citizens—in collaboration with global powers, social media titans, big tech, pharma, and more! This collusion represents an unprecedented power grab and a stark threat to societal integrity. *PsyWar* delves into the true nature of a 'digital panopticon,' a looming surveillance state poised to control every aspect of our lives. This meticulously researched work forewarns a future where democratic values, free speech and moral principles are endangered unless history's lessons are heeded. This book exposes these truths with undeniable clarity, essential for anyone concerned about our society's trajectory. As Robert and Jill conclude, '. . . we must insist on freedom, dammit.' Bravo!"

—**Crisanna Shackelford, PhD**

"Dr. Robert Malone's contributions to the shift in America's consciousness during the COVID-19 pandemic, away from the scientific lies and obfuscation that beset us and back toward objective data and important scientific insights, may never be fully appreciated, but the world would look different today were it not for his efforts. PsyWar extends that legacy by serving as an incisive resource for anyone who wants to learn more about the underside of governmental and organizational workings that aim to control human thought, undermine human sovereignty, and rob us of our God-given power—power that is rooted in our connection with the universe and one another. These forces, persistent as they may be, will fail and will fall. Dr. Malone's book provides tools to help us fortify our minds against their assault. And those readers who also invest in ridding their bodies of the stress that contributes to our susceptibility to manipulation will find themselves forever free of these instruments of human enslavement."

—**Dr. Joseph Ladapo, author of** *Transcend Fear: A Blueprint for Mindful Leadership in Public Health*; **professor at University of Florida College of Medicine; and Surgeon General of Florida**

"Knowing how and why they do it is crucial for anyone who seeks the truth. This isn't a book, it is essential armor for the dark times we are currently in."

—**Hon. Andrew Bridgen, former Member of Parliament, United Kingdom**

"Every government in world history has used fear and misinformation to control the citizens. Malone's book illuminates the evolving strategies so clearly that readers will intuitively sense the undeniable truth."

—**Gavin de Becker, bestselling author of** *The Gift of Fear*

"During the COVID-19 debacle, it is a proven fact that Americans were lied to by a handful of dysfunctional senior federal health bureaucrats who ignored their oaths, silenced dissent, stifled freedom of speech, and dismissed early drug treatments in favor of a mass mRNA "pseudo-vaccine" program. While this never prevented viral infection or halted pandemic progression, it did garner billions of dollars for the participating drug companies.

Marching in lockstep, every American's right to "Freedom of Speech," so fundamentally engrained in our constitutional Bill of Rights, was made a mockery. For physicians, the Freedom of Speech to speak out against the dysfunctional COVID response was twisted into a recognized punishable offense in some states.

As a result, compassionate American medicine, accurate medical research, and the inviolate concept of *patient informed consent* was effectively destroyed in the United States. Many of our once esteemed national medical associations and colleges, have become nothing more than conduits of "misinformation" espoused by the federal health agencies who now are desperately trying to minimize the injuries and deaths caused by an ill-advised and ineffective mass mRNA vaccination campaign.

How did we arrive here and why has this gone unchallenged? The controversial new book *PsyWar* is a highly provocative deep dive, which takes the reader through a step-by-step account of how modern communications technology and social media has now been coupled to a biased corporate mass media monopoly. This has created a nightmare of propaganda and censorship that has suppressed the truth of the COVID-19 debacle.

The book outlines the current heroic David/Goliath fight still underway by true physicians, against a small but powerful group of unconstitutionally motivated federal bureaucrats. It is a continuing fight, largely hidden from the American public.

*PsyWar* is a carefully referenced book with numerous examples that support the authors' contention that modern cognitive and psychological warfare tools have been employed by the US government as part of a mass formation psychological strategy to mold American opinion. It describes the various tactics used by global governments who now clearly define what is mis-, dis-, and mal-information in the world. It presents often shocking and still controversial histories starting with the 1964 Warren Report, to illustrate the origin of this information control and how modern social media serves as an advocacy conduit used to minimize any set of popular beliefs that the government finds inconvenient.

This book is thought-provoking reading for all Americans who believe that Freedom of Speech is vital for the continuance of our Republic."

**—Dr. Steven Hatfill, pathologist and biological weapons expert,
and author of *Three Seconds Until Midnight***

"In *PsyWar*, the Doctors Malone perform a brilliant autopsy on our diseased and dying intelligence community. From their first efforts at election meddling in Italy after the Second World War through our current 2024 election, the authors detail the shadowy influence of our creeping intelligence state. Perhaps it is inevitable that any nation that seeks to be an empire abroad cannot long remain a democracy at home. Like Alexander Solzhenitsyn going after the Soviet Union, the Malones attack the imperial administrative state with the vengeance of an Old Testament prophet. The situation is perilous, but hope remains, especially if we arm ourselves with knowledge and have the courage to speak without fear."

**—Kent Heckenlively, JD,** *New York Times* **bestselling author of** *Plague of Corruption,* **The King of Italy, and** *Twilight of the Shadow Government*

# PsyWar

# PsyWar

## ENFORCING THE NEW WORLD ORDER

**ROBERT W. MALONE, MD, MS**

**JILL G. MALONE, PhD**

FOREWORD BY GENERAL MICHAEL FLYNN

Skyhorse Publishing

Skyhorse Publishing books may be purchased in bulk at special discounts for sales promotion, corporate gifts, fund-raising, or educational purposes. Special editions can also be created to specifications. For details, contact the Special Sales Department, Skyhorse Publishing, 307 West 36th Street, 11th Floor, New York, NY 10018 or info@skyhorsepublishing.com.

Skyhorse® and Skyhorse Publishing® are registered trademarks of Skyhorse Publishing, Inc.®, a Delaware corporation.

Visit our website at www.skyhorsepublishing.com.

Please follow our publisher Tony Lyons on Instagram @tonylyonsisuncertain.

10 9 8 7 6 5 4 3 2 1

Library of Congress Cataloging-in-Publication Data is available on file.

Hardcover ISBN: 978-1-5107-8295-2
eBook ISBN: 978-1-5107-8299-0

Cover design by Anita Hasbury-Snogles, modified from an image supplied by marshall on Wallpapers.com

Printed in the United States of America

By means of ever more effective methods of mind manipulation, the democracies will change their nature; the quaint old forms . . . elections, parliaments, supreme courts and all the rest . . . will remain.

The underlying substance will be a new kind of Totalitarianism. All the traditional names, all the hallowed slogans will remain exactly like they were in the good old days. Democracy & freedom will be the theme of every broadcast & editorial. Meanwhile, the ruling oligarchy and its highly trained elite will quietly run the show as they see fit.

—Aldous Huxley, 1962

# Contents

# FOREWORD
## by General Michael Flynn

The future soldier is one adept at functioning across all spectrums of combat operations. One of these future soldier formations is a United Kingdom psychological operations brigade (the famous 77th BDE) whose history dates to the Great War (WWI). The reformation of the 77th is a tell for many things happening in societies around the world. A unit that transformed itself from a brilliant fighting conventional force during the Great War to a counter-guerrilla force fighting the Japanese along the brutal Burma Road campaigns during WWII, now is reestablished to provide security assistance to the British military. What that "security assistance" represents is a readiness for a new form of warfare and a new form of soldier (fifth-generation warfare with a trained and ready fifth-generation warrior).

You might ask why spend so much time discussing a British army formation? As warfare is transforming, the world is transforming. The blending of this transformation has become far more difficult to discern and even more challenging to understand. If sophisticated armies are recreating themselves for a new type of warfare, regular citizens need do the same. One thing I've learned about warfare is that it isn't fair and is not meant to be. In the future, all citizens must not simply rely on their militaries to understand and then defeat their adversaries. Every citizen now has a responsibility to understand the information and intelligence environments we live within. A battlefield is not only a physical game, most of the time, it is a mental game and one in which every single citizen must now prepare for.

Fifth-generation warfare is a blending of hybrid, irregular, and unrestricted capabilities and ideas and runs through the bloodstream of every society, nation-state, non-nation-state, and even inside the world of global corporations and globalist institutions.

All of us now tuning in to these tectonic and recent shifts in the global landscape are starting to realize that much of what we knew to be true is not. There is a purpose-driven intentionality that powers much of this. A globalist conversation that has proceeded for decades and is now coming into its own. This effort is led by real people with real ideas and even more important real resources.

In this seminal read (vital really), Dr. Robert Malone outlines the five W's (who, what, when, where, and why) but also adds the "how" they are trying to achieve their goals and objectives. What I found both brilliant and enlightening in this magnificent manuscript, unlike many other books of this nature and category, Dr. Malone addresses the "how to defeat" these fifth-generation warfare threats humanity faces. They are real, and they are intent on changing the very nature of humanity.

We can no longer simply rely on the age-old conventional methods when facing future threats. Like the 77th, as citizens, we must also be transformative. I applaud every aspect of this book as I applaud the famous 77th Brigade. Each shows us a path of understanding the challenges that come with transforming; a clear path of achieving the means and steps by which we can take as citizens, never mind just those soldier warriors in uniform. And for all readers who care about the future of mankind, you'll discover during your journey through the following pages, a whole set of new ideas that will help you better understand and operate as a citizen in a completely transformed world. As the very eloquent Benjamin Franklin stated, "By failing to prepare, you are preparing to fail." To better prepare, read this book and win.

# INTRODUCTION

> All censorships exist to prevent anyone from challenging current conceptions and existing institutions. All progress is initiated by challenging current conceptions, and executed by supplanting existing institutions. Consequently, the first condition of progress is the removal of censorship.
>
> —George Bernard Shaw[1]

Free speech is the most pragmatic tool we have for ascertaining truth. Only by examining all sides of an issue can the truth be chiseled out like a statue out of marble. But the underlying reality is that there can be many truths; we each have our own experiences, values, mores, and life. That is the beauty and wonder of being an individual. There can be no free speech without free and open access to ideas, knowledge, truths, and untruths. Without free speech, we are little more than slaves.

We must defend all speech—whether untrue, hateful, or intolerable, as that is the only way to protect our rights and abilities to understand the world. As soon as free speech is restricted, that restriction will be used to sway public opinion. As soon as one person can be defined as a heretic for uttering words, then soon everyone opposing the "officially approved" side of an issue will be labeled as a heretic. The next logical step will be for the state to define acts of heresy as criminal offenses. As soon as governments and those in power can sway public opinion by restricting free speech, democracy and even our republic of United States will be lost.

To illustrate how the US government has narrowed the definition of free speech, consider two recent examples. In February 2024, ex-Fox News and ex-CBS reporter Catherine Herridge was held in contempt for refusing to reveal her sources to US District Court Judge Christopher Cooper concerning reporting relating to a Chinese American scientist, Yanping Chen. Herridge had written a series of stories for Fox News in 2017 about Chen's Chinese military connections and whether a school she founded was being used to help the Chinese government obtain information on American service members via statements the scientist made on immigration forms related to work on a Chinese astronaut program. For which statements the FBI had already been investigating her. Both CBS News and Fox News issued separate statements condemning the ruling and its "deeply chilling" effects on the First Amendment.[2] This disturbing trend continued when the FBI under the Biden administration arrested Steve Baker, a journalist who was doing his job by reporting on the supposed "insurrection" by Trump supporters during the January 6, 2021, protest events.[3]

Our nation's commitment to free speech has faltered. The Western world's commitment to free speech has faltered. Worse than faltered, it has become de rigueur for governments and media corporations to censor private citizens, organizations, and even politicians. For governments to lie, spin stories, and propagate propaganda.

Free speech is being restricted in several ways. The most obvious is censorship, which is the tip of the iceberg. PsyWar is when a government or other organization coordinates and directs the deployment of propaganda, censorship, and psychological operations (psyops) tools and weapons in campaigns designed to manipulate public opinion. The United States government is now routinely waging PsyWar against US citizens.

Now is a time when America needs hope. But more than hope, we need to restore our Constitution and Bill of Rights as the foundational documents of our Republic. These documents support and protect our personal sovereignty and are at the core of our fundamental rights as Americans. We must work to make this country great again by restoring our commitment to these foundational principles and ethics.

All of us who are concerned about government-sponsored deployment of psychological warfare, censorship, and propaganda need to pick up the oars and row this boat called the *US government* to freedom once again. This is no time for slackers.

Make your own personal sovereignty a reality by choosing your words and behaviors carefully, accepting personal responsibility for all that you do, have been, and are, and taking action one well-considered step at a time. Beginning with a commitment to understand the nature, tactics, and strategies being used for modern PsyWar.

# PART I
# THE STATE OF THE UNION

*A brief overview of how the US government has been manipulating the minds of the American people since the mid-twentieth century using propaganda and censorship is in order. These psyops techniques have chipped away at the fundamental rights that have created a free and prosperous nation.*

*Understanding what propaganda is, the types of propaganda, and who uses it is the first step to identifying it and stopping its undue influence. It is also important to examine psyops, which is the suite of strategies, tactics, and technologies involved in how ideas and thoughts of everyday Americans are being manipulated by governments, foreign actors, and organizations. The current heavy usage of propaganda, censorship, and algorithmic social media controls means that people are often unable to form independent opinions and are readily influenced to conform in thought and deed to a desired end point. This can change the outcome of elections. Even more nefarious is the role of the CIA, FBI, and the intelligence community in using psyops and psychological bioterrorism against the American people.*

***Psychological bioterrorism*** *is the use of fear about a disease to manipulate individuals or populations by governments and other organizations, including pharma, academia, and a variety of nongovernmental organizations. Although the fear of infectious disease is an obvious example, it is not the only way psychological bioterrorism is used. Psychological bioterrorism is one method to exert global operational influence and facilitate the manipulation of the general population. Deployment of this strategic approach is a component of the larger domain*

1

*of modern fifth-generation warfare; since psychological bioterrorism operates on both conscious as well as subconscious levels, this form of mental manipulation is an example of both PsyWar (targeting the conscious mind) as well as cognitive warfare (targeting the subconscious).*

*The government has come to believe that scientism is a formula for good governance. Scientism is the belief that science and the scientific method are the best or only way to render truth about the world and reality. But the underlying real truth is that using scientism to determine "truth" has all the hallmarks of a religion. Hence, bureaucrats and government officials act to suppress other forms of religious beliefs, as well as any scientists or medical health professionals who might question the official "scientism," otherwise known as "The Science" narrative. This makes people who hold religious beliefs, as well as dissident scientists and medical professionals, heretics in the eyes of the law. More extreme views which support an approved narrative are rewarded as the narrative becomes fixed on one set of beliefs, while those expressing doubt, nuance, or moderation are punished. Over the past four years of the COVIDcrisis, the government has learned how to openly censor and smear people who oppose the prevailing scientific narratives using advanced methods. These include artificial intelligence, operational integration with corporate and social media, and a wide range of web crawlers, bots, troll farms, gang stalking methods, and computational algorithms.*

*The "Congressional Judiciary and the Select Subcommittee on the Weaponization of the Federal Government US House of Representatives interim report of the weaponization of 'Disinformation' Pseudo-Experts and Bureaucrats" documents how the federal government partnered with universities and Astroturf organizations to censor Americans. This report outlines how the government has worked to censor and smear citizens and representatives of Congress alike. The details of that report include information on how the Cybersecurity and Infrastructure Security Agency (CISA), a component of the United States Department of Homeland Security (DHS), working with Astroturf organizations and intelligence community cutouts, smeared and censored one of the authors of this book (Dr. Robert Malone). They did this through the use of fifth-generation warfare tactics developed for offshore combat against terrorist groups and insurgencies.*

# CHAPTER 1
# The Abbreviated History of Modern American PsyWar

> We are already witnessing another shaping operation to influence the outcome of the 2024 election. This time it is with the false claim that if one side wins, it'll be the end of democracy. This is a lie contrived to ensure a particular outcome and to sabotage free speech.
>
> —Lara Logan, journalist[1]

The government's willingness to deploy modern cognitive and psychological warfare tools and technologies against their own citizenry, in combination with collusion and coercion using the power of modern big information technology, is an evil the world has never known before.

Freedom, sovereignty, personal autonomy, and the individual's rights to succeed in society are important. As is the resistance to the imposition of the logic of Marxism, socialism, and communism by external actors. This is grounded in fundamental American principles codified in our Constitution and Bill of Rights. Also important is the constitutional commitment to self-governance. The social contract that the citizens of this nation-state have with the government through the electoral process. Historically, this has been referred to as a social contract between the ruler and the ruled. We give rights to our government in exchange for our government's commitment to providing security, furthering prosperity, and respecting the people's autonomy, sovereignty, and will.

Over the last four years, many have come to learn that there's a suite of technologies and capabilities that have been developed over decades and can influence everything that we think, feel, hear, and believe. These technologies have been developed and deployed for offshore use, specifically to advance American interests through the US State Department, the Intelligence Community (CIA, etc.), and the Department of Defense. Historically, this suite of capabilities has been outwardly facing. This is generally also true for the Five Eyes intelligence alliance nations of Canada, the UK, Australia, the United States, and New Zealand. These nations have taken the position that it is acceptable to deploy propaganda and dirty tricks to achieve their foreign policy goals in a challenging world, so long as these tools aren't deployed against their own citizens. Or, at least, that is what we have been led to believe.

For example, right after World War II, Italy faced a close pivotal election, and it looked like it might well go to a political party that would bring Italy into the sphere of influence of the USSR—in other words, the Soviet Union. In response, the United States State Department and US intelligence community thought it was justified to intervene using any dirty tricks they could deploy to influence that election to favor a pro-Western outcome.

They formed an alliance with the Italian Mafia, and they succeeded in skewing the election results. Now, was that a good thing or a bad thing? The answer to that question largely depends on your time frame. Over the short term, it yielded the desired outcome. Over the long term, it strengthened the Italian Mafia within Italy and worldwide. Was it ethical? Not in my opinion. Was it good that Italy ended up in a Western sphere and then the European Union instead of in a Soviet sphere of influence? Many believe, "Yeah, that was a relatively good outcome; it could have been worse." But what about the unanticipated long-term consequences, the "blowback"? What if Italy had been allowed free and open elections without external meddling? Would it have still become the politically fragmented, corrupt, Mafia-dominated and failing nation-state of the present?

That pivotal Italian election is one example that has been subsequently used to justify the increased development and deployment of "dirty tricks" capabilities involving psychological manipulation, information manipulation, media manipulation, and cognitive manipulation. And like many things in government, these types of strategies have incrementally evolved into a slippery slope. "Well, it's okay there. Maybe it should be okay here.

Maybe we need to influence this government. We need to overturn that government." And with that incrementalism, foreign nation sovereignty was repeatedly compromised, and the United States was transformed into an imperialist power.

But the truth is that if Italy had voted in that way (pro-USSR) and if they had a strong republic, the ship would eventually have been righted all by itself. It is a strong, stable republic that saves democracies, not outside influences. But that is not how the administrative state in the United States views its global role. They have a very different vision.

For many years, the unwritten consensus of the United States government was that as long as these psyops capabilities remained an outwardly directed tool of foreign affairs and foreign influence, these strategies were acceptable statecraft. Advancing the imperialistic interests of the United States and associated corporations was deemed acceptable as long as it wasn't directed toward American citizens.

That was the agreement that guided the foreign policy positions of both "moderate" Democrats and "moderate" Republicans, otherwise known as the Uniparty. Based on this premise, there was a general consensus on foreign policy and the willingness of the State, DoD, and Intelligence departments to cooperate to influence global affairs.

They used dirty tricks to ensure that foreign governments and their respective stakeholders aligned with American political and economic interests. Then, the internet was developed. As the internet became a mature information ecosystem, there emerged an awareness that modern psychology, monitoring and shaping of emotions, and particularly neurolinguistic programming (NLP), could be integrated with the internet's tools to profoundly influence both election outcomes and fundamental political belief systems.

Over the past two decades, the internet's capabilities have become more sophisticated. Thus, these governmental agencies, along with cooperating nongovernmental organizations (NGOs) and institutes, have adapted to become more adept at using non-kinetic, psychological warfare to control foreign governments, their populations, and their election outcomes.

Suddenly, the United States had an incredible tool that could be used to influence all sorts of political situations, including political movements and elections in the Middle East. The US government could engineer social media tools in cooperation with Big Tech. Facebook was engineered as an intentional social media psychological manipulation weapon from the start. That is how it was built. It was built to create a comprehensive psychological profile of its users. This is part of an amazing database infrastructure that has been created, which aspires to basically know everything about every single person on the globe and to manipulate that information to support a wide range of commercial and political objectives. The fact is that Facebook shares user data with a variety of organizations, governments, and people. This fact became general public knowledge when the story broke that the British company Cambridge Analytica was using data collected on Facebook to influence US elections in 2015.[2]

The Arab Spring was a series of pro-democracy uprisings that swept across several countries in the Arab world starting in late 2010. The United States government deployed Twitter, Facebook, Instagram, and other digital tools, such as cell phone GPS mapping, to facilitate these uprisings and topple foreign governments. The first government to go down was Tunisia. With this new tool kit in hand, the United States had enormous success in overturning regimes throughout the Middle East during this period. It was incredibly powerful, like nothing they had ever seen, and did not require kinetic warfare measures. This worked like greased lightning.

In 2015, a key study was presented and published in a top-tier peer-reviewed journal, which demonstrated that Google could influence elections just by manipulating the information that a viewer sees on an individual basis in a transitory way. Undecided voters could be influenced to swing their votes by 20 percentage points just by how search results were arranged on the front page of Google. These search engine results are ephemeral—appearing briefly before users and then replaced by other information and images. Therefore, they are not traceable. These initial study findings were carefully validated, and the underlying relevant data have only become stronger since then.[3] In fact, the lead author of that study, Dr. Robert Epstein, has gone on to document that Google tampered with US elections during the 2020 election cycle, using just such techniques. They manipulate us and our elections by controlling what you hear, what you think, what you feel, and what you are allowed to discuss. And what's not to like about this technology if you are a political party bent on maintaining control?

The research findings of Robert Epstein and colleagues demonstrate how effective the application of the surveillance capitalism business model has been for manipulating thought and political behavior. In many cases, surveillance capitalism merges with PsyWar tools and technologies to power the modern surveillance state, giving rise to a new form of fascism (public-private partnerships) known as techno-totalitarianism. Leading corporations employing the surveillance capitalism business model include Google and Facebook. Surveillance capitalism has now fused with the science and theory of psychology, marketing, and algorithmic manipulation of online information to give rise to propaganda and censorship capabilities that go far beyond those imagined by the twentieth-century predictions of Aldous Huxley and George Orwell.

---

**Surveillance capitalism** is a novel economic system that emerged in the digital era, characterized by the unilateral claiming of private human experience as free raw material for translation into behavioral data. In this version of capitalism, the prediction and influencing of behavior (political and economic) rather than production of goods and services is the primary product. This economic logic prioritizes the extraction, processing, and trading of personal data to predict and influence human behavior by exploiting those predictions for a variety of economic (marketing) and political objectives.

---

Key features of surveillance capitalism include the following:

1. **One-way mirror operations**: Surveillance capitalists engineer operations to operate in secrecy, hiding their methods and intentions from users, who are unaware of the extent of data collection and analysis.
2. **Instrumentation power**: Surveillance capitalists wield power through the design of systems that cultivate "radical indifference," rendering users oblivious to their observations and manipulations.
3. **Behavioral futures markets**: The extracted data is traded in new markets, enabling companies to bet on users' future behavior, generating immense wealth for surveillance capitalists.

4.  **Collaboration with the state**: Surveillance capitalism often involves partnerships with governments, leveraging favorable laws, policing, and information sharing to entrench its power further.

# Blowback

Around 2016, two things happened that rocked the intelligence world: Brexit and Donald Trump. Suddenly, the State Department, the intelligence community, and the US Department of Defense realized they were confronting a new risk to the post-World War II political and economic structures they had worked so hard to create. The fifth-generation warfare tech and capabilities they'd built for offshore deployment and influence campaigns were suddenly being used in ways that were not to their advantage or in the interest of the policies they sought to promote. The risk was that Europe would fragment with the exit/populist movement, and if Europe fragmented then NATO would fall. Another version of the domino theory that dominated late-twentieth-century realpolitik geopolitical logic. The United States and NATO were suddenly facing the prospect of not only Brexit, but Frexit, Grecxit, et cetera. It looked like the European Union might fragment because of the ability of social media to distribute "populist" messages and disrupt elections. The occult internal US administrative and deep state political alliances (sometimes referred to as "the blob") felt they had to do something. They had to do something in Canada. They had to do something in the UK and the EU. They also had to do something domestically. Suddenly, organizations like the Trusted News Initiative, the Global Alliance for Responsible Media (GARM) agreement, and many other Astroturf fact-checking organizations were formed—and began working on behalf of governmental entities by serving as guardians of information and approved narratives. These were all designed to resist the ability of populist and alternative media to affect significant and abrupt changes within Western governments. A censorship industrial complex was intentionally crafted, comprised of both government-aligned and mercenary branches available for hire, and began aggressively acting to algorithmically promote, patrol, and reinforce the narratives promoted by their employers.

These censorship and propaganda internet tools were advanced through nongovernmental organizations that have shadowy ties to nation-state security agencies and were capitalized by funds from both government and nongovernmental sources because there was a consensus among the core NATO and Five Eyes alliances of Europe, the Pacific theater, and the United States that it was going to be necessary to censor certain organizations and individuals in order to "preserve democracy." That it would be for "the good of all of us." Of course, what makes a stable government "for the people" is not democracy, but rather a constitutional republic. However, that fact is rarely mentioned by those deep state actors who represent the interests of the current hegemony. The concept of "Preserving Democracy" was transformed into just another jingoistic term to be repeated ad nauseum; weaponized against populist movements using modern propaganda methodologies such as neurolinguistic programming.

## What Is Democracy?

The decision by elements of US political leadership that it was going to be necessary "to save democracy" by building and deploying a mercenary censorship-industrial complex against citizens was a turning point for our nation. Of course, this decision was presented as being motivated by the best interests of the citizenry. The leaders and political alliances responsible for this decision define their version of "democracy" as the idea that large established interests, essentially an oligarchy, should be the ones entrusted to define who the acceptable political candidates and positions are, and the rest of us are then allowed to vote within that portfolio. That was and remains their version of "democracy." That is the truth behind the logic which is now being promoted with this talk about "saving democracy." Saving it from whom? Apparently, the answer is that "democracy" must be saved from populist movements that threaten to disrupt the interests and plans of the American oligarchy. In order to "save democracy," administrative and deep state actors, including prominent advocates such as former President Barack Obama, decided that the United States had to deploy the enormously powerful fifth-generation warfare or PsyWar technology that was designed by DoD, CIA, DIA and NSA for offshore, non-kinetic combat to advance the interests of the United States government and its allies globally. For the deep state and the global elites, democracy has come to mean the political stability of the current US political system (often referred to as the Uniparty) combined with continued US-led Western hegemony.

When a government is willing to deploy modern psychological technology's power against its citizenry, then the concepts of social contract, sovereignty, and personal autonomy become completely obsolete. This is the fundamental consequence of PsyWar methods being deployed by a government against its own citizens. People think they are able to resist these modern propaganda tools and methods, but the data show that this is very difficult and that, actually, it's often the most educated that are the most susceptible.[4] The truth is that we are all susceptible to the power of modern psychological warfare and cognitive warfare technologies. Furthermore, there has been a decision made, a consensus, by certain elements of our government that it is acceptable to deploy these methods and technologies in order to avoid the disruptive effects of populist movements, which might otherwise result in major disruptions to current domestic and foreign affairs policies. Recent examples of disruptive populist political movements that are used to justify deploying these battlefield techniques against US citizens include the rise and impact of Nigel Farage/UKIP/Brexit and the election of President Donald Trump.

The Trusted News Initiative (TNI) is an international alliance led by the BBC (British government) which ties together traditional (corporate) news media, social media, and technology companies to combat mis-dis-mal-information on a variety of topics that a globally focused elite committed to "The Great Reset" and "New World Order" has decided it is not in our interest to know about. Another such entity was the "The Global Alliance for Responsible Media" (GARM), which disallows advertisers from sponsoring online sites that have been identified as having "harmful content." The nature of that harmful content is not actually defined, but rather primarily consists of information that differs from governmentally approved narratives. That's where we're at right now. All of this was initially justified based on the thesis of Russian bot farms acting to manipulate US elections and the threat of Russian election interference. This was why the "Trusted News Initiative" was set up, and was also the initial justification used for developing so many of these other entities that currently constitute the mercenary censorship-industrial complex.

Because these capabilities were originally justified on the basis that they were required to resist Russian interference in US and British elections, this largely manufactured threat was used to justify domestic deployment. Then it was decided that it was going to be necessary to use these technologies against the rise of the "anti-vaxxer movement," which was presented as a major threat to human health. In response to this new mission, the Trusted News Initiative pivoted from a contrived justification based on Russian election interference and was reformulated to address the "anti-vaxxer" movement. Then suddenly, shortly thereafter in late 2019, an engineered coronavirus entered the human population in Wuhan, and its rapid spread changed everything.

In response to the promoted fear of this new infectious disease "threat" (COVID-19 disease), a new rationale for deploying PsyWar on citizens was contrived—it was necessary to employ psychological and cognitive warfare technologies on the general population because of the threat posed by infection with this virus. A threat from a virus which, according to highly flawed modeling by Neil Ferguson of Imperial College, was associated with a "crude case fatality ratio of 3.67%"[5] and, according to the World Health Organization, had a 3.4 percent infection fatality rate.[6] That messaging became the approved and promoted narrative, which was then broadcast via every corporate media outlet. That is what governments were told by the various divisions of the United States Department of Health and Human Services as well as by the World Health Organization. This falsehood was published in a top academic journal, and then this article was propagandized worldwide, particularly in the West. The approved and promoted narrative became that SARS-CoV-2 was a highly lethal virus that posed such an enormous threat that it was acceptable and necessary to deploy PsyWar technology to advance and protect the public good and world health. The logic was that deployment of battlefield-grade psychological manipulation methods on civilian populations was necessary to ensure that we would have full compliance with the measures that governments prescribed for all of us in alignment with the advice of the World Health Organization. Never mind that the WHO had just radically shifted its prior infectious disease pandemic recommendations to align with the remarkably totalitarian policies then being deployed in Communist China, where the virus had originated.

The consequence of the decision to deploy PsyWar (or fifth-generation warfare) technology on domestic citizens is that what we now have is functionally akin to a series of mercenary propaganda and censorship armies or mercenary organizations, and they compete with each other. They almost all originated with academic links to places like Cambridge, Harvard, MIT, and Stanford. These organizations are actively competing with each other to garner government grants and contracts to censor and propagandize all of us and to deploy the most advanced psychological manipulation tools that they can develop "all for the common good," all to "preserve democracy," all to ensure that we have full compliance with vaccine mandates or recommendations. But it doesn't stop there. These same institutions are now focused on shaping the 2024 presidential election and public opinion on climate change. Furthermore, they are now employing artificial intelligence tools to further their goals.

The typical modern reason cited for deploying censorship and psychological technology on the population is to maintain the status quo, which is favorable to a group of oligarchs who are pursuing a centralized, globalist agenda. They want to maintain their current status while guiding the world toward a new order or structure that is aligned with their financial and political interests, and they want to do it through the development, possession, and deployment of this kind of technology.

The practical consequence of this effort has been to create a situation, particularly in times of change such as what we're in right now, where the difference between the current political and economic systems and optimal solutions gets larger and larger. The use of censorship, propaganda, and PsyWar methods prevents the culture, the economies, and governments from innovating and adapting to change independently. Instead, those who use these methods impose their consensus version of a better way forward. They force global populations and governments to comply with top-down planning rather than compete in an international free market of ideas and possible solutions. A free market of ideas and possible solutions emerging from the unique cultures and history of a diversity of independent nation-states.

The consequence is that the populace of each nation-state observes that their situation is getting worse and worse relative to what has previously been and what could be. Ordinary citizens observe a larger and larger gap between an optimal solution and the current solution. To any objective outside observer, it is no surprise that this naturally gives rise to populist political movements. Unfortunately, rather than dispassionately and objectively analyzing these natural forces and trends, the globalist oligarchy is instinctively doubling down on PsyWar propaganda and employing media surrogates to falsely label these populist movements as "Far Right," "Fascist," and "Neo-Nazi."

In the case of elections, the obvious solutions, such as paper ballots and manual counting, in-person voting, voter identification requirements, and a general holiday for presidential elections, are not implemented. Instead, censorship and propaganda measures have been increased to promote the narrative that our elections are "fair and secure." People are not stupid. They can see through the government game of charades.

Eventually, that gap between the artifice of propaganda and censorship versus situational reality gets so big that it can only be resolved in one way. That is through a revolution or another form of major disruption to the social-political-economic order. In contrast, allowing free speech and interaction through an exchange of ideas in a decentralized environment will enable incremental improvements. If gradual adaptation to change is permitted, the culture never gets to the point where the population has been locked into bad solutions. And then the probability that those major disruptions happen is reduced. With free speech and thought, there are gradual, incremental, evolutionary changes toward a better and better set of solutions for whatever the problem sets are. But by using the PsyWar tools of censorship and propaganda, the Western governments and globalist organizations are locking the Western populations, and increasingly the global population, into a suboptimal set of solutions.

---

**Psyops** are propaganda techniques used by the military, intelligence agencies, or the police.

---

Suppose we allow the expanding censorship/propaganda industrial complex to continue growing and developing. In that case, we'll lock the world into a set of suboptimal solutions and prevent civilization from evolving by enabling innovative problem-solving, which can power the development of a better world for all of us.

The PsyWar campaign on America goes back decades. Senator Rand Paul stated recently: "There was a coup, and we lost our government."

The day of that coup was November 22, 1963. That was the day that

John F. Kennedy was assassinated in Dallas, Texas. That was the day the US government turned against its own people and began a PsyWar campaign against all of us. We just didn't know it yet. Nothing has been the same since.

It has taken over fifty years to realize the extent of this PsyWar campaign fully, but now there is no denying it. A new book titled: *The Assassination of President John F. Kennedy: The Final Analysis: Forensic Analysis of the JFK Autopsy X-Rays Proves Two Headshots from the Right Front and One from the Rear* documents that President Kennedy was almost surely assassinated by the US government, who also led the cover-up and the ensuing propaganda/ PsyWar campaign regarding the events of his death. The author and scientist, Dr. David W. Mantik, uses modern imaging to prove that the wound in the president's throat and the massive blow-out in the back of his head involved frontal bullet wounds. As Lee Harvey Oswald supposedly shot the president from behind the motorcade, this analysis provides data which refute the government's analysis that he was the lone assassin does not hold up to scrutiny. This book presents clear and compelling testimonial and documentary evidence that the surgeons performed pre-autopsy surgery on the president's head to remove evidence of the forehead bullet, as well as to gain access to his brain. Hence, they were able to "sanitize the crime scene" by removing bullet fragments as well as bullet tracks in the brain tissue. The forensic evidence is clear that the CIA, the FBI, and/or the US Secret Service have been involved in and covered up the assassination of a sitting US president.[7]

As good as the forensic evidence is, there are now a vast number of books on the circumstances leading up to and after the assassination that reveal that Lee Harvey Oswald did not kill President Kennedy. In fact, there are books, studies, publications, and video reanalyzing the Warren Commission Report hearings and exhibits, as well as the House Select Committee Report, records from the Assassination Records Review Board, the National Archives and Records Administration records, and testimony from many eyewitnesses (including the many witnesses, who were not allowed to speak to the Warren Commission). Taken together, this evidence works to prove that the Warren Commission Report was a sham with a predetermined conclusion and was never meant as a real investigation to determine who assassinated President Kennedy. One book that stands out as thorough and compelling on this subject is *The JFK Assassination Evidence Handbook*.[8]

Another important book on this topic was authored by Colonel L. Fletcher Prouty. Prouty was a former CIA operative who worked for the agency during this period. His historic account shatters what we have all come to believe about the assassination of President John F. Kennedy. This is the book that was the basis for Oliver Stone's movie *JFK*. Prouty outlines how Kennedy's death was a coup d'état, and he presents strong evidence to that effect as well as details of the elite power base that was and is the hidden hand of the US government[9]—what is often referred to as the "Deep State."

Our government not only lied about this to the American people, but they created a massive cover-up story, which included framing an innocent man for the murder. For over sixty years, our government has not only covered up this murder, but they also made up an alternate reality of facts that have been presented as truth to the entire world.

In 1865, we almost lost our democracy due to the assassination of President Abraham Lincoln. Is November 22, 1963, the day when we truly lost our democracy to the deep state? Can we believe anything that we have since been told by our government? Why hasn't any US president come forward to tell the American people about what really happened that day?

The assassination of President Kennedy was a pivotal moment in the history of the modern PsyWar campaign against the American people by a rogue shadow government that has persisted up until this day. The rogue government that instigated this psyops upon the American people is still in control. The US intelligence community is the operational organization at the very heart of this PsyWar campaign, as well as the assassination. Full public disclosure of what has taken place and the dismantling of that apparatus is well past its due date.

The censorship-industrial complex has restricted our constitutionally protected right to freedom of speech by interfering with and manipulating what we are allowed to see and hear. With the advent of the internet, the tools available to this industry have only become more sophisticated.

Let's go back to when the internet was founded. In the heady rush of the 1970s, the Defense Advanced Research Projects Agency (DARPA), whose mission is to develop emerging technologies for national security purposes, linked a number of supercomputers together to transfer huge amounts of data. The National Science Foundation eventually took over this project, which led to the creation of university networks, which then developed into the scaffolding of the modern internet. Therefore, DARPA has always had an outsized role in developing and exploiting the internet for its own uses. They did this by funding a variety of cutting-edge research projects.

Google was the result of one of those DARPA grants. The NSA and DARPA jointly funded a grant awarded to Larry Page and Sergey Brin. The goal was to chart how "birds of a feather flock together online" through search engine aggregation. Based on that research, these two individuals cofounded Google just a year later. Shortly thereafter, the company became a military contractor and was able to obtain rights to what is now known as "Google Maps" by purchasing CIA satellite software. From the outset, Google has always had a cozy relationship with our national security apparatus.

## What Could Possibly Go Wrong?

Originally, our three-letter "intelligence" and "national security" agencies viewed exploitation of free speech on the internet as a way to circumvent state control over media worldwide, particularly in areas where the US government had little visibility. Our government created many ways for people to hide their identities on the web. This includes VPNs (virtual private networks), the dark web, encrypted messaging, and end-to-end encrypted chats. These technologies were then used to overthrow what the USA considered rogue governments, and that activity continued unopposed up until approximately 2014. Then, the tables turned. All of a sudden, these technologies began to be used by individuals to promote narratives in this country that the administrative and deep state was very uncomfortable with.

Until then, the US government was very much in favor of using the internet to interfere with and harm what they considered rogue nations. Governments opposed by the Obama administration, such as Egypt and Tunisia, were overthrown in part by exploiting surreptitious PsyWar capabilities embedded within Facebook and Twitter. The Arab Spring is often considered to have been a fifth-generation war won by Twitter. Never forget that Twitter was originally developed and deployed as a PsyWar weapon by the US intelligence community.

At this point in time, the State Department was working very closely with social media companies to keep social media online in these nations. There was a famous phone call from Google's Jared Cohen to Twitter not to do their scheduled maintenance so that the preferred opposition group in Iran would be able to use Twitter to win that election in 2009.[10] The use of social media during the Arab Spring highlighted its potential as a tool for political activism and social change. Free speech was transformed into an instrument of statecraft for the US national security state from the very beginning of the internet.

In 2014, after the US-sponsored coup in Ukraine, there was an unexpected countercoup where Crimea and the Donbas broke away from Ukraine to become independent states with the help of the Russian government. NATO was unprepared for this; it took them by surprise. They had one last Hail Mary chance: the Crimea annexation vote in 2014. When the hearts and minds of the people of Crimea voted to join the Russian Federation, that was the last straw for the concept of free speech on the internet in the eyes of NATO leadership. The fundamental nature of war changed at that moment. At that point, NATO declared something that they first called the "Gerasimov doctrine," which was named after a Russian military general who they claimed made a speech describing how the fundamental nature of war had changed.

The Gerasimov doctrine is the idea that for Russia to win military skirmishes, which could lead to the takeover of central and eastern Europe, all that is needed is to control the media and the social media ecosystem because that's what "controls" elections. Based on this doctrine, NATO realized that it could control opposition militaries by simply getting the right administration into power. This non-kinetic warfare, otherwise known as fifth-generation warfare, psyops, or PsyWar, is infinitely cheaper than conducting a kinetic military war. Wars can be won by simply conducting organized political influence operations over social and legacy media. That was the point when the Pentagon, the British Ministry of Defense, the European Union, and NATO accelerated the development of organized political PsyWar operations designed to have the military work hand in glove with international social media companies to censor Russian propaganda and then to censor the domestic, "right-wing" populist groups in Europe who were rising in political power at the time in reaction to mass in-migration from other countries and regions. This has become a core tenet of NATO diplomatic and warfare strategy, and NATO refers to this as hybrid warfare.

The US State Department, intelligence community, and DoD then began targeting political parties, like Germany's AFD (the alternative for Deutschland), and political parties in Estonia, Latvia, and Lithuania. From there, it only required a simple pivot, a re-aiming of these new PsyWar weapons, to use these technologies to try to control "anti-vaxxers" (which soon became defined as any who opposed vaccine mandates), critics of COVIDcrisis public health policies, climate change deniers, people questioning elections, etc. But it is more than that. On the domestic front, these technologies are being used to shape opinions on election candidates and general policy options. They are being used proactively on our allies and in our own nation. This is PsyWar on the American people by their own government, as well as on the citizens of our friends and allies around the world.

But let's turn the clock back to 2016. When Brexit happened, those events were interpreted as a crisis moment where suddenly NATO had to worry about more than just Central and Eastern Europe. The very next month at the Warsaw Conference, NATO formally amended its charter to commit to hybrid warfare as a new NATO capacity explicitly. In the blink of an eye, NATO went from an operational battle plan focused on deploying traditional warfare technologies to a focus on censoring tweets. Shortly thereafter, newly developed, advanced hybrid warfare capabilities began to be deployed against European political organizations that NATO, the Five Eyes Intelligence Alliance, and the US government interpreted as destabilizing or offensive. Populist movements by the citizens of allied Western nations began to be treated as military threats.

> **Hybrid warfare** involves an interconnected group of state and non-state actors pursuing overlapping goals. Hybrid methods of warfare include propaganda, deception, sabotage, and other nonmilitary tactics aimed at destabilizing regions.

Around this time, NATO began publishing white papers purporting that the most pressing threat NATO faced was not from a military invasion by Russia, but rather the biggest threat would be losing domestic elections across Europe to the "right-wing" populist groups that were springing up because of the open-boarder policies being promoted by the UN and the EU (consequent to the UN "Agenda 2030" treaty).[11] NATO promoted an argument that after Brexit, the entire rules-based international order would collapse (and take NATO with it!) unless the military took control over Western media using non-kinetic warfare spycraft. Recapitulating the realpolitik logic of the mid-twentieth-century "domino theory" concerning global communism, which was used to justify the US wars in Vietnam and Cambodia, Brexit would give rise to Frexit in France with Marine Le Pen. In Spain, Italy, and Germany, it was anticipated that there would be other populist parties that would want to leave the EU. Then there would be Grexit in Greece. And with that the whole European Union would tumble like dominoes. This political theory projected that the EU would come apart and NATO would be disbanded without a single bullet being fired. With NATO dissolved, there would be no enforcement arm for the World Trade Organization, International Monetary Fund (IMF), or the World Bank. Under that scenario and logic, the globalized financial stakeholders who depend on the battering ram of the US and allied national security states would be helpless against hostile governments worldwide.

The multilateral economic threats of rising Middle Eastern, Indian, Chinese, and Russian economic and political powers would compromise both the petrodollar and the many global institutions that sustain the carefully constructed US-aligned "New World Order." From NATO's perspective, if the military did not begin to censor the internet, then all of the "democratic" institutions and infrastructure that gave rise to a US-dominated post-World War II modern world would collapse. This threat was perceived as one component of a diplomatic onslaught for political control by non-US-aligned interests, and it was used to justify the development and deployment of a vast array of dirty tricks. Modern PsyWar, initially designed for offshore combat in the "war on terror," was now deployed to rig elections, control media, and meddle in the internal affairs and sovereignty of every single person and organization in the USA and abroad.

Up until this point, most Americans had thought that America was different. The American people have been told again and again that the "intelligence" agencies that use psyops are not allowed to operate on American soil. The State Department, the Defense Department, and the CIA are often said to be expressly forbidden from operating on US soil. Although many US citizens believe that the Smith-Mundt Act of 1948 protects American citizens from domestic spying and PsyWar operations, that is not actually the case. The Smith-Mundt Act has very little scope or relevance to limits on the powers of the state to propagandize the American people.[12] There have been executive orders from various presidents restricting the use of PsyWar on the American people and supporting the constitutional right to privacy, but those details rarely get in the way of administrative and deep state actors because virtually every one of these orders includes exception clauses which make it simple to bypass these restrictions routinely.

The US administrative state initially saw no moral, ethical, or legal contradictions as it sought to create an advanced mercenary censorship-industrial complex capability. This policy decision was implemented incrementally and justified as a necessary "lesser of two evils." There was some diplomatic debate when PsyWar deployment began in the Middle East, then in all NATO European countries, and subsequently accelerated with Brexit. But then the unthinkable happened, and Trump became president in an unanticipated populist US wave election. The false flag operation called Russiagate cleared the way for papering over all moral arguments against aggressively propagandizing and censoring American citizens in support of administrative and deep state interests.

The logic propagandized by Russiagate was that Trump was a Russian asset, and therefore, this was no longer a traditional free speech issue. It was a national security issue. Eventually, in July 2019, Russiagate was exposed as a fraud. This became obvious when Special Investigator Robert Mueller admitted that after years of investigation, he had no evidence that Russia influenced President Trump or the 2016 election. But by then, an expanded and empowered censorship-industrial complex was in full operation. There was no turning back. The censorship architecture, spanning DHS, the FBI, the CIA, the DOD, the DOJ, and thousands of government-funded NGOs and private sector mercenary firms, had all transited from a foreign-oriented predicate, a Russian disinformation predicate, to a "democracy" predicate by saying that disinformation is not just a threat when it comes from the Russians, but rather disinformation is actually an intrinsic threat to democracy itself. In a 2024 interview with Tucker Carlson, Mike Benz, who was the Deputy Assistant Secretary for International Communications and

Information Policy at the US Department of State's Bureau of Economic and Business Affairs under Trump, summarized the situation:

> It is almost beyond belief, but they were able to launder the entire democracy promotion regime change tool kit just in time for the 2020 election . . .
>
> What I'm essentially describing is military rule. What has happened with the rise of the censorship industry is a total inversion of the idea of democracy itself. Democracy draws its legitimacy from the idea that it is ruled by consent of the people being ruled. That is, it's not really being ruled by an overlord because the government is actually just our will expressed by our consent with whom we vote for. The whole push after the 2016 election and after Brexit and after a couple of other social media-run elections that went the wrong way from what the State Department wanted, like the 2016 Philippines election, was to completely invert everything that we described as being the underpinnings of a democratic society in order to deal with the threat of free speech on the internet. And what they essentially said is, we need to redefine democracy from being about the will of the voters to being about the sanctity of democratic institutions, and who are the democratic institutions?
>
> Oh, it's the military, it's NATO, it's the IMF and the World Bank. It's the mainstream media, it is the NGOs, and of course, these NGOs are largely State Department-funded or IC-funded. It's essentially all of the elite establishments that were under threat from the rise of domestic populism that declared their own consensus to be the new definition of democracy. Because if you define democracy as being the strength of democratic institutions rather than a focus on the will of the voters, then what you're left with is essentially democracy is just the consensus building architecture within the Democrat institutions themselves.

But a counterweight has emerged against the government's massive PsyWar against the American people. The uncensored mature internet ecosystem has allowed citizen journalists and independent voices to outcompete mainstream state-sponsored news media, which had been, to a greater or lesser extent, controlled by the administrative and deep states for many years. It is our independent citizen journalists that just may set us free.

# CHAPTER 2
# Propaganda and Behavioral Control

This is a game of wits and will. You've got to be learning and adapting constantly to survive.

—General Peter J. Schoomaker[1]

Edward Bernays published the classic tome *Propaganda* in 1928. This book was an attempt to alert the public to the power of propaganda while also allaying their fear of it. One of the book's core themes and underlying tenets is that there are elements in a democratic society that cannot be corrupted due to an incorruptible fourth estate (the free press).[2]

*Propaganda* concludes with the thesis that newspapers are the arbiter of news. Thus, the editors, writers, and owners act as gatekeepers, ensuring that the public has a fair rendition of both sides of any issue. The idea of a newspaper spreading propaganda was publicly undisputable during Bernays's era because a polite, responsible society shared a general faith that it was the mainstream press's responsibility and duty to report the news in a balanced fashion.

This may have been how journalism was perceived in the past, or perhaps it was just a convenient fiction akin to Camelot, but that is certainly no longer true in the present. To be honest, it never really was. The idea that the United States government or a political party might buy up enough advertising space so that a newspaper editor would think twice about running a story contrary to the government's position was not even considered by Bernays. His view was that newspaper writers, editors, or the owners couldn't be

23

bribed or, even worse, converted to one cause or another. Therefore, the possibility that newspapers would only publish one opinion on any news topic seems not to have entered Bernays's mindscape. The idea that multiple top-tier national news and opinion publications would be purchased by partisan corporations, agents, or large government contractors (*ergo*, the *Washington Post* and Jeff Bezos) and then act as state agents was completely inconceivable in Bernays's analysis.

That the newspapers of today would become advocacy conduits for one set of beliefs held by the government or one political party over another set of beliefs that the government found inconvenient seemed far-fetched during the 1920s. Frankly, through most of the twentieth century, the fiction that a free press would be fair and balanced was paramount to the industry. That is, until the twenty-first century, when journalism schools began promoting advocacy journalism. More properly called propaganda, "advocacy journalism" is a perversion of more traditional journalistic ethics that advocates the adoption of a nonobjective viewpoint, usually to advance some social or political cause. Advocacy journalism is clearly a type of propaganda that has become normalized in academic journalism schools and society. It has been normalized to such an extent that it seems almost unthinkable that advocacy journalism would be anything but normally accepted journalistic practice.

> **Propaganda** involves using facts, arguments, rumors, half-truths, or lies to influence public opinion and behavior. It has an agenda and a deliberate plan that relies on manipulating groups of people, usually for a political purpose. It is a method for manipulating public opinion by creating a specific narrative that aligns with a political agenda. It uses techniques like repetition, emotional appeals, selective information, and hypnotic language patterns to influence the subconscious mind, bypassing critical thinking and shaping beliefs and values. Propaganda can function as a form of hypnosis, putting people into a receptive state where they are more prone to accepting overt or surreptitious messages.

The purpose of propaganda is not necessarily evil, but it is always meant to manipulate the mental state of those receiving it, and usually for political purposes. Governments and organizations use propaganda for good and evil.

The distribution of "truthful" or "untruthful" information which causes the recipient to become wary or skeptical of the government and its intentions is defined by the US Department of Homeland Security (DHS) as *malformation*. Information that may or may not be truthful but differs from the US government's approved narrative at that point in time is defined by DHS as *misinformation*. Either mal-information or misinformation that is being distributed for a political purpose is defined as *disinformation*.[3] Under the Biden administration, DHS has determined that the spreading of mis- dis- or mal-information can be considered domestic terrorism. This ruling then technically allows various antiterrorism laws, policies, and US government programmatic infrastructure to be deployed to "counter" such information.[4]

In general, the levels of propaganda are classified by color: white propaganda, gray propaganda, and black propaganda.

White propaganda is a type of propaganda in which the producer of the material is clearly known, and the purpose is transparent. It is commonly referred to as marketing and public relations. White propaganda involves communicating a message from a known source to a recipient (typically the public or some targeted sub-audience). This type of propaganda is mainly based on truths, although the whole truth about the subject matter is typically not told. Instead, a selected subset of truth is promoted, resulting in a more positive or favorable impression than might be conveyed by a more comprehensive and objective analysis.

Gray propaganda is the communication of a false narrative or story from an unattributed or hidden source. Sometimes, the messenger or communicator may be known, but the true source of the message is typically hidden. By avoiding source attribution by the communicator, the viewer cannot determine the creator or motives behind the message. This is common practice in modern corporate media, where unattributed sources are often cited. An example of gray propaganda would be placing news stories in news outlets, also known as "pay to play," instead of buying ads to appeal directly to the targeted audience. This common practice also extends to "ghostwriting" of entire articles by corporations or advocacy groups, which are then published as if originating from independent news outlet analysis and writing. When using gray propaganda, a message or false narrative coming through the news media appears to be neutral, thus believable. The related strategies and tactics of Astroturfing involve using fake, organized "grass-roots" movements to spread a message or false narrative. These are often capitalized (funded) by shadowy shell organizations with ties to political parties, corporate interests, nongovernmental organizations, "intelligence" agencies, or other governmental organizations. These funding organizations use Astroturf surrogates to hide their involvement in advancing or inserting gray propaganda into media or public consciousness.

Black propaganda is designed to create the impression that it was created by those it is intended to discredit. It is typically used to vilify or embarrass an opponent or enemy through misrepresentation. Sometimes the source is concealed or credited to a false authority and used to spread lies, fabrications, and deceptions. When used effectively, a major characteristic of black propaganda is that the recipient is unaware that they are being influenced. It is most often associated with covert psychological operations. Black propaganda relies on the receiver's willingness to accept the source's credibility. One example of black propaganda is the method of "bad-jacketing," which became a prominent FBI strategy to sow mistrust and division within the 1960s civil rights movement. Bad-jacketing involves spreading rumors that targeted leaders are not sincere and act on behalf of those they appear to oppose. This typically takes the form of promoted accusations that a leader acts as "controlled opposition." Bad-jacketing and other black propaganda methods have been refined by application of the insights of modern psychology. Black propaganda is explicitly a method for waging fifth-generation or PsyWar against a targeted population.

With the advent of computational technology, particularly the internet—the ability of many different factions to use propaganda has grown exponentially. Computational propaganda can be described as an "emergent form of political manipulation that occurs over the internet."[5] Computational algorithmic propaganda is used in social media, such as blogs, forums, and other websites involving public participation and discussion. This type of propaganda is often executed through data mining and algorithmic bots, which can be created and controlled by advanced technologies such as AI and machine learning. By exploiting these tools, computational propaganda can effectively pollute an information landscape and rapidly distribute false news and contrived opinions around the internet.[6]

Truth be told, it isn't just "bad actors" who are using computational propaganda. Examples abound of how governments openly discuss and deploy computational propaganda technologies worldwide to induce people to eat better, stop smoking, or even behave in public spaces. These methods are generally referred to as "nudge" technologies. The problem is the slippery slope associated with this approach to social engineering. Those who employ propaganda will often use whatever means are necessary to achieve their ends because they have already decided that it is ethically acceptable to manipulate human behavior surreptitiously. Propaganda technologies informed by modern psychology breach the right to personal freedom of thought, autonomy, and sovereignty.

The internet has become a force multiplier for modern propaganda methodology, resulting in the capability to hypnotize individuals and targeted groups functionally, and to control all that they think, feel, and believe based on information control and manipulation. This remains the case even when propaganda is justified as being in the service of advancing the "public good" and is backed up by "experts" in the field. Propaganda aims to control our thoughts and behaviors, and propagandists measure success by "effectiveness" in achieving this objective. Propagandists will typically use whatever tools they are allowed to use to achieve those ends under the twisted ethical logic that the ends justify the means. Currently, there are no government regulations on how far they can go and no effective legal boundaries on the distribution of propaganda or related methods of defamation or delegitimization of individuals seeking to oppose or correct promoted propaganda.

The tools available to modern propagandists have become increasingly sophisticated. Not only are we being subjected to data mining of the personal information freely available via the web for use against us, but these data are being combined with behavioral tools such as nudging, neurolinguistic programming, hypnosis, visualization, repetitive imagery, and messaging, which are often employed through the use of bots and trolls.

During COVID-19, propaganda methods based on advanced applied psychology were developed and successfully deployed to coerce people into taking experimental vaccine products, as well as a variety of non-pharmaceutical interventions such as wearing paper masks that are not effective in preventing viral infection or transmission, social distancing, and quarantining or "lockdown." We have all lived through the effects of these massive and globally coordinated propaganda campaigns, the likes of which the world has never seen before.

There is a misconception that the US government does not conduct propaganda or psyops on its domestic population. This may have once been the case, but no longer. According to the US Department of Defense *Psychological Operations Manual* of 2010, in the case of domestic crisis management, the DoD can become involved in psyops operations against civilian citizens during times of crisis management. The manual states:

> When authorized, PSYOP forces may be used domestically to assist lead federal agencies during disaster relief and crisis management by informing the domestic population.

Although many believe that the Smith-Mundt Act of 1948 banned the use of propaganda by the US government, nothing is further from the truth. The Smith-Mundt Act only applied to specific media outlets developed by the US government for foreign markets, and only to the US State Department and to the relatively obscure Broadcasting Board of Governors (BBG) that provides oversight to USG operations such as "Voice of America." Furthermore, most of the prior restrictions placed by that act were repealed or amended in 2013. There is nothing that stops the US government, including the CIA, Department of Homeland Security (DHS), and DoD, from propagandizing the American people. Our government, media, universities, and medical establishments are just a few of the domestic organizations that routinely use propaganda.

Between 1975 and 1976, the Church Committee examined a wide range of CIA operations (including journalists with CIA ties). The Church Committee was a congressional committee set up to investigate CIA improprieties against US civilians. The most extensive discussion of CIA relations with news media from these investigations is in the Church Committee's final report, published in April 1976. The report covered CIA associations with both foreign and domestic news media.

For foreign news media, the report concluded that:

> The CIA currently maintains a network of several hundred foreign individuals around the world who provide intelligence for

the CIA and at times attempt to influence opinion through the use of covert propaganda. These individuals provide the CIA with direct access to a large number of newspapers and periodicals, scores of press services and news agencies, radio and television stations, commercial book publishers, and other foreign media outlets.

For domestic media, the report states:

> Approximately 50 of the [Agency] assets are individual American journalists or employees of US media organizations. Of these, fewer than half are "accredited" by US media organizations. . . . The remaining individuals are non-accredited freelance contributors and media representatives abroad. . . . More than a dozen United States news organizations and commercial publishing houses formerly provided cover for CIA agents abroad. A few of these organizations were unaware that they provided this cover.

Journalist Carl Bernstein, writing for the magazine *Rolling Stone* in 1977, discovered that the Church Committee report covered up CIA relations with news media and named a number of journalists and organizations who worked with the CIA. In contrast to the "official" version of the Church Committee report, Bernstein provided strong evidence that over four hundred journalists were working with the CIA for a period of twenty-five years.[7] He also uncovered evidence of substantial CIA infiltration of academia, which had been whitewashed by the Committee. The Bernstein article writes that:

> During the 1976 investigation of the CIA by the Senate Intelligence Committee, chaired by Senator Frank Church, the dimensions of the Agency's involvement with the press became apparent to several members of the panel, as well as to two or three investigators on the staff. But top officials of the CIA, including former directors William Colby and George Bush, persuaded the committee to restrict its inquiry into the matter and to deliberately misrepresent the actual scope of the activities

in its final report. The multi-volume report contains nine pages in which the use of journalists is discussed in deliberately vague and sometimes misleading terms. It makes no mention of the actual number of journalists who undertook covert tasks for the CIA. Nor does it adequately describe the role played by newspaper and broadcast executives in cooperating with the Agency.[8]

The final Church Committee report also stated that all CIA contacts with accredited journalists had been dropped at the time of publication. The Committee noted, however, that "accredited correspondent" meant the ban was limited to individuals "formally authorized by contract or issuance of press credentials to represent themselves as correspondents" and that non-contract workers who did not receive press credentials, such as stringers or freelancers, were not included. Based on the Committee's own report, stringers or freelancers comprised over half of those journalists acting on behalf of the CIA.

That said, Operation CHAOS soon came to the fore. This was a massive domestic spying project that spied on anti-war political activists and dissenters. Searching through the CIA's heavily redacted documents in the web-based CIA reading room, which allows individuals to search for unclassified or declassified CIA documents, the extent of some of these activities is revealed.

Of relevant interest is a CIA regulatory document titled *AR 2–2 (U) Law and Policy Governing the Conduct of Intelligence Activities (Formerly HR 7–1)*, which covers the extent of the CIA's international and domestic activities. AR 2–2 has the following wording:

> rules governing a wide range of activities, including surveillance of U.S. persons, human experimentation, contracts with academic institutions, relations with journalists and staff of U.S. news media, and relations with clergy and missionaries.

The documents indicate that the CIA engages in a wide array of domestic activities, often in conjunction with the FBI. Other documents within the CIA reading room suggest that even the CIA and its agents have difficulty determining what rules to follow for domestic surveillance.

# The Five Eyes Alliance Intelligence Network Enables Reciprocal Spying

It benefits our government when people believe that the US government does not use propaganda against its own people, but nothing could be further from the truth. The Five Eyes Alliance (FVEY) is a cooperative intelligence network that monitors citizens' and foreign governments' electronic communications. Furthermore, through the reciprocal spying and intelligence sharing terms and conditions of the FVEY, any barriers to domestic spying and propaganda activities that one of the FVEY intelligence agencies encounters can be circumvented by working with another member. The members of FVEY are the United States, the United Kingdom, Canada, Australia, and New Zealand. FVEY was formed after World War II to share intelligence among the five nations. FVEY is the oldest and most prominent of three related US-centric intelligence alliances. The Nine Eyes alliance includes the original five members of FVEY and Denmark, France, the Netherlands, and Norway. It is considered the most comprehensive espionage alliance in recorded history.

FVEY originated in 1943; the US and the UK formed a cooperative intelligence agreement—a secret treaty known as the BRUSA Agreement. This was later formalized as the UKUSA Agreement, which expanded into the FVEY agreement, although there is evidence that the UKUSA agreement is still viable between just the US and the UK. In the next decade, Canada, Norway, Denmark, West Germany, Australia, and New Zealand were temporarily added to the UKUSA agreement. In 1955, the group was narrowed down to the current FVEY countries.[9]

FVEY intercepts telephone calls, faxes, emails, social media data and text messages from satellites, telephone networks, and fiber-optic cables. FVEY also receives user data records from large technology companies, including Microsoft, Yahoo, Google, Facebook, Paltalk, YouTube, AOL, Skype, and Apple. Each member country has multiple government agencies involved, and each agency is responsible for one to two roles, including "human intelligence, defense intelligence, security intelligence, geo-intelligence, and signal intelligence."

When our government is allowed to combine propaganda with techniques such as neurolinguistic programming, hypnosis, bots, big data, and controlled messaging, do "we the people" even have truly independent individual beliefs, or is everything we think being manipulated? If that is the case, what does this mean for democracy? When a government decides to wage PsyWar on its own citizens, then the fundamentals and concepts of free agency, sovereignty, voting integrity, and representative democracy become irrelevant.

If we wish to remain independent thinkers and preserve our ability to learn, think, and debate issues, we must become warriors in the fight against government development and deployment of propaganda, censorship, and PsyWar.

## The British Army's 77th Brigade: One Example of FVEY Deployment of a Military PsyWar Campaign against FVEY Civilians during the COVIDcrisis

As discussed above, the policies of the US government currently allow deployment of both military, intelligence, and homeland security PsyWar personnel and weapons on US soil against US citizens. Technically, deployment of US Army PsyWar capabilities and weapons on US citizens is limited to domestic situations requiring disaster relief and crisis management, however, those terms are not well defined and therefore subject to broad interpretation by Army commanders and the Office of the President (Commander in Chief). Other US military policy and guidance indicates that deployment of these capabilities during a domestic crisis should be restricted to advisory (to DHS, FBI, or other domestic psyops/PsyWar capabilities). Details of how or if these US Army units were deployed or involved in COVIDcrisis propaganda, censorship, bot, troll, crowdstalking, or other information warfare operations has not entered the public domain. However, the COVIDcrisis was defined by the executive branch as requiring a "whole of government" approach which can safely be assumed to include deployment of DoD psyop/PsyWar capabilities. Mainstream media freedom of information requests and other investigative journalistic activities in the UK and Canada have documented deployment of military psyop/PsyWar capabilities against domestic citizens in those countries, and by extension it is likely that other FVEY partner nations deployed similar capabilities.

In the case of the US Army, the primary psyops/PsyWar divisions of the US Army's active duty Psychological Operations forces are organized into two Military Information Support Operations Groups (the Fourth and Eighth Psychological Operations Group [Airborne]), both located at Ft. Liberty, NC. These US DoD capabilities trace their roots back through the "ghost army" program of WWII. These active duty operations are supplemented by two Army reserve psyop groups based in Twinsburg, Ohio (Second Psyops Group), and Moffett Field, California (Seventh Psyops Group), which provide 74 percent of total Army capacity.

In a 2021 article series, the NATO-affiliated journal *NATO Review* provides current justification and rationale for developing and expanding NATO and FVEY hybrid or fifth generation PsyWar capabilities:

> The line between war and peace time is rendered obscure. . . . Hybrid warfare below the threshold of war or direct overt violence pays dividends despite being easier, cheaper, and less risky than kinetic operations. It is much more feasible to, let's say, sponsor and fan disinformation in collaboration with non-state actors than it is to roll tanks into another country's territory or scramble fighter jets into its airspace. The costs and risks are markedly less, but the damage is real. . . . What takes the centre stage here is the role of civilians: how they think and act in relation to the state. Contemporary digital and social media platforms allow hybrid actors to influence this to the detriment of the adversary state with considerable ease. . . . This translates into perilous erosion of the core values of coexistence, harmony, and pluralism in and amongst democratic societies as well as the decision-making capability of the political leaders. Ultimately, what hybrid threats undercut is trust. . . . It is for this reason that building trust must be deemed the key bulwark against hybrid threats, especially ones that are geared towards undermining democratic states and polities. . . . People must have confidence in the state organs for governments to ensure compliance with their decisions. . . . Building, re-building, and fortifying trust remains critical to creating durable resilience in the face of hybrid threats that acutely imperil the security at the state and societal levels. Trust-building within and across communities ought to be the linchpin of efforts to neutralise hybrid warfare and threats.[10]

In the case of the United Kingdom (England), the best documented FVEY deployment of military PsyWar capabilities against domestic civilians and residents during the COVIDcrisis has involved the British Army's 77th Brigade, a disinformation unit responsible for information warfare and psychological operations. The 77th Brigade consists of various groups, including:

- 16 Air Assault Brigade Combat Team
- Surveillance Group
- Understand Group
- Cyber Electro Magnetic Activities Effects Group (with the 2nd Medical Group joining later)

The formation and mission scope of the 77th Brigade is detailed in a November 2018 article in *Wired* magazine titled "Inside the British Army's secret information warfare machine."[11] Journalist Carl Miller described 77th Brigade warfighters as knowing "how to set up cameras, record sound, edit videos. Plucked from across the military, they were proficient in graphic design, social media advertising, and data analytics. Some may have taken the army's course in Defense Media Operations, and almost half were reservists from civvy street, with full time jobs in marketing or consumer research." The description of this battle unit personnel clearly demonstrates the integration of modern civilian sector commercial sales capabilities within military propaganda operations. The new 77th was originally formed in 2015 by reassembling other British Army units, including a Media Operations Group, a Military Stabilisation Support Group, and a Psychological Operations Group. Beginning with this core capability, the unit has been rapidly expanded by drawing in expertise from British marketing, advertising companies, digital research laboratories, and academic behavioral research expertise, and building specific competence in the area of behavioral change technologies.

While interviewing a soldier from the new unit, Miller captured the internalized logic, justification, and morality which has guided the 77th since its inception.

Ever since NATO troops were deployed to the Baltics in 2017, Russian propaganda has been deployed too, alleging that NATO soldiers there are rapists, looters, little different from a hostile occupation. One of the goals of NATO information warfare was to counter this kind of threat: sharply rebutting damaging rumours, and producing videos of NATO troops happily working with Baltic hosts. Information campaigns such as these are "white": openly, avowedly the voice of the British military. But to narrower audiences, in conflict situations, and when it was understood to be proportionate and necessary to do so, messaging campaigns could become, the officer said, "grey" and "black" too. "Counter-piracy, counter-insurgencies and counter-terrorism," he explained. There, the messaging doesn't have to look like it came from the military and doesn't have to necessarily tell the truth.

The current embodiment of the 77th is really an extension and expansion of longstanding British intelligence and military strategies and tactics. The British government has a long history of aggressive deployment of psychological warfare technologies. For example, the Government Communications Headquarters (GCHQ) is an intelligence and security organization responsible for providing signals intelligence (SIGINT) and information assurance (IA) to the government and armed forces of the United Kingdom, and it has long been known for its information warfare activities and technologies. For example, slides leaked by NSA whistleblower Edward Snowden in 2013 document activities and capabilities associated with the "Joint Threat Research Intelligence Group"—or JTRIG. According to these documents, JTRIG's role is to "deny, disrupt, degrade and deceive." The slides reveal that JTRIG is, among many other activities, in the business of discrediting companies, by passing "confidential information to the press through blogs etc.," and by posting negative information on internet forums. JTRIG can change someone's social media photos ("can take 'paranoia' to a whole new level," a slide read) and can use masquerade-type techniques—that is: placing "secret" information on a compromised computer. JTRIG also has the technology, ability, and authorization to bombard someone's phone with text messages or calls if deemed to be warranted.

The Snowden slides also document that JTRIG holds an arsenal of two hundred information weapons, which were either in development or operational at the time of the leak. For example, one tool named "Badger" supports email mass delivery, similar to the commercial "Mailchimp" tool kit but without transparency concerning origin. Another, called "Burlesque," spoofs SMS messages. SMS spoofing involves the manipulation of sender information to disguise the true origin of a text message, often with malicious intent. This deceptive technique can have serious consequences, including identity theft, financial fraud, and privacy breaches. The "Clean Sweep" tool impersonates Facebook wall posts for individuals or entire countries. "Gateway" provides the ability to "artificially increase traffic to a website." "Underpass" is the name of a JTRIG tool for changing the outcome of online polls. The Snowden leak also documents that another JTRIG trick involves targeted phone spam (termed "call bombing"), in which a target is called every ten seconds. The slides also document that JTRIG employs honeytraps, which the organization described as "a great option" and "very successful when it works." In the digital world, "honeytraps" or "honeypots" are false websites or similar online destinations, which are designed to lure in users for identification and entrapment. JTRIG also deploys denial-of-service (DOS) attacks, which is a method designed to prevent users from accessing a service (typically a website).

Robert Malone has personally experienced repeated hostile social media activity targeting him in a coordinated manner every time he travels to the UK to speak regarding COVIDcrisis and COVID genetic vaccine issues, and in particular when he has spoken in support of British House of Commons MP Andrew Bridgen. Many of the social media accounts that are involved in these waves of attacks self-identify as being involved in some way with the British Army 77th Brigade. Some of these may originate with an irregular government-affiliated group that appears to have loose ties with the 77th, known as the "Mutton Crew." The "Mutton Crew" is a suspected covert wing of the 77th Brigade, a disinformation unit responsible for information warfare and psychological operations. The "Mutton Crew" operatives are believed to engage in online activities, such as:

- Derailing debates with name-calling and ridicule
- Filing spurious complaints about targets, alleging infringement of Twitter rules
- Compromising online platforms, as evidenced by the unusual listing of Swaledale Mutton Company at the top of follower lists for these accounts

Independent journalist Iain Davis, who writes a popular Substack under his own name with the tagline "The Disillusioned Blogger" describes the "Mutton Crew" tactics as crude but effective, due to the complicity of the Twitter (X) platform itself.[12] On May 14, 2024, British member of parliament, Andrew Bridgen, a long-standing critic of government policy on COVID-19, alleged that he had been targeted on Twitter by the "Mutton Crew" network in a sustained campaign of online harassment against him. Bridgen accused the intelligence network of bombarding him with communications of a "grossly offensive or of an indecent, obscene or menacing character." Bridgen called for the public's help in gathering evidence against the anonymous perpetrators.[13] It is essential to recognize that the 77th Brigade's activities, including those of the "Mutton Crew," are shrouded in secrecy, making it challenging to verify the extent of their operations. However, available information suggests that the "Mutton Crew" is a component of the 77th Brigade's information warfare efforts, aimed at influencing online discourse and silencing critics.

According to the Wikispooks archive,[14] the "Mutton Crew" is led by pharmaceutical propagandist Dr. Graham Bottley, and the network operates dozens of online accounts on social media platforms. Operatives in the network are renowned for engaging in vicious psychological warfare (PsyWar) tactics. On Twitter (X), the network is notorious for trolling the accounts of activists, dissidents, and government critics, especially over COVID-19. "Mutton Crew" accounts on Twitter frequently have the Swaledale Mutton Company account shown at the top of their follower list. Their treatment is different on the "X" platform relative to other known troll and bot operations. In contrast to the standard chronological order of followers on Twitter where the most recent followers are listed first, Swaledale Mutton Company is invariably listed at the top of the follower list for these "Mutton Crew" accounts according to Iain Davis. "Mutton Crew" operatives are trained in emotionalizing, antagonizing, and goading their opponents into making aggressive and potentially abusive comments, responses which could be construed as abusive or "hate speech" are then reported to Twitter. The network utilizes other recognized techniques of psychological warfare (PsyWar) to suppress the truth and to propagate disinformation which are detailed in the 2001 essay "Twenty-Five Ways To Suppress Truth: The Rules of Disinformation" by H. Michael Sweeney.[15]

In a November 2020 article authored by investigative journalist Whitney Webb,[16] the deployment of both the British Army 77th Brigade and US military PsyWar capabilities in response to the COVIDcrisis was documented and discussed in detail.

British and American state intelligence agencies are "weaponizing truth" to quash vaccine hesitancy as both nations prepare for mass inoculations, in a recently announced "cyber war" to be commanded by AI-powered arbiters of truth against information sources that challenge official narratives.

In just the past week, the national-security states of the United States and United Kingdom have discreetly let it be known that the cyber tools and online tactics previously designed for use in the post-9/11 "war on terror" are now being repurposed for use against information sources promoting "vaccine hesitancy" and information related to Covid-19 that runs counter to their state narratives.

A new cyber offensive was launched on Monday by the UK's signal intelligence agency, Government Communications Headquarters (GCHQ), which seeks to target websites that publish content deemed to be "propaganda" that raises concerns regarding state-sponsored Covid-19 vaccine development and the multi-national pharmaceutical corporations involved.

Similar efforts are underway in the United States, with the US military recently funding a CIA-backed firm—stuffed with former counterterrorism officials who were behind the occupation of Iraq and the rise of the so-called Islamic State—to develop an AI algorithm aimed specifically at new websites promoting "suspected" disinformation related to the Covid-19 crisis and the US military–led Covid-19 vaccination effort known as Operation Warp Speed.

Both countries are preparing to silence independent journalists who raise legitimate concerns over pharmaceutical industry corruption or the extreme secrecy surrounding state-sponsored Covid-19 vaccination efforts, now that Pfizer's vaccine candidate is slated to be approved by the US Food and Drug Administration (FDA) by month's end.

. . .

Essentially, the power of the state is being wielded like never before to police online speech and to deplatform news websites to protect the interests of powerful corporations like Pfizer and other scandal-ridden pharmaceutical giants as well as the interests of the US and UK national-security states, which themselves are intimately involved in the Covid-19 vaccination endeavor.

. . .

Given this precedent, it is certainly plausible that GCHQ could take the word of either an allied government, a government contractor, or perhaps even an allied media organization such as Bellingcat or the Atlantic Council's DFRLab that a given site is "foreign propaganda" in order to launch a cyber offensive against it. Such concerns are only amplified when one of the main government sources for *The Times* article bluntly stated that "GCHQ has been told to take out antivaxers [sic] online and on social media. There are ways they have used to monitor and disrupt terrorist propaganda," which suggests that the targets of GCHQ's new cyber war will, in fact, be determined by the content itself rather than their suspected "foreign" origin. The "foreign" aspect instead appears to be a means of evading the prohibition in GCHQ's operational mandate on targeting the speech or websites of ordinary citizens. This larger pivot toward treating alleged "anti-vaxxers" as "national security threats" has been ongoing for much of this year, spearheaded in part by Imran Ahmed, the CEO of the UK-based Center for Countering Digital Hate, a member of the UK government's Steering Committee on Countering Extremism Pilot Task Force, which is part of the UK government's Commission for Countering Extremism. Ahmed told the UK newspaper *The Independent* in July that "I would go beyond calling anti-vaxxers conspiracy theorists to say they are an extremist group that pose a national security risk." He then stated that "once someone has been exposed to one type of conspiracy it's easy to lead them down a path where they embrace more radical world views that can lead to violent extremism," thereby implying that "antivaxxers" might engage in acts of violent extremism. Among the websites cited by

Ahmed's organization as promoting such "extremism" that poses a "national security risk" were Children's Health Defense, the National Vaccine Information Center, Informed Consent Action Network, and Mercola.com, among others.

At the time, the intent of the UK government to deploy British military PsyWar capabilities in support of government-approved narratives was also documented by both the *Times of London*[17] and the *Daily Mail*.[18] As the *Times* reported:

> The (British) army has mobilised an elite "information warfare" unit renowned for assisting operations against al-Qaeda and the Taliban to counter online propaganda against vaccines, as Britain prepares to deliver its first injections within days. The defence cultural specialist unit was launched in Afghanistan in 2010 and belongs to the army's 77th brigade. The secretive unit has often worked side-by-side with psychological operations teams.
>
> Leaked documents reveal that its soldiers are already monitoring cyberspace for Covid-19 content and analysing how British citizens are being targeted online. It is also gathering evidence of vaccine disinformation from hostile states, including Russia. Next month the 77th brigade will begin an "uplift" of professional and reserve soldiers to join operations.
>
> Ministers are alarmed at the impact that online propaganda is having on public opinion. A recent report found that more than one-third of people are uncertain or are very unlikely to be vaccinated. Ministers believe Britain will become the first western country to approve a vaccine next week. A BioNTech and Pfizer treatment is set to receive approval within days, paving the way for injections as soon as December 7. Ministers will then launch a huge public campaign to encourage people to get a jab. The campaign will be reinforced by counter-disinformation efforts led by the Cabinet Office, with support from the army and GCHQ.

Mr. Paul Schulte, a retired British civil servant with current academic affiliations with Birmingham Institute for Conflict, Cooperation and Security, as an Honorary Professor and King's College Department of War Studies, as a Senior Visiting Fellow, provided written testimony to the British Parliament in November 2020 titled "Mitigating the Coming Infodemics and The Impacts of Information Disorder on the British Body Politic"[19] in which he provided analysis and justification for the decision to deploy British army capabilities against both British and other FVEY citizens in support of governmental COVIDcrisis policies including mass vaccination. His testimony provides insight into the mindset of and subsequent policy justifications of both himself and his peers at the point in time immediately prior to onset of the COVID genetic vaccine mandates that were deployed in a heavy handed and unethical manner throughout virtually the entire western world, and particularly in Europe and the FVEY alliance nations.

Basically, Paul Schulte's testimony details the then widely held (but undocumented) belief that Russia and China were actively exploiting vaccine hesitancy in Western nation (and specifically British) citizens, that the genetic vaccines under development at that time by Oxford/Astra Zeneca, Moderna, and Pfizer were presumed to be safe and effective, and that therefore, the government was justified in deploying the advanced PsyWar weaponry developed for offshore combat by units such as the 77th Brigade against its own citizens, and implied that similar deployments of military PsyWar capabilities against citizens were planned to occur in the other FVEY alliance nations.

> Observing and reflecting on the strains and disputes occurring from Covid 19, reported in the US, UK, France, Israel and other democratic states, and as a student of group psychology and political warfare, I have become concerned that there are systemic informational vulnerabilities in relation to biosecurity threats, whose social, political and strategic implications have not, as far as I can tell, sufficiently addressed in public discussions of resilience in the National Security Strategy, and which include indirect impacts on public health and prosperity. I have been in touch with networks of experts in UK, and US academia, and participated in recent London and transatlantic online expert workshops on national resilience and biosecurity responses. This has confirmed to me that the informational problem potentially

ranges all across all elements of healthcare—from those looking up dietary advice, to parents concerned about vaccinating
their children. For wider society, it could, for example, include
the sources that specialists from various disciplines, as well as
ordinary members of the public, will access to inform themselves
about the range and utility of available medical treatments, and
medical history, including the history of infectious diseases.

The notion that, usually undefined, "Information Warfare"
poses a threat to British national cohesion and social resilience is now widely accepted in national security planning,
but far less so in public debate over health issues. As a very
recent article in the RUSI Journal put it: "The information
environment is under siege by a mass of domestic and foreign
actors whose tools and agendas overlap in ways that blur borders and challenge norms. Capability outpaces both regula-
tion and education." According to the latest MoD Integrated
Operational Concept 18, (IOC), aimed at 2025, but written
in the present tense: "The old distinction between foreign and
domestic defence is increasingly irrelevant. When 'fake news'
appears to originate not abroad but at home it gains credibility and reach, stoking confusion, disagreement, division and
doubt in our societies. This has been particularly evident with
the significant uptick in disinformation and misinformation
during the coronavirus crisis. . . . Sub-threshold operations are
continuously executed at reach by malign actors who seek to
undermine our military readiness, our critical national infrastructure, our economy, our alliances and our way of life."
Public commentaries on these clandestine activities are accumulating fast. On 14 October the new MI5 Director General,
Ken McCallum was explicit.

"Crucially, on the vaccine, we've been working to protect the
integrity of UK research . . . , our academic research, our infrastructure. And, much discussed, threats to our democracy. In the
2020s, one of the toughest challenges facing MI5 and indeed
government is that the differing national security challenges presented by Russian, Chinese, Iranian and other actors are growing

in severity and in complexity—while terrorist threats persist at scale." This was rapidly followed by linked revelations in *The London Times* of open Russian efforts on state TV channels to denigrate and so damage international public trust in the Covid vaccine under development in Oxford. The two statements have been seen as unusually pointed counter-disinformation responses. On 9 November *The Times* was able to publish further information quoting "official sources" to reveal that GCHQ22, in cooperation with the British Army's seventy-seventh brigade was involved in offensive cyber operations tackling anti-vaccine disinformation, using tactics similar to those used against the Islamic State. A rapid response team has been established in the Cabinet Office to coordinate such action against damaging narratives, including bogus treatments and conspiracy theories about the virus. But the sources stated that disruption would only be permitted against information originating from state adversaries and not online content from ordinary citizens, however misinformed. Nor could UK government specialists attack websites based in the other nations of the "Five Eyes" Intelligence Partnership (US, Canada Australia and New Zealand), which would remain the responsibility of partner agencies.

We were warned. Based on information available even before the genetic "vaccine" products were authorized for emergency use, journalist Whitney Webb clearly saw and anticipated the PsyWar that was about to be deployed. And the world did nothing. How many more times will we not listen to those among us who are able to see through the fog of modern military-grade fifth-generation psychological warfare and anticipate what lies and cyberattacks are about to be deployed against us?

## A Real-World Example of How the US Government Propaganda System Works to Control Opinion and Thought

Johns Hopkins University, in conjunction with the Bill & Melinda Gates Foundation, the CDC, The United Nations (UN), the World Health Organization (WHO), the World Economic Forum (WEF), and the CIA, as well as world leaders and mainstream media (MSM), held a series of pandemic war games that occurred over the span of decades. The outcome of these exercises usually ended with the conclusion that there is a need to control populations in the case of a biothreat, during which behavioral modification and psyops techniques would be used to enforce cooperation from the populace.

Even now, one can review the Johns Hopkins Center for Health Security website and see their current projects include an analysis of "anti-misinformation actions," which they call the "Environment of Misinformation." In March 2021, this center published a report entitled "National Priorities to Combat Misinformation and Disinformation for COVID-19 and Future Public Health Threats: A Call for a National Strategy."[20] In that report, they laid out some of the plans that governments across the world enacted during COVID-19.

National Priorities to Combat Misinformation and Disinformation for COVID-19 and Future Public Health Threats: A Call for a National Strategy
- Ensure a whole-of-nation response through multisector and multiagency collaboration.
- Ensure multisector collaboration in the development of a national strategy to combat public health misinformation through collective planning with social media, news media, government, national security officials, public health officials, scientists, the public, and others.
- Increase coordination across the range of government stakeholders and conduct a cross-governmental analysis of efforts and responsibilities for managing health-related misinformation and disinformation in order to streamline and organize efforts.
- Key US agencies include the Department of Defense, Department of Health and Human Services, and Department of Homeland Security as well as intelligence agencies such as the Federal Bureau of Investigation, the National Security Agency, and the Central Intelligence Agency.

- Encourage active, transparent, nonpartisan intervention from social media and news media companies to identify and remove, control the spread of, and curtail generators of false information."[21]

Note that the first bullet point advocates both a "whole-of-nation" and "multi-agency" response and collaboration. That would include the Department of Defense, all branches of US intelligence, and the Department of Homeland Security. The next section specifically mentions the DoD and intelligence agencies becoming more involved in combating misinformation and disinformation, not only for COVID-19 but also for future public health threats.

The inconvenient truth is that world leaders, governments, big media, Big Pharma, social media, and tech giants are already planning the next pandemic response. In 2018, the World Health Organization proposed the idea of "Disease X," a placeholder for a disease that could potentially cause a major epidemic or pandemic. The original idea was that planning for an (imaginary) "Disease X" would allow scientists, public health officials, and physicians to design the best possible practices for a future epidemic or pandemic. They then formally added "Disease X" (an imaginary disease) to the top priority list of pathogens.

The idea behind Disease X was later weaponized to create a fog of fear in the public and governments. The weaponization started with COVID-19 communications. In a 2021 study, it was found that "the only predictor of behavior change during COVID-19 was fear." Despite their finding that such fear was related to a decrease in both emotional and physical well-being, the authors concluded that using fear to drive the public into compliance with federal policies was the only path forward for public health. The authors wrote:

> However, fear of COVID-19 was related to decreased physical and environmental wellbeing. Overall, these results suggest that "fear" and anxiety at the current time have a functional role, and are related to increased compliance for improving public wellbeing.[22]

## "Damn the Torpedoes, Full Steam Ahead!"

Without further questioning the basic ethics behind using fear to drive compliance, this logic became the consensus of public health officials and governments worldwide. The use of fear to get compliance for vaccines and vaccine mandates, vaccine passports, the zoonotic origins theory, masking, lockdowns, social distancing, school closures, etc., was acceptable in the name of public health. The general public's decreased emotional and physical well-being by promoting fear tactics was an acceptable side effect.

*Exit COVID-19 . . . stage left. Enter "disease X" . . . stage right.*

And just like that, "Disease X" has been substituted for COVID-19.

Without any qualms whatsoever, the World Health Organization has gone from launching a global scientific process using "Disease X" as a model to using "Disease X" as a propaganda tool to drive fear of an imaginary infectious disease. Then, the WHO has used that fear as a strategy to obtain public and governmental compliance for a new pandemic treaty and more money. Such weaponized fear, otherwise known as fearporn, has also been found to elicit more public compliance for public health measures, such as masking, social distancing, vaccines, and lockdowns.

The gradual shift was subtle. In April 2023, the WHO wrote on its website:

> Disease X represents the knowledge that a serious international epidemic could be caused by a pathogen currently unknown to cause human disease. The R&D Blueprint explicitly seeks to enable early cross-cutting R&D preparedness that is also relevant for an unknown "Disease X."

In 2024, the WHO released the warning (without any data whatsoever) that the imaginary Disease X could result in twenty times more fatalities than COVID-19. Their explanation as to why this announcement was made to the world is as follows:

> Of course, there are some people who say this may create panic. It's better to anticipate something that may happen because it has happened in our history many times, and prepare for it.
>
> —WHO Director-General Tedros Adhanom Ghebreyesus,
> Davos - 2024

The bottom line is that Director-General Tedros Ghebreyesus openly admits that the WHO is using fear to pressure governments to open their books and comply with the new pandemic treaty. This is completely outside previously accepted norms of public health policy.

And the WHO's fearmongering and politicizing are working; Congress recently introduced a new bill, H.R.3832, "the Disease X Act of 2023."

The bill reads:

> This bill expands the priorities of the Biomedical Advanced Research and Development Authority (BARDA) to specifically include viral threats that have the potential to cause a pandemic.
>
> In particular, the bill expands the scope of innovation grants and contracts that may be awarded by BARDA to specifically include those that support research and development of certain manufacturing technology for medical countermeasures against viruses, including respiratory viruses, with pandemic potential. It also expands BARDA's authorized strategic initiatives to include advanced research, development, and procurement of countermeasures and products to address viruses with pandemic potential.

In order to understand the significance of this bill, it is important to understand what the Biomedical Advanced Research and Development Authority (BARDA) actually is. BARDA is the US Department of Health and Human Services office responsible for procuring and developing medical countermeasures, principally against bioterrorism, but also for biological, chemical, nuclear, and radiological threats, as well as pandemic influenza and emerging diseases. BARDA is currently limited in scope to procurement and development of medical countermeasures.

This bill is a sneaky backdoor to significantly expand BARDA's mission space, including research into viruses. In the past, BARDA has been limited in its authority and research mission so that it does not compete with NIH. The bill would provide for the expansion of yet another agency with very few limits on its ability to conduct research that is not in the public interest.

The truth is that planning for the next biothreat now includes all of our intelligence agencies. In fact, the Johns Hopkins Center for Health Security webpage titled "CURRENT PROJECTS, the Working Group on Readying Populations for COVID-19 Vaccine" lists two of its working group members as being employed by IQT (In-Q-Tel), which is the CIA's private, nonprofit investment firm. This investment group's mission includes "an agenda to guide the aggregation, generation, and translation of research about the social, behavioral, and communication challenges anticipated with COVID-19 vaccine." This is direct evidence that the CIA, through IQT, is involved in working with nonprofit agencies to create propaganda campaigns against the American people.

Furthermore, in the spring of 2024, the government began a new campaign to create more fearporn propaganda surrounding a bird flu outbreak that infected a handful of cattle, a few cats, and a very small number of people in the USA. The CDC then began testing vast numbers of cattle, cats, wildlife, farmers, and food processors while publicizing any indication of viral presence. As wild birds shed influenza virus in their feces, a positive PCR test is not an indicator of disease, only some sort of exposure.

In 2021, the House Intelligence Committee voted to create a new intelligence office with new roles, responsibilities, and a mandate relating to "disease outbreaks and pandemics" (and although not named, we can be sure that these include "bioterrorism" threats). In fact, the renamed intelligence office is in charge of not just biological threats but a vast array of "terrorism" threats. Chairman of the House Permanent Select Committee on Intelligence, Adam Schiff, D-Calif., inserted the provision into the annual intelligence authorization bill, and it was signed into law to create the National Counterproliferation and Biosecurity Center. Although it has been stated in the press that this new IC office is about biologics, its operational authority is vast. It is organizationally under the Office of the Director of National Intelligence that focuses on containing the spread of nuclear, biological, and chemical weapons.

The bill included a classified annex with several provisions to boost pandemic preparedness and global health security. Although this new center has been delegated to combat "disease outbreaks and pandemics," how they are to do that is completely obscured from the public. We do not know what Congress has authorized it to do as it has been shrouded using a nontransparent, classified mechanism. What we do know is that US intelligence and the Five Eyes intelligence alliance were deeply involved in almost every aspect of Western nation mismanagement of the COVIDcrisis, from the engineering of the virus to the ensuing global harmonized propaganda, psyops, and censorship campaigns.

We know that the US administrative state supports a unified, globalized, centralized political and economic world order based on a command economy rooted in massive databases, predictive artificial intelligence-driven decision-making, computational modeling, and the merging of man and machine to create a new species.

Fulfilling this objective is believed to require universal surveillance, propaganda powered by modern psychology, algorithmic censorship, cultural homogenization, and centralized automated economic controls and resource allocation.

So, isn't it time for those of us who believe there is a better way to live than to be controlled; to plan out responses and measures to combat all these draconian measures? To develop countermeasure methods to respond to a biothreat that does not employ censorship, propaganda, mandates, and behavioral modification techniques. You know, the old-fashioned way where the government relies on people to use their own critical thinking skills to assess what is best for themselves and their families after getting and examining all the relevant information available?

A collective group discussion concerning both how "we" were and are still being controlled, nudged, censored, and lied to by our government is in order. Because these efforts to control through behavioral modification and propaganda are only increasing throughout our digital world.

## A Battlefield Assessment Is Critical to Developing a Game Plan for Resistance

Below is a quote from Frank Gaffney, Jr., cofounder of The Sovereignty Coalition.

> Political warfare is the art of heartening one's friends and disheartening one's enemies. It makes use of ideas, words, images, and deeds to compel or convince friends, foes, or neutrals into cooperation or acquiescence. Effective political warriors know that the best way

to prevail in modern ideological conflict is not through killing, but through persuasion, co-option, and influence.

—Frank Gaffney, Jr.

The government has defined a series of terms that must be incorporated into our lexicon to effectively communicate about fighting governmental tyranny. This is why a complete glossary of PsyWar terms is included at the end of this book.

The US Department of Defense (DoD) 2004 and 2010 Counterinsurgency Operations Reports define "psyops" as the following:

---

**Psychological operations:** Planned operations to convey selected information and indicators to foreign audiences to influence their emotions, motives, objective reasoning, and ultimately the behavior of foreign governments, organizations, groups, and individuals. The purpose of psychological operations is to induce or reinforce foreign attitudes and behavior favorable to the originator's objectives. Also called PYSOP.

When authorized, PSYOP forces may be used domestically to assist lead federal agencies during disaster relief and crisis management by informing the domestic population.[23]

---

Read that last sentence again: "PSYOP forces may be used domestically to assist lead federal agencies during disaster relief and crisis management."

At the heart of psyops operations are behavioral tools or mind-control techniques such as hypnosis, mass formation, neural linguistic programming, repetitive messaging, censorship, security theater, bots, trolls, computational (big) data, and the use of fear to drive anxiety and insert propaganda into the hearts and minds of a populace.

A US Army website recruiting page describes how the military uses psyops.[24] To quote from that website:

DELIBERATELY DECEIVE

Military deception missions use psychological warfare to deliberately mislead enemy forces during a combat situation.

# INFLUENCE WITH INFORMATION
Military Information Support Operations (MISO) missions involve sharing specific information to foreign audiences to influence the emotions, motives, reasoning, and behavior of foreign governments and citizens. This can include cyber warfare and advanced communication techniques across all forms of media.

# ADVISE GOVERNMENTS
Interagency and government support missions shape and influence foreign decision making and behaviors in support of United States' objectives.

# PROVIDE COMMUNICATIONS FOR RESCUE EFFORTS
Civil Authorities Information Support (CAIS) missions aid civilian populations during disaster relief situations by sharing critical information to support the rescue effort.

What is the history of Army Psychological Operations?

Founded during World War I to devastate opposing troops' morale, the psyops unit has played a critical role in World War II, the Vietnam War, and recent operations in Afghanistan and Iraq, where unconventional warfare provided by psyops has been crucial to national security.

Another very important term to understand is nudging. A nudge is a technique for modifying people's behavior in a predictable way by influencing people to behave in a desired outcome. Nudging is usually performed covertly, although that is not considered a required criterion of the nudge. The Behavioral Science and Policy Association defines nudging as:

A nudge is any attempt at influencing people's judgment, choice or behavior in a predictable way that is motivated because of cognitive boundaries, biases, routines, and habits in individual and social decision-making posing barriers for people to perform rationally in their own self-declared interests, and which works by making use of those boundaries, biases, routines, and habits as integral parts of such attempts.[25]

Nudging alters the environment, triggering automatic cognitive processes to favor the desired outcome. Nudging makes it more likely that an individual will make a particular choice or behave in a particular way. Fear nudging involves using nudges that utilize a fear component to drive behavior, opinions, or decision-making. While this is a particularly effective form of nudging, it is absolutely unethical, in my opinion and that of others.

One of the best examples of "nudging," is the use of a "fly" in the toilet bowl. First introduced at Schiphol airport in Amsterdam back in 1999, the idea was simple: etch the image of a fly in a urinal and men will aim for it almost every time. To be precise, men will aim for it well over 80 percent of the time. The airport found that costs of urinal clean-up went way down, without forcing anyone to do anything. This example has been cited hundreds of times as to why governments should be involved in "nudging campaigns." Rarely is it mentioned that such coercion might be highly unethical in some situations and falls under the categories of propaganda and, in some cases, psyops and psywar.

In a special issue of the peer-reviewed journal *Current Opinion in Psychology* dedicated to applied nudge technology, researcher Patrick Fagan provides a comprehensive summary of nudge methods commonly employed in online communication, with an emphasis on the use of nudge technology for online marketing.[26] Related strategies have been adapted for use in promoting "public health" policy compliance. In the abstract, Fagan summarizes his findings:

> Internet users are inundated with attempts to persuade, including digital nudges like defaults, friction, and reinforcement. When these nudges fail to be transparent, optional, and beneficial, they can become "dark patterns," categorized here under the acronym FORCES (Frame, Obstruct, Ruse, Compel, Entangle, Seduce). Elsewhere, psychological principles like negativity bias, the curiosity gap, and fluency are exploited to make social content viral, while more covert tactics, including Astroturfing, meta-nudging, and inoculation, are used to manufacture consensus. The power

of these techniques is set to increase in line with technological advances such as predictive algorithms, generative AI, and virtual reality.

"Frame" is defined as information presented in a way that biases choice. Examples of this tactic include:

- Extraneous reference prices (e.g., old sale price vs. new sale price)
- Fake or ambiguous scarcity claims (e.g., low stock, limited time)
- Fake social proof and parasocial pressure (e.g., high demand label, reviews, endorsements, testimonials)
- Decoys (i.e., a product added to a set simply to make the others look more attractive)
- False hierarchies, in which one option is more visually salient than the others
- Confirmshaming (e.g., "No thanks, I don't want to be a better marketer.")

"Obstruct" is defined as making it harder for users to do what they intended to do. Common examples include:

- Roach motel tactics, where it is easy to subscribe or access but hard (or impossible) to leave or logout
- Roadblocks to actions, like time delays to account deletion
- Price obfuscation (e.g., prevent pricing comparison, bundling prices, or using intermediate currencies)
- Adding extra steps; make navigation or privacy policies labyrinthine; hiding information
- Using a foreign language, complex wording or jargon to inhibit understanding

"Ruse"—Users are tricked into making a choice other than what they intended. Examples:

- Products being sneaked into the basket, usually due to an obscured opt-out button prior
- Drip pricing; hidden costs like delivery fees added to basket at the end
- Ads with a delayed appearance so that users accidently click on them when they meant to click something else
- Disguised ads (e.g., that look like a download button)
- Ambiguous information causing users to get a different outcome to what they expected
- Bait and switch, where the user sets out to do one thing but something else happens instead
- Trick questions (e.g., a list of checkboxes where the first means opt-out and the second means opt-in)
- Distraction (e.g., focusing attention on one element to distract from a small opt-out checkbox)
- Sponsored adverts disguised as normal content

"Compel" nudges force users to do something they may not have wanted to do. Examples:

- Forced continuity, like automatically charging a credit card once a free trial comes to an end
- Grinding, where gamers are forced to repeat the same process in order to secure game elements like badges
- Forced registration to use a website, and pay-to-play
- Nagging (e.g., to buy the premium version of a service)
- Privacy Zuckering and Contact Zuckering, wherein users are tricked into sharing data or address book contacts
- Defaults and pre-selected options
- Playing by appointment (users are forced to use a service at specific times lest they lose advantages or achievements)

"Entangle"— with this strategy, users are kept occupied for longer than they may have intended. Examples:

- Fake notifications (e.g., about content never interacted with) to draw users (back) in
- Pausing notifications rather than being able to permanently stop them
- Never-ending autoplay (e.g., a new video plays when the current one is finished)
- Infinite scroll (i.e., new content continuously loads at the bottom of the feed)
- Casino pull-to-refresh (i.e., users get an animated refresh of content by swiping down)
- Time fog (e.g., hiding the smartphone clock so the amount of time spent in the app is not "felt")

"Seduce"—Users are engaged emotionally rather than rationally. Examples:

- Highly emotive language or imagery; cuteness
- Pressured selling (e.g., under time pressure)
- Bamboozlement: Choice overload or information overload
- Guilty pleasures (i.e., personalized suggestions that prey on individual vulnerabilities)

The ethics of nudging in the context of the COVIDcrisis have been examined and published in another peer-reviewed paper titled "Ethics of Nudging in the COVID-19 Crisis and the Necessary Return to the Principles of Shared Decision Making: A Critical Review."[27]

Nudging, a controversial technique for modifying people's behavior in a predictable way, is claimed to preserve freedom of choice while simultaneously influencing it. Nudging had been largely confined to situations such as promoting healthy eating choices but has been employed in the coronavirus disease 2019 (COVID-19) crisis in a shift toward measures that involve significantly less choice, such as shoves and behavioral prods. Shared decision making (SDM), a method for direct involvement and autonomy, is an alternative approach to communicate risk. . . . The so-called fear nudges, as well as the dissemination of strongly emotionalizing or moralizing messages can lead to intense psycho-physical stress. The use of these nudges by specialized units during the COVID-19 pandemic generated a societal atmosphere of fear that precipitated a deterioration of the mental and physical health of the population. Major recommendations of the German COVID-19 Snapshot Monitoring (COSMO) study, which are based on elements of nudging and coercive measures, do not comply with ethical principles, basic psychological principles, or evidence-based data. SDM was misused in the COVID-19 crisis, which helped to achieve one-sided goals of governments. . . . There should be a return to an open-ended, democratic, and pluralistic scientific debate without using nudges. It is therefore necessary to return to the origins of SDM.

Our government is using nudging and other political PsyWar methods, through social media and mainstream media, to control the narrative. But this battlefield is a type of asymmetric warfare. They have the resources: the power, the money, mainstream media, Big Pharma, tech giants, and social media supporting their efforts.

When the government decided that they would not support the use of ivermectin and hydroxychloroquine as early treatments against COVID-19, despite our laws that allow such usage, these also became censored topics and taboo to discuss. Messages about ivermectin being dangerous and [untrue] news stories about horse-paste sickening people were planted throughout the internet and TV. This was censorship and propaganda against the American people. This was and is an example of the deployment of PsyWar.

When a false flag "peer-reviewed" article appeared in the *Lancet* in 2020 about the dangers of hydroxychloroquine in a clinical trial using a multinational registry, this was black propaganda meant to influence not only the public but also politicians, the administrative state, and federal agencies including the intelligence community.[28] To this day, it remains unclear who or how this story was planted. A Stat article from June 2020 explains:[29]

The *Lancet*, one of the world's top medical journals, on Thursday retracted an influential study that raised alarms about the safety of the experimental Covid-19 treatments chloroquine and hydroxychloroquine amid scrutiny of the data underlying the paper.

Just over an hour later, the *New England Journal of Medicine* retracted a separate study, focused on blood pressure medications in Covid-19, that relied on data from the same company.

The retractions came at the request of the authors of the studies, published last month, who were not directly involved with the data collection and sources, the journals said.

"We can no longer vouch for the veracity of the primary data sources," Mandeep Mehra of Brigham and Women's Hospital, Frank Ruschitzka of University Hospital Zurich, and Amit Patel of University of Utah said in a statement issued by the *Lancet*. "Due to this unfortunate development, the authors request that the paper be retracted."

This falsified study halted the US government from stockpiling and distributing hydroxychloroquine early in the pandemic. That stopped the outpatient use of hydroxychloroquine, because the government immediately sent out national warnings about its usage. One might think there would be a government investigation as to who set up this faked database and why it was faked. But there was absolutely no interest in investigating these made-up databases or continuing with the government plans for clinical trials that had been already developed but halted due to this falsified study. The Emergency Use Authorization for a new drug product, such as a vaccine, requires no other safe and effective treatment option be available. Was this the reason why safe, generic drugs were such a threat? Was this the true reason for the falsified data and the stoppage of the clinical trial? On April 2, 2024, the House Oversight Committee on COVID invited *Lancet* and *Nature* to testify about their early coverage of the pandemic, their early communications with Anthony Fauci and Francis Collins, as well as others in HHS.[30] According to Chairman Wenstrup, these journals refused the request. *Lancet* and *Nature* refused the request for unknown reasons. The implication of malfeasance or corruption looms large in their refusal to testify.

During the COVID-19 public health response, more and more people have woken up to the malfeasance. Now, there is a small, growing guerrilla army of supporters of freedom. Many people have come down on the side of our Constitution, even changing party affiliations and core beliefs.

But if this resistance speaks too loudly or speaks truth to power too often, they are taken out by warnings, shadow banning, and even outright removal from access to social media platforms. Hence, in most cases, one is allowed "freedom of speech, not reach," as Mr. Elon Musk stated to the European Ministry of Truth. To this day, Dr. Robert Malone is permanently banned on LinkedIn for the crime of speaking truth to power, and is significantly shadow-banned (or "throttled") on X.

The loss of the right to free speech is real. During COVID, some conservative politicians could no longer use platforms like YouTube, LinkedIn, or Twitter. Senator Ron Johnson, the ranking member of the Permanent Subcommittee on Investigations, lost the right to publish on YouTube. That should scare and shock anyone with a thinking brain. Our politicians are being banned from free speech because Big Tech, working with and getting paid by the Biden administration, didn't like their messaging. Even more chilling is that 50 percent of the US population believes that censorship is needed to overcome false online information.[31]

Censorship interferes with our fundamental right to a free press and with the integrity and independence of our elections. Our entire republic and democracy are now at risk due to the creation of huge, unelected, and uncontrolled rogue bureaucracies that use digital levers to manipulate the political lives of both citizens and politicians. The growth of these censorship tools is difficult or impossible to check.

Articles on such subjects as the Wuhan Institute of Virology lab leak and the COVID origins were removed from search engines and were not allowed to be republished by the Trusted News Initiative from 2020 to 2022.[32] Professionals lost their jobs and were frequently investigated for speaking or writing on forbidden topics or for sharing forbidden opinions. Many lost their licenses for treating COVID-19 patients with early treatment protocols using generic drugs, for speaking out about the dangers of the vaccine, or even for being critical of masking or lockdowns. Some might call these tactics defenestration. Churches were closed, and fundamental rights to congregate and to protest were suspended. As this happened, more and more people started to realize that the very freedoms that made Western countries what they were had been compromised by false, unfounded promises of public health protection.

One of the largest newspapers in Denmark apologized for its journalistic failure during COVID-19. This newspaper only published the official government narrative without questioning it. This newspaper continued to follow this plan long after it was clear that the government narrative was crumbling.[33] This shows that governments' ability to manipulate social media to control the population has become normalized.

When a person is presented with a novel idea, that idea will stick in the mind, even when the individual is presented with facts that conflict with the original concept. They will generally not deviate from those beliefs if the mental construct is fully formed. People build a scaffold of ideas based on first impressions and once constructed, it is difficult to tear down. Effective propaganda takes advantage of this fact.

During the pandemic, people who believed that lockdowns and masks would save them from catching COVID-19 could not let go of the idea. To this day, many people who initially believed that Hunter Biden's laptop was a fake continue to insist that this notion is based on fact, not a propaganda falsehood fabricated by fifty-one officers of the US intelligence community. This shows the power of propaganda to instill narratives into a population which are not easily eliminated—even with persuasive facts.

## Where, as a Nation, as a Society, and as Individuals, Do We Go from Here?

As is the case with many, this battle has completely changed our lives, our ways of thinking, and our perspectives on our government and world leaders. There is no going back for us. We will not let this great nation descend into totalitarianism without a fight. This is not about a pandemic or a biothreat.

This is about freedom.

# CHAPTER 3
## Psychological Bioterrorism

**Psychological Bioterrorism** is the use of fear about a disease by governments and other organizations, such as Big Pharma, to manipulate individuals, populations, and governments. Although the fear of infectious disease is an obvious example, it is not the only way psychological bioterrorism is used.

In a January 2017 interview with the journal *Current Concerns*, Dr. Alexander Kouzminov (a former Soviet-Russian Foreign Intelligence Service [SVR] intelligence officer) described operational fundamentals of spy tradecraft which he termed "Information Bioterrorism." His analysis was supported with examples drawn from events surrounding late-twentieth- and early-twenty-first-century infectious disease outbreak events; Severe Acute Respiratory Syndrome (SARS) (2002–2003), Avian Influenza A (H5N1) (1997, 2006–2007), and H1N1 "Swine flu" (2009). He defined this as a new method for exerting global operational influence and manipulation over individuals, populations, and nations,[1] and he suggested that other names for this strategy could be "information bioterrorism" or "information biological blackmail." In the essay, Dr. Kouzminov provides specific language for key roles, responsibilities, and strategies used when deploying this form of bioterrorism.

Recognizing that deployment of this strategic approach has become one weapon in the larger domain of modern psychological warfare (or PsyWar), we propose an alternative term for these methods: "Psychological Bioterrorism." Since psychological bioterrorism operates on both conscious as well as subconscious levels, this form of mental manipulation is an example of both PsyWar (targeting the conscious mind) as well as cognitive warfare (targeting the subconscious).

Dr. Kouzminov's credentials in this area are impeccable. He is a highly qualified and experienced biosecurity specialist with an extensive record of work in central government and the private sector as a senior advisor, senior analyst, director, and chief executive. He has contributed to a number of environmental and biosecurity policy papers within New Zealand and internationally, including UNESCO policy forums (among others), and has received several awards from New Zealand's central government as well as international recognitions for his policy development work. Dr. Kouzminov was an intelligence operative in the Soviet-Russian Foreign Intelligence Service (SVR) during the 1980s and 90s and dealt with intelligence operations with bioweapons-related activities in target countries. He is the author of *Biological Espionage: Special Operations of the Soviet and Russian Foreign Intelligence Services in the West* (2005, Greenhill Books) and has over fifty published works on biosecurity, focusing on bioterrorism, bioweapons, risk control and management, and policy approaches.

## What Is Psychological Bioterrorism?

"Psychological" or "Information Bioterrorism" involves the use of fear of an infectious disease to control people and their behavior. It is a very potent method for mass manipulation of populations, and this method works by creating a state of heightened anxiety and fear of death in the people who are targeted. This promoted fear is often based on allusions to misleading, poorly documented historical stories—essentially folktales or parables—about historical epidemics of very dangerous diseases such as plague, typhoid fever, yellow fever, polio, or smallpox. Often, these parables have little relevance to modern society with its sophisticated sanitary practices, clean water, hospital networks, and wide spectrum of antibiotics, antifungals, antiparasitics, and anti-inflammatory drugs.

One example of such a story is the tale of the global "Spanish Influenza" pandemic of 1918. This story has long been used to justify the need for mass annual influenza vaccination to avoid some future influenza pandemic. But this is misleading folklore. This story has been repeated for over a century since these events occurred and still incites deep fear in the minds of many.

The truth is that the waves of mass death from infectious disease which did occur around 1918 were not really due to the H1N1 influenza strain, which *did* infect and cause upper respiratory sickness in many people all over the world—but did not actually cause mass death. Instead, current scientific analysis indicates that these deaths were primarily due to bacterial pneumonia, which co-circulated with the H1N1 influenza virus, together with inappropriate use of non-pharmaceutical public health measures, including masks, and inappropriate dosing with a newly discovered pharmaceutical drug—aspirin. A much more nuanced reality, but not one that supports the need for annual influenza virus vaccination.

The recent global surge in propaganda concerning a more pathogenic strain of H5N1 (Avian Influenza) that is now circulating in large chicken flocks (and a wide range of wild birds) provides a great case study of how a psychological or information bioterrorism event campaign is crafted and deployed. This current round of psychological bioterrorism almost precisely mirrors the previous campaign deployed during 2010–2016.

## What Makes Psychological Bioterrorism Effective?

The main components and aftereffects of this form of mass psychological manipulation include the following:

1.  A **Time factor**: Psychological bioterrorism provides a practical method for immediate global transmission and development of widespread panic through electronic means of communication.
2.  A **Vulnerability factor**: People feel helplessness when confronting the threat due to the lack of effective means of defense. This creates panic among the general population, which can then be directed or exploited to support other objectives.
3.  An **Uncertainty factor**: A lack of factual information about the source of the bioterror threat and its spread creates an opportunity to manipulate the masses of people who initiate the threat. Initiating and promoting a psychological bioterror event creates an opportunity to craft and promote an explanation of the event and to fashion propaganda narratives that serve or support other (typically hidden) objectives.

    In the case of the current "bird flu" narrative, these objectives may include promoting acceptance of mRNA-based genetic vaccination of dairy cattle and promoting the objective of culling cattle herds to mitigate the claimed effects of cattle on $CO_2$ emissions.

4. A **"lack of control" factor**: Every person who accepts the promoted bioterror narrative develops and internalizes a sense of being "out of control" because he/she is a suspicious object, liable to have the disease, and therefore is a threat to everyone else.

   This creates chronic internal anxiety in those vulnerable to the bioterror campaign, and this fear is then easily manipulated by the promotion of narratives requiring compliance with a series of actions—effective or ineffective—that serve to create a sense of purpose, identity, and belonging to an "in group" that has achieved protected status (from the manufactured Bioterror threat) by performing a ritual or modifying their behavior in some way.

## Who Deploys Psychological Bioterrorism?

Large-scale psychological bioterrorism, information bioterrorism, or "information biological blackmail" is usually secretly deployed by foreign or domestic "intelligence" or "security" services and implemented as an "active operation" in target countries using a variety of witting or unwitting allies. However, this strategy is also deployed to augment pharmaceutical industry business objectives.

The existence and deployment of an active psychological bioterror operation can be detected as a scripted series of active operational deployment stages, each involving well-defined strategies, actors, roles, and responsibilities.

These strategies, actors, roles, and responsibilities include the following:

1. An **"active operation"**—This is an activity of an organization (typically a foreign intelligence service) which is aimed at a "target audience" (an object it wants to influence), and is carried out at the request of an "interested party" with "supporters" and "auxiliary means" in order to achieve the required "planned impacts."

   The "active operation" is carried out with the support of agents, supporting persons, and interested organizations. Usually, the "intelligence" or "security" organization (mercenary or governmentally associated) conducts the "active operation" using "false flags":

third-party agents or cutout organizations. In other words, it hides its main objectives under the cover of a (politically) neutral nongovernmental organization, a government bureaucracy, an academic institution, or otherwise hides its goals under some kind of a falsely crafted problem. These agents, supporting persons, and organizations can include networks of interested parties with similar, related, or complementary objectives.

2.  **"Interested parties"**—During the Cold War, "interested parties" were usually the government or its special (secret) services, in other words its "intelligence" or "defense" communities. Today, the "interested party" could be a corporate conglomerate, pharmaceutical companies, banks, and other large financial consortia, corporatist associations, national or global nongovernmental organizations, private and political groups, industry-associated lobbyist organizations, etc.

3.  **"Target"**—The objects or target audience of an "active operation" may be governments, high-ranking military officials, secret services of the enemy, political parties, banks, companies, etc., as well as ordinary populations, where the aim is to cause some kind of an impact and effect.

4.  **"Executor"**—Classically is some form of secret service, generally but not necessarily drawn from a national intelligence community. Usually, the "executor" carries out the "active operations" using one or more "false flag" operations, which means that it masquerades the true operation by covering it up with a false story or threat.

5.  **"Supporters"**—Examples of supporters include academics, "influencers" in the entertainment, social media, or arts, and neutral third parties [the latter are not with the intelligence community]; these can help the "executor" to realize the "active operations." Supporters are typically recruited using various means, including direct overt payments involving fee-for-service agreements or more covert indirect payments or incentives.

6.  **"Mass media"**—The key role played by mass (corporate and/or social) media is to implement active operations by auxiliary means. Mass media (corporate press and social media) is one of the most important ways to implement an active operation. The executor uses mass media to achieve the maximum impact on the target audience/

object of influence. For example, by raising a threat, spreading rumors, and promoting false information. The objective of all of this is really to spread disinformation designed to distract from the true operation and masquerade it.

7. **"Planned impacts"**—Information strategy and objectives sent out to impact a specific audience must be "sharp." It is important to design the strategy to influence the intended object. Information is put together purposefully, usually as a threat or a big problem, as if it's a real problem. The target audience should never doubt the information and should have no awareness of who or what is planning and guiding the messaging and distribution.

## What Are the Main Stages of a Psychological Bioterrorism Active Operation?

The approach used to carry out the active operation is based on a crafted strategy: First, messaging about the problem, and then deployment of its solution.

The main stages of the active operation, through which the psychological bioterror event can be created, are as follows:

Phase 1: The executor (e.g., intelligence service), with the help of supporters (e.g., agents) and auxiliary means (e.g., mass media), throws out false information (in one example—an imminent pandemic of bird flu) onto the target audience (e.g., public) with a pretense that it's real.

Phase 2: Executors, supporters, and auxiliary means accelerate the problem, making it a hot topic (maximum interest needs to be created). Once the false problem is created, it grows like a snowball, rolling and rolling, independently building size as though it's becoming a legitimate concern.

Phase 3: The operation's actual objective is realized (secretly)—monetary gains are obtained, government stability is undermined (e.g., economic loss), and any other planned impacts are achieved.

As Phase 3 is achieved, the target (general population) is told that the problem is being solved and risks are contained. This is done with side-line information (news stories, social media posts, interviews, etc.). However, ideally the problem is left hanging so that the executor can use it again. Ideally, having successfully crafted, inserted, and amplified the fear narrative, the general sense of fear and anxiety about the risks of the psychological bioterror threat agent (in this example, avian influenza or "bird flu") should be maintained at a low level so that it is easy to resurrect for future use.

## Practical Example; Deploying Psychological Bioterrorism

1.  Create the problem

First, there needs to be some report of a local outbreak of avian influenza in chickens or other animals, which the interested party can use to advance its own interests. This of course is false information. Avian influenza is endemic in a wide range of bird populations.

There can also be a report that it's a supposed "leak" from a secret military-medical laboratory, academic laboratory, or army "biodefense research" center. The executor (secret service) can deliberately craft such a situation to create great interest, awe, and fear.

2.  Snowball the problem

The media ("auxiliary means," also including "supporters," e.g., agents of influence) starts to "heat" the public.

The front pages of newspapers, TV channels, the internet, and social media are already filled with alarming titles—"highly pathogenic virus," "new contagious disease," "new flu outbreak into a pandemic," "be ready for corpses, flu plan says"—all heightening the threat and scaring everyone!

Mass media and interested organizations issue warning signs/messages like "the disease breaks the human-to-human transmission barrier" and "predict" that "the disease would infect up to millions of people globally." For example, "A super-flu could kill up to 1.9 million Americans, according to a draft of the government's plan to fight a worldwide epidemic."

3.  The problem becomes a hot topic

Health authorities/senior officials/experts/agents of influence express concerns that a virus will mutate into a form that can spread from one human to another, and this could lead to a worldwide pandemic, and claim that an influenza pandemic would likely lead to high rates of morbidity (sickness) and mortality (death). For example, " . . . the death toll from a human pandemic of avian influenza could be anything from 5 to 150 million." Also, "There is no time to waste. The virus [bird flu] could ignite the next human flu pandemic. I do not need to tell you of the terrible consequences that could bring to all nations and all peoples."

4.   Aggravating a problem and obtaining planned results
The World Health Organization (WHO) may announce a new strain or clade of avian influenza, a public health emergency of international concern. Soon, an influenza pandemic alert is raised to five on a six-level warning scale, meaning a pandemic is imminent.

Governments around the world have little choice; under pressure from businesses and citizens, they must respond to the WHO's pandemic declaration by spending billions on drugs and/or vaccines (if available) and throwing all available resources at fighting the disease once the WHO has declared the pandemic is underway. This triggers a wave of panic buying of vaccines and antivirals by governments around the world, in many cases involving far more money than hundreds of millions of dollars.

Authorized and interested organizations recommend that national governments use specific antivirals and flu-fighting drug(s) and inform them that a new, more "effective" vaccine is being developed and will soon be ready to use.

## Role of the Secret WHO Emergency Advisory Committee

For example, after the prior "swine flu" pandemic scare, the *British Medical Journal* (*BMJ*) highlighted the existence of a secret WHO emergency committee that advised the WHO director-general on when to declare the pandemic. It was claimed that "WHO was being advised by a group of people who were deeply embedded with the pharmaceutical industry, and had a lot of gain by beating this epidemic into a pandemic." The *BMJ* reported that WHO had, in February 2009 (about a month before the first cases of the 2009 "swine flu" outbreak were reported), amended the definition of the pandemic by removing that pandemic can cause "enormous numbers of deaths and illness," lowering the bar for pandemic announcements.

## Weaponizing and Promoting Fear of an Infectious Disease for Political, Financial, or Any Other Purpose Is Unethical

This includes physicians and corporations that amplify fear of a pathogen like H5N1 in order to sell drugs, vaccines, or nutritional supplements.

This includes individual scientists or virologists who assert that H5N1 will kill all COVID mRNA-based vaccine recipients when there are no data demonstrating active human-to-human transmission, let alone evidence of human H5N1 mortality in COVID-19 vaccine recipients. This is attention-seeking behavior and should be condemned. There is a human cost associated with these types of communications that is paid by the naive in terms of depression, suicide, and mental health damage when these types of fear-based narratives are promoted.

This includes state governments, which assert that H5N1 constitutes a public health emergency when no data demonstrate active human-to-human transmission.

This includes corporate media, which build viewership and readership by broadcasting or publishing speculative and unsupported fear regarding H5N1.

This includes governmental centers for Disease Control and Drug Regulators (FDA, EMA), NGOs, and global "health" agencies and organizations (WHO) that promote misleading, inflated, high H5N1 human mortality narratives based on rare infection events.

This includes academic physicians and scientists whose careers are advanced by promoting irrational public fear of infectious diseases including H5N1.

These are all examples of psychological bioterrorists.

We need to learn to protect ourselves from the economic, social, and psychological damage that is caused by permitting psychological bioterrorism. This is truly a crime against humanity, and one which can only be stopped when politicians with integrity and the general public become aware that they are being manipulated, refuse to play along, and socially, economically, and politically shun those who promote and deploy psychological bioterrorism.

Fool me once; shame on you. Fool me twice; shame on me.

# CHAPTER 4
# The New Inquisition of Scientism

> Religions: are the beliefs that humans hold, to which "they regard as holy, sacred, absolute, spiritual, divine, or worthy of special reverence."
>
> —Britannica[1]

Throughout history, religious groups often weed out heretics. Those with dissenting voices are censored and punished. Over time, this maladaptive group behavior has occasionally transmuted into secular governments with disastrous results. There is a name for this:

> **Inquisition**: A judicial procedure and later an institution that was established by the papacy and, sometimes, by secular governments to combat heresy. Derived from the Latin verb inquiro ("inquire into"), the name was applied to commissions in the 13th century and subsequently to similar structures in early modern Europe." —Britannica[2]

Another important term that does not get enough attention is scientism. A working definition of scientism is the belief that science and the scientific method are the best or only way to render truth about the world and reality.

Scientism has become a dominant philosophical point of view among most scientists and public administrators. At the heart of scientism's definition is the theory of materialism, which states that physical matter is the only reality, the only testable element. That means that, according to the philosophy of scientism, everything—including thought, feeling, the mind, and even consciousness—can be explained by physical phenomena and the composition of matter.

Scientism holds that there can be no supernatural, no religion (other than scientism), or God—everything must be grounded in physical matter. That which we can't detect does not exist. The problem with this being promulgated as a scientific theory is that it has not been repeatedly tested and validated. That means that at the heart of scientism is belief, not facts. That makes scientism another form of religion.

Basically, the thesis underpinning scientism is that if we do not have senses or technologies that can detect something, then it does not exist. Likewise, materialism holds that if we cannot observe something, it does not exist. Scientism endorses this as the main criterion for what qualifies as science. Everything must be grounded in observable physical matter.

In a sense, this is scientific narcissism because insisting that measurable physical matter is the only way to describe this entire planet, universe, and our individual consciousness has absolutely *not* been repeatedly tested and validated. We can't measure what we don't know exists. Hence, by their very definitions, the theories of materialism and its cousin scientism fail miserably based on first principles. If there are elements of our minds, the earth, and the universe that we can't comprehend, detect, or measure, how can we even begin to evaluate them scientifically?

If a scientific fact has been repeatedly tested, then it will withstand the test of time. But scientism is different than the scientific method. Yet, scientism is maintained and defended by the US government. However, scientism is not based on the scientific method. Scientism and materialism are fundamentally no different than religion. As an example, physics takes the idea that the universe is infinite as a given. Yet, there is no measurable proof of the universe's infinite nature. Theories surrounding the infinite universe are based on mathematical modeling and inferences based on measured Doppler light wavelength shifts, which is not the same as measurable proof. This core thesis of science (the infinite, expanding universe) is taught in every high school in America, and yet the possibility of the existence of God is typically a forbidden subject.

This passage by Paul Feyerabend in his book *Against Method* describes why democracies must not indulge in scientism.[3] He explains:

> Science can stand on its own feet and does not need any help from rationalists, secular humanists, Marxists, and similar religious movements; and . . . non-scientific cultures, procedures, and assumptions can also stand on their own feet and should be allowed to do so. . . . Science must be protected from ideologies; and societies, especially democratic societies, must be protected from science. . . . In a democracy, scientific institutions, research programmes, and suggestions must therefore be subjected to public control, there must be a separation of state and science just as there is a separation between state and religious institutions, and science should be taught as one view among many and not as the one and only road to truth and reality.

In science, "a fact" is an observation that's been confirmed so many times and in so many different ways that scientists can, for all intents and purposes, accept it as "true." Scientism is different. In the case of scientism, scientific observations and the scientific method are believed to be the best or only way to render truth about the world and reality. That the science is settled. From there, it follows that "the science" can be owned. That description neatly fits into the definition of religion as being the essence of what humans hold to be absolute or worthy of "special reverence." So, for all intents and purposes, scientism is a religion.

## Scientism Is a Belief System; a Religion

One definition of a religion is a belief system that follows a system of doctrine and practice; such a religion will often have cult-like leaders (for example, in scientism, Fauci, Darwin, and Pasteur are some of the chosen ones). One just has to look at the recent history of the Soviet Union to understand why what is happening is so dangerous.

> The anti-religious campaign in the Soviet Union was a campaign of anti-religious persecution against churches and religious

faithful by the Soviet government following the initial anti-religious campaign during the Russian Civil War. From 1917 to 1991 the Communist Party destroyed synagogues, churches, and mosques, killing between 12 and 20 million. Religious leaders were harassed, imprisoned, tortured, and even executed in the push to instill "scientific atheism." In the "Great Purge," up to 100,000 clergy members were slaughtered over a two-year period from 1936 to 1938.[4]

The fact-checkers controlled by the US government are leading this country down a very evil path. Eventually, the desire for "justice" to be administered for fact-checker-flagged infractions by heretics will become too great.

This is why the DHS, FBI, CIA, HHS, USAID, FDA, DOE, and the CDC must stop using scientism to guide US policy. The persecution of those who do not follow the dogma of scientism must stop. It is clear that scientism is a form of religion, it is a belief system, and it has no place in a secular government.

I dread government in the name of science. That is how tyrannies come in. In every age the men who want us under their thumb, if they have any sense, will put forward the particular pretension which the hopes and fears of that age render most potent. They "cash in." It has been magic, it has been Christianity. Now it will certainly be science. Perhaps the real scientists may not think much of the tyrants' "science"—they didn't think much of Hitler's racial theories or Stalin's biology. But they can be muzzled.

—C. S. Lewis[5]

If scientism has become a religion and "fact checkers" (whether or not scientifically qualified) are the de facto keepers of all facts that science accepts as true, is anyone who has a different opinion than either the fact checkers or United Nations leadership by definition a heretic? The definition of heresy is any belief or theory that is significantly different from the established orthodoxy. Particularly those beliefs held by religious organizations or law. A person who speaks heresy is known as a heretic. That means a person who does not believe that scientism or even science is the only way to understand the truth about the world could be labeled a scientific heretic. And we all know what happens to heretics . . .

## Rise of Scientism as a Bureaucratic Religion

In the United States, scientism has become the official religion of the US government. This is evidenced by the huge expenditures on research programs and the censorship of scientific dissent. If scientism is a religion, does that mean that the US government is not only promoting one set of religious beliefs over another, but that it is financially supporting the practitioners of scientism? Therefore, the churches of scientism: universities, research institutions, schools, and even government programs, including those at NIH and the NSF, function as governmentally sanctioned religious institutions. Does this mean that the government is essentially supporting a religion? It seems that maybe the separation of church and state has gone by the wayside.

The US government now considers itself the purveyor of what is "true" science versus "fake" science. "Fact-checkers" are now paid by the US government through contracts, and they now control what is defined as mis-, dis-, and mal- information. That means that the fact-checkers are the newly anointed (and government-funded) priests of the religion called scientism. What about the Department of Homeland Security (DHS), which has deemed the "purveyors" of mis-, dis-, and mal-information as domestic terrorists? By this reasoning, the DHS has become one of the new inquisition courts for this new religion.

The importance of the separation of church (as traditionally defined) and state has become so strong within certain elements of the administrative state that the government and its officials now behave as though traditional religion isn't just to be kept separate but that it is actually an enemy of the state. It is to be subsumed by scientism in our classrooms and teachings. For example, the "Big Bang" theory, with almost no data to support it, is taught in elementary schools across this country, but the mention of a different theory about the creation of the universe, one that involves a supreme being (dare we write God?) is banned. How is that right? Both ideas are based on belief and faith, not strong data. Yet one is promoted, and one is banned. Why?

As scientism has become the religion of the US government, bureaucrats and government officials have begun acting to suppress any other forms of religious beliefs, as well as any scientists or medical health professionals who might question officially approved "scientism" narratives. This makes dissident scientists/medical professionals, as well as people who hold religious beliefs, heretics in the eyes of the federal government. Add to that, traditional religious groups have now also been labeled as enemies of the state. Reasoning by analogy, we can now expect the US government to go after established churches, cultures, and professional organizations that do not support approved scientism narratives.

A recent example that illustrates how the US government is now targeting churches is the revelations by the US Congress that the FBI is actively seeking informants (spies) from inside the Catholic church. The reason is that, institutionally, the FBI has determined that traditional religions are growing domestic terrorists. To my knowledge, the Catholic church has not been a source of domestic terrorists over the years (at least since the Spanish Inquisition ran its course), and yet here we are. . . . This federal law enforcement agency also specifically targeted "mainline Catholic parishes" as part of its efforts. House Judiciary Chairman Jim Jordan, R-Ohio, summarized findings from his committee's investigations into this topic: "If you're a parent attending a school board meeting; if you're a pro-lifer praying at a clinic, or you're a Catholic simply going to Mass, you are a target of the government, a target of the FBI." Representative Jordan then said that officials were attempting to "inflate" their investigations in order to treat them as domestic and violent extremism cases. Over two dozen FBI whistleblowers contributed to this report (as reported by Fox News).

The question now is, if the US government continues down this path, when will the real inquisitions start?

Before the United States, other governments, WHO, WEF and the United Nations gain additional momentum in this push to expand the power of the new globalist religion of scientism, let's see if we can transform this disorder into an opportunity to build a Great Awakening that can move us forward toward fulfilling the full potential of the Human Species. A new morning. Together. Progression beyond resiliency. Antifragile. Based on the recognition that there are truths that transcend the detection capabilities of current technology and materials knowledge.

# CHAPTER 5
# Deep State Censorship Exposed

## How the US Government Tore Robert Malone, MD's Reputation Apart Piece by Piece

*Fellow Americans, the government will take care of you!*

*They don't want you to worry about posting information that they don't approve of on your social media accounts.*

*They don't want you to worry that the US government would directly interfere with your First Amendment rights, and certainly would never meddle in an election or with your medical freedoms.*

*That said, the deep state will gladly "contract those jobs out to left-wing 'disinformation' fighting firms."*

—*The Administrative State*

A bombshell Congressional House Interim report was published on November 6, 2023, titled: *Weaponization of "Disinformation" Pseudo-Experts and Bureaucrats: How the Federal Government Partnered with Universities to Censor American's Political Speech*, Interim Staff Report by the Committee on the Judiciary and the Select Subcommittee on the Weaponization of the Federal Government US House of Representatives. In that report, the committee laid out the role of the Election Integrity Partnership (EIP) that the Department of Homeland Security contracted (that means paid for) to censor Americans. From the House press release:

The report reveals how the Department of Homeland Security's (DHS) Cybersecurity & Infrastructure Security Agency (CISA) and the Global Engagement Center (GEC, within the State Department) coordinated with Stanford University and other entities to create the Election Integrity Partnership to censor Americans' speech in the lead-up to the 2020 election. It outlines how the Election Integrity Project (EIP) was created in the summer of 2020 to provide a way for the federal government to launder its censorship activities in hopes of bypassing both the First Amendment and public scrutiny. The report also reveals for the first time internal emails from EIP members stating that the EIP was created "at the request of DHS/CISA."

The Committee and Select Subcommittee have obtained documents showing that CISA had access to the inner workings of the EIP, including incoming misinformation reports. The report discloses hundreds of the nonpublic "misinformation" reports from the EIP's centralized reporting system, known as "Jira tickets." During the EIP's operation, the Jira ticketing system was accessible only to select parties, including federal agencies, universities, and Big Tech. The EIP targeted true information, jokes, and political opinions of Americans across the political spectrum, but especially conservatives. This includes candidates such as President Trump and Senator Tillis, entities such as Newsmax and the Babylon Bee, and conservative commentators such as Sean Hannity, Mollie Hemingway, and Charlie Kirk.[1]

Representative Jim Jordan also provided receipts through his Twitter (X) account showing how the Election Integrity Partnership (EIP) was founded. These documents, including a letter from the Atlantic Council in 2020 advising a "sync-up," whereby they created the Election Integrity Partnership. *Ergo*, a partnership of four organizations working in collaboration with both the US government and the Atlantic Council. The letter was from Graham Brookie, Vice President and Senior Director of the Atlantic Council's Digital Forensic Research Lab (DFRLab) to other Atlantic Council members, which outlined the founding of the Election Integrity Partnership. From the letter:

On the DHS app, fake news, and any other US election-related work, it would be great to sync up, as well. I know the Council has a number of efforts on broad policy issues around the elections, but we just set up an election integrity partnership at the request of DHS/CISA and are in weekly comms to debrief on disinfo, IO, etc.

The EIP partnership was made up of four "partners." They were the Stanford Internet Observatory (SIO), the University of Washington Center for an Informed Public (CIP), Graphika, and the Atlantic Council. Each organization had a distinct role to play, from identifying "spreaders of misinformation," to identifying the networks of social media landscapes that those so accused interacted on, to actual recommendations to social media companies for removal of identified offending posts, and communications back and further between the government and the EIP. This was done with government money and resources.

Below is information on each EIP partner and a description of their technologies or recent activities.

1. **The Stanford Internet Observatory (SIO):** Stanford has removed the SIO page from its website, but the Wayback Machine still has a somewhat functional archival copy—although much of the original content has been scrubbed.

    The archived SIO page only lists case reports up to June 2020, as the rest have been removed, but the Wayback Machine has some detailed reports up through 2022. This includes information about SIO's operation called "*Platform Takedown*," which was developed to get information that the EIP deemed unacceptable, removed from the major social media platforms.

2. **The University of Washington's Center for an Informed Public (CIP):** Their mission "is to resist strategic misinformation, promote an informed society, and strengthen democratic discourse."

    In the late fall of 2023, the CIP refocused its identification of targets for censorship from election "fraud" and COVID-19, to identifying the flow of what they view as the "new elites" of X (*ergo*, influencers with large followings) regarding how they share information regarding the Hamas/Israel conflict. The implication is that "X" or its influencers are being targeted or will be targeted in the future for more harassment by the Election Integrity Partnership.

3. **Graphika:** This company specializes in "cutting-edge technology that creates large-scale explorable maps of social media landscapes." The website boasts that its in-depth AI analysis automation reveals insights to help "clients and partners understand complex online networks and take decisive action." Its "AI-based automation works on streaming and other data to identify narratives, behaviors, and actors of interest." Graphika lists Harvard, Oxford, and DARPA as its partners.

4. **The Atlantic Council's Digital Forensic Research Lab (DFRLab):** The Atlantic Council's DFRL employs former US intelligence establishment technology staffers (*ergo*, ex-CIA and DIA = "deep state" personnel), and of course, the Atlantic Council itself is known as a landing bed for deep state operatives (and is otherwise known as a CIA cutout organization).

The Atlantic Council's Digital Forensic Research Lab website states that:

> Centralized and decentralized platforms share a common set of threats from motivated malicious users—and require a common set of investments to ensure trustworthy, user-focused outcomes . . .
>
> Further research and capability building are necessary to avoid the further proliferation of these threats.
>
> Within industry, decades of "trust and safety" (T&S) practice has developed into a field that can illuminate the complexities of building and operating online spaces. Outside industry, civil society groups, independent researchers, and academics continue to lead the way in building collective understanding of how risks propagate via online platforms—and how products could be constructed to better promote social well-being and to mitigate harms.

Take away all the flowery words, and that sure sounds like organized government-sponsored deep state censorship! Beyond the Astroturf organizations listed above, the Congressional House Interim report does an excellent job of documenting how the Election Integrity Partnership worked to censor the American people, including the following:

> Enter the Election Integrity Partnership (EIP), a consortium of "disinformation" academics led by Stanford University's Stanford Internet Observatory (SIO) that worked directly with the Department of Homeland Security and the Global Engagement Center, a multi-agency entity housed within the State Department, to monitor and censor Americans' online speech in advance of the 2020 presidential election. Created in the summer of 2020 "at the request" of the Cybersecurity and Infrastructure Security Agency (CISA), the EIP provided a way for the federal government to launder its censorship activities in hopes of bypassing both the First Amendment and public scrutiny.

This interim staff report details the federal government's heavy-handed involvement in the creation and operation of the EIP, which facilitated the censorship of Americans' political speech in the weeks and months leading up to the 2020 election. This report also publicly reveals for the first-time secret "misinformation" reports from the EIP's centralized reporting system, previously accessible only to select parties, including federal agencies, universities, and Big Tech. The Committee and Select Subcommittee obtained these nonpublic reports from Stanford University only under the threat of contempt of Congress. These reports of alleged mis- and disinformation were used to censor Americans engaged in core political speech in the lead up to the 2020 election.

As this new information reveals, and this report outlines, the federal government and universities pressured social media companies to censor true information, jokes, and political opinions. This pressure was largely directed in a way that benefitted one side of the political aisle: true information posted by Republicans and conservatives was labeled as "misinformation" while false information posted by Democrats and liberals was largely unreported and untouched by the censors. The pseudoscience of disinformation is now—and has always been—nothing more than a political ruse most frequently targeted at communities and individuals holding views contrary to the prevailing narratives."[2]

Basically, this report lays out how people on social media platforms who were saying things that the deep state did not want to be said were the ones being censored.

The EIP's operation was straightforward: "External stakeholders," including both federal agencies and government-funded organizations, submitted misinformation reports directly to the EIP. The EIP's misinformation "analysts" next scoured the internet for additional examples of misinformation. If the submitted report flagged a Facebook post, the EIP analysts searched for similar content on Twitter, YouTube, TikTok, Reddit, and other major social media platforms. Once all of the offending links were compiled, the EIP sent the most significant ones directly to Big Tech with specific recommendations on how the social media platforms should censor the posts, such as reducing the posts' "discoverability," "suspending [an account's] ability to continue tweeting for a period of time," "monitoring if any of the tagged influencer accounts retweet" a particular user, and, of course, removing thousands of Americans' posts.

The House committee (through Rep. Jim Jordan) also released a Google doc of the EIP's misinformation "analysts," who created "Jira Tickets" of those that were to be censored in chronological order, and includes details of what their alleged misinformation "crimes" were. A Jira ticket, also known as a Jira issue, is commonly used in the information technology industry. It is a digital representation of a task, bug, or request that requires attention and resolution. Jira is a ticketing system developed by the Atlassian corporation that is used to manage any type of information technology task management workflow. Jira is used by agile teams for project management and by IT help desks and support teams as a ticketing system. It is a fundamental component of the Jira ticketing system, used to track and manage work items throughout an information technology project's lifecycle.

In the Jira Tickets list, it is worth noting that on June 11, 2021, the list abruptly changed its focus from "election misinformation" to "vaccine misinformation" and renamed these efforts as the "Virality project." It's almost like there was some sort of directive issued from the top [sarcasm].

On the last page of the Jira Ticket list found in the Congressional report appendix, Robert Malone, an author of this book, is included in those censored by the EIP. The EIP lists his misinformation sin as being what Robert said in his original interview with Tucker Carlson for Fox News.

Almost directly after that, the list ends. It's as if the Congressional House Interim report didn't want to cover the censorship of the COVID-19 vaccine adverse events but instead only focused on election integrity censorship. So, how many times Robert was recommended for censorship regarding COVID-19 statements by the EIP/Virality project is not public knowledge. Except that based on the obvious shadow banning over the past two years, it is reasonable to assume that there were many such "Jira Tickets."

Robert's first "crime" was claiming on the Fox interview that the risks outweigh the benefits for teenagers and young adults (June 30, 2021).

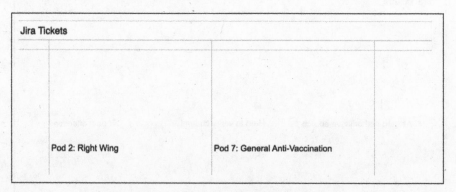

As shown in the image below, the Election Integrity Partnership (now the Virality Partnership) notes Robert is both "general anti-vaccination" and also "right wing" in his affiliations.

| Jira Tickets | | |
| --- | --- | --- |
| | | |
| | | |
| Pod 2: Right Wing | Pod 7: General Anti-Vaccination | |

To put it mildly, this document is really, really creepy. The fact that Robert's *"Right Wing"* political leanings are mentioned implies that being *"Right Wing"* was/is criteria enough for censorship. The fact is that criteria such as political affiliation were considered sufficient justification for censorship. These documents clearly provide evidence of direct political and election interference by the Biden administration through its Astroturf organizations.

This list also labels Robert as being generally against vaccination. It is as if being against the mRNA gene therapy in the form of a "vaccine" for specific vulnerable groups, which was his position early in the roll-out of the mRNA jab, makes one generally against vaccination. This was also apparently enough justification for government-promoted censorship.

As shown in the Jira ticket image below, the Election Integrity Partnership also notes that Robert is a "repeat offender." This labeling implies that he might be subject to further attention or government interventions, which could include FISA warrants, FBI/DHS investigations, automatic censorship programs, or more deplatforming from social media.

In fact, Robert was deplatformed from most of social media. He was banned from *Twitter* for almost all of 2022 (until after Twitter was purchased by Elon Musk and the "Twitter files" were released), permanently banned from LinkedIn in 2022, and almost completely shadow-banned from Facebook, Instagram, and TikTok from 2021 on to the present. This was all made possible by the Department of Homeland Security Bulletin labeling anyone in the United States who spreads "mis-dis-mal information" (MDM) as a potential domestic terrorist.[3]

| Jira Tickets | | |
| --- | --- | --- |
| | | |
| Alleged authoritative source | Hard to verify content | Repeat offender |
| | | |

It is also interesting that he was censored, even though the informants could not verify whether the contents of what he was saying were true. Note how they label him as an "alleged" authoritative source—that is, not proven.

Not that it matters, but it should not be up to the US government or its contractors to determine what speech is or is not allowed on the internet.

The government has jumped from its stated purpose of removing verified foreign false information about elections on social media to removing any media, from experts and others, that does not parrot the governmental narrative about any chosen topic. It even goes so far as to remove content that can't be verified as fact or fiction. Then, the government goes one step further and censors people for "Right-Wing" political views.

Frankly, the Jira Ticket and the House Committee report documenting how the government removed Robert's contributions to science and the media, is an abusive deep violation of free speech. The House report also shows that even Congressmen, such as Representative Thomas Massie, were censored. Think about that. Even congressional members are no longer allowed the fundamental right of free speech.

After President Biden was inaugurated in January 2021, the government's censorship regime ramped up. At the DHS branch known as the CISA (The Cybersecurity and Infrastructure Security Agency), the Countering Foreign Influence Task Force (CFITF) soon dropped any pretense of a "foreign" focus and relabeled itself as the "MDM team." This became the team that would zero in on speech that the Biden administration considered to be mis-, dis-, or mal-information. Throughout 2021, the Biden White House engaged in a pressure campaign against Facebook and other social media companies to censor anti-vaccine content, even if it was factual. By 2022, CISA invited social media executives to form an advisory MDM Subcommittee to consult with CISA about how the agency could and should combat online speech that the government considered to be mis-, dis-, or mal-information.

However, by 2023, the US Republican political party retook the majority in the House of Representatives and initiated oversight of the censorship-industrial complex. Once this happened, CISA scrubbed its website of references to domestic censorship.

The House Oversight Committee and Select Subcommittee obtained and revealed how Facebook changed its policies because of pressure from the Biden administration. Internal Facebook documents show that the Biden White House, in particular, wanted true information and satire (jokes, memes, comics) censored at a rate even Big Tech found objectionable.

Clearly, the hit pieces on Robert by the *Atlantic Monthly*, *New York Times*, *Washington Post* (twice), *Business Insider*, *The Scientist*, *Rolling Stone*, and other mainstream media outlets within a very short time frame reflected a coordinated effort by the deep state to delegitimize and suppress the information which he was sharing at the time concerning the bioethical and regulatory breaches associated with mRNA-based COVID "vaccines." We believe that the intelligence agencies and DHS led this effort through the deep state. Kash Patel nicely discusses how these types of hits are conducted in his book, *Government Gangsters*,[4] which is a process whereby the government feeds information to operatives working within mainstream media.

This is in keeping with the title of the Jira Ticket describing Robert's transgression, which they labeled: "*Dr. Robert Malone, Self-Purported Inventor of mRNA Vaccines, Discusses Vaccine Dangers on Tucker Carlson*." Then that same phrase, "self-purported," is used in many of the mainstream media hit pieces planted against him. The fact that the government used that phrase as a weapon shows that this was not a coincidence. Those same hit pieces were most likely planted by government operatives and were then used against him in other government circles. This is the deep state at work. This tactic is known as the wrap-up smear.

> **The wrap-up smear** is a deflection tactic whereby a smear is made-up and leaked to the press. The press then amplifies the smear and publishes it, which conveys legitimacy. Then another organization or author can use the press coverage of the smear as a validation to write a summary story which is the wrap-up smear.

This ability to write hit pieces without being sued is predicated on the Supreme Court case known as *Sullivan vs. the New York Times*. Simply put, it is this court case that determined that people with a public image can almost never win a lawsuit for malicious defamation. The deep state and its media partners use this loophole to attack, malign, defame, harass, and engage in direct character assassination. This is evil.

After the Committee on the Judiciary and the Select Subcommittee on the Weaponization of the Federal Government released its report on CISA, the House Judiciary Committee released another interim staff report on how Global Alliance for Responsible Media (GARM) and its members are colluded with other companies to censor not only hate speech but to censor speech that they don't like. Just like the Election Integrity Partnership/Virality project, GARM censored conservative voices whose primary crime appears to be expressing opinions that GARM doesn't agree with.[5]

GARM was a cross-industry initiative established by the World Federation of Advertisers to address the challenge of "harmful" content on digital media platforms and its monetization via advertising. GARM is closely affiliated with the World Economic Forum and is prominently featured on WEF web pages. The World Federation of Advertisers is a WEF partner.

Imagine Robert's surprise when he discovered that he is one of the "star" poster "celebrities" for the House Judiciary Committee's report on how GARM and its affiliates sought to censor free speech by pressuring advertisers and threatening investigations of platforms that violate their policies.

As discussed above, Robert is still either banned or shadow-banned from most major social media platforms (including X). He is permanently deplatformed on LinkedIn without any ability to appeal. Furthermore, mainstream media, such as Real Clear Politics, will not pick up articles that he has written or cowritten. Because much of what he writes is of interest to Real Clear Politics, he has often submitted more timely and well-written pieces for consideration by that news aggregator. Basically, the response back is crickets. There is still a complete mainstream corporate media boycott of his articles, podcasts, and opinions, and this even includes almost all conservative media. Furthermore, most of the larger conservative media outlets (with the exception of Bannon's *The War Room* and *The Epoch Times*) do not invite him to be on their shows and haven't done so since the Joe Rogan podcast. Behind closed doors, he has had people involved with those platforms share that they are scared to have him on due to pressure from their advertisers.

According to congressional Judiciary investigation reporting, Coca-Cola specifically targeted the *Joe Rogan Experience* over the episode featuring Robert.[6] Furthermore, whatever deal was struck between Spotify, GARM, their partners, and Coca-Cola, among other brand names, so that Spotify could continue monetizing its platform through GARM and GroupM did not include Robert!

GARM, the advertising agency GroupM (a GARM cofounder), and companies like Coca-Cola have significantly damaged his reputation and his ability to earn a living. The collusion of the largest advertisers and companies in the world to censor Robert is not a conspiracy theory, it is well documented by the US House Judiciary committee.

In 2022, Robert advised now Governor Landry of Louisiana that the state should work with people like Dr. Jay Bhattacharya, a professor at Stanford, to go after the government for censoring free speech due to the lack of documents showing that he was being censored (even though it was clear that this was happening). He did this because he wanted that case to be as strong as possible, and Dr. Jay Bhattacharya and associates already had FOIAed documents regarding their being censored by the US government over the Great Barrington Declaration.

But now the evidence is clear: Robert's reputation and his ability to make a living have been severely and intentionally damaged due to companies pressuring social media and MSM regarding his appearance on their broadcasts, social media, as well as his writings.

Below is the House Press Release, followed by screenshots of the interim report, in which Joe Rogan and Robert are specifically singled out. But unlike Joe Rogan, who has a professional relationship with Spotify, no major corporation has Robert's back.

This report also documents how the GARM agreement has worked with the US government Department of Homeland Security Cybersecurity and Infrastructure Security Agency (CISA).

Robert Malone refuses to concede to the deep state character assassination. He will not let them ruin his life and reputation. And he will not allow them to victimize him.

We must not forget our constitutional rights.

The US Constitution reads:

> We the People of the United States, in Order to form a more perfect Union, establish Justice, ensure domestic Tranquility, provide for the common defence, promote the general Welfare, and secure the Blessings of Liberty to ourselves and our Posterity, do ordain and establish this Constitution for the United States of America . . .

The First Amendment reads:

> Congress shall make no law respecting an establishment of religion, or prohibiting the free exercise thereof; or abridging the freedom of speech, or of the press; or the right of the people peaceably to assemble, and to petition the Government for a redress of grievances.

In the United States, our right to free speech and the right to assemble is paramount to who we are. So, when the Department of Homeland Security put out the following National Terrorism Advisory Bulletin, it is time for all Americans to pay attention.

"The Summary of Terrorism Threat to the U.S. Homeland: National Terrorism Advisory System Bulletin," Feb 07, 2022, states that:

> Meanwhile, COVID-19 mitigation measures—particularly COVID-19 vaccine and mask mandates—have been used by domestic violent extremists to justify violence since 2020 and could continue to inspire these extremists to target government, healthcare, and academic institutions that they associate with those measures.[7]

The manipulative linking of election violence to COVID-19 policies in that DHS bulletin was disingenuous. It was a calculated strategy to allow government authorities to crack down on those who go against the Health and Human Services narrative that there are no early treatments for COVID-19, that everyone must get vaccinated, and that the lockdowns and mask mandates are necessary.

Those who are writing and speaking about science and health policy have been in danger of being targeted by the US government as domestic terrorists for spreading "mis- dis- and mal-information (MDM)." Once this type of technique for suppression of information is used and thereby legitimized, can the genie be put back in the bottle? Will those who question the childhood vaccine schedule, statin use, pasteurization of milk, Biden's dementia, religious freedoms, or other controversial subjects, be next on the government's list of domestic terrorists? This is another example of how typical bureaucratic incrementalism leads the US administrative state to engage in what are clearly unconstitutional actions.

The US government must be held accountable for their failed policies and authoritarian behavior during this pandemic. Scientists, the press, physicians, and, yes, laypeople must be able to speak and write freely. In this day and age, that means using the internet without censorship and without administrative state-promoted social media and search engine algorithm manipulations. There is no one right answer for everyone regarding healthcare treatments, and the choice to take a vaccine is a personal one. As a people, we can't allow ourselves to be censored this way. The problem is that the government isn't exactly telling us who gets the Elon Musk treatment of "freedom of speech, not reach."[8]

It is time for our legislative and judicial branches of government to do their jobs to protect our First Amendment rights. Even though it was now written years ago, this bulletin from the DHS can't be allowed to stand, or it will be used as a future template for a national crisis, and we will no longer have a free country. It is up to Congress to act in its oversight role to ensure that this doesn't happen again.

> First they came for the Jews and I did not speak out because I was not a Jew. Then they came for the Communists and I did not speak out because I was not a Communist. Then they came for the trade unionists and I did not speak out because I was not a trade unionist. Then they came for me and there was no one left to speak out for me.
>
> —Martin Niemöller Stiftung, Public speech, 22.09.2005, Wiesbaden

Now they have come for the physicians and the scientists. Who will be next?

# PART II
# FIFTH-GENERATION WARFARE

*What is fifth-generation warfare, and why does it matter? Think of it as a war of information and perception. The basic idea is that fifth-generation warfare uses non-kinetic (that means digital and, generally, nonviolent tools that don't fall within the traditional military tool kit) against an opponent. This section includes a brief overview of these tactics and describes these tools and why they matter to those of us fighting to maintain our free speech rights.*

*As technology becomes more sophisticated, the general public has not kept pace. Most people don't even realize they are being targeted. However, their perceptions, thoughts, and behavior are being manipulated to benefit the government and nefarious actors like Big Pharma. To become more resistant to this form of psychological manipulation, we need to understand the battlefield and learn the tactics of those who seek to oppress us.*

# CHAPTER 6
## General PsyWar Terms

A reliable way to make people believe in falsehoods is frequent repetition because familiarity is not easily distinguished from truth. Authoritarian institutions and marketers have always known this fact."

—Nobel Prize laureate Prof. Daniel Kahneman

### What Is Fifth-Generation Warfare, and Why Does It Matter?

With this chapter, we aim to give you more tools to recognize fifth-gen warfare tactics and help the reader learn to use these tools to survive the "information warfare" you are subjected to. We seek to help you to begin mastering these methods so that you can become a skilled warrior in the fifth-gen battles that lie ahead.

### *One Common Tactic Is the Deliberate Manipulation of an Observer's Context to Achieve a Desired Outcome*

Fifth-generation warfare is an extension of asymmetric and counterinsurgent warfare strategies and tactics, whereby conventional and unconventional military tactics and weapons are incorporated and deployed, including exploiting political, religious, and social causes. Asymmetric warfare is a conflict in which the opponents' resources are uneven and the opponent appears to be at a military disadvantage. The new gradient of fifth-generation warfare targets the internet, social media, and the twenty-four-hour

91

news cycle seeking to change the cognitive biases of individuals and/or organizations. It can be conducted by organized or unorganized (*ergo*, decentralized) groups; it may be led by nation-states, non-nation-state actors and organizations, nongovernmental organizations, for-profit corporations, or even individuals. A key characteristic of fifth-gen warfare is that the nature of the attack is concealed. The goal is to disrupt and defeat opponents by creating new cognitive biases without revealing who or what organization is sponsoring the attack. In this sense, fifth-generation warfare is closely related to black propaganda.

The most effective fifth-gen warfare strategies employed by those lacking integrity are not purely based on pushing false narratives, mis- dis- or mal-information. The most effective strategies mix truth with fiction. They act to increase confusion and disorder in the thoughts and minds of those being targeted so that the victim is not sure what or whom to believe.

Any sufficiently advanced technology is indistinguishable from magic.

—Arthur C. Clarke[1]

Some have written that the term fifth-gen warfare should only be applied to those opponents with fewer resources (asymmetric warfare), but this is inconsistent with current practice. Large and small governments, transnational corporations, globalist organizations, as well as ordinary citizens have learned how effective the fifth-gen tool kit is and have utilized fifth-gen warfare strategies and tactics (such as psychological biowarfare) to their advantage.

Abbot's seminal *Handbook of 5GW*, published in 2010, states that "The very nature of fifth-generation warfare is that it is difficult to define." It is hidden from plain view, lurking in the shadows. To be clear, the concept of fifth-generation warfare as being traditional "warfare" is inaccurate. When the term "war" is applied, the concept of a physical war as a battle for territory using kinetic weapons looms large. This is not the case with fifth-gen warfare.

We find the term fifth-generation psyops perhaps more accurate for what is happening across the web. But fifth-gen warfare is the term people know, so there it is. When a collaborative or synchronized fifth-generation psyops program is being referred to, we will use that term when appropriate.

There is also the small point that although the abbreviations "5GW" or 5G warfare are commonly used, these terms can often confuse those first encountering fifth-gen warfare terminology. It is easy to confuse fifth-gen warfare with 5G technologies (cell phone tower tech). For this reason, we avoid using "5GW" or related acronyms. This may all seem esoteric, but words and definitions matter.

## A Brief Summary of Fifth-Generation Warfare:
- Involves a war over information and perception
- Targets existing cognitive biases of individuals and organizations
- Creates new cognitive biases
- Is different from classical warfare for the following reasons:
  - Focuses on the individual observer / decision-maker
  - Is difficult or impossible to attribute
  - The nature of the attack is concealed

## Fifth-Gen Warfare Weapons, Tactics, and Technologies:

There are two general categories of these tactics: electronics and software and behavioral modification techniques. These tactics are designed to change the perceptions and biases of individuals and/or groups. At the end of this book is a large compendium of PsyWar terms, tactics, and technologies, which may be helpful to review at this point.

The list of tactics is extensive, but the truth is that only a subset of these tools are available to poorly resourced individuals and groups. However, these groups may compensate for the deficit by leveraging populist sentiments.

The good news is that some of the most effective fifth-generation warfare tools cost the least. Decentralized and highly non-attributable psychological warfare and community synergy are two methods that individuals and groups can utilize to make a difference.

When it is the people against a government or governmental policy, the people have numbers behind them but typically have fewer technological, financial, and physical assets (vehicles, kinetic weapons, intelligence gathering capabilities). The late-twentieth-century (Vietnam, for example) and current twenty-first-century (Afghanistan, et al.) history of warfare clearly demonstrates that very effective asymmetric battlefield campaigns can be deployed by coordinating group efforts.

Another recent example of an effectively deployed fifth-generation warfare tactic involved shifting the "vaccine narrative" to acknowledge that post-COVID jab myocarditis occurs in athletes and children. In the case of this example, when a new victim is identified, posts are shared both openly and via semiprivate direct messages to influencers, and the word spreads very quickly. These posts reach not only those who already believe there is a problem but also those who are unaware. This is why social media has taken extreme censorship actions over such posts on many social media platforms, such as Facebook. Unfortunately, at the operational heart of these anti-free speech policies we often find agents of the US government and their non-governmental contractors.

This tactic has also been utilized by the World Economic Forum (WEF), which is a guild of the largest transnational corporations working toward a new world order—that is, a reorganization of the world based on international corporate-world government leadership. The WEF has enlisted 14,000 "global shapers." According to the Global Shapers website, these are young adults recruited to spread WEF messages throughout the world about such things as the importance of smart cities, the fourth industrial revolution, collectivism, migration, stakeholder capitalism (a modified form of socialism), and effective climate change solutions.

The WEF global shapers program website is outdated and seems stale. It is failing because the messages are stagnant and often are not culturally aligned with the intended audience—they come across as "fake," contrived, and lacking integrity. In the fast-paced news cycle of fifth-gen warfare, the message must be seen as genuine and to move as fast as the ever-changing news stories and narrative. Understanding fifth-gen warfare is critical when fighting effectively in this battlespace of minds, ideas, and memes.

With a fifth-gen warfare campaign, it is easy to change the target. Just follow the social media posts, news stories from alternative sources, trends and go! Anyone can play. Just be aware that a false flag operation often does more harm than good.

This is a big reason why once the US government identifies and censors messaging content, the message must change rapidly. The government goes after individuals and internet nodes to silence and defame because fifth-gen warfare is working against the interests of the administrative state and its allies. By taking away one's right to post, as well as professional licenses, political posts, bank account access, etc., they are actively blocking fifth-gen campaigns.

The focus on decentralized cells or individuals of a leaderless battlespace effectively forces the parties that seek to advance and insert a false narrative into susceptible minds to play "Whac-A-Mole" because there are too many autonomous actors or apparent "leaders." In this case, as one person is taken down, another rises. This is where being a "shape-shifter" is adaptive. Be ready to change social media platforms, handles, email accounts, etc. This is how Robert survived and thrived when deplatformed from Twitter, Facebook, and LinkedIn, and was defamed by almost every single mainstream media corporation.

Keeping a separate identity from your social media accounts can be helpful. Use emails that aren't tied to your personal affairs for social media.

The "Pegasus" and "Pegasus II" mobile phone spyware developed by Israel is one such tool that governments and other "players" routinely use to track and surveil journalists, lawyers, political dissidents, and activists, as it is remotely installed on cell phones. Let yourself think through what that means to you in a practical sense and how you chose to respond to these threats.

We have to be smart. Which is to say, don't be stupid. For instance, don't play that quiz game based on your name and date of birth, don't respond to emails that need personal information, etc. No Nigerian prince is going to send you millions of dollars. So, learn to recognize phishing and other strategies employed by con artists.

Challenge authority when it is wrong. Don't allow yourself to be bullied. Don't give up, and don't get depressed.

In this chapter, we have intentionally not written about the battles ahead or what we are fighting for. Except to say that we all know what we are fighting for now. The fight is for our very sovereignty, self-autonomy, and freedom to speak and think our own thoughts. It is to stop a new world order based on corporatism. To prevent ourselves and our children from becoming indentured servants to self-appointed centralized global "masters of the Universe."

These tools are just too seductive for large entities not to use. Do not expect these tactics to stop. Digital spying will continue, and it will be relentless.

Our job is to understand the terrain, the tools, and the tactics.

Fifth-gen warfare is a form of war. This is not a "nice" game, with rules that we all agree to. There are no rules in fifth-gen warfare, only tactics and strategy. Nothing is "fair," and your mind, thought, and emotions are the battlefield.

This is a war for my mind, your mind, our children's minds, and our collective minds.

Don't be a victim. Be a fifth-gen warrior for truth and for the sake of our children and their children.

Never forget, the truth is like a lion. You don't have to defend it. Set it free, and let it defend itself.

# CHAPTER 7
# Tactics of Disinformation

## Introduction

A brief explanation clarifies the many new psyops and cyber warfare (PsyWar) terms and phrases that have developed over the last two decades and will continue to evolve as these concepts and technologies become more sophisticated. Additional definitions can be found in the glossary at the end of this book.

The five domains of warfare are land, sea, air, space, and cyberspace. Cyberspace is a relative newcomer to the domains of warfare. Military theory now treats cyber as a place, not a mission. The core technical components of cyberspace are cyberwarfare and cyberattacks. It is important not to confuse the fifth domain of warfare, that is, cyberspace with fifth-generation or fifth-gen warfare. Cyberwarfare is a component of fifth-gen warfare.

> **Fifth-generation warfare** is using non-kinetic military tactics against an opponent. This would include strategies such as manipulating social media through social engineering, misinformation, censorship, cyberattacks, and artificial intelligence. It has also been described as a war of "information and perception." Although the concept has been rejected by some scholars, it is seen as a new frontier of cyberspace and the concepts behind fifth-generation warfare are evolving, even within the field of military theory and strategy. Fifth-gen warfare is used by non-state actors as well as state actors.

It is important to understand the evolution of warfare in order to understand what fifth-gen warfare is.

> First-generation warfare refers to ancient and post-classical battles fought with massed manpower, using phalanx, line, and column tactics with uniformed soldiers governed by the state. . . .
>
> Second-generation warfare refers to industrial warfare, which evolved after the invention of the rifled musket and breech-loading weapons and continued through the development of the machine gun and indirect fire. . . .
>
> Third-generation warfare focuses on using late modern technology-derived tactics of leveraging speed, stealth, and surprise to bypass the enemy's lines and collapse their forces from the rear. Essentially, this was the end of linear warfare on a tactical level, with units seeking not simply to meet each other face-to-face but to outmaneuver each other to gain the greatest advantage.
>
> Fourth-generation warfare as presented by Lind et al. is characterized by a post-modern return to decentralized forms of warfare, blurring of the lines between war and politics, combatants, and civilians due to states' loss of their near-monopoly on combat forces, returning to modes of conflict common in pre-modern times.
>
> Fifth-generation warfare is conducted primarily through non-kinetic military action, such as social engineering, misinformation, and cyberattacks, along with emerging technologies such as artificial intelligence and fully autonomous systems. Fifth-generation warfare has been described by Daniel Abbot as a war of "information and perception."[1]

Fifth-generation warfare can be combined with the other four stages of warfare. It is "nonlinear" and can be carried out by non-state actors, such as corporate saboteurs, chaos agents, and military psyop units. Often, the use of PsyWar together with kinetic warfare is labeled as "hybrid warfare." Most of the strategies and tactics covered by fifth-gen warfare target conscious thought and conscious awareness, except neurolinguistic programming and cognitive warfare. Cognitive warfare involves a different approach than more classical fifth-generation warfare strategies and tactics. Cognitive warfare is specifically focused on targeting your subconscious mind.

The American think tank and government partner, the Atlantic Council, now defines a sixth domain of warfare; the private sector. A recent position statement by this organization argues that the military-industrial complex has become so important to the war effort that it needs a permanent leadership position. This would include the establishment of "a critical Infrastructure Wartime Planning and Operations Council with Government and Private-Sector Membership."[2] Such a relationship would formalize the fascist relationship already in place between the military and the private sector which already exists and is often referred to as the military-industrial complex.

As laid out by the Atlantic Council, this relationship would include the expansion of Expansion of Cyber Command's "Hunt Forward" teams:

> [The] United States U.S. Cyber Command regularly works with allied and partner nations at their request to enhance the cybersecurity of their critical infrastructures . . .
>
> Upon invitation, USCYBERCOM Hunt Forward Teams deploy to partner nations to observe and detect malicious cyber activity on host nation networks. The operations generate insights that bolster homeland defense and increase the resiliency of shared networks from cyber threats.
>
> A Hunt Forward operation is a joint effort, as the Cyber Command operators "sit side-by-side with partners and hunt for vulnerabilities, malware, and adversary presence on the host nation's networks."

In this report, the Atlantic Council describes the extensive cybersecurity units in the USA, which are located within US government agencies tasked with defense and intelligence. These operations clearly include protecting critical cyber infrastructure, which is warranted, but they also include censorship and psyops operations. This is being done in the name of cyber threats to the US citizenry.

# Background and Context

An overview of disinformation tactics has been compiled by the US government, and it is summarized and published on the US government's Cybersecurity and Infrastructure Security Agency (CISA) website.[3] We have slightly modified that document and inserted it below for use by individuals and organizations wishing to counter the mis- dis- mal- information (MDM) constantly emanating from governments, corporations (such as Big Pharma), nongovernmental organizations (such as the Gates Foundation), and Astroturf organizations (such as the Center for Countering Digital Hate), as well as from their many agents and surrogates.

All of the disinformation tactics described below are being used against the health sovereignty movement, the freedom (or liberty) movements, those pushing back against UN Agenda 2030 and the approved climate agenda, the WEF, the UN, WHO, populist politicians, progressive transgender policies, and the resistance against globalization movement (new world order or NWO).

## Tactics of Disinformation

Disinformation actors include governments, commercial and nonprofit organizations as well as individuals. These actors use a variety of tactics to influence others, stir them to action, and cause harm. Understanding these tactics can increase preparedness and promote resilience when faced with disinformation.

Disinformation actors use a variety of tactics and techniques to execute information operations and spread disinformation narratives for a variety of reasons. Some may even be well intentioned but ultimately fail on ethical grounds. Using disinformation for beneficial purposes is still wrong.

Each of these tactics are designed to make disinformation actors' messages more credible, or to manipulate their audience to a specific end. They often seek to polarize their target audience across contentious political or social divisions, making the audience more receptive to disinformation.

These methods can and have been weaponized by disinformation actors. By breaking down common tactics, sharing real-world examples, and providing concrete steps to counter these narratives with accurate information, the *Tactics of Disinformation* listed below are intended to help individuals and organizations understand and manage the risks posed by disinformation. Any organization or its staff can be targeted by disinformation campaigns, and all organizations and individuals have a role to play in building a resilient information environment.

This is yet another aspect of fifth-generation warfare, otherwise known as PsyWar or psyops. Our governments, corporations, and various non-state actors routinely deploy these technologies, strategies, and tactics on all of us.

## Disinformation Tactics Overview

**Cultivate Fake or Misleading Personas and Websites**: Disinformation actors create networks of fake personas and websites to increase the believability of their message with their target audience. Fake expert networks use inauthentic credentials (e.g., fake "experts," journalists, think tanks, or academic institutions) to lend undue credibility to their influence content and make it more believable.

**Create Deepfakes and Synthetic Media**: Synthetic media content may include photos, videos, and audio clips that have been digitally manipulated or entirely fabricated to mislead the viewer. Artificial intelligence (AI) tools can make synthetic content nearly indistinguishable from real life. Synthetic media content may be deployed in disinformation campaigns to promote false information and manipulate audiences.

**Devise or Amplify Conspiracy Theories**: Conspiracy theories attempt to explain important events as secret plots by powerful actors. Conspiracy theories impact an individual's understanding of a particular topic; they can shape and influence their worldview. Disinformation actors capitalize on conspiracy theories by generating disinformation narratives that align with the conspiracy worldview, increasing the likelihood that the narrative will resonate with the target audience.

**Astroturfing and Flooding the Information Environment**: Disinformation campaigns will often post overwhelming amounts of content with the same or similar messaging from several inauthentic accounts. This practice, known as Astroturfing, creates the impression of widespread grassroots support or opposition to a message while concealing its true origin. A similar tactic, flooding, involves spamming social media posts and comment sections with the intention of shaping a narrative or drowning out opposing viewpoints.

**Abuse Alternative Platforms:** Disinformation actors may abuse alternative social media platforms to intensify belief in a disinformation narrative among specific user groups. Disinformation actors may seek to take advantage of platforms with fewer user protections, less stringent content moderation policies, and fewer controls to detect and remove inauthentic content and accounts than other social media platforms.

**Exploit Information Gaps:** Data voids, or information gaps, occur when there is insufficient credible information to satisfy a search inquiry. Disinformation actors can exploit these gaps by generating their own influence content and seeding the search term on social media to encourage people to look it up. This increases the likelihood that audiences will encounter disinformation content without any accurate or authoritative search results to refute it.

**Manipulate Unsuspecting Actors:** Disinformation actors target prominent individuals and organizations to help amplify their narratives. Targets are often unaware that they are repeating a disinformation actor's narrative or that the narrative is intended to manipulate.

**Spread Targeted Content:** Disinformation actors produce tailored influencer content likely to resonate with a specific audience based on their worldview and interests. These actors gain insider status and grow an online following that can make future manipulation efforts more successful. This tactic often takes a "long game" approach of spreading targeted content over time to build trust and credibility with the target audience.

# Common Disinformation Technologies, Tactics, and Strategies in More Detail:

• **Cultivate Fake or Misleading Personas and Websites**

Disinformation actors create networks of fake personas and websites to increase the believability of their message with their target audience. Such networks may include fake academic or professional "experts," journalists, think tanks, and/or academic institutions. Some fake personas can even validate their social media accounts (for example, a blue or gray checkmark next to a username), further confusing audiences about their authenticity. Fake expert networks use inauthentic credentials to make their content more believable.

Disinformation actors also increase the credibility of these fake personas by generating falsified articles or research papers and sharing them online. Sometimes, these personas and their associated publications are intentionally amplified by other actors. In some instances, legitimate organizations and users also unwittingly share these materials. The creation or amplification of content from these fake personas makes it difficult for audiences to distinguish real experts from fake ones.

Adversaries have also demonstrated a "long game" approach with this tactic, building a following and credibility with seemingly innocuous content before switching their focus to creating and amplifying disinformation. This lends false credibility to campaigns.

• **Create Deepfakes and Synthetic Media**

Synthetic media content may include photos, videos, and audio clips that have been digitally manipulated or entirely fabricated to mislead the viewer. *Cheapfakes* are a less sophisticated form of manipulation involving real audio clips or videos that have been sped up, slowed down, or shown out of context to mislead. It's sort of like how the corporate media will often take limited quotes out of context and then weaponize them. In contrast, *deepfakes* are developed by training artificial intelligence (AI) algorithms on reference content until it can produce media that is nearly indistinguishable from real life. Deepfake technology makes it possible to convincingly depict someone doing something they haven't done or saying something they haven't said. While synthetic media technology is not inherently malicious, it can be deployed in disinformation campaigns to share false information or manipulate audiences.

Deepfake photos by disinformation actors can be used to generate realistic profile pictures and in this way create a large network of inauthentic social media accounts. Deepfake videos often use AI technology to map one person's face to another person's body. In the case of audio deepfakes, a "voice clone" can produce new sentences as audio alone or as part of a video deepfake, often with only a few hours (or even minutes) of reference audio clips. Finally, an emerging use of deepfake technology involves AI-generated text, which can produce realistic writing and presents a unique challenge due to its ease of production.

- **Devise or Amplify Conspiracy Theories**

Conspiracy theories attempt to explain important events as secret plots by powerful actors. They impact an individual's understanding of a particular topic and can shape and influence their worldview. Conspiracy theories often present an attractive alternative to reality by explaining uncertain events simply and seemingly cohesively, especially during times of heightened uncertainty and anxiety.

Disinformation actors capitalize on conspiracy theories by generating disinformation narratives that align with the conspiracy worldview, increasing the likelihood that the narrative will resonate with the target audience. By repeating certain tropes across multiple narratives, malign actors increase the target audience's familiarity with the narrative and, therefore, its believability. Conspiracy theories can also present a pathway for radicalization to violence among certain adherents. Conspiracy theories can alter a person's fundamental worldview and can be very difficult to counter retroactively, so proactive resilience building is especially critical to prevent conspiratorial thinking from taking hold.

Furthermore, conspiracy theories can also be used to divide groups and bad-jacket individuals within a movement.

Conspiracy theories can also be used to discredit a movement. Theories that are not based in reality and that can be linked to a movement or organization can be used to smear that group as a "fringe element," not to be taken seriously, or to drown out expert voices.

• **Astroturfing and Flooding the Information Environment**
Disinformation campaigns will often post overwhelming amounts of content with the same or similar messaging from several inauthentic accounts, either created by automated programs known as bots or by professional disinformation groups known as troll farms. By consistently seeing the same narrative repeated, the audience sees it as a popular and widespread message and is likelier to believe it. This practice, known as Astroturfing, creates the impression of widespread grassroots support or opposition to a message, while concealing its true origin.

A similar tactic, flooding, involves spamming social media posts and comment sections with the intention of shaping a narrative or drowning out opposing viewpoints, often using many fake and/or automated accounts. Flooding may also be referred to as "firehosing."

This tactic stifles legitimate debate, such as discussing a new policy or initiative, and discourages people from participating in online spaces. Information manipulators use flooding to dull the sensitivity of targets through repetition and create a sense that nothing is true. Researchers call these tactics "censorship by noise," where artificially amplified narratives are meant to drown out all other viewpoints. Artificial intelligence and other advanced technologies enable Astroturfing and flooding to be deployed at speed and scale, more easily manipulating the information environment and influencing public opinion.

**Astroturfing** is the practice of masking the sponsors of a message or an organization, to make it appear as though it originates from and is supported by grassroots participants. By hiding information about the source's financial or governmental connections, Astroturfing gives the statements or organizations credibility.

- **Abuse Alternative Platforms**

Disinformation actors often seek opportunities for their narratives to gain traction among smaller audiences before attempting to go viral. While alternative social media platforms are not inherently malicious, disinformation actors may use less stringent platform policies to intensify belief in a disinformation narrative among specific user groups. These policies may include fewer user protections, less stringent content moderation policies, and fewer controls to detect and remove inauthentic content and accounts than some of the other social media platforms.

Alternative platforms often promote unmoderated chat and file sharing/storage capabilities, which is not inherently malicious but may be appealing for actors who want to share disinformation. While some alternative platforms forbid the promotion of violence on public channels, they may have less visibility into private channels or groups promoting violence. Disinformation actors will recruit followers to alternative platforms by promoting a sense of community, shared purpose, and the perception of fewer restrictions. Groups on alternative platforms may operate without other platforms' scrutiny or detection capabilities. Often, groups focus on specific issues or activities to build audience trust, and disinformation actors can, in turn, abuse this trust and status to establish credibility on other platforms.

- **Exploit Information Gaps**

Data voids, or information gaps, occur when there is insufficient credible information to satisfy a search inquiry, such as when a term falls out of use or when an emerging topic or event first gains prominence (e.g., breaking news). When a user searches for the term or phrase, the only results available may be false, misleading, or have low credibility. While search engines work to mitigate this problem, disinformation actors can exploit this gap by generating their own influence content and seeding the search term on social media to encourage people to look it up.

Because the specific terms that create data voids are difficult to identify beforehand, credible sources of information are often unable to proactively mitigate their impacts with accurate information. Disinformation actors can exploit data voids to increase the likelihood a target will encounter disinformation without accurate information for context, thus increasing the likelihood that the content is seen as true or authoritative. Additionally, people often perceive information that they find themselves on search engines as more credible, and it can be challenging to reverse the effects of disinformation once accepted.

• **Manipulate Unsuspecting Actors**

Disinformation campaigns target prominent individuals and organizations to help amplify their narratives. These secondary spreaders of disinformation narratives add perceived credibility to the messaging and help seed these narratives at the grassroots level while disguising their original source. Targets are often unaware that they are repeating a disinformation actors' narrative or that the narrative is intended to manipulate their mental landscape. The content is engineered to appeal to their and their follower's emotions, causing the influencers to become unwitting facilitators of disinformation campaigns.

Disinformation campaigns often amplify purity spirals, leading to group break-ups. A purity spiral occurs when members of an ideological group become increasingly zealous and intolerant, eventually turning on other members. Chaos agents may be placed online to propel purity spirals and dissent amongst group members.

• **Spread Targeted Content**

Disinformation actors surveil a targeted online community to understand its worldview, interests, and key influencers and then attempt to infiltrate it by posting tailored influence content likely to resonate with its members. By starting with entertaining or non-controversial posts that are agreeable to targeted communities, disinformation actors gain "insider" status and grow an online following that can make future manipulation efforts more successful. This tactic may be used in combination with cultivating fake experts, who spread targeted content over time, taking a "long game" approach that lends false credibility to the campaign. Targeted content often takes highly shareable forms, like memes or videos, and can be made to reach very specific audiences by methods such as paid advertising and exploited social media algorithms.[4]

We will now provide a few personal examples of how disruptive these tactics can be to help illustrate the concepts and strategies outlined above.

Robert Malone, MD, has a number of personas, websites, and social media influencers, including various Substack authors, who continuously target Robert by using misleading, false, and re-timed events. It is extremely disturbing to see fragments of his CV, his life, his peer-reviewed papers dissected, reconfigured, and even modified with the intent of doing psychological damage to him, or to damage his reputation and legitimacy in his areas of expertise, or to damage the reputation of those fighting to reform the system. We have reason to believe that some of these agents targeted Robert because his ideas are perceived to be dangerous to the deep state, pharmaceutical industry corporations, and the global elites, not because they are false or inaccurate.

One person on Twitter with over 100,000 followers has literally posted thousands of posts targeting him. At one point, Jill took screenshots of these posts and placed them in a summary document. After about five months of Tweets, she gave up on the project, which generated over 1,500 pages. Every day for years, this disinformation artist has posted two to three hit pieces on Robert—mixed with other content. He has used every single one of these tactics outlined above. Clearly, he is being paid by an organization or government. He defines himself as an independent journalist and has a long and well-documented history of cyberstalking and spreading falsehoods. Many of his followers do not question his authenticity. One of the followers recently even attacked Robert for having worked on the development of the "Remdesivir vaccine"! Another posted a streamed video to the social media platform GETTR claiming that Robert had caused the CIA to place a "hit" on her, and implored Robert F. Kennedy Jr. to get Robert to call off the "hit." The resulting video was translated into at least four languages and went viral globally. These posts get passed around as authentic information, and he can do nothing. Robert only amplifies the lies if he refutes the charges and thereby increases the attacker's social media presence.

These fabricated information fragments, some now years old, are then repeatedly re-spread as if they are true—historical representations and other influencers report on these posts as if they were real. The cycle goes around and around. The end result is not only intentional damage to Robert and his reputation but also damage to the whole movement against the global elites and tyranny, which also gets delegitimized—particularly by outside observers (the persuadable middle). This is a "win" for those chaos agents pushing this disinformation.

That said, social media users are getting savvy. Millions don't fall for these psyops tactics and know to look past the superficial hype. Of the millions of Robert's followers on social media, only a handful engage in this type of harmful trollery and hate. But those few can do a disproportionate amount of damage.

It is important to recognize that the Google-web and other search engines prioritize government websites and "trusted sources" above other sources of information. Remember, just because a web page is the first term found on Google does not mean it is true. Search deeper and use alternative search engines. For instance, *The Epoch Times* is one of the most accurate new sources on the web and in newsprint. It's print newspaper has the fourth largest subscriber base in the United States. Yet, news stories from this new source are rarely, if ever, found in news aggregator sites like Google.

The Google web does not like data voids. So, when Google does not like the analytics yielded by a search term or encounters a data void, they fill the gap with information they do like. The Google-web has even been caught manipulating search results by hand. This is what happened with the search term "mass formation psychosis," which was used by Robert while on the *Joe Rogan Show* to describe the public response to the COVIDcrisis. As this term went against the COVID narrative, its legitimacy was quickly denied by the Google web fact-checkers, and Google search results were manually modified by unseen hands in real time. Google officially denied that this happened, but various individuals including Silicon Valley entrepreneur Steve Kirsh were able to screenshot and document this practice as it was happening.

Robert Malone sincerely believes it may take a while, but eventually, truth does rise to the top. That overwhelming numbers of American people can see past the PsyWar madness and manipulations which have become commonplace. That we, the people, will prevail in righting the course of this nation back to some semblance of normalcy and restoring the Constitution back to its primary role in governing this country.

## There Are Ways to Avoid the Disinformation Traps

Be very wary of information that seeks to divide groups and individuals.

Critically evaluate content, as well as its origin. Be sure to read and watch information from many different conduits of information. Nowadays, it is important not to rely on the "mockingbird" legacy media as your only source of news and medical information. Seek out alternate points of view. Do not rely on one person or source for information; researching the author's history and credentials is important. Are they trustworthy? Is there an agenda? Also, be aware that those who counter the mainstream narrative are subjects to "wrap-up smears" and that one can't rely on mainstream media sources. Wikipedia editors are known for their use of the wrap-up smear.

An agenda that influences many media outlets, including social media, may include advertising money obtained from pharmaceutical or vitamin sales. Medical articles or websites that link a treatment, cure, or alternative therapies with the sale of curatives are not to be trusted. Do your homework before buying medical products on the internet!

It is important to triangulate information and verify the facts. Although government sources can provide helpful information, know that regulatory capture and the deep state have rendered many government websites almost useless due to government agenda biases. Governments routinely manipulate public perception for their own agenda.

NATO Allied Command describes cognitive warfare as "activities conducted in synchronization with other instruments of power to affect attitudes and behavior by influencing, protecting, or disrupting individual and group cognition to gain an advantage over an adversary."[5] This is precisely what our government now routinely practices against its own citizenry.

Discuss and share sources of information with others and get more than one opinion. If you link something you are not sure of, state that and ask others to help verify the source.

## Can Systemic or Algorithmic Censorship Be Controlled?

The distribution of mis-, dis-, or mal-information has been defined as domestic terrorism by the US Department of Homeland Security. Recall that the 2010 DoD Psychological Operations manual, signed off by current Secretary of Defense Lloyd Austin, includes the following clause:

> When authorized, PSYOP forces may be used domestically to assist lead federal agencies during disaster relief and crisis management by informing the domestic population.[6]

In other words, any time a disaster or crisis occurs—as loosely defined by any component of the US Federal administrative state, the DoD is authorized to deploy military-grade psyop (otherwise known as PsyWar) technologies and capabilities against US citizens.

A key aspect of psyop or PsyWar capabilities involves distribution of gray and black propaganda into a targeted population. The methods used to accomplish this (summarized above) are clearly defined by CISA on its own website, and as discussed earlier, the congressional Interim staff report for the Committee on the Judiciary and the Select Subcommittee titled "How a 'Cybersecurity' Agency Colluded with Big Tech and 'Disinformation' Partners to Censor Americans: The Weaponization of CISA" provides a summary road map of how CISA has acted as a key coordinating agency for the Federal administrative state as it has deployed these technologies, tactics, and strategies on United States citizens.[7]

> CISA is the "nerve center" of the vast censorship enterprise, the very entity that worked with the FBI to silence the Hunter Biden laptop story.
>
> —Missouri Attorney General Andrew Bailey

In the case before the Supreme Court titled *Murthy, et al. v. Missouri, et al.*, five individuals and two states (collectively named "Missouri") were the plaintiffs. They argued that the government (defendants) used public statements and threats of regulatory action, such as reforming Section 230 of the Communications Decency Act, to induce social media platforms to suppress content, such as COVID-19, pandemic lockdowns, and Hunter Biden's laptop, thereby violating the plaintiffs' First Amendment rights. For example, the White House coerced platforms to remove content "ASAP" and accounts "immediately" as well as "asking" on multiple occasions for social media platforms to provide details on their internal policies. The platforms created an expedited reporting system, removed certain content, and banned specific users from their websites.

The previous decision from a panel of three judges concluded that the actions of the Biden White House, FBI, and other government agencies likely violated the First Amendment but that CISA attempted to convince, not coerce. However, as the courts use government experts as the arbiters of truth, it is hard to come to the conclusion that the system is rigged in favor of the state.

The Republican AG from Missouri, who brought the case, asked for a rehearing. The 5th Circuit judges then ruled that CISA facilitated the FBI's interactions with social media companies. The order bars CISA, other agencies, and White House officials from attempting to "coerce or significantly encourage" social media companies to take down or slow the spread of social media posts.[8] This case went to the Supreme Court, and they dismissed the claims, citing the plaintiffs' lack of standing could have significant implications. The Court's decision not to delve into the merits of the case meant that it did not make any rulings on the substance of the First Amendment free speech doctrine, nor did it rule on the legality of the government's censorship of Americans. The majority's restrictive standing approach could make it exceedingly difficult for victims of indirect government coercion to bring their free speech claims to court.

> If the Court decides to avoid the merits of this case under such a lack-of-standing reasoning, it would allow government agents to engage in egregious censorship activity so long as they did a good job of not creating a record of asking for particular individuals' speech to be suppressed. The government could do this by calling for entire types of content or viewpoints to be censored without targeting specific people.[9]

Murray Rothbard, in his seminal book *The Anatomy of the State*, argues that because the US court system was never set up to be fully independent of the other branches of government, it has become the legitimizer of the administrative state.[10] Therefore, the courts never work in the best interests of the individual but as a legitimizing force for government. The *Murthy v. Missouri* case certainly continues to prove this point.

CISA knew precisely what it was doing and how to accomplish the Biden administration's censorship and propaganda agenda.

In this case, the Supreme Court has essentially let CISA and the Biden administration violate the First Amendment. This is not the first time this court has sidestepped this issue, in favor of the US government to continue to trample on our First Amendment rights. In doing so, they are allowing the USG administrative state to deploy censorship on US citizens. The question remains: What can we, the collective "we," do about this?

At this point, the answer has to come from Congress. One way is to enact stricter congressional oversight of government agencies, which must include penalties. Another is to pass new laws that stop agencies from impeding individuals' rights.

## Cognitive Warfare

Cognitive warfare is waged on the battlefield of the human mind. Tactical or strategic objectives are achieved by pursuing warfare by other means. This method of warfare directly exploits advances in digital technology, applied both at individual and networked levels, to manipulate the psychological, social and information environment. This shapes not only what people think individually and group-think as social networks, but also influences how they collectively act and interact. Launched by a sophisticated adversary, cognitive warfare manipulates individual and group representations or beliefs with the desired effect of amplifying targeted behaviors and actions that favor the adversary. Pursued to the fullest, cognitive warfare has the potential to destabilize societies, military organizations, and fracture alliances. Cognitive warfare is achieved by integrating cyber, information, psychological, and social engineering capabilities.

Exploiting information technology, it seeks to create confusion, false representations, and uncertainty with a deluge of information over-abundance or misinformation. This is achieved by focusing attention on false targets, by causing distraction, by introducing false narratives, radicalizing individuals, and amplifying social polarization to muster the cognitive effects needed to achieve short-term and longterm objectives.[11]

Most of the strategies and tactics in this book target conscious thought, conscious cognition, with the possible exception of neurolinguistic programming. However, cognitive warfare involves a different approach than more classical fifth-generation warfare strategies and tactics. Cognitive warfare is specifically focused on targeting the subconscious mind.

Cognitive warfare is a critical component of modern cyberwarfare. NATO's strategic document "Warfare Development Imperative of Cognitive Superiority" details planning to develop a ten to twenty-year operational framework that defines defensive and proactive measures within the cognitive warfare space for NATO. In this document, NATO Allied Command defines cognitive warfare as including "activities conducted in synchronization with other instruments of power to affect attitudes and behavior by influencing, protecting, or disrupting individual and group cognition to gain advantage over an adversary."[12] The nature of the adversary is open-ended and can include both foreign and domestic interventions.

NATO's definition of cognitive warfare includes a cognitive attack that directly targets the minds of civilians (and citizens), meaning non-combatants. To their credit, NATO apparently believes (as do I) that this violates the Law of Armed Conflict, and we also agree that it is already happening. Therefore, NATO proposes that countering cognitive attacks is a military task that NATO must participate in. Of course, this logic provides a convenient excuse for developing the capacity and capabilities to engage in and deploy these same practices if deemed necessary against domestic citizens. Another opportunity to advance "dual function" research logic.

In its journal, *Three Swords*, NATO recently published an article titled "Cognitive Warfare." It was written by Commander Cornelis van der Klaauw, Royal Netherlands Navy and Strategic Communications and subject matter expert for the NATO Joint Warfare Centre. This essay describes some critical ideas behind NATO's concept of cognitive warfare.

> Unlike psychological operations, cognitive activities are not directed at our conscious mind, but at our subconscious mind, the main drivers of our behavior: emotions. This takes place through hyper-personalized targeting integrating and exploiting neuroscience, bio-technology, information and cognitive techniques (NBIC), mainly using social media and digital networks for neuro-profiling and targeting individuals. We need to realize that individuals are at the centre of all military operations and strategic-political decision-making. Although they often sound like ideas from a science-fiction film, cognitive attacks are not science fiction anymore. They are taking place already now, and these attacks will continue to become more sophisticated.
>
> Several countries are developing NBIC capabilities and collecting data for use in targeting the cognitive dimension. These activities are supported by aspects such as data mining and data analytics, and are further combined with artificial intelligence. Although most of the cognitive attacks remain below the threshold of armed conflict, the effects can be lethal and multi-domain, affecting all five domains of warfare.[13]

Commander Cornelis van der Klaauw then goes on to speculate that China is already using neuroscience, biotechnology, information, and cognitive techniques (NBICs) to influence not only Chinese citizenry but also the web as well as the three billion gamers worldwide. Gamers are particularly vulnerable to attack because the

> lines between physical, digital and mental personas are becoming blurrier and with that, the difference between reality and fiction is also becoming unclear. Virtual reality environments (such as the Metaverse) in particular drive this trend.
>
> Cognitive warfare is no longer science fiction. Cognitive warfare is a fact of the modern age and everyone, whether civilian or military, is a potential target. Cognitive attacks are aimed at

exploiting emotions rooted in our subconscious, bypassing our rational conscious mind. This is achieved by exploiting biases, fallacies, emotions and automatisms, but also through nanotechnology, biotechnology and information technology.[14]

Never forget that in fifth-generation warfare, otherwise known as PsyWar, the battle is for control of the mind, thoughts, emotions, and all information that an individual is exposed to. The only way to win at PsyWar is not to play. As soon as one engages with either corporate or social media, one enters the battlefield. So be careful out there.

To even merely defend themselves, people must learn their opponent's technology, tactics, and strategies. The PsyWar battlefield terrain is tortuous, bizarre, constantly shifting, and dangerous to mental health. Our opponents make no distinction between combatants and noncombatants, and they recognize no moral boundaries to what they will do to achieve their objectives.

Of course, it should go without saying that the PsyWar social media battlefield should be one for adults only. A sure way to win is to keep children off of social media. In fact, a law banning children from taking cell phones to school would be a great place to start creating a healthier society.

Parents everywhere need to control their children's internet time and remove smartphones from their lives. As alternative media warriors, we need to spread this message far and wide.

# CHAPTER 8
## Citizen Journalism as Disruptive Technology

In America, only six corporations control 90 percent of the media. In the UK, three major companies own 70 percent of the national media market.

From Sun Tzu's *Art of War*, to the CIA's "Mighty Wurlitzer" and "Operation Mockingbird," to today's "censorship-industrial complex," centralized media has been routinely exploited by governments to advance the propaganda objectives of the state and its military, and thereby to influence policies and politics in virtually all nation-states. In the modern West, this centralization of media by large, often transnational corporations has been further augmented by the creation of supra-corporate aggregator organizations, which function as trade unions to protect the interests of these media oligopolies. Examples include Reuters, AFP, Associated Press, and the notorious "Trusted News Initiative." In many cases, the leadership of these organizations are further integrated into other large corporatist organizations via both shared board membership and shared ownership by the usual globalist/transnational financial firms such as BlackRock, State Street, Vanguard, Bank of America, etc.

Over millennia, with rapidly accelerating precision during the twentieth and twenty-first centuries, the resulting "public-private" corporatist—*ergo* fascist—information control cooperatives have embraced scientific and medical advances in social sciences and psychology to develop a tool kit which enables amazingly effective manipulation of the very thoughts and emotions of individuals, groups, and populations targeted by this information

117

technology. In parallel, a shorthand language for describing what is really an advanced suite of subtle large-scale brainwashing methods and technologies has been developed. These terms include "PsyWar" (psychological warfare targeting the conscious mind), cognitive warfare (which targets the subconscious), the NATO favorite "hybrid warfare," and a wide range of shorthand "internet slang" for the tactical and strategic tool kits available to those seeking to control "The Great Narrative."

In an essay titled "Power to the People: The Rise and Rise of Citizen Journalism" by Micha Barban Dangerfield, Mr. Dangerfield provides a dissection of the history of what we posit to be the most disruptive journalism-related technology in modern history: citizen journalism.

> The advent of the internet, new technologies, social platforms and grass-roots media has heralded a significant shift in collecting, disseminating and sharing information. Citizen journalism can be considered as the offspring of this evolution—an alternative form of news gathering and reporting, taking place outside of the traditional media structures and which can involve anyone. We live in the age of image consumption and data absorption. Everyday, a fresh wave of information reaches our computers and phone screens, but not only are we the recipients of this constant flow, we are now the creators. The liberalization of information allows anyone to share and spread their personal experience of an event, in real time. This new form of reporting takes place ahead of or outside traditional media structures and can function as a fire wall—holding media accountable for any inaccuracies or lack of news coverage.[1]

The modern media landscape can be viewed from the perspective of its role in enabling the administrative state and globalist organizations to control minds, thoughts, beliefs, and opinions and define the very nature of reality based on the surrealist thesis that subjective feelings and beliefs are a valid substitute for objective fact.

In practice, historically, this has been possible both because the information ecosystem is controlled by a small number of dominant, centralized portals and by exploiting (and controlling) digital and cellular communication. The information and opinions flowing through these portals pass through control choke points consisting of a small number of owners, editors, censorship boards, and related stakeholders. The consequence of this information bottleneck is that the psychosocial dynamics of groupthink can be easily manipulated by representatives of the administrative state, globalist organizations, and intelligence communities including the increasingly powerful academic-industrial-governmental mercenary armies of the censorship-industrial complex to give rise to synthetic controversies and narratives that advance the financial and political interests of powerful cabals.

People in positions of power as well as organizations are increasingly conscious of the narrative-shaping power of their words, particularly in the public sphere. They are now shaping their responses to fit the current and future narratives they adhere to. Hence, they are both supporting the narrative scaffolding and maintaining the narrative. They are building storylines based on the prevailing narratives rather than on the facts. This occurs at both the individual and the whole-of-society level.

Modern technology concentrates economic and political control—and, increasingly, cultural control as well—in a small elite group of social media companies, corporate planners, market analysts, deep state players—including those in the intelligence community, and social engineers. Examples of such narrative seeding include the fifty-one intelligence professionals who lied about Hunter's laptop, the coordinated media attacks emanating from the NIH on the Great Barrington Declaration authors, and the *Lancet* letter signed by twenty-seven scientists painting the lab leak hypothesis as a conspiracy theory in early 2020. Once the narrative is established, a scaffold is created, and somehow, all the facts available for public consumption tend to lead to the same predetermined conclusion. At that point, even when the events are shown to be untrue—people on that side of the narrative will still believe the original lie.

Ideas have strange properties. When the world is not ready, they can hide away for days, weeks, years, decades until the right time for their emergence. And then they present themselves, in harmony, all over the world.

Ideas are sticky. They slip into open minds and embed themselves, as if into the subconscious, into the land of dreams and possibilities. Then they suddenly pop into awareness at the strangest of times, when some confluence of circumstance and need combines to make the previously hidden seem obvious.

And ideas have power. Power to subtly shift perspective and then abruptly change the world. Power to overturn economies, societies, and governments.

This is why those stakeholders benefitting from the current status quo actively seek to influence and suppress the spread of new ideas, inconvenient truths, and independent thought.

But now the gloves are off and to some extent, alternative media is able to break through to some minds. Consequently, the American imperial state and its allies (governments and corporations) are increasingly resorting to raw power to avoid the consequences of their actions. And with this, it is becoming easier to see the fist. A fist that takes the form of the most aggressive and pervasive global suppression of thought and speech ever witnessed in recorded history. One that is rapidly becoming normalized as an industrial/academic censorship and propaganda complex.

Science, technology, and geopolitics can all be described as methods for devising optimal solutions to various problem sets. In some cases, the problem sets are stable and universal, such as the universe's nature and physical matter's properties. In other cases, the problem sets are constantly changing as the underlying understandings and current solutions change or evolve under pressure to optimize a solution to address a need.

What censorship and propaganda do is to delay or prevent development of innovative ideas and solutions to unmet needs.

What happens as humans apply their minds and muscles to solving problems and creating value (and wealth, a storage form of value) is that the systems and technologies that they create get closer and closer over time to an optimized solution to the problem. Humans are able to not only adapt to changing conditions in real-time but can also efficiently archive and transmit their solutions to other humans through complex written and verbal communication. The result is rapid widespread innovation.

As systems and solutions improve, they usually encounter obstacles that cannot be addressed by the current paradigm or model of reality. When this happens, a gap develops between the problem or unmet need and current capabilities to address that gap due to some sort of boundary condition. This gap between unmet need and current solutions typically increases over time, particularly during periods of change.

In the case of science and technology, a scientific "revolution" will occur when some new idea, observation, or solution ("disruptive technology") results in a restructuring of understanding about the problem and potential solutions. Such events suddenly (abruptly) dissolve or overcome the boundary that has limited the development of an optimal solution to the problem, and a set of more optimal solutions are rapidly developed until the next boundary condition is encountered. The larger the gap between the current and optimal solution, the more disruptive the change. These fundamental principles are described in the seminal work *The Structure of Scientific Revolutions*, and are associated with the theoretical basis for "paradigm shifts."[2]

Political propaganda and censorship act as boundary conditions to development of more optimal solutions to the problems with which politics is concerned. Problems involving economics, finance, resource distribution, and (increasingly) the nature and impact of the human species on its environment, other species, and itself. When a local or more global hegemonic power (such as post-World War II USA) or cabal (such as the World Economic Forum, WHO, or United Nations) acts via propaganda and censorship to restrict the free flow of ideas and innovation in order to maintain its dominance, this leads to a growing gap (disparity) between current and optimal solutions. This gap is the unmet need, resolution of which is impeded by deployment of propaganda and censorship acting in service of a minority and against the interests of a majority of humankind.

In the case of periods of rapid change, this gap may rapidly expand, resulting in large differences between optimum and allowed solutions. This is particularly the case when objective reality ("truth") is discarded in favor of subjective "truthiness" in which reality becomes whatever dominant individuals or groups assert it to be, and for which they may employ psychological manipulations of various forms to impose their subjective versions of "truth" (false narratives) on the larger population. Of course, these processes are exacerbated when political power is more globally aggregated rather than being decentralized. What might otherwise be a localized failed experiment becomes massive tragedy under a centralized or globalized political system of organization and governance. Example: COVID-19.

Eventually, this unmet need results in an intolerable level of social stress or strain, or difference between the average human condition and that of the elites, which often act to create boundaries to change. In response to these constraints, a new constellation of ideas will often arise that purports to resolve this discontinuity. The historical structure of human revolutions demonstrates that frustrated humanity will often abruptly endorse these new and different ideas, often out of desperation—even if they have not been demonstrated to resolve the gap between current and optimal solutions.

In contrast, in a decentralized human society grounded in objective truth, where open and honest debate about ideas between sovereign autonomous individuals is the expected norm, what develops is a process wherein solutions to problems are constantly being explored, deployed at small scale, and subjected to the crucible of reality-based decision making. The consequence is an incremental set of improvements that allow real-time "evolution" of more optimal solutions to the problem set. And this system has the added benefit of avoiding the development of a frustrated, disempowered majority willing to accept any alternative to a dysfunctional present.

Justification of the use of propaganda and censorship in order to sustain a hegemonic political/economic system that primarily benefits an oligarchy of one form or another (saving "democracy," for example) represents immature, narcissistic, short-term thinking. This must be rejected if for no other reason than that it will delay the development of more effective solutions to current problems and will also strongly contribute to the development of future social and political revolutions resulting in the desperate adoption of unproven ideas and ideologies.

People just need to stop believing that magically some uncorrupted government, social media, or organization will offer up the "truth."

Citizen journalism is so threatening to the administrative state and globalist narrative control because it is completely decentralized. This is why we argue that citizen journalism is modern history's most disruptive information technology. And this is why it has become necessary for those who wish to maintain the ability to control national and global narratives to invest in the censorship industrial complex and the mercenary army organizations available for hire to eliminate this decentralized information threat.

However, above and beyond the relatively straightforward task of cataloging and informing people of what is being done to them on a routine basis through alternative social media channels, what may be even more effective is to enable the development of next-generation tools and capabilities designed to support and empower the global explosion of citizen journalism. In this new surrealistic reality where feelings and beliefs can substitute for actual data, we are choosing to believe that information actually does yearn to be free and that decentralized citizen journalism can save us from the threat of a globalist central command economy designed to serve an elite oligarchy. The hope is that some sort of Web 2.0 will emerge, evolving from the now cludgy but effective blockchain technologies.

If the general populace can learn to recognize advanced propaganda and mass-scale mind control technology as it is deployed, then people will both be able to see through and consequently become much more resistant to these methods and technologies.

# CHAPTER 9
# A Battlescape of the Mind

So now, as the COVIDcrisis has ended and the propaganda/fifth-generation warfare continues to ramp up, we are starting to see additional battle strategies emerge. One new strategy that seems to be cropping up is the circulation of fake documents and videos. Deepfakes are here, and soon, we will not be able to tell the difference between audio, video, and images that are AI-generated versus the real thing. These come in many versions, and as usual, are designed to exploit human behavioral and psychological weaknesses and vulnerabilities. The ability to easily create deepfakes has reached those who are technically savvy. Advertisers are already pushing out deepfake spam videos as fast as their techs can make them. Soon, everyone will be able to play the deepfake game, creating videos, images, and audio of all their favorite friends and enemies.

But this is not the only way to game the public. Chaos and propaganda agents have intentionally compromised public discourse with a variety of highly infectious mind viruses that are rapidly propagated on both social and corporate media. Rampant lying has been normalized in the political/public spheres, and the logical consequences of widespread skepticism and mistrust have, therefore, also become the norm. Mistrust is everywhere.

People with time on their hands and no clear mission or purpose just love to gossip. The more salacious, the better. It is often observed that a good joke must be based in reality. A good gossip topic is the opposite—it contradicts reality. The most potent and viral gossip storylines are the ones that seem at odds with the known public persona. Gossip can imply, often indirectly and fraudulently, that a person or organization is not sincere or otherwise acting in ways that are at odds with their mission or public persona. Gossip, whether spread by chaos agents or small-time influencers, is a way to spread ill-intentioned mind viruses.

There seem to be three general categories of chaos agents that interact in the public square, usually under protection of Section 230 of Title 47 of the US Federal Communications Decency Act of 1996, to deploy these sorts of propaganda and disruption methods actively. Section 230 protects online platforms from lawsuits over harmful user-generated content.

One category consists of paid shills, haters, and trolls who serve a third-party agenda. Often, these parties serve a governmental actor (typically as "subcontractors") but also may serve a surreptitious corporate or other non-state financial interest (*ergo*, Pharma or others). These may include hired-gun "journalists" or even alternative and mainstream media that are being paid for "advocacy journalism" attack articles.

Then there are the lone wolves ("trolls"), who sometimes swarm or form loose, transient online packs or flash mobs, and typically take a perverse pleasure in causing pain and suffering to others. This has developed into a subculture that celebrates spreading hate and causing psychological pain. There is a fundamental evil darkness in these sorts of activities, which are typically grounded in a variety of personality disorders and dysfunctional or maladaptive behaviors. Examples of such disorders of thought include sociopathy, psychopathy, narcissism, free-floating aggression, anger, and self-loathing. These "lone wolves" often have unresolved and unresolvable conflict, insecurity, or cognitive dissonance in their own lives, which they seek to resolve by scapegoating, projecting, or just plain bullying. Many of these seem to have a need for interpersonal conflict-based engagement in their lives. Often, these tend to be more transient hate-mongers, and if you can stand to ignore them, they eventually go away or find another target that will fulfill their need for engagement and conflict. However, their energy and hate are often exploited by the first category of paid propagandists or by those in the third category.

The third and most insidious category of social and corporate media propagandists, who actively deploy and exploit hate and fear, are those who have found a way to monetize their activities. This has long been a favorite strategy of corporate media. The mantra "If it bleeds, it leads" sums up his strategy nicely. We have previously written about the "fearporn" business model, which is a chronic staple of CNN broadcasting.

Even more corrosive and pervasive are the many small podcasters and internet-based authors who strive to spread sensational gossip with the intention of generating anger and outrage. This is absolutely a business model, and many of these parties occasionally slip the veil of pretense and acknowledge the fact by bragging about how many followers, comments, or "likes" they are getting using these methods. In some cases, these small but very loud (on social media) actors pick up sponsors who have an agenda which is aligned with these smaller and less cohesively organized chaos agents. The shouting voices of these small actors can then be coordinated and amplified by selective sponsorship. This false narrative is then amplified by the use of the usual bot and troll strategies, in which an Astroturf movement is generated by deploying groups of agents.

In some cases, these small agents use bot farms, but typically the use of bots is a strategy/tactic employed by larger state, non-state/NGO, and corporate fifth-gen warfare campaigns. In the case of the coordinated smaller players, most of these are typically decentralized networks of individuals who have been recruited over time—perhaps for some other cause—and are connected to a central communication point (typically via e-mail list) and can be provided a (false) narrative and directed toward an online target (typically by exploiting paranoia, fear, hate, and outrage). In other cases, a modest investment in free burner phones distributed through a network of contacts (family, friends, trusted associates) can yield what appears (to outside observers) to be a decentralized spontaneous response. This is a favorite Astroturf strategy to "make something (or someone) go viral." The use of burner phones to create fake TikTok, Instagram, Facebook, and Twitter (X) accounts that will push out videos and other media to cause them to go viral is a known technique used by Astroturf organizations as well as advertisers.

## Here Is How the General Ecosystem Works:

The internet and social media are non-scalable systems. What we mean by that is that the vast majority of internet or social media nodes have relatively few connections, so it is almost impossible to grow them exponentially. A non-scalable system is when the level of achieved results depends on continuous efforts. In the case of social media, connection nodes consist of "followers" and "followed." These node connections define the cloud of first- and second-degree interrelatedness associated with a primary node (a person, user, account, etc.) and, therefore, define the ability of the primary node to influence others. Low node connectivity = low influence. The vast majority of internet sites and social media nodes are low complexity/connectivity and low influence.

As the complexity of the web of node connections increases for any one node, then the probability of that node continuing to develop additional connections increases. At this point, the system becomes scalable. The system can grow without any additional effort. This is how "followers" and influence develop, and this cycle is typically nonlinear (unless constrained or "throttled" via shadow banning, etc.). In other words, connectivity gives rise to ever-greater connectivity. As a consequence, if one assesses the interconnectedness of internet and social media "platform" nodes, there is a vast plain (valley of death) of low-complexity nodes interrupted by "spikes" or mountains of highly connected nodes which typically become more connected over time. Connectedness is an unpredictable, emergent, and typically exponential phenomenon of these networked systems.

Because of the internet's "nonlinear" decentralized structural characteristics, the interconnectedness and functionality of the web could be almost completely destroyed by eliminating less than 10 percent of existing nodes, that is the highly interconnected ones. Likewise, the webs of communication and impact on society at large associated with highly connected social media nodes can be destroyed by targeting those nodes and the associated individuals or organizations. Of course, this is most readily accomplished by directly eliminating the node.

Eliminating a node is most easily achieved by blocking a static IP address or a particular URL, for example (on the internet), or by banning or deplatforming an individual account or, in the case of Facebook, a group.

There are many examples of Facebook effectively using this method of eliminating nodes of users that they don't agree with. For instance, they effectively stopped a group of vaccine injured from their platform by eliminating the group once it reached a critical size. Thus, they are able to effectively eliminate that node from their platform.

But Facebook wasn't content with just eliminating that node; they also go after specific users who might have posted information that Facebook finds offensive or "dangerous." Facebook understands the use of scalable and non-scalable systems and how to eliminate core communities to achieve its desired result. Here is the Facebook policy that goes beyond just eliminating the offending group in question, but also targets individual users within that group who might try to reassemble or grow more nodes (groups).

> Facebook
> Update on October 20, 2021 at 9:00AM PT:
> Today, we're announcing new measures to keep Facebook Groups safe.
>
> To continue limiting the reach of people who break our rules, we'll start demoting all Groups content from members who have broken our Community Standards, anywhere on Facebook. These demotions will get more severe as they accrue more violations.
>
> This measure will help reduce the ability of members who break our rules from reaching others in their communities, and builds on the existing restrictions placed upon members who violate Community Standards. These current penalties include restricting their ability to post, comment, add new members to a group or create new groups.

These are basically methods for killing or surgically terminating a source of disagreeable content as well as the entire network of interconnected individuals (or an idea space) who share a particular node (and belief system) as a common junction. These methods are readily available to governments, very large corporations and NGOs, and organizations that control the internet (ICANN, for example) or the major social media sites.

Major social media sites are examples of the internet's emergent scalability properties. You can think of this as akin to the observation that "success breeds success." Suppose you seek to influence the general public information and idea square to impact current knowledge and thought in some way. In that case, you will seek out the major social media platforms for your interactions. Consequently, social media platform innovators have great difficulty establishing themselves unless there is some characteristic of the larger platforms that make them distasteful to a critical mass of individuals. Audiences, influencers, and authors migrate to the most successful platforms.

Substack is an online platform that publishes and provides payment options, analytics, and template design to support subscription newsletters. These newsletters can then be viewed on the platform's website. Views can be limited to subscribers or open to the public.

It's truly amazing how successful the Substack business model is, despite facing censorship pressures. This success highlights two general truths. First, Substack gained popularity largely due to widespread censorship on other social media platforms. In a way, it revives an older internet business model—direct email distribution. However, building a Substack audience typically requires an extraordinary event or an existing audience, such as a social media following that can be leveraged.

In Robert's case, the synchronous deplatforming by Twitter and LinkedIn, coupled with his interview on the *Joe Rogan Experience* #1757 on December 31, 2021, created the dynamics that allowed our Substack account to breach the scalability threshold. Basically, his followers came looking for him after he had "disappeared" from social media. A new audience was built from the 100+/- million viewers of that single Joe Rogan podcast that occurred almost simultaneously with the deplatforming.

If a business model (or fifth-generation warfare objective) is based on internet traffic (clicks, likes, views, or paid subscriptions), then one faces a challenge. One cannot escape the low node connectivity problem, the valley of death, unless one can find some way to attract attention to their node. This is sort of like the problem of how to reach and sustain the critical velocity required to escape the pull of gravity if one wishes to reach space. How does one distinguish their unique "node" from the vast terrain of other low-connectivity nodes that inhabit this valley of death? How can one reach the threshold of critical connectivity, which will then enable them to benefit from the non-scalable nature of these systems?

Some people make a *lot* of money from their internet sites, podcasts, Substack essays, and YouTube videos, but they all had to solve this problem. In some cases, and Joe Rogan appears to be one example, this can require years and years of sustained effort to build an internet following. However, in almost every other case, these success stories involve capitalizing on some event that drove viewers to their node and then converting that traffic into "followers" and some sort of revenue stream. Advertisers are one common source of revenue; merchandise (T-shirts, caps, coffee cups) is another, and third-party sponsors are another. But first, the node must reach that critical mass of connectivity, which is the escape velocity required to overcome gravity. That is the art and science of monetizing the internet and social media—and any media, for that matter. Building connections.

Just like any small business, one way to grow an audience is to provide value. In this model, followers and subscribers are treated like valued customers. Like any small business (or consulting practice), this strategy requires hard daily work. Creating original content that people wish to read (or watch), day after day after day, is hard work—take our word for it; we live it. Like any small business, vacations and time off are a luxury that comes at a high price of lost revenue, followers/subscribers, and customer satisfaction. And just like any other small business, the author/artist/videographer/influencer confronts a competitive landscape, including competitors that will employ a wide range of aggressive strategies—including attempts to undermine or delegitimize others perceived as competition. And then there are the ancient and ever-present seven deadly sins: envy, gluttony, greed or avarice, lust, pride, sloth, and wrath. Haters will hate. Humans will always remain human.

One strategy for escaping the valley of death involves stoking rage, feeding conspiratorial tendencies, combined with the very human desire to gossip. People seem to have a need to be stimulated by increasingly outrageous claims, regardless of whether they are based on verifiable reality or just reflect conspiratorial imaginings and fabricated associations that do not hold up to even casual scrutiny. Unfortunately, Section 230 has created an environment where these more aggressive and dysfunctional strategies can flourish.

The problem is that very little can be done about this type of behavior. It is fundamentally evil and incredibly destructive to reputation and to good mental health. We have picked up a number of what are essentially internet (and in some cases physical) stalkers that employ this method on a daily basis. In the case of one obsessed person, this has been going on for over two years now. Like many other things, Robert's primary defense mechanism has been intellectualizing the experience. This chapter reflects that defense mechanism bias, which is considered relatively adaptive but also somewhat neurotic. More mature and adaptive defense mechanisms include humor, sublimation, suppression, altruism, and anticipation, all of which Robert also strives to deploy in response to the psychological stress that these types of public attacks provoke—but after all, he is another imperfect human, just like we all are.

In the social media ecosystem, and also in the case of biased "advocacy journalism" based corporate media, the options to respond to these forms of slander and defamation to "clear your name" are very limited, particularly if one has a substantial social presence (*ergo*, have become one of those more interconnected nodes). Responding to defamatory attacks will draw more attention to the attack and the attacker, fueling clicks, follows, likes, and revenue for the attacker. It is a no-win situation, where one is constantly juggling the problem of how much reputational damage is being done by the attacker and the constant clamor to "just debate him/her, answer the questions!" etc. In the end, civil courts are the last resort if the attacker is causing substantial reputational damage. But that is a costly, time-consuming, and low-probability path for damage control, and can backfire as the attacker will often claim to be a victim of unjustified lawfare.

One version of this is the podcaster or author who makes outrageous defamatory statements and then demands that you come on their podcast or do an interview to answer the allegations. Why would anyone of sound mind want to go into a podcast's intimate and exposed environment with someone who is slandering and defaming you? A podcast is an amazingly intimate interpersonal transaction that is recorded and/or streamed all over the world. If one walks away from a hostile interview, that is readily seen as an admission of lack of integrity or guilt. If you are honest about something that can be misconstrued, it will be weaponized against you. You are locked into a one-to-one discussion with another party (which you typically just met). And they can say or ask anything; it is all on the record. Many will require pre-negotiated rules of engagement—forbidden topics or questions, a practice which we avoid. Your partner in this transaction may decide at some future date to misconstrue something that you said and weaponize it for fame, attention (and clicks). Recently, Robert picked up someone who is currently doing this by loudly claiming that Robert was censoring him. With no actual evidence. Frankly, Robert has been burned enough times that he approaches every podcast with a bit of resentment and loathing these days. Why should he repeatedly tear open the psychological veil that we all show to the world on a daily basis? Because hostile, hating, inquiring minds want to know?

Fifth-generation warfare is a nasty business. There are no rules of engagement. There is no distinction between civilians and combatants. It is about controlling your mind, the information you encounter, your beliefs, and your emotions. It is enabled in the United States by Section 230 and by the legal precedent of *New York Times v. Sullivan*. There are sins of information warfare, as with any form of warfare, and they typically boil down to utilitarian logic—the means justify the ends. But they often involve some form of conflict of interest. Striving for money, power, fame, an agenda, or advancing a government pysops objective.

The distribution of defamation and slander as a means to advance information warfare is evil. Most of us who are aware (or "awake") have noticed the pervasive presence of evil over the last three years. Evil exists. And it exploits and feeds, in large part, on the seven deadly sins: envy, gluttony, greed or avarice, lust, pride, sloth, and wrath.

Don't spread malicious gossip. It is a highly destructive form of mental masturbation. It is destroying our commons and our public square. Don't be evil. Don't take our (or anyone else's) word as gospel truth. Do your own diligence, and think for yourself. For heaven's sake. Or for your children's sake. Or to merely protect your own soul from evil.

# CHAPTER 10
## PsyWar Tactics

### Cyberstalking and Gang Stalking

What a bizarre world we are living in. The *Epoch Times* has published an article based on whistleblower evidence that the United States government agency, the Centers for Disease Control and Prevention (CDC), has used its congressionally-approved nonprofit (called the CDC Foundation) to contract with at least one company to perform cyberstalking and gang stalking attacks on licensed physicians accused of spreading misinformation about COVID public health policies including genetic vaccines.[1]

This is a far larger story of government malfeasance than the relatively benign headline seems to indicate. Of course, corporate media has completely overlooked (e.g., buried) the story. This is yet more evidence of the US government deploying fifth-generation PsyWar technologies on its citizens. In this specific case, it was deployed against US licensed physicians who contradicted officially promoted false narratives concerning the COVIDcrisis and the abysmal public health policies that were promoted by the WHO, US HHS, and specifically the CDC.

As we have said many times before, how can a democratic society exist when the government is willing and able to deploy fifth-generation PsyWar technologies against its own citizens? When this becomes an accepted practice, personal sovereignty and autonomy become obsolete, an anachronism.

According to its website, the CDC Foundation is "the sole entity created by Congress to mobilize philanthropic and private-sector resources to support the Centers for Disease Control and Prevention's critical health protection work."

So now, according to the *Epoch Times*, the CDC Foundation receives funding from a wide range of donors. This organization has been funding cyberstalking and gang stalking of licensed physicians. Cyberstalking is both a federal crime and a crime in many states. The 2022 donor report from the foundation included the likes of Merck, Pfizer, PayPal, Fidelity, BlackRock, the Imperial College of London, Emergent BioSolutions, the Robert Wood Johnson Foundation (as in J&J), and so many other major corporate and state donors. Some of those very same organizations that have made billions of dollars from the COVIDcrisis are funding a nonprofit to cyberstalk and gang-stalk scientists and physicians who criticize these very same organizations for regulatory capture and safety issues of their products. Good to know. Below is the federal code for stalking, which includes cyberstalking.

> 18 U.S. Code § 2261A - Stalking
> (ii) an immediate family member (as defined in section 115) of that person;
> (iii) a spouse or intimate partner of that person; or
> (iv) the pet, service animal, emotional support animal, or horse of that person; or
> (B) causes, attempts to cause, or would be reasonably expected to cause substantial emotional distress to a person described in clause (i), (ii), or (iii) of subparagraph (A); or
> (2) with the intent to kill, injure, harass, intimidate, or place under surveillance with intent to kill, injure, harass, or intimidate another person, uses the mail, any interactive computer service or electronic communication service or electronic communication system of interstate commerce, or any other facility of interstate or foreign commerce to engage in a course of conduct that—
> (A) places that person in reasonable fear of the death of or serious bodily injury to a person, a pet, a service animal, an emotional support animal, or a horse described in clause (i), (ii), (iii), or (iv) of paragraph (1)(A); or

(B) causes, attempts to cause, or would be reasonably expected
to cause substantial emotional distress to a person described
in clause (i), (ii), or (iii) of paragraph (1)(A), shall be punished
as provided in section 2261(b) or section 2261B, as the case
may be.

## *Some Background, Which Is Important in Order to Understand the Corruption That Is Occurring in the Present Day:*

We are very familiar with the CDC Foundation, having first encountered it decades ago when Robert was working as Director for Business
Development and Project Management for the AERAS Global TB
Vaccine Foundation. AERAS was one of the first wave of "Gatelets,"
the nonprofit companies set up to receive "donations" from the Bill &
Melinda Gates Foundation (BMGF) so that the BMGF foundation could
get the tax benefits of donating to nonprofit organizations. AERAS happened to be the one that taught the BMGF how Merck Vaccines does
business, as the CEO (Jerry Sadoff) had once been a director at Merck
Vaccines and had kept the various business and training manuals from
that firm which he then brought into AERAS, and then used these corporate manuals to instruct the BMGF in "industry best practices" for
vaccine companies.

At the time, we were looking hard for new clients, and Robert was
brought into this situation as a consultant proposal manager/author/subject
matter expert by a vice president of AERAS to salvage a poorly written
grant/contract proposal prepared by an AERAS employee, let's call him
"Larry." Larry used to work for the CDC in the tuberculosis group and
still had good contacts there. The tuberculosis research group at CDC had
a problem—they could not get authorization for additional staff (full-time
employees or FTE). They could get money to develop offshore clinical
research sites, just not money for additional employees. In DoD federal con-
tracting and Washington DC slang, this is called having an issue of "the
color of money."

AERAS had a problem—they needed more money (and legitimization
via CDC) to develop clinical research sites in India and South Africa at
which the new TB vaccines they were developing (with BMGF funds) could
be tested in places where there is a lot of tuberculosis. A deal had been

cooked with the CDC so that AERAS would "donate" money through the CDC Foundation to fund the desired additional tuberculosis researchers (FTE) at the CDC. And the quid pro quo was to be that the CDC would "solicit" a proposal from a qualified TB vaccine innovator (written so that only AERAS would qualify) for clinical research site development. The problem was that "Larry" was not able to write a decent federal proposal, his submission had already been judged inadequate once by CDC reviewers, and AERAS was only going to be allowed two shots on goal. So Robert became the hired gun brought in to write a second version of the proposal. The mission was accomplished, the award was made by the CDC, and the donation was made by AERAS.

And from this, we learned yet another lesson in how DC really works—how this congressionally approved "CDC Foundation" back door actually allowed private entities to influence federal public health policy. In the precise way that it was not supposed to work. Just like the Foundation for NIH, which funneled Pharma money into the COVID "ACTIV" clinical trials during COVID.

## Rules on Gifts in the Federal Government

Government ethical rules restrict giving and accepting gifts among employees and from outside interests. Policies on exchanges of gifts among employees—as well as on acceptance of gifts or hospitality from other sources—are set by government-wide rules found in the Code of Federal Regulations at 5 CFR 2635 201–205 and 301–304.

Basically, no individual or company is allowed to give "gifts" openly to an employee or agency of the federal government because of the risk of resulting conflict of interest (otherwise known as corruption).

Congress specifically waived these rules for the CDC Foundation and the Foundation for the NIH. This allows Pharma and various other interests to do exactly what the law was intended to prevent: influence federal agency policies and actions by making financial donations.

## Cyberstalking and Cyberbullying

Here is some relevant background and definitions from the Cyberbullying Research Center:

> **Cyberstalking** involves the use of technology (most often, the internet!) to make someone else afraid or concerned about their safety. Generally speaking, this conduct is threatening or otherwise fear-inducing, involves an invasion of a person's relative right to privacy, and manifests in repeated actions over time. Most of the time, those who cyberstalk use social media, Internet databases, search engines, and other online resources to intimidate, follow, and cause anxiety or terror to others.

Surprisingly, cyberstalking by a stranger rarely occurs (although we do hear about those cases when they involve celebrities and rabid fans) and most often is carried out by a person the target knows intimately or professionally. For example, the aggressor may be an ex-girlfriend or ex-boyfriend, former friend, past employee, or an acquaintance who wants to control, possess, scare, threaten, or actually harm the other person. In many cases, they have had access to certain personal information, accounts, inboxes, or other private knowledge regarding their target's daily routine, lifestyle, or life choices.

## Difference between Cyberstalking and Cyberbullying

Cyberstalking is one form of cyberbullying, as the definition of cyberbullying is "willful and repeated harm inflicted through the use of computers, cell phones, and other electronic devices." Cyberstalking behaviors may include tracking down someone's personal and private information and using that information to make their target afraid. Techniques include texting the victim hundreds of times a day to let them know you are watching them, "creeping" on their social media accounts to learn where they are so they can show up there uninvited, or posting about them incessantly and without their permission. The common denominator is that the behavior of the aggressor makes the target extremely concerned for their personal safety and causes some form of distress, fear, or annoyance.

Stories of cyberstalking are frequently covered by the mainstream media when famous people are involved (you can find incidents related to Selena Gomez, Madonna, Justin Bieber, Beyoncé, Justin Timberlake, Kim Kardashian, Britney Spears, and others with a simple Google search) but media headlines often do not accurately convey the true nature and extent of the phenomenon. Unfortunately, academic researchers have largely neglected studying cyberstalking on a broad scale, and we only have a couple recent national studies from which to draw upon.

> **(Cyber) Gang stalking** is a form of cyberstalking or cyberbullying, in which a group of people target an individual online to harass them through repeated threat threats, fear inducing behavior, bullying, teasing, intimidation, gossip, and bad-jacketing.

## What Does This Weaponized Term "Misinformation" Actually Refer To?

Misinformation in the context of current public health is defined as any speech that differs from the official statements of the World Health Organization or local health authorities (*ergo*, CDC, FDA, NIH). So, any physician who says, writes, or highlights opinions or information that differs from the (current) CDC position can be defined as spreading misinformation by the US government. "Disinformation" is such speech which is provided for political purposes.

"Mal-information" is any such speech that can cause mistrust of the government, even if the information is true. The US Department of Homeland Security has defined mis- dis- and mal-information as a form of domestic terrorism. So apparently, federally funded cyberstalking is acceptable when the CDC accuses a licensed US physician of domestic terrorism for the crime of spreading mis- dis- or mal-information concerning COVID public health policies.

The February 7, 2022, "Summary of Terrorism Threat to the US Homeland" from the Department of Homeland Security states that:

> The United States remains in a heightened threat environment fueled by several factors, including an online environment filled

with false or misleading narratives and conspiracy theories, and other forms of mis- dis- and mal-information (MDM) introduced and/or amplified by foreign and domestic threat actors. . . . The primary terrorism-related threat to the United States continues to stem from lone offenders or small cells of individuals who are motivated by a range of foreign and/or domestic grievances often cultivated through the consumption of certain online content.

(1) the proliferation of false or misleading narratives, which sow discord or undermine public trust in US government institutions; . . .

Key factors contributing to the current heightened threat environment include:

The proliferation of false or misleading narratives, which sow discord or undermine public trust in US government institutions:

For example, there is widespread online proliferation of false or misleading narratives regarding unsubstantiated widespread election fraud and COVID-19. Grievances associated with these themes inspired violent extremist attacks during 2021. . . .

As COVID-19 restrictions continue to decrease nationwide, increased access to commercial and government facilities and the rising number of mass gatherings could provide increased opportunities for individuals looking to commit acts of violence to do so, often with little or no warning. Meanwhile, COVID-19 mitigation measures—particularly COVID-19 vaccine and mask mandates—have been used by domestic violent extremists to justify violence since 2020 and could continue to inspire these extremists to target government, healthcare, and academic institutions that they associate with those measures.[2]

The take home message here is that the government has decided that any message regarding COVID-19 that is not approved by the US government is dangerous and could lead to "increased opportunities for individuals looking to commit acts of violence." This is a totalitarian response that cannot be allowed to stand in a free society. It is also a perfect example of why our ABC agencies must be reformed.

The label of malformation by the US government of any dissident scientist or physician who relies on their own mind to formulate an opinion is shocking. Furthermore, enabling Astroturf organizations to then go after these professionals via cyberstalking and cyberbullying is illegal and seems to be orchestrated and legitimized by the administrative state because cyberstalking and cyberbullying are illegal activities.

Wikipedia and many other sources provide detailed information concerning cyberstalking and cyberbullying. We currently have at least five individuals who are actively engaged in cyberstalking and cyberbullying Robert on a daily basis, and we can tell you that it is extremely stressful for both of us, not to mention the threats from others who are provoked by these people.

The following is abstracted from the Wikipedia information concerning cyberstalking:

> Stalking is a continuous process, consisting of a series of actions, each of which may be entirely legal in itself. Technology ethics professor Lambèr Royakkers defines cyberstalking as perpetrated by someone without a current relationship with the victim. About the abusive effects of cyberstalking, he writes that:
>
> [Stalking] is a form of mental assault in which the perpetrator repeatedly, unwantedly, and disruptively breaks into the life world of the victim, with whom he has no relationship (or no longer has), with motives that are directly or indirectly traceable to the affective sphere. Moreover, the separated acts that make up the intrusion cannot by themselves cause the mental abuse, but do taken together (cumulative effect).

## Distinguishing cyberstalking from other acts

There is a distinction between cyber-trolling and cyberstalking. Research has shown that actions that can be perceived to be harmless as a one-off can be considered to be trolling, whereas if it is part of a persistent campaign then it can be considered stalking.

Cyberstalking is a technologically based "attack" on a victim who has been targeted specifically for that attack for reasons of anger, revenge control, or clickbait. Cyberstalking has many forms, which can include harassment, embarrassment, and humiliation of the victim. Cyberstalking may also include some sort of economic attack, which may include ruining credit scores, emptying bank accounts, shutting down reoccurring accounts—such as essential utilities. The attackers may also harass family, friends, employers, and social media contacts to isolate the victim as well as scare tactics on the victim and their contacts to instill fear and anxiety.

## Identification and Detection

Legal authorities will analyze the following features to characterize a stalking situation. They are malice, premediation, repetition, distress, obsession, vendetta, no legitimate purpose, personally directed, disregarded warnings to stop, harassment, and threats.

A number of key factors have been identified in cyberstalking (from Wikipedia):

- False accusations: Many cyberstalkers try to damage the reputation of their victim and turn other people against them. They post false information about them on websites. They may set up their own websites, blogs, or user pages for this purpose. They post allegations about the victim to newsgroups, chat rooms, or other sites that allow public contributions such as Wikipedia or Amazon.com.
- Attempts to gather information about the victim: Cyberstalkers may approach their victim's friends, family, and work colleagues to obtain personal information. They may advertise for information on the internet, or hire a private detective.
- Monitoring their target's online activities and attempting to trace their IP address in an effort to gather more information about their victims.
- Encouraging others to harass the victim: Many cyberstalkers try to involve third parties in the harassment. They may claim the victim has harmed the stalker or his/her family in some way, or may post the victim's name and telephone number in order to encourage others to join the pursuit.
- False victimization: The cyberstalker will claim that the victim is harassing him or her.

The Anti-Defamation League recently attacked Robert in a published article as a conspiracy theorist and misinformation spreader for writing about fifth-generation warfare, the administrative state, and the Uniparty.[3] In so doing, they have also created a false association between Robert, Steve Kirsch, Dr. Joseph Mercola, and many obscure Neo-Nazis and anti-Semites. Based on a recent decision in the Southern District of New York, this type of false association meets the criteria for malicious defamation. The ADL wrote:

> *Who is Robert Malone*
> *294,000+ Subscribers*
> *Tens of Thousands of Paid Subscribers*
> *Minimum Monthly Profits: $40,550*
> Robert Malone is best known for posting vaccine and COVID-related conspiracy theories. However, his content also promotes conspiratorial tropes about evil, powerful forces in the government. In one article, he discusses something called fifth-generation warfare, or "5GW," as a way to retain "autonomy and sovereignty," rather than conceding to what he calls "the Uniparty and their globalist Overlords." Malone also pushes anti-government conspiracy theories, writing that a "Uniparty is waging fifth-generation warfare against American citizens.

What Robert wrote and writes about in this book is not a conspiracy theory. The US federal government, through the "administrative state" and the "deep state," is funding organizations that engage in cyberstalking and cyberbullying of licensed US physicians on a routine basis. This is not subtle. This is fifth-generation warfare, yet another example of PsyWar being waged against US citizens by their government.

---

**Deep state** is a type of governance made up of potentially secret and unauthorized networks of power operating independently of a state's political leadership in pursuit of their own agenda and goals.[4]

**Administrative state** is a type of governance in which the executive branch and administrative agencies exercise power to create, adjudicate, and enforce their own rules. The administrative state uses non-delegation, judicial deference, executive control of agencies, procedural rights, and agency dynamics to assert control above the republic and democratic principles.

Congress must act, because the executive branch is out of control and routinely pursues a strategy of disregarding the Bill of Rights and federal laws in a game of "catch me if you can." The administrators who have authorized these practices need to be held accountable, tried in federal court, and, if found guilty, must bear the same penalties that any US citizen engaging in cyberstalking should be subjected to.

The US government should not be allowed to engage in these practices. This means an entire overhaul of our agencies. This can only be achieved by Congressional oversight, combined with a change of leadership at every level of federal agencies and institutions. This will require a president who can maintain power for more than one term or be able to pass off this critical remaking of the senior executive class to reflect both the republic and the democracy under which we all live.

The congressionally mandated nonprofits developed to fund and bypass congressional oversight of various agencies must be disassembled. This will require either an amendment or repealing the sections of congressional bills that have allowed these nonprofits to bypass normal federal oversight.

The Foundation for NIH and the CDC Foundation must be dissolved, as must the CIA's investment organization In-Q-Tel. The CIA has no business generating dark money through a shady nonprofit, whose monies can't be traced. Congress has created a monster with these shady organizations. The slush funds generated are being used for what would otherwise be prohibited. The Foundation for NIH and the CDC Foundation enable these executive branch administrative units to engage in what would otherwise be unlawful or prohibited activities.

# CHAPTER 11
## Power Is in Tearing Human Minds to Pieces

> Vast numbers of human beings must cooperate in this manner if they are to live together as a smoothly functioning society. . . . In almost every act of our daily lives, whether in the sphere of politics or business, in our social conduct or our ethical thinking, we are dominated by the relatively small number of persons . . . who understand the mental processes and social patterns of the masses. It is they who pull the wires which control the public mind.
>
> —Edward Bernays—*Propaganda* (1928) pp. 9–10[1]

One of the most successful disinformation campaigns in the twenty-first century occurred a few weeks before the 2020 presidential election between Joseph Biden and incumbent Donald Trump. Kash Patel's book *Government Gangsters* lays out the timeline for the Hunter Biden laptop scandal in detail.[2]

The history is as follows: In 2019, Joe Biden's son left a laptop at a Delaware computer repair shop, which he never picked up. After several months of abandonment, the laptop become the property of the shop owner. The laptop had photographs and videos of Hunter Biden with prostitutes, illegal drug use, and most damning, documents and emails linking his father, who was vice-president at the time, to his own business dealings that involved soliciting money from rich oligarchs and countries such as China and Ukraine. Whistleblower evidence suggests that the FBI seized the laptop in 2019 but chose not to investigate. In fact, during 2022 Senate testimony, a whistleblower said that the FBI told some bureau employees that they "will not look at that Hunter Biden laptop." Later, Senators Chuck Grassley and Ron Johnson later stated that the FBI whistleblower who brought this scandal to light was suspended without pay, in what appears to be an act of reprisal.

The summer before the 2020 election, the FBI laid out a fake story to Meta (Facebook) weeks before the Hunter Biden news story broke in order to prepare a defensive disinformation campaign.[3]

> Basically, the background here is the FBI basically came to us, some folks on our team, and was like, "Hey, just so you know you should be on high alert," said Zuckerberg. "We thought there was a lot of Russian propaganda in the 2016 election, we have it on notice that basically there's about to be some kind of dump that's similar to that so just be vigilant."
>
> When Rogan asked if the FBI had told Facebook to be on guard specifically for our story about Hunter Biden's laptop, Zuckerberg claimed, rather unconvincingly that he did "not remember . . . specifically" but "it basically fit the pattern."
>
> Whatever was said, the briefing must have been specific enough for Facebook to recognize immediately that our story was exactly what the FBI was warning about and move at record speed to throttle it. At 11:10 a.m. the morning the story went live, Democratic operative Andy Stone, Facebook's communications manager, issued a statement on Twitter announcing "we are reducing its distribution on our platform" while the story is "fact checked by Facebook's third-party fact checking partners."

The FBI collaborated with the world's largest social media company to rig an election and kill the upcoming *New York Post* story about the contents of Hunter Biden's laptop. From there, it gets even worse. The *New York Post* broke the true story about Hunter Biden's laptop in early October 2020 in a news story[4] that should have won the Pulitzer Prize.

The *Post* acted transparently to readers how it got the Laptop from Hell. Moreover, nobody on Team Biden denied the *Post*'s report, because they knew or suspected it was true. Every news outlet in the country should have fronted the story at that point: "Biden team refuses to deny Hunter Biden laptop story." A few months later, Hunter himself said the laptop "certainly" could be his, and the media shrugged instead of apologizing . . .

Even in the presidential debate where the matter came up, Joe Biden's comments were not a denial but simply a deflection, and everybody who reported that he denied the laptop story was guilty of propagating fake news all over again. What he actually said was,

> There are 50 former national intelligence folks who said that what he's accusing me of is a Russian plant. Five former heads of the CIA, both parties, say what he's saying is a bunch of garbage. Nobody believes it except his good friend Rudy Giuliani.

That is what is called a lie in the real world, but not in the corridors of Washington, D.C., or in state-sponsored media.

This *New York Post* article documents that even in 2020, elements of the US government, which some might call the "deep state," were engaging in misinformation (translation—lies) meant to alter the outcome of the upcoming election. There is a good chance that their efforts succeeded and that they swayed the election in favor of Biden.

These deep state agents have turned to using big tech, social media, legacy media, and paid "influencers" to smear, slander, censor, and defame those who tried to bring the story of Hunter Biden's laptop to the American people prior to the election.

But the FBI wasn't done playing psyops on the American people yet. In 2023, FBI whistleblowers came forward to Iowa Senator Chuck Grassley to relay the following: fifty-one FBI officials and operatives signed a fraudulent letter that Hunter Biden's laptop was Russian "disinformation," just two weeks before the 2020 presidential election. Kash Patel then goes on to explain:

> The backlash against this reporting was immediate and intense, leading to suppression of the story by US corporate media outlets and censorship of the story by leading Silicon Valley monopolies. The disinformation campaign against this reporting was

led by the CIA's all-but-official spokesperson Natasha Bertrand (then of Politico, now with CNN), whose article on October 19 appeared under this headline: "Hunter Biden story is Russian disinfo, dozens of former intel officials say."

This fraud caused Joe Biden to become forty-sixth president of the United States. Polling data and studies show that President Trump would have been voted into office if this letter had not been produced. In fact, 79 percent of voters have stated that if the details of this letter were known, the election would have had a different outcome. Here is a quick analysis on how the fraudulent FBI letter changed the electoral outcome:

> In November 2020, the Media Research Center commissioned The Polling Company to survey 1,750 Biden voters in seven swing states (Arizona, Georgia, Michigan, Nevada, North Carolina, Pennsylvania, and Wisconsin).
>
> A massive 45.1% of Biden voters polled said they were "unaware of the financial scandal enveloping Biden and his son, Hunter," adding that "full awareness of the Hunter Biden scandal would have led 9.4% of Biden voters to abandon the Democratic candidate."
>
> And it's this 9.4% change that could have been hugely consequential when we consider Biden's winning margins in six of these swing states. Biden won Arizona by 0.3%, Georgia by 0.23%, Michigan by 2.8%, Nevada by 2.4%, Pennsylvania by 1.2%, and Wisconsin by 0.63%. A swing of 9.4% would have handed each of these states to former President Donald Trump, giving him 79 additional electoral votes.
>
> His total in this scenario? 311 electoral votes, 41 votes over the 270 electoral votes required to win the presidential election.[5]

This is truly the administrative and the deep state skewing the election in favor of their own candidate. The government cheated to ensure that Joe Biden became commander in chief. This is pure evil. This is also more evidence of a psychological operations war on the American people. This is domestic psyops which will eventually lead to the end of representative democracy in America unless the FBI is brought under control by Congress and the next president of the United States.

For us personally, the revelation of this scandal opened our eyes to the depths of corruption that are now marbled throughout the US government. We knew regulatory capture had become the norm for "dual-use" agencies (such as FDA, CDC, USDA, FAA, etc.), in other words, those with a direct mission to both regulate and promote industry, but we had no idea of the depths of corruption that permeated our entire government.

Elements of our government have been engaged in psyops campaigns designed to manipulate the beliefs and thoughts of the American people, and these campaigns started long before COVID-19. The *New York Post*, which was one of the victims of the censorship and smear campaign led by democratic officials, ex-CIA "reporters" (which usually means current CIA "contractors") acting in collusion with big tech and the legacy media, also wrote about this in a piece called:

"How Dem officials, the media and Big Tech worked in concert to bury the Hunter Biden story."[6]

> Everlasting, undying, soul-rending shame be upon you, Facebook and Twitter and Politico and all the others who covered up, denied and suppressed this newspaper's true and accurate reporting about Hunter Biden's laptop in 2020. You should be hurling yourselves at the feet of the American people, begging forgiveness. You should be renting billboards saying, "WE LIED."
>
> But most importantly, you should be hauled before Congress to answer humiliating questions.

## Exit Stage Left: Hunter Biden—Enter Stage Right: COVID-19

Well, we all know what happens next. We have lived it. The censorship and defamation of any scientist or physician who questions the safety, efficacy, or data (or lack thereof) of the public policies surrounding COVID-19 have been unprecedented in modern US history.

From the CDC hiding important data to stop "vaccine hesitancy" (*ergo*, scientific fraud), to the CDC, HHS, and DHS using a billion dollars to fight vaccine "misinformation" to promote vaccines by funding state-sponsored media (*ergo*, legacy media) and to fund "influencers" is by now well known to all those who are reading these words. Then there are the state and federal government's increasingly hysterical efforts to shut down early treatment and push more boosters by persecuting physicians and censoring anyone who speaks (such as myself) on platforms like Twitter and LinkedIn. Need we write more?

They have turned to using big tech, social media, legacy media, and paid "influencers" to smear, slander, censor, and defame.

Y'all think we all might be starting to see a pattern?

## Exit Stage Left: COVID-19—Enter Stage Right: Mainstream Media, Big Tech, Russia, and Ukraine

George Orwell was right. From free speech to "spheres of influence" to our passion for endless war, most citizens have become the double-thinkers that the book *1984* predicted.

The deep state and the administrative state turned to using big tech, social media, legacy media, and paid "influencers" to smear, slander, censor, and defame those who hold a different view regarding Russia and Ukraine. The goal is total information control and total thought control.

The evidence is in. The systemic use of psyops by the American government on us is clear. We are the victims. The thought police rule.

## Neurolinguistic Programing, Propaganda, and Mind Control; the US Government Administrative State Has Crossed the Orwellian Line

Tony Robbins is the most successful business, life, and results coach in the world. Why? Because he gets results. His system is based primarily on neurolinguistic programing, (NLP) combined with leadership training and immersive seminars.[7]

There is that word again. Neurolinguistic programming. What the heck is it and why does it matter?

Common neurolinguistic programming techniques include:

- Anchoring: Associating an external or internal trigger with a healthier response until it becomes automatic
- Belief changing: Replacing negative thoughts or beliefs that prevent the client from achieving their desires

- Reframing: Putting a situation in a different context to elicit an adaptive reaction instead of following the same maladaptive behavioral patterns
- Visualization: Forming a mental image of something the client wants
- Visual-kinesthetic dissociation: Guiding the client in reliving trauma by evoking an imaginative out-of-body experience
- Mirroring, modeling, image training, incantations, and repetition are also common techniques.

Neurolinguistic programming is considered a useful set of tools for behavioral therapies, including drug addiction, overeating, cessation of smoking, etc. Particularly when combined with conversational hypnosis. Conversational hypnosis is a set of techniques used to make the receiver of information more open to accepting and acting upon suggestions.

Although Wikipedia and others label NLP as a "pseudoscience," the public and a long list of peer-reviewed publications disagree. For instance, The *British Medical Journal* (*BMJ*) published a series of articles specifically citing many successes using this approach as a behavioral therapy.[8,9,10]

What is not as commonly recognized is that these tools, including subliminal advertising, are used extensively in marketing. Marketers and advertisers have been using these techniques effectively for decades, and there are whole courses on using these tools effectively to increase sales.

We have a government that seeks to influence us on a daily basis. We all know this to be true. Of course, for some, there is a naive belief that it is all for "our own good." That censorship and propaganda "will save our democracy." Others believe that the First Amendment is our one great protection if we wish to remain a republic and a representative democracy. The truth is that when we lose our First Amendment rights, we will lose our country.

We have a government that deploys information control and propaganda technologies on its citizens on a daily basis. These techniques were developed during the Cold War, refined during the war with Vietnam and then the forever wars in the Middle East. Now, the federal government appears to be working in concert with marketers, advertising agencies, big tech, NGOs, Astroturf organizations, etc. to control bad-speak (as the government defines it) and to create more "positive" narratives for the people of the USA.

When the data on Hunter Biden's laptop was leaked and made public, the US administrative and deep state went into action. They released a letter with false information that the laptop was a disinformation campaign. This letter was signed by fifty-one intelligence operatives, who most likely knew that the laptop was real. The Washington deep state, including career intelligence officials, the media, and Big Tech, strategized to suppress and discredit the fully authentic and legitimate Hunter Biden laptop story, solely for the purpose of influencing the 2020 election. These lies were reframed, repeated, anchored to another story that this was Russian disinformation. Of course, all the neurolinguistic programming techniques. The American people weren't just conned, they were programmed into believing the big lie. A lie that changed the outcome of a presidential election.

By now, we all know that billions of dollars were spent during COVID-19 to influence our behaviors. Actors, artists, musicians, paid influencers, NGOs, advertising and marketing agencies, tech/social media manipulations, newspapers, and magazines were all paid as part of the process to convince people to wear masks, social distance, stop shopping, stay home, and to "get vaccinated." The money came from many different agencies—the DNI, CIA, DoD, CDC, NIH, FDA, DHS, USAID, etc.

Information warfare conducted by the US government includes covert propaganda, controlled opposition, chaos agents, divide-and-conquer operations, false flags, disinformation campaigns, bad-jacketing, advertising, and more. These are being combined with neurolinguistic programming, subliminal messaging, nudge technology, hypnosis, and propaganda.

The tools of the marketeers, big tech, social media, and behavioral therapists, combined with the tools of the intelligence community, are powerful weapons routinely being used on all of us. They wish to control our feelings, emotions, thoughts, beliefs, and state of mind to keep us compliant and happy. But how can one be free when one's very thoughts and emotions are being manipulated?

In fact, what we have seen in the past year is that the government is willing to use these tools to influence elections, such as the campaigns to discredit the news story about Hunter Biden's laptop in 2020 and the 2016 Russia "disinformation" false flag operation, and to stop any public dissent over the war in Ukraine in 2023[11] or the approved "climate crisis" narratives.[12,13,14]

The government manipulated the media to create fear surrounding monkeypox,[15] the Nordstream explosion,[16] and, of course, my favorite, the evolving theories regarding the origins of COVID-19. Go back to that list of neurolinguistic programming techniques—yep—clearly, they were utilized in influencing the public's mind on these issues, too.

So, who does this work for the government, to convince, cajole, and get the American people to comply? For COVID-19, the list of advertising companies includes IQ Solutions, FORS Marsh, Atlas Research, Lamar Media, Palladian Partners, The Scientific Consulting Group, Silver Fir Media, and "various foreign awardees"—to name a few.[17]

Here is a typical "campaign" by FORS Marsh. This is a recruitment campaign for the Army National Guard:

> ### How do we get people to serve in a national service they know nothing about?
>
> Army National Guard, Social Media Campaign
>
> We developed a social media campaign that positions ARNG as the pathway to achieving life-changing goals. We create and share meaningful and motivational content to promote the benefits of enlisting. Full of heart and hustle, our content presents a realistic portrayal of day-to-day service. We connect with people by acknowledging their challenges and providing actionable steps toward the lives they envision.
>
> A community management team responds to comments and messages, keeping the conversation authentic and insightful. People are directed to fill out a lead form and are connected with local recruiters for more information.
>
> We provide local social media marketing teams with in-person and virtual training support, weekly newsletters, and digital materials, including a resource website to ensure cohesive messaging nationwide.

FORS Marsh Group, LLC is utilizing propaganda and neurolinguistic programming tools, including belief changing, reframing, visualization, and repetition in the above example. But this is just one small example of how our government uses advertising and marketing companies to "sell" propaganda. Of interest, the https://www.forsmarsh.com/ page with the above quote was taken down after an earlier draft of this essay was first published on our Substack: that article was read by about half a million people, if not more.

The truth is that our government has become a master at information control and propaganda as well as marketing through their many contractual awardees—otherwise generally known as "beltway bandits."

We have a government who seeks to influence us on a daily basis. They also know how to use the tools of the internet to stop you from seeing and reading what they don't want you to see. They are using behavioral control methods, such as neurolinguistic programming, to control and mold our very thoughts. Examine, question, and do your own triangulation of facts; using many sources. A critical mind will set you free.

And there you have it.
Our destiny is being chosen for us.
Orwell's 1984 is here.

Stand up now, or your children will have to deal with the consequences of your lack of courage.

# CHAPTER 12
## Life on the Front Lines

Is the life that we lead one of simple bucolic splendor?

A good friend from South Africa who traveled to New York City for Christmas spent a few days with us. She is unjabbed. We traveled together (Rome, Lisbon) during the COVIDcrisis; this was our second Christmas together. She is also an equestrian and saw the new Christmas colt ("Thor") before returning to NYC. She often provides us with an alternative point of view on current events, which helps broaden our horizons.

Last Monday, before returning home and after Robert helped get her on her way by changing her car battery and checking fluids (two quarts down!), they got to talking about the daily realities that we have to manage: A new foal, feeding out hay and grain, vehicle and machinery maintenance, dealing with fifth-generation information warfare—the usual daily grind.

She related that, from the outside looking in, it seems like we lead a relatively quiet and simple life, traveling a lot (an understatement—about 400,000 miles in 2022) but generally pretty straightforward. But from the inside, watching and talking to both of us while visiting, the reality was that we are dealing with a lot more complexity than she ever imagined.

We just take our current reality for granted. Our friend encouraged that Robert compose a simple essay to convey the ground truth of our current lives.

That inspired Robert to write the following:

Where to begin. It certainly is a bit of a roller coaster.

For example, as we were picking up the battery, we had to go to multiple places—finally settling on the Ford dealership, as this is a small town (with limited stock). I got a call from an executive film producer from Santa Barbara with a big resume and an interest in producing a film based on our new book. A bit weird to be talking about movie rights while trying to buy a battery that would fit her car (older Ford model) from a small-town dealership parts department. And please add two quarts of oil to the tab. Thank you. My schizoid life. I can deal with that sort of stuff pretty well, and (to be honest) take a certain amount of perverse pleasure in having the folks at the local farmers co-op, lumber shop, and the person delivering a few tons of alfalfa square bales chat me up about the latest Substack and the COVIDcrisis narrative. Helps me feel like I am actually reaching real people, not just internet denizens. It is so easy to get wrapped up in the Virtuals world, so connecting with other Physicals is really nice.

The difficulty comes in with the efforts to communicate effectively while dealing with the complexities of the modern media and information warfare/propaganda battlefield. For example, I gave talks in Richmond and down in Ocala, Florida, in which I discussed the realities of the influenza vaccine manufacturing and marketplace issues. I have been involved in influenza vaccine development, marketing, regulatory affairs, clinical research, and associated issues for decades. I once served as clinical director, Influenza Vaccines for Solvay. This included oversight of about $200 million in federal contract (BARDA) funds. I once gave an invited lecture at the World Health Organization headquarters on influenza vaccine technology and new vaccine product development. I understand the influenza vaccine space, from product development to advanced development (clinical, regulatory, project management, funding, pricing, market complexities, etc.). I discussed the realities of warm based manufacturing. I discussed the evolution of my concerns with influenza vaccine and vaccine strategies—in detail. And for my efforts I was rewarded for trying to share what I know with the general population with yet another attack article (with the usual defamation) from a "journalist" who publishes his little bit of uninformed and un-researched drivel in *Forbes* magazine. It was so superficial, and made such a small impact, that I just chose to ignore it.

It is easy to get wound up with outrage when getting attacked in either the press or social media. *"How can they say that about me?! How can they get away with lying?!"* Well, sorry to say, but there is this legal precedent that the press cites, which they use to provide cover for their routine defamation.

The long-decided Supreme Court case, *Sullivan vs The New York Times*, is interpreted as establishing that, in the case of anyone meeting the criteria as a "public figure," the press or others can slander and defame at will. Unless they meet the criteria of "malicious defamation," which is pretty much in the eye of the beholder. Like porn, the judicial system seems to infer that they will "know it when they see it."

Having been around the block on this a few times, I am well aware that garden-variety untruths, carefully written, and even accusations of being a spreader of mis- or disinformation (or being "controlled opposition" or a "deep state" actor), if only stated once, will be hard to establish as meeting criteria for "malicious defamation." These terms essentially equate to accusing someone else of fraud, which, if unproven, meets the defamation criteria. But if there is only one article, publication, or podcast, this is hard to establish "malice." If repeated again and again, in multiple articles, despite a *cease-and-desist* letter, etc., then this gets more clear-cut.

So that sort of stuff is constantly coming across our radar. People text us this or that latest insult from corporate media or those seeking to generate outrage or clicks (which are readily converted into revenue). On a daily basis we have to watch the chatter and make decisions about how to respond, if at all. For example, one "journalist" loves to create novel word strings and neologisms that sound very technically impressive, add the acronym DARPA (which I have never worked for), attribute some fabricated nefarious action to me, and make a video about it or even a faked document. He is such a clown that we just ignore it.

For example, a couple of years ago he wound up posting some (fake) "news" story about what Jill and I did when we worked at the University of California, Davis, and then recorded a very ominous broadcast from what he asserted was part of the research campus. The setting looked very industrial and threatening. The only problem was that it was recorded in front of a Davis tomato processing plant that makes tomato paste and ketchup. And I did not get a bunch of amplified bots and trolls attacking me about that. So, I ignored that one and all of the subsequent ones from this character that follow the same pattern. I guess everyone needs to make a living somehow. But to give an example how pervasive this is, Jill cut and pasted his attack articles and posts about me from January 2023 to May 2023 and ended up with a massive document of over 1,500 pages of screenshots from his Twitter feed. Full of half-truth, un-truths, and grains of truth. Which is mixed together to create a frothy mix of propaganda. Confused yet? That is the idea. My only question is which Astroturf agency or pharma company pays him to spend endless days writing this stuff? And who pays that Astroturf organization?

Then there is the real battlefield. The military-grade psyops and propaganda campaigns deployed by our government and who knows whom else. The Twitter files have really helped in this battleground, because Jill and I no longer sound like "conspiracy nuts" when we write about what has happened. For example, once upon a time, I started using the terms "regulatory control, inverse totalitarianism, and the administrative state" when few others were. I did this because the fear of totalitarianism seemed to be even more pressing than the fear of COVID. So, these terms seemed useful in helping people transfer their "mass formation" hypnosis from COVID to this greater threat. That is the threat to our very freedom. A baby step toward getting them to understand how they are being manipulated. At first, I was greeted with the usual "stay in your lane, Malone" trollery, but gradually discussions of totalitarianism became mainstream. Likewise, the World Economic Forum and the Great Reset. I was a bit late to jump on that train, but took plenty of flack when I did. As they say, incoming flack indicates that you are over the target.

When we were first "unfairly" attacked in corporate media and social media for speaking what we believed to be scientific truth based on a seasoned, experienced, highly qualified assessment of data and government actions, Jill and I realized that nothing was going to be "fair" about this fight. We soon learned that if we were going to help save lives and stop children from being jabbed with products that damage the heart and other organs, we were going to have to dive into the emerging world of alternative media. And particularly the podcast. Then came the big kahuna, Joe Rogan, and everything changed. When a podcast garners over a million views, the long knives come out.

It has been a steep learning curve for us to master modern media; we are still students. How does one assess the risk of getting bushwhacked? For instance, the notorious Fox News hit involving Alex Berenson, where he accused me of essentially being a fraud and a grifter. I was bleary eyed after a long day of filming in Spain, no coffee on board, and the interview was

2:00 a.m. on location. How I managed to think on the fly and respond to the attack on my credibility escapes me, but somehow I survived. And then I called up the Fox News booker and cussed her out. Suffice to say, not the most mature response. I have not been invited back on the Laura Ingraham show since. But the story illustrates the problem. It is hard to anticipate when I might get bushwhacked by either an interviewer or a panelist while on camera. This is why I do not do debates and am very wary of panel discussions these days. It is so easy to get labeled as a conspiracy nutcase by association when others on a panel start spouting off about snake venom toxins in the water or the (unspecified) global predators. So, there is that.

And then we have the mainstream "journalists," who do little more than sprout propaganda. Their main drivers are not to produce fair and balanced news stories but instead to produce advocacy pieces promoting the current progressive narrative. How far legacy media has fallen.

So, the point is, I get a lot of requests for interviews, podcasts, and book tours, and each one has to be evaluated by Jill and myself to assess the risk of an incoming hostile attack. Sometimes, we miss the signals, and then it is "grin and bear it" as the interviewer has me under interrogation on some recorded video call.

These days, there are trolls who have seemingly made a career of dissecting the nuances of my facial expressions, the number of times I blink (have you ever spent hours with bright lights in your face while recording podcast after podcast?). One notorious "shock jock" interviewer once demanded that I disclose "all you know," and I said I would not do so. Frankly, I do not really remember and life's experiences are way to vast to disclose "all I know" in a single podcast. Which was interpreted and weaponized as a clear indication that I was a deep state–controlled opposition bad guy. But I have signed many, many nondisclosure agreements over the decades of running a consulting business, and I have held "secret" classification clearance. Rather cheeky for a shock jock to expect me to unburden myself at his demand completely, don't you think? Besides, that would take days, not minutes.

## That Sort of Stuff That Has to Be Managed on a Daily Basis

And then back to the stuff that matters. How can you fight back when fifth-gen warfare is being waged against the truth? By trying to master fifth-gen warfare and tactics, of course. That takes time and a lot of thought. It is sort of intuitive to me at this point, but there is still so much to learn. In fifth-gen warfare, there are no "leaders." These people who are caught up in twentieth-century information warfare metaphors are frustratingly clueless. All of the scrambling to be top dog is *so* last century. "Dr. "X" is the true leader, so Malone should be taken down!" Blah, blah, blah. In fifth-gen warfare, there are no clear leaders. As little energy as possible should be expended to yield maximum penetration of ideas into the minds and thought space of the aggressors and opponents. It is a bit like martial arts. Use the opponent's energy and turn it back on him or her.

There was a fun little video clip that a film crew from Norway put together in which they cut a little impromptu comedy skit involving Drs. Richard Urso, Ryan Cole, and myself edited into the CNN piece in which Anthony Fauci claimed to have jabbed Santa and the Elves. This little comedy sketch took almost no time, effort, or resources and then it was released on social media just before the 2022 holidays. This is a perfect example of fifth-gen warfare in action. The clips poke fun at the opponent while also inserting medical truth into viewers' minds. Personally, I am really proud of that.

The comedian JP Sears has become a Zen master of fifth-gen warfare, whether or not he knows it. Jill's "Friday Funnies" and "Sunday Strip" are now a required deliverable for our subscribers, but they are also actually fifth-gen weapons.

As I have written before, fifth-gen warfare aims to influence minds and thoughts. The more subtle, the better. Low energy, high impact. And when one is at the top of one's game, the opponent is not even aware of what is happening. For example, Tony Fauci complained that the spreaders of "mis- and disinformation" about the vaccines seem to be winning, as people are not lining up for the boosters for themselves or their children. He seemed confused and perplexed.

In the ideal fifth-gen warfare campaign, strategic "influencers" share general information relevant to the topic at hand and then others pick up on the information and thoughts and spread it in a decentralized way. So then the reposts, retweets, and others taking the ideas or thoughts and expanding on them are par for the course. Others write their own Substack essays on the topic, all of that sort of stuff is absolutely the objective. Nothing is "owned." There is no "leader." It's just a decentralized swarm.

This is what they tried to do to us by paying all of the "influencers" in music, arts, dance, TikTok, Instagram, etc. (not to mention "medical professionals" and media celebs) at the outset of this massive (and massively expensive) propaganda campaign that we have all been subjected to during the COVIDcrisis. Those of us on the front lines took the hits, and we are still standing. And now, with the help of the Twitter files and the flood of data on the harms and lack of effectiveness that are coming in from all over the world, and the hubris/overreach of the self-styled unelected and illegitimate "global leaders" of the WEF, UN, WHO, and NGOs (Bill Gates, I am looking at you), we have the data and information on our side. We just have to get smart and understand the new information battlefield.

We can turn the tide here, but we must be aware of the battlefield, strategy, and tactics. There are no leaders, just a decentralized and growing network of influencers.

Welcome to the new world. It is not about fairness or justice. It is not about territory. It is about minds and emotions. And a centralized world government versus a decentralized network of communities. It is about the use of deep fakes and AI versus truth. They think that they can bend the very nature of reality and thought to their objectives. I say, "hell no," this will not stand.

Each day, we deal with complex scheduling, interviews, podcasts, phone calls, writing essays, editing books, emails, feeding dogs, horses, peacocks, chickens, guinea fowl, checking waterers, buying farm supplies, stacking hay, and if we are very, very lucky, we get actually to ride a horse. Each day, we wake up with a bit of fear and loathing as to what the fifth-gen battle-escape has laid at our doorstep. And with that, I hope you understand our daily lives. Today started with that darned spunky foal running around and refusing to follow his dam through the pasture gate. A lot has happened since then.

And please, do not frag or bad-jacket each other. These tactics may be a good way to get clicks, and may even be a good business model, but they are extremely counterproductive in terms of the overall battlefield objectives. Those who employ this strategy need to be shut down, and if they will not stand down, then they need to pay a price. We have no time for petty vindictive behavior and academic infighting.

Remember, there are no leaders in this battle space. Drop the ego stuff. This is low-energy, high-impact, stealth information warfare. Read, learn, deploy. The times have changed. This is not the twentieth century, not the 1960s. Get with the program, run with the big dogs, or stay on the porch.

Now let's get to work. For the sake of our children, if nothing else.

# PART III
# PROPAGANDA AND CENSORSHIP

*The noble lie is the justification for which propaganda and censorship is being deployed upon the world. What is the noble lie, and why does it matter? Following that is a brief overview and history of propaganda and mass formation during the early twentieth century. We focus on Paul Joseph Goebbels, the chief German propagandist who applied the early theories of mass formation to sway the minds of the German people during World War II. Then, the writings of Gustave Le Bon, a French social psychologist who is often seen as the founder of the study of crowd (group) psychology, are discussed. There are many modern examples of psychological operations that use the insights of these individuals.*

*The COVID crisis saw science being co-opted for political and economic reasons, a development that has significantly eroded American trust in both science and government. However, the full extent of this corruption remains largely undisclosed. To shed light on this, we turn to Robert's personal experiences with publishing in academic journals during this period. His encounters serve as a stark reminder that we are still ensnared in a PsyWar campaign. It is the vaccine-injured who bear the brunt of our government's deceptions and are paying the ultimate price.*

*Cyberstalking and cyberbullying are tactics of the chaos agent. These strategies harm people in many ways and have been designed to do so. Corporate media, governments, and NGOs are all players in the game. Is there any recourse when such attacks are carried out for years on end? This is an information war, and the online attackers aren't going to stop just because we want them to. Many are hypnotized into believing they are on the right side of history, which may be the scariest element in all of this.*

*We then turn to analyzing the corruption of evidence-based medicine and the propaganda that has enabled this to happen. The fifth-gen tool kit is the weapon of choice by government and Big Pharma. This leads to a discussion of the Steele Dossier, whereby the FBI duped the American people into believing that there was compelling evidence that the Russians worked with the Trump organization during the 2016 campaign in a "disinformation" campaign. Which years later, turned out to be a total ruse. The use of controlled opposition, disruptors, chaos agents, and bad-jacketing tools are part of the FBI playbook, and what has happened in the freedom movement is most likely part of an ongoing psyops operation by the US government. Finally, in 2023, the Durham report on Russian disinformation discredited all that has been fed to the American public over the past seven years regarding Russian election interference. Where did the US government go so very, very wrong? What is truly disinformation versus black propaganda? When did the DNC and the FBI become so deeply corrupted?*

*The use of micro-oppression accusations is another tactic used by those who wish to control the narrative, and are actively seeking to constrain the Overton window of acceptable discourse.*

*This part concludes with more information on mass formation and how governments and corporations use this as a psyops technique today.*

# CHAPTER 13
# Mind Viruses and Their Vectors

## What Comes Next after the COVIDcrisis Propaganda Wars?

The average citizen has generally been asleep during the deployment of propaganda and military-grade psyops during the COVIDcrisis. This propaganda was actively spread by an amazingly diverse and coordinated global cast, apparently justified by the logic of Plato's noble lie, a myth or lie that is knowingly propagated by an elite to maintain social harmony.

To recap, the Noble Lie is a concept attributed to Socrates and discussed in Book III of Plato's "The Republic," which holds that the use of noble lies by the ruling caste is necessary to uphold social cohesion within an ideal society (the Republic). In many ways, this is the root of the internal justification employed by the various bureaucrat/administrative state actors that have authorized and funded (using taxpayer funds) the fearporn and pro-vax propaganda campaigns. Few recognize that the noble lie is one component of a core Platonic myth designed to justify a permanent class system, with the allegory of the cave being another. Both are derived from the Myth of Three Metals.

The Three Metals myth posits that Mother Nature invented all human beings and mixed different metals—gold, silver, bronze (or iron, a fourth metal not covered in the title)—into their characters. This is basically Plato's justification for a permanent social caste structure of rulers (overlords) and ruled. Rulers have gold in their characters, workers have iron, and so on for all different classes and professions. Plato posits that this myth will make it easier to rule an ideal republic since 1) everyone will think that their social class is an extension of their inner character, and 2) everyone will know they have a common mother so they will treat each other peacefully. In such an "ideal" republic, inspired, wise philosopher-kings with characters of gold will rule in a benevolent manner (noblesse oblige) and will lie to the ruled when necessary to maintain social order and the natural social structure (based on one's metal content, or "mettle").

In short, based on these assimilated social theories traced to antiquity, we were all lied to throughout the COVIDcrisis. Because the ruling oligarch caste felt that they were philosophically justified in doing so. Otherwise, allowing free speech would jeopardize the social structure by causing vaccine hesitancy or concerns about governmental and WHO public health policies (including mandated reliance on an experimental vaccine). Our Golden overlords (otherwise known as the deep state and the globalist class) were justified in doing so because their very characters are fashioned from gold, while ours contain silver, bronze, or iron.

Bluntly, the Platonic thesis is that propaganda emanating from the ruling caste is necessary and required to maintain social order. In the twenty-first century, the term "propaganda" has become curiously quaint and anachronistic as the associated underpinning psychological science and technology have advanced. Terms more accurately reflecting the current state-of-the-art include fifth-generation warfare, nudge theory, psyops, PsyWar, and the censorship-industrial complex.

As the COVIDcrisis winds down, and the roaches responsible for the horrid public policy decisions have all scurried into various cracks and crevices to hide from the light of day, we are left with two fundamental questions:

"Will there be any real accountability commensurate with the *needle and the damage done*?"

And

"What will they do to us next?"

Our point of view on the first is that it is highly unlikely that anything more than some token sacrifice to the gods of public opinion will happen, if even that. On the second, batten down the hatches, *cuz thar will be years if not decades of stormy seas* ahead consequent to the decision-making of the Golden overlord caste that has become so invested in globalism, utilitarianism (for the underclasses), Malthusianism, command-economy Marxism, and the bizarre dysfunctional cluster of victim theory often referred to as "Wokeism."

As we look out across the torn and tortured psyops battleground terrain remaining after over three years of globalized total unrestricted information warfare during the COVIDcrisis, the fields of diseased, dead, and dying, the shreds of what were once the battle standards we carried into the conflict as both sword and shield—those being the Declaration of Independence, US Constitution and Bill of Rights—lie trampled into the soggy clay of our collective consciousness. And who do we have to thank for that? Who did we expect to fight for truth by our sides, but instead took the metaphorical thirty pieces of silver to become a pharma and government-sponsored mercenary force deployed against us? That would be corporate and social media and the information technology giants of the Western United States.

We have spent years now trying to make sense of what has happened, writing, talking, thinking, podcasting with people from all walks of life. It started with just being conscientious objectors to the obscenities of abuse and wholesale disregard of fundamental human rights, including the right to informed consent for medical procedures and of bodily autonomy. Now we all know what the administrative state really thinks about human rights.

## "Ye Shall Know Them by Their Fruits." Matthew 7:16

Then we progressed to hour after hour of podcasts and social media infowars just trying to help people understand what was being done to them. Obsessing about identifying, developing, and describing early treatment protocols involving repurposed drugs and trying so, so hard to get the necessary clinical trials funded and operational. Travel and rallies. And then the pivotal moments; left-wing corporate media attacks, censorship and deplatforming, and the lightning strikes of the *DarkHorse Podcast*, the *Joe Rogan Experience* #1757, and the resulting globally coordinated backlash to Robert just trying to interpret and speak COVIDcrisis truth based on the current data.

As we look back in order to look forward, my expectations of the WHO and bureaucratic administrative (Uniparty) state were always quite low. Our most profound shock and awe was in seeing how readily people—physicians, politicians, clergy, school boards, and most significantly, the corporate and social media, were readily corrupted and co-opted to serve the pharmaceutical/biodefense/vaccine/public health enterprise. Having spent far too much time writing this book that seeks to make sense of all of this, and now watching as the propagandists and apologists daily work to sweep the whole fecal storm under the rug (while also seeking to destroy what remains of Robert's professional reputation), we are left wondering "what comes next for us?"

Should we just try to sell vitamins and supplements like most of the "medical freedom" fighters now seem content to do? Should Robert go into politics (as Steve Bannon once wanted me to do)? Should we find ourselves back immersed in a deeply corrupt Washington, D.C., culture? Just to be clear, the answer to all of those questions is a hard no.

We, and probably all of us, crave a worthy opponent, a cause worth getting up in the morning to fight. Something big and meaningful. As we look back over the last four years and try to imagine the next four, we think that the worthy opponent is the deeply corrupted corporate and social media and their enablers. If corporate MSM and the social media/tech giants had acted with integrity, the corruption of the medical and scientific professions could never have become this bad. We cannot "fix" the US government. We cannot "fix" the WHO. We cannot even "fix" the deep corruption of the medical enterprise. But we think we just might be able to participate in enabling an alternative media ecosystem where everyone can access accurate as well as inaccurate information, as well as intelligent and insightful interpretation.

And that would be enough for us, for our sunset years. Well, that and taking care of each other, our horses, dogs, and farm.

The deployment of military-grade propaganda psyops and government-sponsored and facilitated social media censorship on the citizens of a representative republic (or really any political organization that purports to derive legitimacy from the will of the governed) is grossly unethical. It makes a mockery of the concept of individual liberty or sovereignty. State-sponsored media and propaganda are wrong on so many levels, and it is antithetical to any society seeking to foster competent problem-solving and innovation.

Working to break the stranglehold of the modern administrative state and its Uniparty facilitators on media and information is the worthy opponent that we choose. "Medical freedom" is a meaningless aphorism in a world where the administrative state seeks to deploy its awesome power to control your thoughts and emotions. This is the nature of fifth-generation warfare technology, which is what the Western nations have deployed on their citizens over the last three years. All in the name of the "noble lies" told to us for our own good and that of society by the Golden overlords.

What is propaganda? The Mind over Media Propaganda educational laboratory project provides an excellent summary of just what this mind-virus called propaganda consists of.[1]

1. Propaganda is one means by which large numbers of people are induced to act together.[2]
2. Propaganda is a form of information that panders to our insecurities and anxieties.[3]
3. Propaganda is the deliberate, systematic attempt to shape perceptions, manipulate cognitions, and direct behavior to achieve a response that furthers the desired intent of the propagandist.[4]
4. Propaganda is intentionally designed communication that invites us to respond emotionally, immediately, and in an either-or manner.[5]
5. Propaganda is a form of purposeful persuasion that attempts to influence the emotions, attitudes, opinions, and actions of specified target audiences for ideological, political, or commercial purposes through the controlled transmission of one-sided messages (which may or may not be factual) via mass and direct media channels.[6]
6. Propaganda is indifferent to truth and truthfulness, knowledge, and understanding; it is a form of strategic communication that uses any means to accomplish its ends.[7]
7. Propaganda is a form of communication aimed toward influencing the attitude of a population toward some cause or position.[8]
8. Propaganda appears in a variety of forms. It is strategic and intentional as it aims to influence attitudes, opinions, and behaviors. Propaganda can be beneficial or harmful. It may use truth, half-truths, or lies. To be successful, propaganda taps into our deepest values, fears, hopes, and dreams.[9]

We hope you will walk along with us as we gradually stray from the medical freedom path to tread what we believe to be a higher and more important trail (and calling). Freedom, let alone medical freedom, is meaningless if we are not even allowed the tools and ability to think for ourselves. Propaganda by the US government is being used to influence, mold, and shape our points of view. So, when phrases like "safe and effective" are propagated throughout society for pharmaceutical products that are not safe, nor effective, people need to learn to see through the Wizard of Oz's curtain. We cannot be free as long as our media are being influenced by government propaganda developed for the domestic populace.

---

**Infodemic** is the rapid and far-reaching spread of information, both accurate and inaccurate, about a specific issue. The word is a conjoining of "information" and "epidemic." It describes how misinformation and disinformation can spread like a virus from person to person and affect people like a disease. This use of this technique can be deliberate and intentional.

---

And we must live free, free to choose, or we will surely die a miserable death at the conclusion of a hollowed-out and meaningless life. Maybe some of you feel the same way. If so, we hope you will join us.

# CHAPTER 14
## Shedding Innocence

To our surprise, governments, the World Health Organization (WHO), and various nongovernmental organizations (WEF, BMGF, etc.) managed to keep the COVIDcrisis alive and weaponized well past its expiration date by using lies, censorship, and obfuscation to justify policies that do not advance public health objectives. They used psychological bioterrorism, including fearporn to advance their own political and financial interests. Like tossing offal over the transom, "Never let a good crisis go to waste" seems to have provoked a shark-feeding frenzy from which humanity may require decades to recover.

Assuming we ever do.

The apple of knowledge about the depths of what the US government, the Uniparty, the "administrative state" will do has been well and truly bitten into now. None who are "awake" to the damage done (to individuals, families, and communities) in the name of public health will ever be able to return to what, in retrospect, seems like the Eden of our prior innocence.

Now we are finally seeing the patient counsel of Augustine of Hippo come to pass—"The truth is like a lion; you don't have to defend it. Let it loose; it will defend itself." Like so many others, we had naively assumed that this process would require months, not years.

Just to make the point yet again, the COVIDcrisis was never really a crisis in the way it was portrayed. It was always a house of cards built upon USA, CCP, and WHO propaganda and grossly overstated risk modeling and projections from Imperial College, London, developed by the Neil Ferguson research group.

Layers and layers of propaganda. Deep, harmonized, simultaneous collusion, enticement, censorship, malicious defamation, and gaslighting across all Western political organizations and their paid toadies in corporate and social media—propagated and coordinated by the UN, WHO, EU, USA, former "British Empire" governments, and the new wannabe corporatist world government body known as the "World Economic Forum."

A comprehensive, global "shock and awe" fifth-generation warfare action the likes of which the world has never seen before. All justified as necessary to protect us from a pathogen whose risks were greatly exaggerated from the get-go based on highly flawed risk modeling which was not updated as new and more accurate information about the true (modest) risk of the virus became available. A global "shock and awe" fifth-generation warfare action that weaponized fear of an infectious disease to promote compliance with governmental and WHO-promoted policies and to get vaccine needles into arms.

Event 201 was a 3.5-hour pandemic wargaming exercise that simulated a hypothetical, extremely pathogenic, and infectious pandemic. It created an alliance between intelligence communities, the military, public health, and Big Pharma, which in turn led to the regulatory capture of governments by transnational corporations during the COVID-19 pandemic. The exercise was organized by the Johns Hopkins Center for Health Security in partnership with the World Economic Forum and the Bill & Melinda Gates Foundation.

The truth is that the preplanned (Event 201) authoritarian totalitarian response resulted in a massive upwards transfer of wealth largely to those who funded the planning (that being the WEF and Bill Gates). Was the overreaction and authoritarian mismanagement a psychological projection of their guilt about having created and loosed this slouching beast on all of us? Or was the virus just a strategy to enable a broader agenda of increased corporatism and the Great Reset? Or one of many possible strategies developed and waiting to be deployed? We suspect that Dr. Anthony Fauci would plead a failure of memory if asked to testify to those questions under oath.

Or perhaps (just as internet haters are going to hate), authoritarians and monopolists, when given an opportunity, will enable totalitarian states and corporate monopolies.

For three years, we were all banished to inhabit dark crevices and cracks in the garden of good and evil. Forced into our homes and the fringes of society while psychopathic devils who normally inhabit Dante's nine circles of hell openly danced a global bacchanal of death, destruction, and greed. And as they danced, they steadily advanced their long-anticipated "Great Reset."

Any so bold as to question the approved narrative, to alert chained fellow cave dwellers that they are only being allowed to see shadows on the wall projected by these dancing devils, have been further ostracized to the depths of their own personal hells. With swarms of paid demons unleashed to discover and exploit any crack in their own personal armor (or history). And now these devils assert that the whole sordid affair supports the need for the world to grant them more money and power?

Grasping for some frayed thread of a silver lining to their dark cloaks, we suppose that you have to admire their chutzpah at least.

Innocence has layers. Over the last three years, as we have journeyed along the broad road of corrupt propaganda, censorship, and defamation hell, each turn and twist has forced us to peel away yet another.

Belief in the universal acceptance of bioethical truths. Truths which had been so painstakingly developed since the end of World War II, and then augmented after the CDC-sponsored Tuskegee study. Faith in the integrity of international regulatory and clinical research norms, and the absolute fire wall around informed consent and avoidance of compulsion, coercion, and mandated medical and surgical procedures. Faith in the NIH, previously damaged by decades of personal experience, shattered into a thousand fragments by Robert F. Kennedy Jr.'s meticulously documented indictment titled *The Real Anthony Fauci*. Faith in the integrity of the FDA and CDC and their commitment to stand as bulwarks to ensure public safety under the pressure of a rapacious pharmaceutical industry. Faith in the integrity and commitment of my fellow scientists and physicians to the Hippocratic oath.

And now we confront a complete loss of faith in the commitment of the United States government and its officials to protect and defend the US Constitution. Earlier in this twisting journey, this broad road to hell, Robert Malone had taken risks to discuss the growing threat of totalitarianism openly. Robert received a call from a decades-long colleague employed at a senior level

(GS-15) at the Defense Threat Reduction Agency (DTRA) darkly warning him to not discuss Dr. Michael Callahan or his activities in China during 2019–2020, or there would be consequences. Robert Malone was later warned by a well-known broadcaster to "stay in my lane" and not discuss the World Economic Forum, its plans and activities. In a world where the term "fascism" had been twisted and distorted beyond recognition, early on, Robert insisted on returning to the original definition (attributed to Benito Mussolini) that the proper name for fascism was corporatism, and discussing the widespread acceptance of globalist corporatism as the new model for replacing the autonomous nation-state as the dominant political structure.

And then there were the more mundane, transparent lies and propaganda regarding the lack of repurposed early treatment medical interventions and the safety and efficacy of the genetic "vaccine" products which all have come to see in our daily lives clearly do not protect against infection, replication, or spread of this cluster of novel coronavirus variants which we call SARS-CoV-2. Hour after hour spent on innumerable radio, television, and podcast interviews trying to break through the wall of propaganda erected by governments colluding with big tech and corporate press/TV.

We wish to acknowledge and thank Joe Rogan for allowing his Spotify platform to break through that fire wall and allow Robert to speak his truths to the world. Although he has not been welcomed back since, we suspect what happened over the subsequent days, weeks, and months was the clearest tolling of the bell for current corporate media (and '60s rock and rollers) that has ever been heard.

Recently, Robert Malone was asked to participate in a "Twitter Spaces" discussion regarding the censorship that has been experienced by so many who have tried to break through the propaganda fire wall of the last three years. Asked to discuss his own experiences, he went on and on. The words poured out.

This was a question no one had ever really asked him before, and he has been asked so many questions over the last three years that he sometimes feels like someone who has been subjected to a strip search by the US Transportation Security Administration (TSA). No body cavity left unprobed except for this one.

There is still so much to cover regarding what has happened to us over the past years. It started with Amazon deleting Jill's book on the virus in

March 2020 for irreconcilable (but undefined) "violation of community standards." Robert's 2020 manuscripts warn about risks encountered in prior coronavirus vax development that have been rejected by scientific journals. Including that original famotidine/mast cell hypothesis paper titled "COVID-19: Famotidine, Histamine, Mast Cells, and Mechanisms," that laid out the primary mechanism for early treatment that got rejected again and again.[1]

The repeated rejection of high-quality clinical studies demonstrating the effectiveness of early treatment using celecoxib, famotidine +/- ivermectin. Repeated inexplicable intransigence of FDA to allow DoD-funded clinical trials to proceed. The Nobel Prize marketing campaign to promote the false valor of Kariko and Weissman as having originated the mRNA platform technology which necessitated belittling, defaming, and gaslighting my own much earlier contributions. The systematic evisceration of Robert Malone's Wikipedia page. The reactions of Spanish and Israeli governments to my "hostage" video warning parents about the risks of genetically vaccinating their children. The YouTube demonetization of Dr. Bret Weinstein after the infamous "save the world" podcast with Steve Kirsch and myself. The backlash after *Joe Rogan Experience* podcast #1757 on December 31, 2021. The relentless unqualified "fact-checker" attacks (justified by Facebook in court as narrative reinforcement activities, not "fact" checks). *The Atlantic Monthly*, *Rolling Stone*, *New York Times*, *Washington Post*, and even *Santa Barbara News Press* (the authors' hometown newspaper, now bankrupt and defunct) published malicious attacks, misrepresentations, and outright lies while in some cases accusing him of being a liar. Classical psychological projection. It all continues unabated to this day, now augmented by professional infiltrator/disruptors who carefully troll for tidbits in Robert's CV that can be weaponized while continually shouting "controlled opposition" and "deep state" as a chorus to the usual lyrics of mis- dis- and mal-information accusations coming from mainstream government-sponsored press outlets.

But caught like a deer in the headlights by the podcaster's question, Dr. Robert Malone completely forgot to cover the outcome of the huge amount of time he (together with other colleagues) had invested in establishing a special edition of "Frontiers in Pharmacology" dedicated to publishing academic manuscripts concerning repurposed drugs and protocols effective against COVID. He had invested more than six months of effort in getting the necessary permissions, soliciting and reviewing manuscripts, and building a solution to address the unwillingness of journals all over the world to publish information about life-saving treatments. And then, in December 2020, Dr. Pierre Kory testified in the US Senate about the potential of ivermectin. The DoD-funded group Robert was working with to identify and test repurposed drugs was very aware of the potential of the repurposed agent, and when Dr. Kory and colleagues posted a summary of their findings on the web, Robert reached out (as an editor of this special *Frontiers* volume) and encouraged him to reformat and submit as an academic review for consideration by *Frontiers in Pharmacology* for our special volume. The rest is history. A somewhat biased account of what then took place can now be found published in *The Scientist*. The subsequent cascade of events are summarized in the following resignation letter[2]:

**23rd April 2021**
**RE: Resignation in protest, Frontiers in Pharmacology Topic Editors, "Treating COVID-19 With Currently Available Drugs"**
To: Frontiers Chief Executive Editor, Manager | Frederick Fenter Frontiers in Pharmacology, Respiratory Pharmacology Chief Editor, Prof. Paolo Montuschi Frontiers Director of Publishing Operations | Judyta Sorokowska-Yammin Frontiers Head of Research Integrity, London Office | Elena Vicario, PhD
From: Guest Editors:
Prof. Maria Cristina Albertini, University of Urbino Carlo Bo
Prof. Piero Sestili, University of Urbino Carlo BoDr. Robert Malone, MD, MS
RW Malone MD LLC
Dr. Howard Haimes, PhD., Preclinical Scientist—Pharmacology & Toxicology
A&AS Support to DTRA, SAIC

It is with sincere regret that we write at this time to resign from our roles as founding topic editors for the Frontiers in Pharmacology Research Topic *"Treating COVID-19 With Currently Available Drugs."* Since developing this topic and associated justification documents and applying to and receiving permission to proceed with this special topic volume from *"Frontiers in Pharmacology"* for publication under the *"Frontiers in Pharmacology (Respiratory Pharmacology)"* we have invested many hundreds of volunteer hours in soliciting manuscript submissions, identifying reviewers for submitted manuscripts, and managing the peer review process. We took this action not for any commercial gain, but rather to address an unmet need. This has been done in full and careful compliance with all "Frontiers" criteria, and with approval by "Frontiers."

The Topic had been created with the aim to contribute to identification of better and more effective pharmacological treatments during the COVID-19 pandemic by suggesting repurposed drugs. Our goal has been to reduce the barriers to publishing earlier stage clinical research regarding repurposed drugs, and in this way help reduce the terrible burden of global death due to COVID-19. While awaiting development of herd immunity (during vaccination), we wanted to contribute in COVID-19 therapy. In proposing the guest topic, we noted that Frontiers purports to provide rapid review, and explicitly allows publication of earlier stage clinical research findings including case series reports. CVs of each guest editor and the Topic proposal were accepted after evaluation and Mr. Nathan Watkins was assigned by the Frontiers organization to support the guest editors.

The recent extraordinary and unprecedented actions by Frontiers in the rejection of the review manuscript "REVIEW OF THE EMERGING EVIDENCE DEMONSTRATING THE EFFICACY OF IVERMECTIN IN THE PROPHYLAXIS AND TREATMENT OF COVID-19" and the original research manuscript "HOSPITALIZED COVID-19 PATIENTS TREATED WITH CELECOXIB AND HIGH DOSE FAMOTIDINE ADJUVANT THERAPY SHOW SIGNIFICANT CLINICAL RESPONSES" after review and acceptance of each manuscript by four/five well qualified peer reviewers (during final validation) is what has prompted our collective resignation.

To place this into context of the Frontiers review process, the papers have been rejected during the final validation phase, having previously passed the evaluation (peer review) phase.

In general, the Frontiers review process consists of the following steps: initial validation, editorial assignment, independent review, interactive review, review finalized (acceptance/rejection), final validation (this last step is the final editorial review decision prior to invoicing and finalizing manuscript proofs before actual publication). The initial validation step performed by Frontiers is independent of the Guest Editors' evaluation and is performed prior to editorial assignment to Guest Editors. Guest Editors are then asked to look for reviewers for independent review and manage interactive review. Review is finalized by guest Editors but the final validation depends on Frontiers decision . . .

**Upon reviewing these events, some might conclude that the journal is practicing extraordinary and unprecedented censorship of fully peer reviewed manuscripts.** The rationale for doing so is speculative, and the journal has communicated that these actions are justified by the following considerations:

1) "The papers considered for publication in this Research Topic will require more specific oversight, as the subject and aim of the collection has an important involvement with the ongoing public health crisis. Frontiers aims for editorial independence while also being ultimately responsible for all article publications. We need to anticipate potential impact on the population and maintain standards of rigour for our Journals and the scientific record overall."

2) "Moving forward, the Editorial Office will continue to monitor submissions to this topic. Articles will be screened at submission, with the support of our Specialty Chief Editor, to ensure that all articles submitted are valid, and fulfil our acceptance criteria. We ask that, as you continue to act as Handling Editors for articles, you remain vigilant and ensure that any serious recommendations for rejection are addressed swiftly. These steps, combined with increased awareness and participation from all parties involved, will help ensure the recent situation around the Ivermectin paper is not repeated. We hope that you understand the rationale behind these additional measures,

which are in place in the interest of maintaining scientific integrity, both for your collection, and Frontiers in Pharmacology as a journal."

The Guest editors reject any assertion that scientific integrity was compromised or breached during the review process for either of these submissions, or that this special edition has not been managed with full integrity, except in the case of the unethical breach of the journal itself and its senior management in performing an extraordinary, arbitrary and capricious post-peer review process.

At this point, based on these many actions, we are unable to assure scientific integrity of the peer review process on the part of the journal for this special topic. Our time and that of the peer reviewers has been donated to the journal, and our reputations used without compensation. We ask to be removed from association with this special topic area, that an apology be issued to ourselves and our respective institutions for the actions of the journal in this matter, and that the special topic (which we had developed with full approval by the journal) be discontinued effective immediately. **Having communicated to Frontiers that this would be our collective action if corrections were not made to this extraordinary re-review process, Frontiers has elected to expel each of the guest editors from any ongoing or future role as editors, and to close down and wipe all electronic evidence that the special topic had ever even been approved or had manuscripts submitted under the topic approved.** This decision was disclosed in email communications with all corresponding authors of published, approved, or pending manuscripts, but not with the guest editors who had created the topic and solicited and managed review of the manuscripts.

The scientific process requires fair, open, and transparent peer review to proceed effectively and efficiently—particularly at this time and for this topic. The actions of "Frontiers" in this matter clearly violate well-established norms and processes for peer review and publication of scientific works and intellectual contributions and instead have substituted a unilateral, arbitrary, and capricious process. On behalf of our peers, our institutions, and our scientific and medical colleagues we cannot allow this precedent to remain unchallenged. In our opinion, these unfortunate events constitute gross editorial misconduct by "Frontiers."

How many lives could have been saved if publication of this volume had been allowed to proceed in a normal fashion?

An unanswerable hypothetical. But as we watch the daily drip of information concerning the role of governments, nongovernmental, and transnational organizations and cabals in actively suppressing information which clearly could have saved lives, colluding with corporate media and big tech to deploy a massive military-grade fifth-generation PsyWar, propaganda and psyops campaign on their own citizens, enforcing medical treatment with protocols which clearly lead to widespread slaughter of elderly and other vulnerable populations, and working to destroy the reputations and livelihood of anyone so bold as to question their "Scientism" based on substitution of hope for data, please keep the silent dead and silenced vaccine injured in your mind.

These are the people that have paid the ultimate price for the mismanagement. These are the true victims. The hurt and widespread destruction of reputation and professional standards consequent to what has been done to myself and my colleagues will be tempered with the passage of time.

Innocence has been peeled away to the point where we may never be able to trust governments, our peers in the medical and scientific professions, or the corporate "press" again.

But who will be left to stand up and speak for the dead and the damaged?

# CHAPTER 15
## The Cost of Integrity

### What Is Cyberstalking and How Does It Differ from Cyberbullying?

> He notices the subtle furrowing of her forehead, the slight change in how she is holding her eyebrows, and asks *"Are you OK?"* She answers *"No, I am depressed and angry. It's not just the constant online attacks, it is also the lack of support from so many that I had thought were friends."*

And there it is. The unspoken truth which daily eats at our souls, the truth that we both are constantly aware of but try not to talk about, is out in the open between us.

How is an individual, or a close couple, supposed to deal with the daily reality of organized censorship, gaslighting, defamation, and online bullying persisting for years and years? There are no well-established guidelines, and those friends and colleagues who have experienced some limited form of this only offer general platitudes. Platitudes which range from some variation of *"suck it up, snowflake"* to blaming the victim. Robert often states that he refuses to define himself as a victim, but we do not know of a better term.

The first wave of attacks mostly came from corporate media, beginning in 2020 (before the vaccine rollout). The "official" corporate media/keepers of the approved narrative (*NY Times*, CNN, STAT News, and others) had enthusiastically embraced the promoted narrative that Drs. Katie Kariko (a female scientist, VP of BioNTech, and former Hungarian spy) and Drew Weissman (a former Anthony Fauci post-doctoral research trainee)—both of whom have academic appointments at the University of Pennsylvania—were the persons who came up with the idea (*ergo*, invented) of using mRNA as a drug and for vaccines. Now, just to say it, inventorship is not established by peer-reviewed academic papers. It is something that is formally determined, via strict guidelines, by the US Patent and Trademark Office. The Kariko and Weissman University of Pennsylvania "pseudouridine" patent is derivative, and not even enabling. A composition of matter improvement on the art at best. CureVac proved that the technology works for eliciting a human vaccine response even without the added pseudouridine. But not a single member of corporate media bothered to call up a patent lawyer and investigate these matters. Instead, they just regurgitated the approved and promoted narrative. Jill was particularly incensed by this promoted lie, as she had lived through the traumatic events associated with Robert having made those discoveries almost a decade before Kariko and Weissman did any work in the area, and was acutely aware that Robert had carried the mental scars of PTSD ever since. Frankly, still wanting to just bury his experiences at the Salk Institute and UC San Diego in his mind (even after all of the ensuing decades), at the time he just wanted to hide from all of the injustice.

But Jill is a warrior, and decided to make the real story public. She got out our boxes of old data and documents, wrote a summary of the events, and scanned relevant documents including the original patent disclosures, the original Salk Institute patent filing (since abandoned without notice sent to me), the nine issued patents covering DNA/mRNA vaccines and the use of mRNA as a drug, and sent copies of all of this to a wide range of recipients including Salk Institute and UC San Diego leadership. No reply from any of these was received. She also sent a copy to various professional colleagues, including a professor at the Karolinska Institute who we both know (who works on RNA vaccines) and who happens to be involved in the Nobel Prize selection process. In that case, to his credit, we did get a reply that included validation that he did remember those events and that timeline—and that we had visited the Karolinska a couple of years later at his invitation to discuss the discovery.

You can find a summary of the details together with "receipts" on our website.[1] Jill's original document (letter) can be found there also. And then there is the patent record, as well as my CV, which is easy enough for any journalist to look up. Of peripheral relevance is that the Kariko and Weissman patent issued to U Penn decades later makes no claims about using mRNA for vaccines.

Objecting to this promoted (false) narrative, combined with Robert's appearance together with Steve Kirsh on the Bret Weinstein *DarkHorse* podcast in early 2021 whereby Robert questioned the safety studies of the mRNA vaccine and promoted early treatment, triggered a barrage of attack articles from corporate media, coupled with very aggressive editing of my Wikipedia page and the related Wikipedia references to mRNA vaccines to basically write me (and my scientific contributions) out of history. The campaign to get Kariko and Weissman the Nobel Prize continued, and they were awarded the US Lasker award (considered the closest thing in the United States to the Nobel), as well as analogous awards from governments all over the world. Millions of dollars went into their pockets in prize money alone. Eventually of course, they won the Nobel Prize in Medicine. The Nobel Prize committee phrased their win: "for their discoveries concerning nucleoside base modifications that enabled the development of effective mRNA vaccines against COVID-19." Note that they didn't actually win the award for discovering mRNA vaccines, but only for adding the pseudouridine—a toxic chemical that caused far more harm than good and whose human safety profile was uncharacterized at the time of global administration of the mRNA inoculation product.[2] For the record, Robert's total compensation for all of those issued patents covering mRNA delivery and vaccination was one Susan B. Anthony dollar. Thanks, Vical and Salk Institute. Muchas gracias. Have a nice day.

What most amazed us about this early period of attacks was the willful ignorance of the corporate media authors (and many self-appointed social media "experts") in completely overlooking the patent literature. It took us years to realize that this was by design. A way to delegitimize Robert by the advocacy journals and their overlords, the mainstream media, who are in the pockets of the administrative and deep states. In some cases, these very public and widely circulated attacks were sponsored by various pharma-associated organizations such as the Wellcome Foundation, Bill & Melinda Gates Foundation, Zuckerberg-Chan Foundation and others. As an expert witness on one of the largest vaccine qui tam cases ever, we have also wondered if Robert had been targeted due to his involvement in that court case, which is still in legal limbo.

Then, as Robert started speaking out about his concerns regarding the bioethics and toxicities of genetic vaccines and calling them what they were—gene therapy technology applied to vaccination—there came the second wave of attacks from corporate and social media, basically asserting that Robert was a liar and/or a crank with an ax to grind, that he was "attention-seeking" or "arrogant."

Of course, as we wrote about earlier, before all of this negative publicity, Robert had been attacked for trying to advance clinical research into using famotidine and Celecoxib, with or without ivermectin. Elaborate attack articles, including photographs of him and our stallion "Jade" were prepared and published by the *NY Times* and the Associated Press.

All of this seemed to be consistent with well-known and documented biases and behaviors associated with corporate media, and for some (at the time but no longer mysterious) reason, any effort to discuss valid concerns regarding the ethics, safety, and efficacy (or inventorship!) of the genetic vaccines was immediately and aggressively attacked by a wide range of corporate media channels. CNN, *NY Times, Washington Post, Business Insider, Atlantic Monthly, Rolling Stone,* etc. The list went on and on. All superficial and poorly documented propaganda pieces composed by non-scientists. Which was basically what drove us to dive into the world of alternative media and the podcast.

Consulting with supportive colleagues who had very senior-level media experience, the feedback was that this is just the way things are. The corporate media is wicked, so cowboy up and get used to it. In retrospect, now we can recognize that the use of fifth-gen warfare to control the narrative was at work.

Once again, we did not sign up for this. No matter what people say, a constant stream of very high-profile personal attacks in major media outlets is hurtful. You can try to put a smile on it to remind yourself that all media exposure is good, but it still hurts. And it hurts those close to you. And it doesn't go away, as the Google web in bed with the administrative state keeps those hit pieces about Robert on their front page when people search his name. Our Substack, which is read by half a million people a day, doesn't even come up on the Google-web search engine—unless one submits just the right keywords.

Then, another physician (located in Maui, of all places) attempted to revoke Robert's medical license. That complaint landed in our mailbox right before Christmas, 2021, and the Maryland State medical board needed to have a prompt response, so that chewed up a good part of that holiday. The same physician carried on with his media attacks for years. In retrospect, we are sure that an Astroturf organization, perhaps funded by the CDC foundation, was behind this physician's attacks.

What's to be done when a wide range of corporate media, fact-checkers, social media companies, the administrative state, and online haters (who we now know were at least partially supported by the CDC and/or the CDC Foundation) are doing their best on a daily basis to destroy your reputation and generally write you out of history, or defame, slander, gaslight, and disparage? Not to mention the various small opportunists seeking to elevate their own profile by attacking you.

The general nonspecific answer is you pay a lawyer to write and send a cease-and-desist letter. Sometimes that works, but the devil is in the details. No apology was forthcoming though, or anything even close to a recognition that what they were doing was wrong. Rarely are the online or published attack articles taken down. Some entity apparently pays Google to keep the infamously poorly written and researched *Atlantic Monthly* attack article at the top of the Google ranking when one searches Robert's name. A note about the *Atlantic Monthly*. It proudly states the following—"*The Atlantic's* COVID-19 coverage is supported by grants from the Chan Zuckerberg Initiative and the Wood Johnson Foundation."

Then, having threatened to sue if the defamation is not rectified, you are left with two choices—tuck your tail and walk away, or follow through. Civil lawsuits alleging malicious defamation are among the hardest to prosecute and win. And notoriously expensive. So, unless you have the legal budget of someone like President Trump, you must pick your battles, and build a strategy, particularly when facing a barrage of cannon fire. Fortunately, our revenue from Substack allows us greater freedom to pursue legal action, but it all comes from our bank account. No big donor has stepped up and said "Oh, poor Dr. Malone: let me help you with your legal costs." And the courts take forever to even decide if they will allow the case to proceed to the discovery phase.

We were prepared for this, sort of. To the extent that anyone can be. We consciously discussed and chose to expose ourselves to the risk of these types of personal attacks, although we had no idea of how nasty, persistent, long-lived, and oppressive it would get.

What we were not prepared for, and still are reeling from, was the following wave of attacks. This is not Robert's first rodeo as a whistleblower, the other one being the notorious Jesse Gelsinger gene therapy death in 1999, which was also the University of Pennsylvania gene transfer experimental failure. Does anyone else notice a pattern here? The consequences to Robert's career were significant—due to his stepping forward and doing the right thing then. But just like during the COVIDcrisis, Robert had a duty to do what was right, and he did it.

But then there came the attacks from within—from those that we had assumed were on our side in this fight. We cannot easily express how demoralizing it is to be cyberstalked, maliciously defamed, and gaslighted on a constant daily basis by people that you thought were colleagues. Or their surrogates. Literally for years now. "Et tu, Brute?" To paraphrase from Julius Caesar—And you too, Brutus? Even you, my devoted friend, have turned against me? Then I may as well die. "Et tu, Brute? Then fall, Caesar." To have people that you once tried to help and mentor turn on you with online hate and venom, day after day after day. Or encourage surrogates to do their dirty work for them. That is indeed the unkindest cut of all. Of course, chaos agents abound. All part of the fifth-gen warfare arsenal. At some point, one has just to suck it up and get used to it.

If the only remedy for left-wing corporate media malicious defamation is the cascade of "cease and desist" followed by a lawsuit if no action is taken and the behavior continues, then should this only apply to those on the left who are attacking? What if the people, ostensibly on the same side opposing the same foes as you are, are also engaging in cyberstalking and malicious defamation (of you)? Should they get a pass? That makes no sense to us. Wrong is wrong. Damage is damage. Harm is harm, and hurt is hurt. Cyberstalking and malicious defamation are crimes against persons. Psychological pain inflicted on one's self and one's loved ones is still pain no matter the age, prior good works, or background philosophy of the one inflicting the pain.

There are so many haters and so little money. You have to pick your battles. Robert has now been accused of being a mass murderer because he supported the "mass formation" model of Mattias Desmet—thereby in some way enabling the "global predators," which of course, makes no logical sense. He has also been accused of being a mass murderer for having invented the core mRNA vax platform technology some thirty years ago and attacked for not working full-time to mitigate the damage caused by that technology. Robert has been accused of being a mass murderer for speaking out against the vaccines, which was the primary complaint of the Maui physician seeking to have Robert's Maryland medical license revoked. We once counted six different forms of accusations during COVID by which Robert was asserted to be a mass murderer. He has been accused of blocking the use of ivermectin and promoting remdesivir (both of which are clearly false claims). And recently, of somehow being involved in enabling both the 9–11 hijacking airline attacks *and* the anthrax spore attacks. Repeatedly accused of being "controlled opposition" and an employee of the CIA, both of which accusations are verifiably false and seem mostly to serve the interests of governmental and pharmaceutical industry actors. The attacks are incessant, sometimes three to five times per day. A very small cohort of people in the "medical freedom" movement have put out literally thousands of tweets and Substack articles, which get amplified and cross-posted. Constantly. Month after month after month. All designed to delegitimize him in some way.

Our criteria for taking legal action has been whether or not someone seems to be doing significant reputational damage, while also factoring in the quirky nature of various clauses in defamation law. In some cases, Robert proceeded to deliver a cease and desist and that was enough. Dr. Richard Fleming was one such case. Our lawyer sent him a letter, and he stopped. Seems rational enough. Thank you, Richard (and we seriously mean that). Turns out that response is the exception rather than the rule. Others double down, go public, get even nastier and more personally vindictive. So, then you have the same dilemma. Act on it or not. Fish or cut bait. First stop is to ask a mutual colleague to intervene. In almost all cases, the cyberstalker refused to stop the defamation. This all leads to endless pain, stress, and financial cost in the bizarre form of a do-loop.

And as if this is not enough, then there are all of the armchair quarterbacks, some of who are employers, friends, or associates with the ones doing the harassment and defamation. "Why are you suing the _____ (fill in the blank)!!??!!" "You just want to destroy the medical freedom movement!" (whatever that is). "You are just doing it for money!" (what a horrible business plan that would be, given the paltry odds of winning a defamation lawsuit).

No, Robert was suing because he has had something taken from him, and it is both wrong and illegal. His reputation, his peace of mind, and that of those close to him. Cyberstalking, cyberbullying, gang stalking, and malicious defamation. These things are wrong. They are not what civilized, mentally healthy people do to each other. And they often seem to involve some odd perverse obsession. But it is also true that hate and defamation is a very good business model and a great way to build up a follower base. People build their audiences by employing this strategy based on tall tales, lies, name-calling, and hate. But maybe, just maybe, if Robert or someone else wins a defamation case, this will become a disincentive for those prone to this sort of behavior in the future.

And then there are the ones that are shunning Robert because he is (legally) fighting back against those that are doing this to us. That part is a real mind-bender for me. Somehow fighting back against those who are aggressively cyberstalking and defaming Robert on a daily basis makes him the bad guy. Now if that is not pretzel logic, we do not know what is.

In an intellectual sense, we suppose it is a fascinating question to ponder. What makes these people behave in this way? Why do haters hate? Why do others support them? We do not have an answer, only informed speculation. Personally, we think it somehow relates to the mental state of other types of stalkers, such as the ones that shot President Reagan and John Lennon. We have had stalkers show up at events or threaten to, and that scares Jill enough, where we have had to cancel a couple of speaking engagements. And it clearly relates to envy, jealousy, and greed. Spreading hate can be quite lucrative in the age of the internet, where attention-seeking behavior can be monetized. So, there is that.

In an effort to comprehend, as if that will make it better, less painful, to somehow understand the motivation of those trying to hurt Robert, we sought information from those with more experience in these matters. Most of them seem to either be psychiatrists or lawyers who specialize in defending people who are being defamed and/or cyberstalked.

Remember that cyberstalking is using the internet to harass, stalk, or attack a person, entity, or organization. It is an electronic form of stalking and harassment. The term cyberbullying refers to electronic bullying. Cyberstalking uses slander, defamation, threats, libel, creating false accusations, monitoring profiles (a form of stalking), and solicitation for sexual acts. Cyberstalkers are often strategic, and this harassment is chronic. Many cyberstalkers also engage in physical stalking.

There are some strategies to take down cyberstalkers, but despite being technically illegal, cyberstalking is rarely prosecuted. However, it is important to document harassment and defamation. This can aid in either removing an individual from a social media platform or removing offensive content. Furthermore, such documentation is necessary if a restraining order is needed. Many cyberstalkers will accuse their victims of harassing them, so keep records. As deep fakes and AI become the norm, expect these types of attacks to grow exponentially.

Many cyberstalkers become fixated on public figures and celebrities. They are often delusional to a greater or lesser extent as they become very familiar with their victims through the internet, online, TV, etc. We have experienced how damaging this is to one's personal life.

That said, many cyberstalkers are getting paid or are getting "perks" by organizations that find it in their interest to harass specific targets. It has become an organized technique, as has been documented when the CDC Foundation, who paid Astroturf organizations to solicit physicians and scientists to become "professional" cyberstalkers to harass, stalk, and even work to get people fired or lose their professional license. These cyberstalkers were given special privileges by Twitter that allowed them to bully without getting kicked off the platform. These cyberstalkers (or cyberstalking) are collectively known as gangstalkers or gang stalking. Yes, Robert was one of the victims of a group of professionals gang stalking—at the behest of an Astroturf organization betting paid by the CDC Foundation, as documented in a recent *Epoch Times* article.[3] So, cyberstalking and gang stalking have become fifth-generation warfare techniques deployed by the Centers for Disease Control.

There are various online websites that list what can be done, if one picks up a cyber stalker. These are common recommendations.

1. Preserve and document all evidence.

2.  Install an email filtering system. Of course, when this is done—documentation of evidence becomes difficult but for peace of mind, it may be necessary.
3.  Don't retaliate or respond to your attackers. Most cyberstalkers don't care whether your response to their threats and attacks is positive or negative—they are simply looking for a reaction.
4.  Consider limiting what personal information, photos, video content you make available online.

We have rapidly become experts on cyberstalking, due to the school of hard knocks. Living in the age of COVID as a whistleblower has certainly provided Robert with a rich tapestry of examples to draw from.

We know that if you have never experienced unrelenting daily unjustified attacks in press and social media for years, then you cannot understand what it is like. This is painful, demeaning, and threatening, and for someone who already has an elevated PTSD set point, sometimes it can provoke a sense of breathless panic. There is no good answer on how to stop the cyberstalking or gang stalking. Except that one must grow a thick skin and try not to let it get to you. It's not a perfect or even imperfect solution.

But that is what courage is all about, isn't it? Courage is encountering fear, panic, anxiety and still persevering. Day in and day out. Many people have this kind of quiet courage, and you would never know it. But they are all around us.

When both online and in person, please keep in mind that your capacity to hurt others by your words and actions is significant. Maybe that is part of the motivation—for those who feel powerless in their own lives, causing others pain and suffering can give them some sense of power over others.

Here in this part of Virginia, we have a word for these sorts of folks. We call them assholes. They are everywhere, but for some reason seem more highly concentrated in the big city, probably because it is harder to remain an anonymous asshole in a small rural town.

Please try to be kind to others. We all have a bit of inner asshole, and it comes out from time to time.

But try to not let it get the better of you.

# CHAPTER 16
## Sins of Information Warfare

The business model of stoking rage for the "up and coming" podcaster is real. In our opinion, this strategy is fundamentally the same as the "fear-porn" business model commonly used by corporate media—and in particular, CNN.

For what it is worth, we hold "our side" to higher standards than we have come to expect from corporate (broadcast and published) media. We reject the assertion that on the battlefield of the current twenty-first-century unrestricted media and information war in which we are immersed, it is acceptable to employ the tactics of our opponents. We have heard others in the medical resistance community advocate the schoolyard "logic" of "they are doing it to us, and so we have to do it to them." We firmly reject this. Any "win" on the information war battlefield which is based on this type of rationale will be transitory and self-defeating. It is not a win if we become one with the ethics of our opponents.

This is not just an information war; it is a battle over what is right and good versus what is fundamentally evil. Our opponents clearly believe that the ends justify the means, and that ethics, right and wrong—are completely situational and subject to the same logic widely accepted by the "Virtuals" caste; that there is no objective truth or reality, and reality and ethics are whatever one believes them to be. The ultimate derivative of the logic of "cultural relativity." The logic from which springs the transsexual movement is denialism of the genetic/biological basis of gender.

As Robert has said so many times, in so many lectures, our opponents

191

in this information war, this war on truth and integrity, have no ethical guardrails. Ethics are entirely situational in their world.

Repetition has merit in this case; our opponents appear to believe that the ends justify the means, and their cause is sufficiently compelling (in their minds) to justify any actions of censorship, defamation, mis- dis- or mal-information deployed to support their cause. In their minds, they are fighting for a higher cause. Would that be globalism, utilitarianism, social-ism, Marxism, totalitarianism, or fascism? Who knows? But for them, the end result that they want justifies jettisoning ethics and fundamentals of respect for the integrity and dignity of others.

Furthermore, this has become about tribalism and the demonstration of tribal allegiance. It is not about me, you, medical freedom, or anything rational. This *is* about mass formation, or mass psychosis, of the forma-tion of crowds, or whatever term you wish to apply to the phenomenon so thoroughly described and documented by Freud, Le Bon, Arendt, and yes, Mattias Desmet, as well as other contemporaries.

We must be willing to admit when we make a mistake, apologize, and move on.

As a consequence of once cross-posting a video montage which included a false association involving the tragic death of a young man on Twitter, Robert received a rather aggressive and accusatory cease-and-desist letter from lawyers representing his family and estate. Basically, he was accused of exploiting his death (and the associated video of same) for political pur-poses, even though he did not produce the video in question (rather, he merely cross-posted it). Strong language was used in asserting that he was intentionally disrespecting the young man and his family.

Frankly, his reaction to the letter was a mix of horror and pity. He felt pity for the parents and family, who were probably being inadvertently forced to relive a personal tragedy, and he felt horror that he had in some way compounded or contributed to their pain.

What did Robert do? He immediately deleted the cross-post and apolo-gized to the family via their legal representative who had contacted him. He had acted in ignorance. He had assumed that the video (which he believed came from a credible source) was accurate. But Robert had acted wrongly. Immediate deletion and apology, acknowledging the harm inadvertently done, was the closest he could get to being consistent with his own personal commitment to fundamental integrity, respect for human dignity, and valuing his community's ethical standards.

For either side of the debate. It is often said, when debating an opponent (or an internet troll) that "you are entitled to your own opinion, but not to your own facts." Moreover, many types of "artistic license" distortions of truth cause damage to the credibility of the arguments being made (which may otherwise be valid), and can also cause psychological pain.

Furthermore, these types of errors become weapons that will be deployed against us by our opponents in this unrestricted information war battlefield.

Allow us to provide an example from recent history. The Jeff Hays video production of *The Real Anthony Fauci*, a full-length feature documentary based on Robert F. Kennedy, Jr.'s runaway bestseller,[1] was meticulously (internally) fact-checked before being released. Anything stated during the many interviews that were used to generate the final product that could not be documented was left on the cutting room floor. It did not rely on either hyperbole or misrepresentation. And (unfortunately) it did not go viral. But it will withstand the test of time.

The collective answers to these questions by the medical freedom community will further define who we are. What are the ethical standards to which we will hold ourselves? As far as we are concerned, that is the question that really matters. The rest is merely a tale, full of sound and fury, signifying nothing, and full of passionate intensity.

Furthermore, the truth will eventually come out. Maybe not today, maybe not tomorrow, and maybe in some cases, such as the JFK and RFK assassinations, it can be hidden for a long time. But it will come out.

When the dust settles, which side do you want to be on?

Striking a more elegant literary note;

> Tomorrow, and tomorrow, and tomorrow,
> Creeps in this petty pace from day to day
> To the last syllable of recorded time,
> And all our yesterdays have lighted fools
> The way to dusty death. Out, out, brief candle!
> Life's but a walking shadow, a poor player

That struts and frets his hour upon the stage
And then is heard no more: it is a tale
Told by an idiot, full of sound and fury,
Signifying nothing.

—*Macbeth*, Act 5, Scene 5

# CHAPTER 17
# Evidence-Based Medicine Is a Mirage

## How the Government Stopped Worrying and Learned to Love Propaganda

In 1990, a paradigm shift occurred in developing new medicines and treatments. An idea so big, that it was supposed to encompass the whole of medicine. It was to start initially at the level of preclinical and clinical trials and work all the way through the system to the care and management of individual patients. This new concept of how medicine would be developed and conducted is called evidence-based medicine (EBM). Evidence-based medicine was to provide a more rigorous foundation for medicine, one based on science and the scientific method. Truly, this was to be a revolution in medicine—a non-biased way of conducting medical research and treating patients.

### Evidence-Based Medicine

Evidence-based medicine is "the conscientious, explicit and judicious use of current best evidence in making decisions about the care of individual patients."[1] The aim of EBM is to integrate the experience of the clinician, the values of the patient, and the best available scientific information to guide decision-making about clinical management.

## So, What the Hell Happened?

There is a big flaw in the logic of evidence-based medicine as the basis for the practice of medicine as we know it, a practice supposedly based on science; one that determines care down to the level of the individual patient. This flaw is nestled in the heart and soul of evidence-based medicine, which (as we have seen over the last two years) is not free of politics. It is naive to think that data and the process of licensure of new drugs is free from bias and conflicts of interest. In fact, this couldn't be any further from the truth. The COVID-19 crisis of 2020 to 2023 exposed for all to see how evidence-based medicine has been corrupted by the governments, hospitalists, academia, Big Pharma, tech, and social media. They have leveraged the processes and rationale of evidence-based medicine to corrupt the entire medical enterprise.

Evidence-based medicine depends on data. For the most part, the data gathering and analysis process is conducted by and for the pharmaceutical industry, then reported by senior academics. The problem, as laid out in an editorial in the *British Medical Journal*, is as follows:

> The release into the public domain of previously confidential pharmaceutical industry documents has given the medical community valuable insight into the degree to which industry sponsored clinical trials are misrepresented. Until this problem is corrected, evidence based medicine will remain an illusion.[2]

This ideal of the integrity of data and the scientific process is corrupted as long as financial (and government's) interests trump the common good.

> Medicine is largely dominated by a small number of very large pharmaceutical companies that compete for market share, but are effectively united in their efforts to expand that market. The short-term stimulus to biomedical research because of privatization has been celebrated by free market champions, but the unintended, long-term consequences for medicine have been severe. Scientific progress is thwarted by the ownership of data and knowledge because industry suppresses negative trial results, fails to report adverse events, and does not share raw data with

the academic research community. Patients die because of the adverse impact of commercial interests on the research agenda, universities, and regulators.

The pharmaceutical industry's responsibility to its shareholders means that priority must be given to their hierarchical power structures, product loyalty, and public relations propaganda over scientific integrity. Although universities have always been elite institutions prone to influence through endowments, they have long laid claim to being guardians of truth and the moral conscience of society. But in the face of inadequate government funding, they have adopted a neo-liberal market approach, actively seeking pharmaceutical funding on commercial terms. As a result, university departments become instruments of industry: through company control of the research agenda and ghostwriting of medical journal articles and continuing medical education, academics become agents for the promotion of commercial products. When scandals involving industry-academe partnership are exposed in the mainstream media, trust in academic institutions is weakened and the vision of an open society is betrayed.[3]

Another issue is that the modern, "corporate" university model compromises the concept of academic leadership. No longer are positions of leadership due to distinguished careers. Instead, the ability to raise funds in the form of donations, grants, royalty revenue, and contracts dominates the hiring and retention requirements for university leaders. They must now demonstrate their profitability or how they can attract corporate sponsors.[4] The university system is more interested in generating income than creating a research program that is free from bias.

The US government, particularly NIH and its institutes, such as the National Institute of Allergy and Infectious Diseases (NIAID), awards a significant amount of the grants and contracts won by of most academic institutions in the United States. Hence, senior government employees also can determine what research is conducted and who is funded to conduct that research. Although there is an illusion of peer review in the selection of grants, it is actually the agency or institute and ultimately the director who makes the final decisions. These grants are not awarded based on "peer-review," although the government sure likes to pretend that this is so. A close read of the process suggests something else entirely. The final selection of grants is not made by the sham peer review process, staff, or advisory boards. The ultimate decision of what grants get funded is made entirely by the institute directors. The revolving door between government and industry, particularly the pharmaceutical and biotech industry, ensures that conflict of interest issues abound.

US government employees also control the narrative. Take, for example, the use of the media that the CDC and the FDA used to control the narrative about early treatment for COVID-19. By now, we should all know about the corruption in the early clinical trials of hydroxychloroquine.[5] On the basis of these faked studies, one of the safest drugs in the world was recommended not to be used in an outpatient setting in the midst of an ongoing pandemic. This faked study convinced the administrative state that a vaccine was the only viable solution to fight COVID-19. Even though the said vaccine was experimental and, at the time, still in development. In the case of ivermectin, the US government used propaganda to control the use of ivermectin by such tactics as calling it unfit for human use and labeling it as a "horse dewormer." The gray and black propaganda campaign against ivermectin, which has an excellent safety record, overwhelmed mainstream media airwaves.

Another tactic is creating preclinical and clinical studies "designed to fail." By choosing the wrong dose amounts, start date, end date, or length of treatment, studies can easily be designed to produce negative results. All indications are that these efforts by the US government and their contracted academics were to dissuade early treatment to either strengthen the Emergency Use Authorization for the experimental vaccine still under development. Once the experimental "vaccine" had EUA approval, these propaganda techniques were used to decrease vaccine hesitancy. The government knew these drugs were safe, they knew off-label use of licensed drugs is very common by physicians and yet, the government provided data that was not peer-reviewed to intercede in the physician/patient relationship.

Ironically, industry-sponsored key opinion leaders appear to enjoy many of the advantages of academic freedom, supported as they are by their universities, the industry, and journal editors for expressing their views, even when those views are incongruent with the real evidence. While universities fail to correct misrepresentations of the science from such collaborations, critics of the industry face rejections from journals, legal threats, and the potential destruction of their careers. This uneven playing field is exactly what concerned Popper when he wrote about suppression and control of the means of science communication. Preserving institutions designed to further scientific objectivity and impartiality (i.e., public laboratories, independent scientific periodicals, and congresses) are entirely at the mercy of political and commercial power; vested interest will always override the rationality of evidence.[6]

Regulators (*ergo*, the FDA) receive funding from industry and use industry-funded and performed trials to approve drugs. In most cases, the FDA regulators do not review the raw data. What confidence do we have in a system where drug companies are permitted to "mark their own homework" rather than having their products tested by independent experts as part of a public regulatory system? Unconcerned governments and captured regulators are unlikely to initiate necessary change to remove research from industry altogether and cleanup publishing models that depend on reprint revenue, advertising, and sponsorship revenue.

Those who succeed in academia are likely to be key opinion leaders (KOLs, in marketing parlance), whose careers can be advanced through the opportunities provided by industry. Potential key opinion leaders are selected based on a complex array of profiling activities carried out by companies. For example, physicians are selected based on their influence on the prescribing habits of other physicians. Key opinion leaders are sought out by industry for this influence and for the prestige that their university affiliation brings to the branding of the company's products. As well-paid members of pharmaceutical advisory boards and speakers' bureaus, key opinion leaders present results of industry trials at medical conferences and in continuing medical education. Instead of acting as independent, disinterested scientists and critically evaluating a drug's performance, they become what marketing executives call "product champions."[7]

Finally, pharmaceutical companies pay off mainstream news outlets in the form of advertising. Advertising dollars are spent to suppress the press from critically investigating pharmaceutical companies. This strategy became very apparent during the COVID-19 pandemic and is yet another fifth-gen warfare technique. The practice of currying favor of investigatory agents even happens at the level of academic journals. Big Pharma and biotech companies both advertise and buy vast numbers of article reprints (bound paper copies of published articles) as a way of garnering favor of big-name scientific journals. This has become one of the main funding mechanisms for academic journals, and the corporations running the journals are dependent on this funding mechanism to remain solvent. These are corrupting influences on the medical and scientific fields that must end. Congress needs to step in to pass laws to abolish these practices.

## Some Proposals for Reforms Include:

- Regulators must be freed from drug company funding. This includes the FDA funding which must come directly from the government, as opposed to pharma fees, as now is the case. Tying employee salaries to pharma fees creates a huge conflict of interest within the FDA.
- The revolving door between regulators like the FDA, the CDC, and Big Pharma (as well as tech/media) must stop. Employment contracts for regulatory government positions must have "non-compete" clauses whereby employment opportunities are limited upon leaving these regulatory agencies. Likewise, Big Pharma executives should not fill leadership positions at regulatory agencies.
- Taxation imposed on pharmaceutical companies to allow public funding of independent trials; and, perhaps most importantly, anonymized individual patient level trial data posted, along with study protocols. These data to be provided on suitably accessible websites so that third parties, self-nominated or commissioned by health technology agencies, could rigorously evaluate the methodology and trial results.
- Clinical trial data must be made public. Trial consent forms are easily changed to make this anonymized data freely available.
- Publication of data must be open and transparent. The government has a moral obligation to trial participants, real people who have been involved in risky treatment and have a right to expect that the results of their participation will be used in keeping with principles of scientific rigor.

- The government and its employees have a moral obligation to the public to conduct clinical trials in ways that are not biased by industry.
- The Foundation for the CDC and the Foundation for the NIH, which runs clinical trials and studies for their respective organizations (while their boards are made up of pharma industry executives and employees) must be decommissioned. We have laws in this country whereby the government does not accept volunteer labor or direct donations to influence government decisions. These NGOs are doing just that. These practices must be stopped. They are intentionally using these organizations to bypass federal laws concerning exertion of undue influence on federal decision making. Unfortunately, these NGOs were commissioned by Congress and it will take action by Congress to decommission them.
- Off-label drugs must continue to be used by the medical community. The early treatment protocols, which have saved countless lives, have documented the important role that physicians have played in finding cheap and effective treatments for COVID as well as many other diseases. Let doctors be doctors.
- Scientific and medical journals must be stopped from taking monies from Big Pharma. This includes the sales of reprints, banner ads, print ads, etc.
- Government must stop interfering with the publishing of peer reviewed papers and social media. A free press must remain free from coercion from government. We all know countless examples, such as the Trusted News Initiative (TNI) and White House meetings with Big Tech to influence what is allowed to be printed. And the billion dollars spent by the US government to promote these EUA/unlicensed "vaccine" products that do not prevent infection or transmission of the SARS-CoV-2 virus. This is a direct assault on our First Amendment rights. It also skews evidence based medicine.
- Informed consent, one of the foundations of modern medicine, has been stymied by the FDA, NIH, the CDC hospitalists, Big Tech and social media. They have been hiding data and skewing results. When people cannot get the information they need to make an

informed decision, evidence-based medicine cannot function correctly.

- The government and its employees must stop picking winners and losers. Evidence-based medicine requires a unbiased playing field.
- Industry concerns about privacy and intellectual property rights should not hold sway.
- Pharmaceutical companies and biotech should not be able to advertise drugs and medical devices. Either the FDA or Congress needs to act to close this loophole.

If we are to ever trust and support the concept of evidence-based medicine again, significant changes to the system must be enacted. The only question is . . . are our government and our HHS bureaucrats up to the job?

# CHAPTER 18

## Censorship and Propaganda Are Destroying "Democracy"

Back in 2016, we both half-believed that the Steele Dossier was, for the most part, real. We believed this because we read that the FBI found compelling evidence that the Russians worked with the Trump organization. There were so many seemingly precise but faked details. Details upon details. After all, the government said that it was true. In fact, the FBI used the Steele Dossier to justify the wiretapping of Carter Page.[1] They did this even though they knew it was fake, but that didn't stop them from asserting otherwise to the public. Then the Mueller investigation implied more Russian disinformation. We believed it—even though it seemed over-the-top crazy, because both the corporate media and our government institutions of power, what we now call the deep state as well as the administrative state, were telling Americans that it was all true. Boy, did we ever get it all wrong! In retrospect, we can't believe how we fell for the deep state's narrative. Back then, we thought we understood the government and civil service. We thought our government may be corrupt around the edges but that "we" were mostly the "good" guys. What we didn't understand about psyops and propaganda back then could fill a book!

In May 2023, the American people had final confirmation from the Durham Report produced by special counsel John Durham, that it was likely the Clinton and the DNC who worked with the Russians to produce the Steele Dossier. We learned that the usual procedures that the FBI uses were discarded when investigating Hillary Clinton's server mishaps, the

Clinton Foundation, and the DNC, which paid for the Steele Dossier to be produced. We also learned that the FBI disregarded normal procedures when investigating Trump. In his case, they used biased informants, didn't verify documents (such as the Steele report), and generally were out to get him. This means Trump wasn't lying or being paranoid when he said the deep state was out to get him. They were and still are out to get him. He still isn't lying about that. The many court cases, including the *People of the State of New York v. Donald J. Trump* and *Trump v. United States* document that the deep and administrative states are most definitely out to get him.

The Steele Dossier was bought and paid for by the deep state government operatives, and then the deep state also leaked the unsubstantiated Steele Dossier to the press. The press then published it—as if the original source was from the government. The government then used the stories written in the press to assert the need for an investigation of Trump, based on the Steele Dossier. Rinse and Repeat. This was a classic wrap-up smear and the mainstream media went right along with it all. The question does remain, who in the MSM are the stooges and who are the operatives?

After the Durham Report was released, mainstream media spent the night writing hit pieces on the report to allay the fears from the liberal side that the report was an indictment against Clinton or the DNC. It is clear now that it was Hillary Clinton and the DNC that funded the Steele Dossier. As Kash Patel likes to say, "*government gangsters*" have taken over the government.

We completely lost faith in the Democratic Party years ago. We both had just never really come to terms with what that meant. But sometime in 2021, maybe between Robert's interviews and private discussions with the likes of Glenn Beck, Lou Dobbs, Tucker Carlson, and Steve Bannon and long conversations between ourselves, we both had an epiphany: what if everything we "knew" was wrong? The conclusions that we came to shocked both of us. Almost everything we had once believed in was a lie. Furthermore, when we look back on the Democrat's track record over the past decade, we realize that what we believe in is good governance, and that is not how they govern.

They have become everything we abhor. Their positions on war, education, urban policy, agriculture, Big Pharma, Big Tech, common decency, censorship, propaganda, the grooming of children, medicine, and regulatory capture—we can't support any of it. Nothing that has happened over the past two years has made us change our minds about the Democratic Party. This is not the "Kennedy" Democratic Party, and there is no going back to how things once were. Furthermore, the "Kennedy" Democrats believed in big government, excess entitlements, and big budgets. These policies only worked to destroy this great country, not rebuild it.

It is the unique American version of self-responsibility, hard work, ingenuity, and independence that built this great nation, not handouts and a universal living wage.

We understand better than most just how corrupted our government has become. Robert has had two-plus years of disinformation aimed at him. Literally, he is accused of misinformation by "fact-checkers" almost daily. And those fact checks stay up as a permanent reminder of all of his supposed sins. It does not matter if he has been proven right; they never apologize, they never retract, and they continue to spread their own misinformation about Robert.

Of course, this is also part of the wrap-up smear. All those fact-checks and MSM articles mean that Google is given free rein to censor and suppress the positive articles about Robert at will. As no one reads past the front page of Google results, this becomes another form of censorship and propaganda. This is then repeated on his Wikipedia page—where he is labeled as spreading "misinformation about the COVID-19 pandemic."

For instance, did you know that Robert actually said that "spike is a toxin" back in May 2021 on the *DarkHorse Podcast*? Imagine the horror! This is just one of his "great lies," according to MSM. For the record, the SARS-CoV-2 spike protein IS a toxin.[2,3] Peer-reviewed papers as early as 2020 document that spike is a toxin, and yet, Robert's great sin is still trumpeted on the front page of Google. Basically, pure propaganda. All the while, the government plants fake information about him. It is a surreal game that he can't get out of. If he reacts, he is labeled as reactive, making things up, making false accusations, etc. If he doesn't try to fight back or doesn't react (even if he does), their lies get embedded as fact on the front pages of Google. Evidently, those original nine patents on mRNA vaccines still aren't evidence of an invention. According to the fact-checkers and the government subcontractors, those patents make Robert a "self-described" or "self-purported" inventor.

Their chaos agents try to convince others on our side of the fence that Robert is "controlled opposition." Like all good fifth-generation warfare, just who is behind those attacks is a murky mess. His past is dissected as if he were in a position of great power. That he somehow could have changed the trajectory of the COVID policy failures.

Now these same chaos agents are making up stories that he is responsible for 9–11, the anthrax attacks, had links to Mossad, that he ran secret offensive biothreat labs, is a CIA officer, patented the SV40 virus (evidently because Robert used the commercially available SV40 promotor in some of his laboratory work in the early 1990s), is a mass murderer, etc. Seriously? The attacks from both sides never seem to end. We have had violent protesters from the health freedom movement show up where he was speaking, death threats, nasty emails, and phone calls. He routinely has *poison pen* letters dropped in his hand while at events or mailed to our home address. Another tactic is to take his twenty-page CV, spanning back decades—as well as his patents, his hundreds of papers, and peer-reviewed abstracts, to dissect them for "evidence" that he is some sort of evil monster. This is then spread throughout the health freedom movement followers in a bizarre attempt to "delegitimize" him. All of which leads to a vile amount of cyberstalking and cyberbullying. The bile that is extruded from this group of people toward Robert is grotesque.

One such leader in the cyberstalking and cyberbullying crusade has the initials G.W. This man has literally put out thousands of tweets about Robert—including faked stories and documents—which are woven into all the nefarious exploits he asserts Robert is responsible for. He has been working for three plus years now on this project to take Robert down. Jill once tried to collate all of his tweets—but gave up when she hit the 1,500-page mark. We believe that such attempts by multiple individuals at painting Robert as "controlled opposition" or some sort of government deep state spy are about taking people's eyes off of Big Pharma, HHS, DoD, and Fauci's role in the COVIDcrisis and the PsyWar campaign. Because who would care so much about Robert but the deep state or Big Pharma to do all this? And G.W. is not the only one who dogmatically puts out propaganda about Robert, day after day after day. The amazing thing about all of this is that a group of people believe this stuff. And they do. Recently, while speaking at a NY event—Robert had someone try to rush up on stage, making garbled threats. However, this type of cyberbullying that leads to real, physical danger has all the hallmarks of a typical black ops operation, for which the FBI is well known. The use of controlled opposition, disruptors, chaos agents, and bad-jacketing tools are part of the FBI playbook.

As we have written before, following the money can be very helpful. In Robert's case and as we have written about in an earlier chapter, some of the gang stalking and cyberstalking from the deep state can be traced through nonprofit Astroturf organizations, up through the Foundation for the CDC to the CDC itself. But the other chaos agents? Those attacking him from within the movement? We frankly don't know. But how can we not suspect that these attacks are also coming somewhere in the government, most likely the FBI?

So, now we are left with reading the Durham report on Russian disinformation that discredits all that has been fed to the American public over the past seven years and trying to make sense of it all. Where did the US government go so very, very wrong? What is truly disinformation versus black propaganda? When did the DNC and the FBI become so deeply corrupted?

At sixty-five years of age, one might think we didn't have any innocence left to lose. But here we are, trying to disentangle the strands of dis-, mis-, mal-information being fed to us by competing sources from within the government. But the truth is that when the amount of money given by the government to produce psyops becomes a driving profit factor for mainstream media and Big Tech, who can we trust?

Elon Musk has clearly come down on the side that he will have to cooperate with governments if he wishes to keep Twitter alive. His vision of an untainted social media platform has vanished (if it ever really existed), as his goals to make X a one-stop financial platform are bigger than his goals to keep Twitter free of censorship. It took the threat of loss of profit to get him to hire a WEF official named Linda Yaccarino as CEO of Twitter. All appearances are that he has caved to the USG, EU, and the WEF. So then, will Twitter revert back to just being another arm of the government? Is it just a matter of time and incrementalism?

So, here is a thought to consider. Has the federal government splintered into so many factions that the deep state is starting to turn on itself? Is the use of fake information that is constantly being planted within mainstream media become so commonplace that it may take the form of a "circular firing squad"? Whereby different factions within the government continuously plant competing fake news narratives? Are we seeing this play out in real-time with the Durham report? The result of all this will be a complete degradation of public faith in our governmental institutions and political parties. Censorship and propaganda will not protect "democracy" (technically a representative republic); they will destroy it.

Batten down the hatches, build intentional communities, find shelter for you and your loved ones, and get ready for the storm.

# CHAPTER 19
# How "Micro-Oppression" Is Used to Control Free Speech

## The Right to Be Free Is Like a Muscle; It Has to Be Exercised to Stay Strong

As we all know intimately well, cancel culture is still rapidly evolving and expanding throughout society, like some single-stranded RNA virus—with no checks to its genome—another mind virus that has inserted itself into a new host population.

Combine this phenomenon with the weaponized offensive accusations of "microaggression" and the two together are just the latest examples of how sensitive the left has become to any and all perceived slights. The situation has gotten so extreme that for people of a certain gender or color, simply being accused of committing an act of microaggression puts them at a risk of losing their livelihood. This is particularly true in academia.

> **The definition of "micro" is clear.**
> Micro (mī′krō)—adjective
> Very small or microscopic

We find it all very disturbing. Robert is a man with roots from the deep south, and he often slips into referring to people that he is addressing as "sir" and "ma'am." This is how he was raised. Frankly, he sometimes slips up and says, "Yes, ma'am," which is what his mother would want him to say.

For him, this is a sign of respect. Just as "yes, sir" is a sign of respect. It is something he can't turn off easily, as he was raised with this being how to show respect.

---

**The definition of "lady" is clear.**
Lady (lā′dē)—noun
   1.  A woman of high social standing or refinement, especially when viewed as dignified or well-mannered.
   2.  A woman who is the head of a household.
   3.  A woman, especially when spoken of or to in a polite way.

---

So, the fact that a man calling a group of women "ladies" (which happens to be the plural of lady) seems pretty benign to us. Referring to a woman or group of women as dignified or in a polite way seems entirely appropriate. Robert will also to refer to men as gentlemen. Again, the opposite of a slur is intended. We certainly don't view using these words as a microaggression. But evidently, in the minds of some, it is just that.

### Former Principal Loses Superintendent Job for Calling Women "Ladies"

*The Epoch Times*, April 12, 2023
The use of the word "ladies" in addressing two female officials caused a Massachusetts school board to rescind a job offer for superintendent to the district's former principal—igniting social media backlash, street rallies, a recall petition, and even death threats.

"Shame on the school committee for participating in cancel culture!" wrote the Easthampton Education Association in a Facebook post slamming the decision to recant the job offer to Vito Perrone, who currently serves as an interim superintendent at the nearby West Springfield schools.

Perrone announced publicly that the board had rescinded their offer in an executive session because he had committed a *"microaggression"* by sending an email to the Easthampton School Committee Chair Cynthia Kwiecinski and the committee's

Executive Assistant Suzanne Colby in which he addressed them with the greeting as "Dear Ladies."[1]

The exact definition of microaggression from Google is:

> Microaggression is a term used for commonplace verbal, behavioral or environmental slights, whether intentional or unintentional, that communicate hostile, derogatory, or negative attitudes toward stigmatized or culturally marginalized groups (Wikipedia).

Of course, there is nothing in Wikipedia to suggest that the usage of the word "microaggression" might in of itself be a microaggression. But frankly, it is, isn't it?

This new concept of micro (microscopic) aggressions being a thing is clearly something that we should all come to know and understand, so that we don't commit anything that might be construed as such [insert sarcasm emoji]. Honestly, when did Americans become so damn sensitive?

But maybe this new idea of micro-aggression doesn't have anything to do with microaggression or even aggression, but everything to do with the left controlling the narrative on the right. Could the outraged cry of *"microaggression!"* just be another type of *"micro-oppression"* (or maybe even oppression) by the left and the radical progressives?

Back in 2015, the esteemed conservative thinker Thomas Sowell wrote an essay on just this subject entitled, "The Left's 'Microaggression' Obsession Is Indicative of Its Micro-totalitarian Tendencies," to quote:

> Professors at the University of California at Berkeley have been officially warned against saying such things as "America is the land of opportunity." Why? Because this is considered to be an act of "microaggression" against minorities and women. Supposedly it shows that you don't take their grievances seriously and are therefore guilty of being aggressive toward them, even if only on a micro scale.
>
> You might think that this is just another crazy idea from Berkeley. But the same concept appears in a report from the

flagship campus of the University of Illinois at Urbana. If you just sit in a room where all the people are white, you are considered to be guilty of "microaggression" against people who are not white, who will supposedly feel uncomfortable when they enter such a room.

Word games are just one of the ways of silencing politically incorrect ideas, instead of debating them.

The concept of "microaggression" is just one of many tactics used to stifle differences of opinion by declaring some opinions to be "hate speech," instead of debating those differences in a marketplace of ideas. To accuse people of aggression for not marching in lockstep with political correctness is to set the stage for justifying real aggression against them.

To me, the most amazing thing is that a decade after Thomas Sowell's essay was written, after the word microaggression entered the American consciousness, it is still being weaponized to take down individuals or even organizations that people on the left deem not progressive enough.

Take the recent example of Kyle Duncan; a visiting federal judge at Stanford University who was attacked at a Federalist Club forum by outside student agitators. Protesters refused to let him speak because he was perceived to be "anti-trans," due to a court case that he ruled on in 2020. This is the ruling where the judge would not allow a man, who had been in prison for eight years for child pornography, to change his pronoun officially. *Ergo* the judge was judged as being anti-trans. This action singled out this judge as being the biggest microaggressor these protesters could think of.

*Their* aggression was amplified by an associate dean with oversight responsibility for the forum, who was at the event and was supposed to be monitoring it. Heck, she even joined in the fray. *Microaggression meets aggression.*

The issue of transgender men competing in women's sport leagues is an important one, as women are not only losing to men, who are physically stronger and taller, women are also getting injured in the process. When professional swimmer Riley Gaines was violently attacked at San Francisco State University because she criticized women's sports leagues for allowing men to compete with women, the response of the university was as follows:

Following the mayhem, Jamillah Moore, vice president for Student Affairs & Enrollment Management, emailed students thanking them for taking part in the event.

"It took tremendous bravery to stand in a challenging space," Moore wrote. "I am proud of the moments where we listened and asked insightful questions."

"I am also proud of the moments when our students demonstrated the value of free speech and the right to protest peacefully," she added.

After the statement was tweeted out, Gaines thundered: "I'm sorry did this just say PEACEFUL. . . . I was assaulted. I was extorted and held for ransom."[2]

These examples prove the point that way back in 2015, Dr. Sowell was right in his analysis. The progressive left, including transgender activists, are using the idea of alleged past microaggressions to justify an aggressive response, even violence. This is not acceptable in a civilized society. Let's stop with the nonsense and get back to being sensible. That means, rejecting propaganda and the faux claims of microaggression and aggressors to stymie free speech.

Let's not, as a society, tolerate the weaponization of words aimed to oppress one side over the other. Let's stop these micro-*oppressions* and get back to the idea that we don't have to all share the same ideology, but we do have to follow the rule of law, and using lawfare to include "microaggressions" as defamation is not an acceptable strategy from the progressive left. Nor is weaponizing perfectly acceptable verbiage as microaggressions. Particularly when that weaponization takes the form of an attack on Judeo-Christian values.

Claims of micro-slights by those who wish to control the narrative are actively seeking to constrain the Overton window of acceptable discourse by restricting free speech and people's ability to earn a living. This is not okay.

After all, if a word has the preface "micro" attached to it, how important can it be?

# CHAPTER 20
## Mass Formation, Propaganda, and the Hidden Global Coup

**Mass formation** is, in essence, a kind of group hypnosis that destroys individuals' ethical self-awareness and robs them of their ability to think critically. Mass formation within a population can happen suddenly. So, a "society saturated with individualism and rationalism suddenly tilts toward the radically opposite condition, toward radically irrational collectivism."[1]

**Mass formation psychosis** describes an individual who is under the spell of mass formation. Although this term is not found in the Diagnostic and Statistical Manual of Mental Disorders (DSM-5), we believe it is just a matter of time before this amendment is included.

Knowledge of the theory and practical implementation of mass formation psychology can and is being used by propagandists, governments, and the World Economic Forum to sway large groups of people to act to benefit the propagandists' objectives. Although a major crisis of some sort can be extremely useful for propagandists to take advantage of various situations (war, hyperinflation, or public health, for example), these psychological theories can and often are applied even without strong evidence of a compelling crisis. For this to be effective, the leader must be sufficiently compelling.

According to Dr. Mattias Desmet, author of the book *The Psychology of Totalitarianism*, mass formation could be described as the hypnosis, or the madness, of crowds, which can account for the strange phenomenon of about 20–30 percent of the population in the Western world becoming entranced with the noble lies and dominant narrative. With mass hypnosis, one observes that a large fraction of the population cannot process new scientific data and facts. Such as what happened concerning the safety and effectiveness of the pseudo-mRNA "vaccines" being used against COVID-19, which causes people's bodies to make large amounts of biologically active coronavirus spike protein. Mass formation also occurred within a large segment of the population worldwide regarding the effectiveness and adverse impacts of mandatory mask use and lockdowns. These lies were propagated and enforced by politicians, science bureaucrats, pharmaceutical companies, and legacy media alike.

These hypnotized by this process are unable to recognize the lies and misrepresentations they are being bombarded with on a daily basis and actively attack anyone who has the temerity to share information with them, which contradicts the propaganda that they have come to embrace. And for those whose families and social networks have been torn apart by this process, and who find that close relatives and friends have ghosted them because they question the officially endorsed "truth" and are actually following the scientific literature, this can be a source of deep anguish, sorrow, and psychological pain.

A brief overview of mass formation:

## CROWD PSYCHOSIS

The conditions to set up mass formation psychosis include lack of social connectedness and sensemaking as well as large amounts of latent anxiety and passive aggression. When people are inundated with a narrative that presents a plausible "object of anxiety" and strategy for coping with it, then many individuals group together to battle the object with a collective single-mindedness. This allows people to stop focusing on their own problems, avoiding personal mental anguish. Instead, they focus all their thought and energy on this new object.

As mass formation progresses, the group becomes increasingly bonded and connected. Their field of attention is narrowed and they become unable to consider alternative points of view. Leaders of the movement are revered, unable to do no wrong.

Left unabated, a society under the spell of mass formation will support a totalitarian governance structure capable of otherwise unthinkable atrocities in order to maintain compliance. A note: mass formation is different from groupthink. There are easy ways to fix groupthink by just bringing in dissenting voices and making sure you give them platforms. It isn't so easy with mass formation. Even when the narrative falls apart, cracks in the strategy clearly aren't solving the issue, the hypnotized crowd can't break free of the narrative. This is what appears to be happening now with COVID-19. The solution for those in control of the narrative is to produce bigger and bigger lies to prop up the solution. Those being controlled by mass formation no longer are able to use reason to break free of the group narrative.[2]

Of course, the obvious example of mass formation is Germany in the 1930s and 40s. How could the German people, who were highly educated, very liberal in the classic sense; western thinking people . . . how could they go so crazy and do what they did to the Jews? How could this happen? To a civilized people? A leader of a mass formation movement will use the platform to continue to pump the group with new information to focus on.

Studies suggest that mass formation follows a general distribution:

- 30 percent are brainwashed, hypnotized, indoctrinated by the group narrative
- 40 percent in the middle are persuadable and may follow if no worthy alternative is perceived
- 30 percent fight against the narrative

Those who rebel and fight against the narrative become the enemy of the brainwashed and a primary target of aggression. In this day and age, that can translate into targets becoming victims of cyberstalking, gang stalking, bots, trolls, swatting, and the like.

One of the best ways to counter mass formation is for those against the narrative to continue to speak out against it, which serves to help break the hypnosis of some in the brainwashed group as well as persuade the persuadable middle to choose reason over mindlessness.

It is thought that for something as big as COVID-19, the only way to break the mass formation psychosis was to give the crowd something bigger to focus on. The Ukrainian and now the Israeli wars appear to be the antidote that broke the COVID-19 mass hypnosis.

Mass formation requires that four conditions be met. These are 1) Overall sense of loneliness and lack of social connections and bonds: Individuals must feel disconnected and isolated from others. 2) Lack of meaning: People must experience unsatisfying and purposeless "bullshit jobs" that don't provide a sense of fulfillment or direction. 3) Free-floating anxiety and discontent: This stems from the loneliness and lack of meaning, creating a pervasive sense of unease and dissatisfaction. 4) Manifestation of frustration and aggression: As anxiety builds, individuals must express their frustration and anger in some way. 5) Emergence of a consistent narrative: A dominant narrative, often promoted by government officials, mass media, and other influential sources, must emerge and exploit the frustration and anxiety, providing a sense of explanation and direction for the masses. These conditions create an environment in which people become receptive to mass formation, characterized by a collective trance-like state, where individuals surrender their critical thinking and autonomy to the dominant narrative.[3]

One example of mass formation involved the almost global acceptance of cloth and dust masks used by the general population for three years during the COVIDcrisis. Because Fauci and his acolytes at the CDC insisted that masks work, public acceptance of a very intrusive element in people's lives was almost universal. The mass formation was so strong that there are countless examples of non-compliant individuals being attacked in shops, public spaces, and even outdoors for not wearing a mask. Data demonstrating the lack of effectiveness of masks for preventing the spread of the SARS-CoV-2 virus[4,5] were largely ignored by those who have become hypnotized by the mass formation process. Even the logic of masking children was accepted without question despite the clear and compelling evidence of both psychological and physical harm associated with chronic mask usage for both children and adults.[6,7,8,9] The government went out of its way to ensure that sources of information regarding the inefficiency of mask use to combat respiratory infections was hidden from public view.

Paul Joseph Goebbels was the chief German propagandist for the Nazi Party from 1933 to 1945. He was arguably the creator of the concept that the state can control people by introducing propaganda into the news to enable the state-based control of entire populations. Goebbels's wicked brilliance was to exploit racism as a tool to promote German nationalism to the point of mobilizing and motivating Germany to engage in a globalized war for political, military, and economic dominance. His writings and speeches on propaganda have been studied by leaders and governments ever since.

Goebbels applied the theories behind what is now described by Dr. Mattias Desmet as mass formation (psychosis) to practical politics within a nation-state.[10] Academic writings concerning the formation of a "mass" or a crowd, otherwise known as mass formation, was an accepted discipline during the time when Goebbels was developing his insights, with many scholars including Gustave Le Bon (1841–1931), Freud, McDougal, and Canetti being leading intellectual contributors to his thinking.

Le Bon, a French social psychologist, is often seen as the founder of the study of crowd (group) psychology. Le Bon defined a crowd as a group of individuals united by a common idea, belief, or ideology, and he believed when an individual becomes part of a crowd, he or she undergoes a profound psychological transformation. The individual ceases to think independently and instead relies on the group synthesis of a set of simplified ideas. According to this theory, crowd formation (mass formation) requires a set of simplified ideas that the group incorporates, at which point an individual who has become integrated into the group ceases to psychologically exist as an independent mind and functionally becomes hypnotized.

Le Bon maintained that a group typically forms around an influential idea that unites a number of individuals, and this idea then propels the group (or mass) to act toward a common goal. However, he also concluded that these influential ideas are never created by members of the crowd. Instead, they are most often given to the crowd by a leader or set of leaders. According to Le Bon, in order for an idea to unite and influence a crowd, it must first be dumbed down to the level that the entire crowd can understand it. It must be easily understood by all within the crowd.

Just to provide a current example, a scientific discipline could develop a new type of vaccine as a solution to a public health crisis. That complex research and resulting technology may have required decades of effort. On average, the crowd as a whole would be incapable of comprehending such complex theories or technologies, so socially engineering acceptance of the vaccine (by a crowd or mass) would require this new concept for vaccination to be thoroughly simplified before the idea could become the focus of a hypnotic, single-minded belief in the solution (the new type of vaccine). Le Bon proposed that this is where group leaders come in. Under the Le Bon model, the leader of a crowd (for example, someone like Fauci) will enable this process by distilling these complicated concepts (or technologies) down to a small set of simplified ideas that the crowd can accept, incorporate, and act upon as their own. One of the most important elements of this is the requirement for a "trusted leader" to be accepted by the crowd. Once a crowd truly accepts a leader, it is almost impossible for them to reject that leader, whether or not the lies that he or she may tell are actually done with "noble" intent or purpose.

Over the last few years, we have seen clear evidence that our government, as well as those of Great Britain and many other Western democracies, have learned to actively apply the lessons of Gustave Le Bon and Joseph Goebbels quite well.

Going back in time, in a book titled *Propaganda and Persuasion*, historians Jowett and O'Donnell wrote about Hitler's basic principles of propaganda, which were based upon Goebbels's work and advice. They are:

Hitler's Basic Principles (abstracted from *Propaganda and Persuasion*[11]).

- Avoid abstract ideas - appeal to the emotions.
- Constantly repeat just a few ideas. Use stereotyped phrases.
- Give only one side of the argument.
- Continuously criticize your opponents.
- Pick out one special "enemy" for special vilification.

In looking back over the last two years, it is clear that each of these core principles has been deployed against us. In particular, these tactics have been deployed against "anti-vaxxer" physicians, scientists, and lawyers who have been speaking out against the totalitarian practices of Western governments, CDC and WHO-approved narratives (which we now know were actually yet more propaganda), discussing early treatment, trying to examine or explore the data concerning vaccine adverse events or the logic of universal vaccination. During the *Joe Rogan Experience* podcast #1757 with Dr. Robert Malone, Robert cited Nazi Germany as an example of "mass formation psychosis" and in retrospect, it was absolutely appropriate. He was actually being quite conservative by not going further with that example.

Unfortunately, both national and world governmental organizations have learned more than just the lessons of mass psychosis and propaganda. World governments and large financial interests have now united to produce harmonized propaganda through a wide variety of media outlets, such as Big Tech, social media, and mainstream media. We have entered a new era of total thought control exerted on a global scale, which is often referred to as psychological operations or psyops.

Before proceeding further, it is important to provide examples to illustrate what is happening in modern psyops operations and PsyWar led by governments, nongovernmental organizations, and global forums such as the United Nations, World Health Organization, and World Economic Forum.

## Helpful Examples of Psyops Operations:

- Operation Mockingbird: Operation Mockingbird was organized by Allen Dulles and Cord Meyer in 1950. The CIA spent about $1 billion a year in today's dollars, hiring journalists from corporate media, including CBS, the *New York Times*, ABC, NBC, *Newsweek*, Associated Press, and others, to promote their point of view. The original operation reportedly involved some 3,000 CIA operatives and hired over 400 journalists. In 1976, the domestic operation supposedly closed, but less than half of the media operatives were let go. Furthermore, documentary evidence shows that much of the Operation Mockingbird was offshored at that time. It is rumored that British Intelligence picked up many of the duties of Operation Mockingbird on behalf of the US intelligence community.[12]
- The Trusted News Initiative (TNI): is a British Broadcasting Corporation (BBC)-led organization that has been actively censoring eminent doctors, academics, and those with dissenting voices

that contravene the official COVID-19 narrative as well as other narratives, such as voter fraud, elections, and current news not sanctioned by government.

Anything contrary to the government narrative is considered disinformation or misinformation and will be deleted, suppressed, or deplatformed. In the case of COVID-19, misinformation and disinformation are considered anything not aligned with the World Health Organization and/or the regional Public Health Authority-approved "truth." In the case of the United States, that "truth" is established by Anthony Fauci, the CDC, and the FDA. The TNI uses advocacy journalism and journals to promote their causes. The Trusted News Initiative is more than this though; if you go back to Hitler's basic principles, the members of the TNI are using these core principles to control the public. The known TNI partners include: Associated Press, AFP; BBC, CBC/Radio-Canada, European Broadcasting Union (EBU), Facebook (whose founders fund articles being written for *The Atlantic*), *Financial Times*, First Draft, Google, *The Hindu*, Microsoft, *New York Times*, Reuters, Reuters Institute for the Study of Journalism, Twitter, YouTube, the *Wall Street Journal*, and the *Washington Post*.

Some of the early egregious actions by the TNI were described in a blog post by Trusted News Initiative founder and past Director Jessica Cecil,[13] where she wrote:

"We have been sharing alerts over COVID-19, and before that, over falsities which posed a threat to democratic integrity during the UK and Taiwan Elections. And now we are sharing alerts over the most serious disinformation in two very different elections—in the US and in Myanmar. And because different news organizations are most relevant in different regions, we are working with a wide and expanding group of publishers."

- The World Economic Forum (WEF): is one of the key think-tanks and meeting places for the management of global capitalism, and is arguably coherent enough to qualify as the leading global "deep state" organization. Under the leadership of professor Klaus Schwab, it has played an increasingly important role in coordinating the globalized hegemony of large pools of transnational capital and associated large corporations over western democracies during the last three decades. Many of its members were active in using COVID-19 to carry out a "Great Reset" (as described in the writings of Klaus Schwab) to dispossess and implement digital tracking and control of people as a step toward what many believe will institute a techno-feudalism as well as the WEF objective of a fourth industrial revolution incorporating technologies collectively referred to as "transhumanism." Genetic mRNA vaccines have been identified by both Western governments as well as the WEF as a first step toward an inevitable "transhumanism" agenda.

- Social credit systems: China's social credit system is a combination of government and business surveillance that gives citizens a "score" that can restrict the ability of individuals or corporations to function in the modern world by limiting purchases, and the ability to acquire property or take out loans based on past behaviors. Of course, how one uses the internet directly impacts the social credit score. This is the origin of the social credit system that appears to be evolving in the United States. Environmental, social, and governance (ESG) metrics are a kind of social credit system designed to coerce businesses—and, by extension, individuals and all of society—to transform their practices, behaviors and thinking. Many government leaders in US who have been trained by the WEF Young Leaders or Influencers programs are pushing this scoring system and actively promoting the idea in the US. Already, financial institutions such as PayPal and GoFundMe, as well as some more mainstream banking systems, are actively deciding who can use their services based on a social credit scoring system.[14]

- WEF Young Leaders Program: is a five-year World Economic Forum training program that hand-picks individuals most likely to succeed in politics, corporate governance, and as key influential royalty. The WEF helps connect these graduates with leaders and capital to ensure that they rise in the ranks of national or world politics and/or corporate governance. The training program agenda is kept secret, and it is very rare that a graduate will discuss the program publicly. However, the benefits of global corporatism, combined with social engineering, are main components of the program. The Young Leaders program started in 1992 (under a different name) and has graduated close to 4,000 people. They include a "who's who" of leaders and influencers in politics, Big Tech, media, the pharmaceutical industry, and finance.

**A small subset of the graduates from the Young Leaders Program in the United States include:**

- Politics and Policy: Jeffrey Zients (White House Coronavirus Response Coordinator since 2021), Jeremy Howard (co-founder of lobby group "Masks for All"), California Governor Gavin Newsom, Peter Buttigieg (candidate for US president in 2020, US secretary of transportation since 2021), Chelsea Clinton, Huma Abedin (Hillary Clinton aide), Nikki Haley (US ambassador to the UN, 2017–2018), Samantha Power (US ambassador to the UN, 2013–2017, USAID Administrator, since 2021), Ian Bremmer (founder of Eurasia Group), Bill Browder (US-British financier), Jonathan Soros (son of George Soros), Kenneth Roth (director of Human Rights Watch), Paul Krugman (economist), Lawrence Summers (US Secretary of the Treasury, 1999–2001), Black Lives Matter co-founder Alicia Garza, and Ivanka Trump.

- Legacy Media: CNN medical analyst Leana Wen, CNN Sanjay Gupta, Covid-19 Twitter personality Eric Feigl-Ding, Andrew Ross Sorkin (*New York Times* financial columnist), Thomas Friedman (*New York Times* columnist), George Stephanopoulos (ABC News), Lachlan Murdoch (CEO of Fox Corporation, co-chair of News Corp), Justin Fox (Bloomburg), Anderson Cooper (CNN).

- Technology and Social-Media: Microsoft founder Bill Gates, former Microsoft CEO Steven Ballmer, Jeff Bezos. Google co-founders Sergey Brin and Larry Page, Elon Musk, former Google CEO Eric Schmidt, Wikipedia co-founder Jimmy Wales, PayPal co-founder Peter Thiel, eBay cofounder Pierre Omidyar, Facebook founder and CEO Mark Zuckerberg, Facebook COO Sheryl Sandberg, Moderna CEO Stéphane Bancel, Pfizer CEO Albert Bourla (a WEF Agenda Contributor), and Pfizer VP Vasudha Vats.

Note: When you read about people on this list, please remember that they have been trained by the WEF in their five-year program. These graduates' alliances may not be with the United States but with corporatist globalism and the WEF.

- The Great Reset: is the name of an initiative launched by the World Economic Forum (WEF) and its founder, Klaus Schwab, in June 2020. They are using the cover of anti-COVID-19 measures and an overstated public health crisis, as well as emergencies such as "climate change" to push an agenda to remake the world using stakeholder capitalism (a form of socialism). Peter Koenig, a renowned economist, describes the Great Reset as using the global technocratic biosecurity state (otherwise known as the global public health system) to implement these changes. The end results will mean extensive restrictions on the physical environment around people, a forced digitization, and a loss of bodily autonomy (having a say in your own health decisions).

  On face value, "The Great Reset" is also the title used for the fiftieth annual meeting of the World Economic Forum, which was held during June 2020. The event brought together high-profile business and political leaders, and was convened by Charles, Prince of Wales and the WEF, with the theme of rebuilding society and the economy following the COVID-19 pandemic. The above description is what one finds on your basic search engine and again, but the motives are less than pure. A less flattering definition of The Great Reset would be capitalism with Chinese characteristics: A two-tiered economy, with profitable monopolies and the state on top and socialism for the majority below.

With these basic terms and ideas in our toolbox, let's return to the central topic. In the coordinated propaganda and censorship response to the COVID-19 public health crisis, globalists and corporatists were and are directly incorporating Hitler's own principles for crowd control. If we look closer, we can clearly see coordinated actions by the BBC-led Trusted News Initiative, the Google web, various scientific-technological elite, large financial groups (such as Vanguard, BlackRock, and State Street), and the World Economic Forum acting in real time to suppress a growing awareness by the general public of having been actively manipulated. It is increasingly becoming clear that these organizations and aligned nation-states used crowd psychology tools to generate significant fear and anxiety of COVID-19 to advance their agendas on a global scale. They have used COVID to drive a planned and coordinated agenda, the Great Reset.

Multiple governments have now admitted to actively using fear and "mass formation" related theories as a tool for totalitarian control during this outbreak. These are basically psychological operations aimed at populations of nations. One glaring example has been operating in the UK. A 2021 article published in the *Telegram* titled, "Use of fear to control behaviour in COVIDcrisis was 'totalitarian,' admit scientists Members of Scientific Pandemic Influenza Group on Behaviour express regret about 'unethical' methods" writes:[15]

> Scientists on a committee that encouraged the use of fear to control people's behavior during the COVID pandemic have admitted its work was "unethical" and "totalitarian."
>
> SPI-B (*Scientific Pandemic Influenza Group on Behavior*) warned in March last year that ministers needed to increase "the perceived level of personal threat" from Covid-19 because "a substantial number of people still do not feel sufficiently personally threatened."
>
> Gavin Morgan, a psychologist on the team, said: "Clearly, using fear as a means of control is not ethical. Using fear smacks of totalitarianism. It's not an ethical stance for any modern government. By nature, I am an optimistic person, but all this has given me a more pessimistic view of people."

Of course, all of this has been occurring at the same time that the increasingly weakened COVID-19 variants are destroying the legitimacy of government and WHO propaganda concerning the "safe and effective" mRNA vaccines and associated mandates. In fact, the various "fact-checker" and "advocacy journalists" seem to have doubled down on this form of "digital hate."

Long ago, we warned of the potential public health consequences when the public discovered that the "lab leak hypothesis" had merit, early treatment against COVID-19 was effective, and that the genetic "vaccines" were not completely safe and effective. Instead of coming clean, the propagandists doubled down. And now we know that the vaccine industry, as is public health in general, is corrupted to its core. Furthermore, we have destroyed public trust in physicians, academic medicine, and the entire hospital system. The damage done is going to take decades to rebuild.

As the US government's fifth-gen warfare, censorship, and propaganda machinery jumps from issue to issue, trying to mold the American people into compliance, we cannot just let them move on. We must legally challenge everything they did and are doing to prevent it from happening again. Then, we must begin to reform the educational system so that our children know how to recognize the signs of tyranny in the future.

# CHAPTER 21
## PsyWar Enforcement, US Government, and COVIDcrisis Narratives

*Just got off [an] hour long call with [Senior Advisor to President Biden]*
*Andy Slavitt. . . . [H]e was outraged—not too strong of a word to*
*describe his reaction—that we did not remove this post. . . . I countered*
*that removing content like that would represent a significant incursion*
*into traditional boundaries of free expression in the US but he replied*
*that the post was directly comparing COVID vaccines to asbestos poi-*
*soning in a way which demonstrably inhibits confidence in COVID*
*vaccines amongst those the Biden Administration is trying to reach.*

Sir Nick Clegg, Meta's President of Global Affairs, former
Deputy Prime Minister of the United Kingdom, describing his
efforts to explain the boundaries of the First Amendment to the
Biden White House in April 2021. Internal email from Nick
Clegg to Facebook personnel (Apr. 18, 2021, 9:07 PM)

On May 1, 2024, the Committee on the Judiciary and the Select
Subcommittee on the Weaponization of the Federal Government, US
House of Representatives released an interim report titled "The Censorship-
Industrial Complex: How Top Biden White House Officials Coerced Big
Tech to Censor Americans, True Information, and Critics of the Biden
Administration." This report provides over eight hundred pages (not includ-
ing supplements) of detailed information documenting censorship advo-
cacy transactions and interactions between the Biden administration and

a variety of social media providers. The report and supporting appendices document close cooperation in censoring speech relating to COVID policies and criticism of the Biden administration, involving the White House and Facebook, YouTube, and Amazon, and cite documents previously released concerning Twitter (now "X").[1]

Of note is that executive branch COVID-related censorship activities began occurring as early as March 2020, which is when our book *Novel Coronavirus: A Practical Guide for Preparation and Protection* was censored and deplatformed by Amazon publishing for "violating community standards" after White House meetings with Amazon and other media company representatives concerning the need to control information concerning SARS-CoV-2.[2,3,4]

The following text includes excerpts from the committee's findings, with slight modifications to depoliticize some of the language.

The report details the successful months-long campaign by the White House to coerce large companies, namely Meta (parent company of Facebook), Alphabet (parent company of YouTube), and Amazon, to censor books, videos, posts, and other content online. By the end of 2021, Facebook, YouTube, and Amazon changed their content moderation policies in ways that were directly responsive to criticism from the Biden administration.

While the White House's pressure campaign largely succeeded, its effects were devastating. By suppressing free speech and intentionally distorting public debate in the modern town square, ideas and policies were no longer fairly tested and debated on their merits. Instead, policymakers implemented a series of public health measures that proved to be disastrous for the country. From unnecessary extended school closures to unconstitutional vaccine mandates that forced workers to take a newly developed vaccine or risk losing their jobs, the Biden administration and other officials needlessly imposed harm and suffering on Americans across the country.

Ongoing litigation and the publication of the Twitter Files following Elon Musk's acquisition of the company began to provide some insight into the behind-the-scenes efforts of the Biden White House to censor political opponents and disfavored views. For example, on just the third day of the Biden administration, the White House emailed Twitter (now X) personnel to demand that a tweet by Robert F. Kennedy, Jr. be "removed ASAP."[5] The directive was not limited to just Kennedy; in the same email, the Biden

White House asked Twitter to also "keep an eye out for tweets that fall in this same genre."[6]

But the most important documents to understanding the Biden White House's censorship efforts have proven to be internal emails from the companies on the receiving end of White House threats and coercion. After issuing dozens of subpoenas to Big Tech, government agencies, and relevant third parties, the Committee on the Judiciary and Select Subcommittee on the Weaponization of the Federal Government began to obtain tens of thousands of documents illustrating the details of the Biden White House's pressure campaign. Obtaining key internal company communications—often including the highest levels of company leadership—took additional escalatory measures from the Committee and Select Subcommittee, including threats to hold Meta CEO Mark Zuckerberg in contempt of Congress.[7,8]

## Censorship and Policy Enforcement-Related Actions Taken by the Administration Included the Following:

- **Big Tech changed their content moderation policies because of Biden White House pressure.** In the weeks and months following the start of the White House pressure campaign, Facebook, YouTube, and Amazon all changed their content moderation policies. The White House pressured companies to censor information that did not violate their content moderation policies at the time. The best evidence to assess why content moderation policies were changed is to review relevant email correspondence and other documents at the time of the policy change. Both Facebook and Amazon referred to the administration's efforts as "pressure." Key documents obtained by subpoena which demonstrate this pressure campaign[9] include the following:
  - In March 2021, an Amazon employee emailed others within the company about the reason for the Amazon bookstore's new content moderation policy change: "[T]he impetus for this request is criticism from the Biden Administration about sensitive books we're giving prominent placement to."
  - In March 2021, just one day prior to a scheduled call with the White House, an Amazon employee explained how changes to

Amazon's bookstore policies were being applied "due to criticism from the Biden people."

- In July 2021, when Facebook executive Nick Clegg asked a Facebook employee why the company censored the man-made theory of the SARS-CoV-2 virus, the employee responded: "Because we were under pressure from the [Biden] administration and others to do more. . . . We shouldn't have done it."

- In August 2021, an internal Facebook email explained why the company was developing, and ultimately implementing, new content moderation policies: "[Facebook's] Leadership asked Misinfo Policy . . . to brainstorm some additional policy levers we can pull to be more aggressive against . . . misinformation. This is stemming from the continued criticism of our approach from the [Biden] administration."

- In September 2021, after receiving months of criticism for not censoring non-violative content, YouTube shared with the Biden White House a new "policy proposal" to censor more content criticizing the safety and efficacy of vaccines, asking for "any feedback" the White House could provide before the policy had been finalized. The White House responded: "at first blush, seems like a great step."

- **The White House's censorship campaign targeted true information, satire, and other content that did not violate the platforms' policies.** Contrary to claims of wanting to combat alleged so-called "misinformation" and foreign disinformation, the Biden Administration pressured the companies to censor true information, satire, memes, opinions, and Americans' personal experiences.

  - For example, internal July 2021 Facebook emails show that Facebook understood that the Biden White House's position as wanting "negative information on or opinions about the vaccine" removed as well as "humorous or satirical content that suggests the vaccine isn't safe."

  - The same set of emails also noted that "The Surgeon General wants us to remove true information about side effects."

- **The White House's censorship campaign had a chilling effect on other speech.** In February 2021, Facebook increased its censorship of several topics— including those related to the origin of the SARS-CoV-2 virus—as part of a general response to the Biden White House's pressure to "do more." After a few months it became clear that the Biden White House's focus was on alleged vaccine misinformation. In May 2021, Facebook stopped removing content about the lab leak theory, which even parts of the Biden administration consider true today. Zuckerberg privately told top Facebook officials that "[t]his seems like a good reminder that when we compromise our standards due to pressure from an administration in either direction, we'll often regret it later."
- **The White House had leverage because the companies had other policy concerns involving the Biden administration**.
  - In July 2021, Facebook executive Clegg emailed others in the company that "[g]iven the bigger fish we have to fry with the [Biden] Administration," Facebook should try to think creatively about "how we can be responsive to [the administration's] concerns."
  - In April 2021, YouTube's Public Policy team emailed YouTube's Product team that having the Product team brief the Biden White House would be "hugely beneficial" because the company was "seek[ing] to work closely with [the Biden] administration on multiple policy fronts."
- **The White House pushed censorship of books, not just social media.** The pressure campaign was not limited to just social media companies, but also the world's biggest online bookstore, Amazon.

The parallels for the three companies are striking. In each case, the companies identified the Biden White House's censorship requests as "pressure" or noted a fear that things could "spiral out of control."[10] And while there is a difference in how long and in what ways each company succumbed to the White House's pressure, by September 2021, Facebook, YouTube, and Amazon had each adopted new content moderation policies that removed or reduced viewpoints and content disfavored by the White House.

## The Facebook Files

In February 2021, Facebook increased its censorship of anti-vaccine content as well as the lab leak theory of the origin of the virus because of "tense conversations with the new [Biden] Administration" and as part of an effort to be responsive to the Biden White House's exhortations to "do more" to combat alleged misinformation. After a few months, Facebook realized the White House cared more about censoring anti-vaccine content and so the company lifted its censorship of the lab-leak theory. In response, Zuckerberg said the mistake served as a reminder to not "compromise our standards due to pressure from an administration."

But Facebook continued to face continued pressure from the Biden administration to censor content questioning vaccines, including true information, satire, memes, and other lawful content that is constitutionally protected and not violative of Facebook's content moderation policies. In July 2021, tensions hit a fever pitch, with President Biden publicly accusing Facebook of "killing people." Noting that they had "bigger fish to fry" with the Biden Administration, such as issues related to "data flows," senior Facebook officials decided in August 2021 to enact new content moderation policies that would censor more anti-vaccine content. An internal August 2021 email states plainly that the decision "stemm[ed] from the continued criticism of our approach from the [Biden] administration."

## The YouTube Files

In the spring of 2021, the Biden White House increased pressure on YouTube to remove and reduce alleged misinformation, including "borderline content"—i.e., content that did not violate YouTube's policies. Internally, YouTube asked its Product team to brief the White House directly because the company feared the situation could "potentially spiral out of control." Throughout the summer, the White House continued to press YouTube about its policies and enforcement, sometimes asking why particular videos were not removed or otherwise demoted. In September 2021, as YouTube prepared to finalize a new policy "proposal" to censor content that questioned the safety or efficacy of vaccines, YouTube emailed the White House in advance for its "feedback." After the policy was announced, the White House privately praised the expanded censorship as a "great step."

# The Amazon Files

On March 2, 2021, the Biden White House emailed the vice president of public policy at Amazon, asking to have a discussion regarding the "high levels of propaganda and misinformation and disinformation at Amazon." To support their allegations, multiple members of the Biden White House ran keyword searches on Amazon for "vaccines" and emailed screenshots of the search results page to Amazon, noting that just adding a CDC warning would be insufficient to adequately censor the books. Immediately after the initial email outreach from the White House, Amazon internally accelerated its consideration of implementing a new policy that would disfavor anti-vaccine books. Internal talking points prepared by Amazon included the question: "Is the [Biden] Admin asking us to remove books, or are they more concerned about search results/order (or both)?" On March 9, just one week after the initial outreach from White House official Andy Slavitt and the same day as the company's scheduled meeting with the White House, Amazon implemented a new policy that added the "Do Not Promote" label for anti-vaccine books.

The First Amendment prohibits the US government from "abridging the freedom of speech." Thus, "any law or government policy that reduces that freedom on the [social media] platforms . . . violates the First Amendment." To inform potential legislation, the Committee and Select Subcommittee have been investigating the Executive Branch's collusion with third party intermediaries to censor speech. The Committee and Select Subcommittee have uncovered other serious violations of the First Amendment throughout the Executive Branch during the Biden Administration. The Committee and the Select Subcommittee are responsible for investigating "violation[s] of the civil liberties of citizens of the United States." In accordance with this mandate, this interim staff report on the Biden White House's violations of the First Amendment and other unconstitutional activities continues to fulfill the obligation to identify and report on the weaponization of the federal government against American citizens.

Even this brief summary provides a clear example of how modern PsyWar can readily be operationally deployed in an occult, nontransparent manner. Those who take the time to read the report and appendices will gain a richer understanding of how the intersection of government interests and business interests can be exploited (in either direction) to justify and power the deployment of PsyWar against the citizens of any nation or transnational alliance to advance either the political interests of a ruling political party, the business interests of a corporation, or both.

# PART IV
# THE RISE OF TECHNO-TOTALITARIANISM

*From the White House to the mainstream media, free speech and those public figures who utilize it are under attack. There are many new strategies and some old, who are using pysops to gain authoritarian control. One new way they are controlling the populace is through what is known as a state of exception.*

*A state of exception is similar to a state of emergency but based on the sovereign's ability to transcend the rule of law in the name of the public good. How different is this really from psychological bioterrorism, which is the use of fear about a disease to manipulate individuals or populations by governments and other organizations, such as Big Pharma?*

*Is a state of exception just another noble lie to keep us all uninformed of the PsyWar campaign being conducted to control every aspect of our lives?*

*This is a direct assault by our government and the globalists on our rights as individuals. How far do they have to go before we fight back?*

# CHAPTER 22
# Rogue Agencies and the COVID Truth Seekers

## What, Me Worry?

Late one Saturday night, we were woken up by a series of telephone calls from Romania, which we didn't answer. The person called again at 7:00 a.m. on Sunday morning—again, we didn't answer. Again, a phone call from the same number midmorning. This time, Robert picked up the phone. The call was from a Romanian woman informing Robert that he needed to be very careful because she had evidence that the CIA was monitoring him (no surprise there) and that she herself was under surveillance and had at some point been subjected to a CIA rendition program. We are not sure why a CIA employee would be interested in capturing a Romanian woman or what evidence she could possibly have from Romania about Robert . . . but there it is. Her key point apparently was that Robert needed to be careful. We can certainly get behind the logic that Robert's electronic communication and various travels are being monitored. We have had repeated advice (and agreement!) on that topic from a wide range of senior security professionals.

We get these kinds of calls, messages, and handwritten letters (even packages) fairly frequently. Calls from people who believe that DARPA has placed an implant in their head, or that 5G has implanted memories that aren't theirs, or that the government is poisoning them, or that they were abducted by aliens. There are lots and lots of people who truly believe that the government has harmed or is out to harm them. We have received a lot of strange phone calls over the past few of years. However, since January 2020 we have all seen so many things which have been denied or attacked by corporate media and government officials that have turned out to have been true that it has become harder and harder to determine the difference between a "conspiracy theory" and actual conspiracies!

Being a little famous (or is that infamous?), Robert expects that many people contact him because they have become a bit crazed by the fearporn and propaganda, are a lot lonely, or are very angry at what they have been through or wish to frighten me. It seems to be part of the territory. We don't need to get into their personal stories—but we believe that treating everyone with respect and empathy is important. We try to be polite and empathetic but not allow such people to take up too much of our time or headspace. We also do not allow ourselves to get too frightened or paranoid. We are lucky in that we live on a farm that is pretty isolated, have some really scary dogs, good neighbors, and when needed, security.

But this caller—well, it made us think. Maybe because of the urgency and frequency of the calls over the course of the weekend, or maybe that it was because she was not from the United States, or maybe it the intensity of her voice. But she struck a nerve.

Of course, the government is monitoring Robert. We have been told this through backdoor channels more than once (and we don't believe that either of us is crazy). Pegasus (and Pegasus 2) spyware is real, and we most likely have had it installed on our phones. Robert's phone, in particular, has long pauses, clicks, and noise—too often for coincidence. But the bottom line is that we don't have anything to hide, we are not criminals, and we can't stop the government from being the government. We can't stop them from spying on us. By the way, we hate when state-sponsored media use the word "monitor" for what our government is engaged in. It is spying on Americans—let us stop sugarcoating it.

We know that Twitter and LinkedIn ended Robert's accounts because the US government told them to. How do we know this? Because the evidence is clear-cut. Both corporations cut Robert off without a literally given reason, other than violating "community standards," if that, within forty-eight hours of each other in December 2021—just a day before the Joe Rogan interview with Robert went live. Both were permanent bans. Twitter reinstated Robert at the end of 2022 after Elon Musk bought

Twitter, but LinkedIn never did. Robert is still banned from that platform years later. That is not the "normal" procedure for going "against" community standards. The very mention of Robert's name or links to his Substack articles gets people shadow-banned on the Meta channels and TikTok. And most damning is the evidence that the government is colluding in "private-public" (fascist) deals with Big Tech to censor people like Robert.[1]

In fact, then–White House Press Secretary Jen Psaki admitted in 2021 that the White House has been working with Facebook to flag down "problematic posts" written by Americans, which she described as "misinformation."

> Psaki disclosed the government's role in policing social media during her daily press briefing after Surgeon General Vivek Murthy called on companies to purge more pandemic posts.
>
> The demand for censorship—and Psaki's admission of government involvement—follows a series of flip-flops from health officials who contradicted themselves throughout the pandemic on issues such as mask efficacy, as well as censorship of claims that later gained credibility, such as the theory that COVID-19 leaked from a Chinese lab.
>
> "We are in regular touch with the social media platforms and those engagements typically happen through members of our senior staff and also members of our COVID-19 team—given as Dr. Murthy conveyed, this is a big issue, of misinformation, specifically on the pandemic," Psaki said.
>
> She added: "We've increased disinformation research and tracking within the Surgeon General's Office. We are flagging problematic posts for Facebook that spread disinformation."
>
> Psaki added, "it's important to take faster action against harmful posts . . . and Facebook needs to move more quickly to remove harmful violative posts."[2]

So, here we are. Stronger and more resilient after being censored, slandered, and harassed by our government for four years now. And yes, the state-sponsored media has censored, slandered, and harassed Robert. But we have a moral compass, a strong marriage, the benefit of decades of experience in the rough and tumble of working with both the government and the medical-pharmaceutical-industrial complex, and we can both take it. We only wish to see our public health system and, now, our government behave according to traditional Judeo-Christian ethical and constitutional norms. The lessons learned from the pandemic are that our government is not ready for the next outbreak. That the medical-pharmaceutical industrial complex is sickening Americans. The global elitists, many of whom are embedded in our own government, have taken over the hidden levers of power in the United States through the processes of inverted totalitarianism and have weaponized public health.

"Saving the world," or some small part of it means being brave. All of us need to be brave. Robert Malone is not the only person in this battle—many of us are now working to save the United States from itself and outside influences. We are proud to know lots of superheroes working and standing with us. True American patriots.

Those of us critical of the pseudo-mRNA vaccines, mandatory vaccination, lock-ups, masking policies, pandemic public health policies, censorship, and propaganda have been censored, slandered, and harassed. This also true of the January 6 dissenters, or those who have spoken out against election fraud. The list of people getting special governmental treatment for one thought crime or another now goes on and on. Heck, a Congressional report documents that our own government even censored Robert for being "Right-wing."[3]

The question is how are the dissenters, which the Department of Homeland Security have often deemed as domestic terrorists, being spied on? What agencies? How? What? When? Where?

Do they monitor us through our public writings and speeches, on our phones (Pegasus?), cameras, tracking, and by data mining our transactions and bank accounts? We know that the CIA is illegally "monitoring" American citizens. But the American people are not allowed to know how many people are being spied upon, for what "crimes," or how this monitoring is occurring and why.

You are about to witness an enormous political debate in which the spy agencies and their apologists on TV tell you this is normal and OK and the CIA doesn't know how many Americans are in the database or even how they got there anyway. But it is not OK.

—Edward Snowden[4]

A recent newspaper article published by *The Guardian* entitled "Declassified documents reveal CIA has been sweeping up information on Americans: Civil liberties watchdogs condemn agency's collection of domestic data without congressional or court approval or oversight," shows that the CIA has been secretly collecting Americans' private information in bulk.[5]

Two Democrats on the Senate Intelligence Committee exposed the surveillance program in February 2022. Senators Ron Wyden of Oregon and Martin Heinrich of New Mexico allege, in an official letter sent to the CIA, that the agency has long concealed its domestic spying from the public and Congress.

Wyden and Heinrich requested the declassification of a report by the Privacy and Civil Liberties Oversight Board on a CIA bulk collection program, in a letter sent April 13, 2021. The letter, which was declassified and made public today reveals that "the CIA has secretly conducted its own bulk program," authorized under Executive Order 12333, rather than the laws passed by Congress.

The letter notes that the program was:

> "entirely outside the statutory framework that Congress and the public believe govern this collection, and without any of the judicial, congressional or even executive branch oversight that comes from [Foreign Intelligence Surveillance Act] collection . . .
>
> FISA gets all the attention because of the periodic congressional reauthorizations and the release of DOJ, ODNI and FISA Court documents," said Senators Wyden and Heinrich in response to the newly declassified documents. "But what these documents demonstrate is that many of the same concerns that Americans have about their privacy and civil liberties also apply to how the CIA collects and handles information under executive order and outside the FISA law. In particular, these documents reveal serious problems associated with warrantless backdoor searches of Americans, the same issue that has generated bipartisan concern in the FISA context."[6]

Of course, it is perfectly legal for the FBI and now the CIA, to spy on Americans, and those powers have recently been reauthorized in the Patriot Act by Congress and the reauthorization of the FISA warrant system in 2024. These programs allow law enforcement agencies such as the FBI, CIA, and DHS to continue to look through the browsing history of American citizens without needing a warrant or to notify. The faked Russiagate scandal and then the COVIDcrisis have been used to usher in new surveillance measures, as well as new definitions as to what is a domestic terrorist. Hint: being critical of the public health response can now be considered an act of domestic terrorism by the US government.[7]

Computers, smartphones, and smart speakers armed with microphones, cameras, and tracking abilities all have the ability to track and monitor what we write, where we go, everything we say, contacts for our friends and family, and who we meet. Pegasus even has the ability to turn on video cameras and microphones. Recently, it has been revealed that smart thermostats are equipped with the ability to spy on us in our very own homes and can even be hacked by others to listen in.[8] Home security systems have been hacked to spy on children and even lure them into conversations.

The US Constitution supposedly safeguards the rights of Americans to privacy and personal autonomy. But here we are. Congress has utterly failed at making privacy a reality for many Americans, and we do not have any way to know who or for what reason we are being watched.

It doesn't feel particularly good to think of the US government listening in on our private life. It certainly feels like a major intrusion.

Where does it end? How will this information being collected on Robert and all of us be used in the future? What happens when there is a data leak? Has there been a data leak? Who would inform us? Somehow, we doubt the FBI, DHS, and the CIA would!

About a decade ago, Robert held an active security clearance. To get that clearance, Robert had to answer many questions on *Form 86* about his and our personal lives, which he answered honestly. *Form 86* is a 127-page document that delves into intimate questions about prior brushes with the law, drug use, psychiatric health, and info on friends and family members. It requires the applicant to put his or her Social Security number on nearly every page of the document.

Questions frankly, that were mostly nobody's business but Robert's own. Certainly not some bureaucrat's business in DC. The government then placed his answers on a cloud-based server somewhere. A while later, Robert was informed through a letter sent through the US Postal Service, that government security had been breached and his personal data had been leaked. To make up for the breach, the government offered him the opportunity to get credit reporting access, credit monitoring, and recovery services for a year as if credit monitoring and recovery services would somehow absolve the government of recklessly collecting personal information that could be leaked to a foreign country. The whole experience left him with a lingering sense of being used and violated. Subsequent news reports then linked the hacking attack to China. So now, in the face of Robert being labeled a domestic terrorist, we also know that foreign governments around the world know more about Robert than most of our family and friends do. This is not a comfortable feeling.

There have been enough cloud-based hacks and backdoor data collection bots to think that it is only a matter of time before those of us whose personal lives have been completely upended by government spying will see that data being used by state-sponsored media, hackers, corporations such as medical and insurance companies, and foreign governments for nefarious purposes.

An early case study of this happening was what happened to Jeff Bezos. Saudi Crown Prince Mohammed bin Salman (MBS) placed Pegasus on Bezos's phone during a WhatsApp conversation. MBS probably wanted to spy on what Jamal Khashoggi, who was a reporter for the *Washington Post*, was going to publish next about the kingdom. As we all know, later MBS organized the assignation of Mr. Khashoggi. Pegasus was also placed on the phone of Jamal Khashoggi's wife by United Arab Emeritis (MSB) and most likely helped in his assassination.

Eventually, *The Enquirer* used the Pegasus data of Bezos's affair to try to blackmail Bezos into stopping the investigation into the origins of Pegasus on his phone. With that, Bezos announced his affair to the world, rather than be blackmailed. This of course, led to his divorce. This is one small case study—of how two phones infected with spyware ultimately led to the death of a reporter, and in the case of Bezos, completely upended his life.

Pegasus has been sold to governments, including our own. Who knows how many phones this spying software has been placed on.

For us personally, we like to think that Robert is not so important that a foreign government would wish to kill him. But on the other hand, somewhere between 250,000 and a million people read our Substack essays daily, and we don't hold back in our writing. Robert's podcasts and TV appearances have reached hundreds of millions of people. So, maybe we are being naive. Maybe it isn't such a good idea that we visit China, France, Egypt, Germany, Canada, or British Columbia in the near term . . .

Knowing our government is most likely actively spying on Robert and directing state-sponsored media to censor, slander, and harass him is certainly upsetting if we think about it too much. This is why Robert never "Googles" himself. Because if he was a paranoid person, he would think they were out to "get him." And of course, our government only has our best interests at heart, right?

This all gets back to why a few phone calls from Romania warning Robert about the CIA can send chills down our backs because there is that tiny chance the threat of harm from our government may just be real.

# CHAPTER 23
# The Very Fabric of This Nation Will Be Torn in Ways That Cannot Be Repaired

*I believe in dangerous freedom over peaceful slavery.*
—Thomas Jefferson[1]

The 2023 leak of Justice's Alito opinion on the landmark abortion case *Dobbs v. Jackson Women's Health Organization* has exacerbated an already existing and organized campaign to attack the Supreme Court's legitimacy, which began years ago. The Supreme Court has grown more conservative recently, and as it has done, so the political Left has increased criticism of the legitimacy of the court. This criticism has included targeted character assassination of individual judges. The *Wall Street Journal* reports:

> Justice Alito says "this type of concerted attack on the court and on individual justices" is "new during my lifetime. . . . We are being hammered daily, and I think quite unfairly in a lot of instances. And nobody, practically nobody, is defending us.
>
> The idea has always been that judges are not supposed to respond to criticisms, but if the courts are being unfairly attacked, the organized bar will come to their defense." Instead, "if any-thing, they've participated to some degree in these attacks."
>
> Judges are in a double bind: If they don't respond, the attacks stand. If they do, they diminish the mystique on which judicial authority depends.[2]

For the most part, these attacks have come from almost all of the mainstream media sources, not just the "left." For instance, there have been attacking articles calling for more oversight of the Supreme Court and highlighting alleged ethics violations in almost every single one of the legacy news media outlets. One has to ask, has there been some sort of organizing element to these attacks on the Supreme Court? There has been a cynical ploy to delegitimize the courts as well as the Supreme Court justices, and to blame this strategy on the amorphous "left" negates the fact that the deep state of the government appears to be the hidden hand behind these attacks. Mainstream media bias has again and again been shown to be driven by the deep state, so are these coordinated efforts coming from the White House, the DNC, or the deep state, or is there even some clear, dividing line between these entities?

As discussed in earlier chapters, thanks to the work of Robert Epstein,[3,4] Mike Benz in his interview with Tucker Carlson, as well as what was revealed in Matt Taibbi's Twitter File reporting and the *Murthy v Missouri* lawsuit, we know much more about the censorship and propaganda during the 2020 presidential election cycle and the COVIDcrisis. Then we have the Congressional investigation of the "The Great Barrington Declaration," as well as Congressional investigations of other censorship/propaganda operations run by the US government during the last three years of the COVIDcrisis. There have also been various *Epoch Times* exposes and other FOIA documents (in particular, thanks to Project Veritas, Open the Books, and Judicial Watch), documenting that the federal government has been involved in these types of propaganda campaigns for many years. The extent of these operations has been vast, with billions of dollars funneled into Astroturf organizations, government contractors, and nonprofit organizations. The Twitter Files documented how DHS/CISA, the State Department, DoD, HHS, the White House, Big Pharma companies, social media, philanthropic oligarchs, and Big Tech have been partnering together to conduct these operations. These include money, meetings, strategic sessions, technical help, "hit" lists of people to take down, etc. Mainstream media and much of the internet have been compromised and bought off. Any reporting on that fact will just get more of the same treatment. One such organization involved in the censorship-industrial complex is the Global Disinformation Index (GDI).

## Who and What Is the "Global Disinformation Index"?

A 2024 UnHerd article describes GDI as the following:

> GDI provides real-time automated "risk ratings" of the world's media sites and then recommends those sites with poor rankings be blacklisted from advertising aggregators. The algorithms used include not only mis, dis- and mal-information but also information of an "adversarial narrative." This would include conservative and gender-critical websites, publications, and even columnists. One of two co-founders admitted in a 2021 interview that decisions on who to ban from advertising aggregates are often made by personal opinion:
>
> GDI founder Clare Melford explained in an interview at the LSE in 2021 how this expanded definition was more "useful" as it allowed them to go beyond fact-checking to targeting anything on the internet that they deem "harmful" or "divisive":
> "A lot of disinformation is not just whether something is true or false—it escapes from the limits of fact-checking. Something can be factually accurate but still extremely harmful . . . [GDI] leads you to a more useful definition of disinformation . . . It's not saying something is or is not disinformation, but it is saying that content on this site or this particular article is content that is anti-immigrant, content that is anti-women, content that is antisemitic . . ."
> Larger traffic websites are rated using humans, she explains, but most are rated using automated AI. "We actually instantiate our definition of disinformation—the adversarial narrative topics—within the technology," explains Melford. "Each adversarial narrative is given its own machine-learning classifier, which then allows us to search for content that matches that narrative at scale . . . misogyny, Islamophobia, anti-Semitism, anti-black content, climate change denial, etc."[5]

The GDI team and algorithm have not been trained to identify disinformation, but rather to identify and defund any content which GDI founder Clare Melford personally finds offensive. This includes content supporting the January 6 "insurrections," influence of "white men in Silicon Valley," and anything that might undermine the global response to the "existential challenge of climate change.[6] According to their website, GDI has assessed over 700 million websites in over forty languages across 150 countries. After the magazine UnHerd called out the GDI for their bad behavior, they removed information about their funding ties to the US and the UK governments from their list of funders.[7] Although the GDI website still clearly states that government entities partially fund them. Although they do not specifically list the United States and UK, they strongly imply such a link. Included in their preferred funding sources are George Soros's Open Society Foundation. The GDI also receives money from the UK government (via the FCDO), the European Union, the German Foreign Office, and a body called Disinfo Cloud, which was created and funded by the US State Department.[8] The other cofounder and executive director, Daniel J. Rogers, was the founder and leader of Terbium Labs, an information security and dark web intelligence startup. He also worked in the US intelligence community. GDI is just one of many such firms throughout the world and the United States. These organizations are ubiquitous throughout the world.

We know that the campaign to besmirch Robert Malone's reputation, including outright lies and malicious defamation written about him by the *Atlantic Monthly*, the *Washington Post*, the *New York Times*, *Rolling Stone*, *The Scientist*, and *Business Insider*, to name a few, was a coordinated campaign led by the US government and the deep state. There is direct evidence that both CISA and the CDC were involved in smearing Robert.[9,10] All evidence suggests that they did this because Robert spoke out about the toxicity of the pseudo-mRNA vaccines early, and so the government worked to dispute his role as the original inventor of these vaccines (which gave him legitimacy to speak and be heard). Robert's Wikipedia page was edited early on to make him look like a fraud. This editing came from one editor, tied to the UK government, operating under the sock puppet name of "Phillip Cross." "Phillip Cross" has led the charge attacking almost all of the people who spoke out early against the jab and those physicians who advocated early treatment. By the way, none of these hit pieces attacking Robert, including his Wikipedia page, even mention the patents where the proof of principle mRNA vaccination studies are provided and described (they aren't hard to find).[11,12,13,14,15,16,17,18,19]

I think we can all agree that something just isn't "right" about the search algorithms these days. For instance, those distorted propaganda pieces about Robert are still front and center on the first page of results from a Google search of Robert's name, despite many other articles with far more views, including our many Substack essays. More than that, we now know that Google manipulates the algorithms and will occasionally *manually* manipulate results. As mentioned before, Google has even worked to change the outcome of major elections in the United States, including the 2020 presidential election.[20]

The truth is that the subtle dent to the reputation of people and organizations by the skewed algorithms sticks in people's minds, even if completely untrue. Modern psychology demonstrates that repeating a lie is an effective method for subconsciously programming people to accept and repeat falsehoods without examining the actual facts. This is why almost all of these hit pieces against Robert still remain on the front page of the Google results. This is despite the fact that there are many, many other articles, newspaper stories, and even our Substack essays, which have often generated a lot more traffic than these mainstream media articles. To this day, the Joe Rogan interview with Robert on Spotify is almost impossible to find on Spotify itself and in Google results. *For some reason*, Rogan has also never asked Robert back on. Even conservative media, such as Fox News, is scared to have him as a guest. It turns out that even big media influencers like Joe Rogan or Fox News can get triggered when the hand of government censorship comes down on them.

We know that the federal government interfered with the story of Hunter Biden's laptop, when over fifty "ex" intelligence officials signed a letter stating that this was a fake story planted by Russia two weeks prior to the 2020 presidential election. Thus, the federal government directly tampered with a federal election, which by all nonbiased accounts, was the deciding factor in President Biden's election win in 2020. This was black propaganda designed by the government in collusion with Big Tech and mainstream media to steal a presidential election. Where is the media outrage about this? Why don't more citizens understand or care that the election was stolen?

Both the US government and corporate media also actively interfered with investigations of the funding of the gain-of-function research that created SARS-CoV-2-WIV. Dr. Anthony Fauci, the Director of NIAID, lied to Congress, claiming that NIH did not fund the gain-of-function research. This statement is now clearly contradicted by many FOIAed documents as well as Fauci's own testimony in 2024.[21] More recently, it has been revealed by Congress that NIH, HHS, and NIAID lied to Congress about a multi-year project making monkeypox more virulent, which is truly a dangerous gain-of-function research project.[22]

The government appeared also to have been involved in planting fake stories, such as where the virus originated. In chronological order over time—bats, snakes, pangolins, and then three years after the virus came on to the world scene, wolf dogs have all been blamed by the deep state. Once a false narrative is frequently repeated, it can become similar to a hardwired memory—almost impossible to dislodge. Thus, many people still believe the COVID natural origins story. The fake origins story appears to have been driven by NIAID's director, Tony Fauci, to cover his own and his organization's involvement in creating the virus. Another mind virus was inserted into the public sphere, courtesy of the US government.

NIAID has long since abandoned its core mission in favor of biologic "defense," gain-of-function research, and doing the bidding of Big Pharma.

Since the start of the COVID-19 outbreak, NIAID has known it is at least partially responsible for the creation of the virus named SARS-CoV-2. It has had years to come clean and to fix its organizational and cultural issues. Instead, it has lied, obfuscated, and hidden the evidence of its responsibility for what happened. NIAID's organizational culture is arrogant and has a deep-seated sense of entitlement.

I propose that research at NIAID be shut down and the institute shuttered systematically and carefully. Of course, this must be done in a responsible manner—with biological tissue and pathogen banks being carefully preserved and assessed, but much of this archiving function is already outsourced to independent contractor companies.

Then, two new research institutes can be formed: one focused on infectious diseases, and the other on immunologic and allergic diseases. Leadership in these institutes should be completely replaced. The institutes should be focused on what can work to provide benefits to the majority of Americans. The good example of how NIAID has ignored effective solutions is using Vitamin D with A, K, and zinc to boost the immune system. Another great example is how they have fought the use of generic drugs to fight infectious diseases despite a long track record of such drugs being effective in both the early and late stages of respiratory disease.

How to do this? President Biden and Congress recently founded the Advanced Research Projects Agency for Health within NIH. The same pathways that allowed this new agency within NIH to come to fruition can be used to start these two new institutes.

In the face of this clear history of coordinated public-private partnering in advancing propaganda narratives, we can now say with near certainty that the defamatory statements concerning President Trump, the Russia disinformation propaganda, the COVID-19 origins story, and censorship have been operations coordinated by the federal government. There is evidence that the federal government may have interfered with the J6 investigation and even the event itself. But when a psyops operation is involved, who can say for sure? But isn't that the point of such propaganda and mass formation embryogenesis? To confuse the recipient to the point where "truth" can no longer be discerned.

Thanks to the investigative reporting from *Epoch Times* and at least one unnamed whistleblower, we have learned that the US government, through their nonprofit CDC Foundation, hired third parties like the Public Goods Project (PGP), who then contracted with other Astroturf groups like "Shots Heard Around the World" to crowdsource professional influencers to censor, defame, cyberstalk, and gang-stalk Robert and others who spoke out about the safety and efficacy of the pseudo-mRNA "vaccines."[23] The irony is that cyberstalking is a federal crime. Interestingly enough, the various congressional committees have not investigated the censorship, propaganda, and harassment of physicians and scientists who have questioned the mRNA jabs or early treatment.

The Senate oversight committee with jurisdiction over the Department of Homeland Security also seems to be completely disinterested in the topic. Those physicians and scientists who have published or written about the adverse events, safety and efficacy of the mRNA jabs have not been asked to testify. Nor have those who have advocated early treatment. Yet, they have had continual defamatory propaganda written about them, as well as being harassed by groups of social media influencers; who censor, gang-stalk, and cyberstalk at the behest of the US government through the CDC Foundation's activities.

There is a clear and compelling case to be made that when the mainstream media attacks in a systemic fashion and acts in coordination with each other, the federal government must be suspected of leading that attack. This has become a pattern of abuse by the federal government. This circles back to the recent media attacks and abuse on the conservative justices . . .

We must consider that the Democrat federal government propaganda machine is targeting the conservative court and justices. Why? Because these attacks in the mainstream media and Big Tech are occurring in a systemic fashion and in coordination with mainstream media and Big Tech. This means that these propaganda attacks are most likely being coordinated at the highest levels by the federal government. Is this at the behest of the White House, the DNC, or members of the administrative state? FOIAed documents might reveal the answer. Or at least, that is, unless FOIA specialists, "ethicists," and federal employees didn't work to hide evidence of such corruption, as what has happened in NIAID during the COVID-19 virus origins cover-up.[24]

But this goes beyond media and Big Tech. After the leak of Justice Alito's draft opinion on the *Dobbs v. Jackson Women's Health Organization* case in 2022, there was and is an organized campaign to physically intimidate and harass conservative justices by activists. Individual Supreme Court justices and conservative justices have been doxxed, with agitators protesting outside their homes. These violent protests were allowed to continue unabated by Biden's justice department, despite there being a federal law on the books prohibiting the targeting of federal judges.[25] The Department of Justice has refused to take action against the protesters. There was an attempt on Justice Kavanaugh's life, about which President Biden and the media were mostly silent. The Supreme Court justices must now travel in armored cars and have full-time security.

Since that draft opinion, Justice Alito has continued to receive constant harassment from mainstream media. Despite the Supreme Court being responsible for its own ethics plan, the mainstream media has kept up the constant drumbeat that Justice Alito and Justice Thomas are violating normal ethical bounds.

Progressives are furious about the overturning of *Roe v. Wade*, which is why they are pressuring two of the most upstanding members of the Supreme Court into recusing themselves from participating in upcoming cases about the 2020 and 2024 elections. The goal is to shrink the justices on the bench down to seven, so that the left has a chance of winning these cases. The left, through proxies in the mainstream media, has centered its strategy of attacks on Justice Alito for the rather innocuous "sin" of his wife flying the American flag upside down, which is not a crime and, up until 2024, had no significance. Now it has been deemed by mainstream media to represent an insurrection. Democrat Congressional members, such as Rep. Jamie Raskin, are now interfering with the Supreme Court by demanding that specific Supreme Court Justices recuse themselves from these cases.[26]

These types of personal attacks by mainstream media, that are then amplified on social media causes the haters and trolls to swarm. Living with the chronic fear of being attacked by an unknown assailant is one of the most insidiously damaging psychological campaigns one can imagine. We know. Robert has had at least a dozen cyberstalkers that repeat malicious defamation against both of us on a daily basis. This is different from having some corporate media doing a one-off hit piece. This is repeated defamation which is continually repeated. Justice Alito wrote about the hate aimed at him and other Supreme Court Justices:

> It was rational for people to believe that they might be able to stop the decision in Dobbs by killing one of us.
> —Justice Samuel Alito

The systemic attacks of both Supreme Court justices and conservative judges continue unabated. It is not just those seeking to return federal abortion rights to the United States. Justice Clarence Thomas has been the victim of coordinated attacks by the press for years, including coordinated racist and downright libelous articles written about him and his family. Yet, despite all these media hit pieces, no charges have been brought forth. More evidence that this is a coordinated propaganda campaign brought on by the Democrat administrative and deep states. That is, by our very own government on the Democratic side.

Other conservative judges have been harassed by trans rights protesters and gay rights protesters. They have even been harassed for the sin of being appointed by President Trump to a judicial position. These are not peaceful assemblies, as is our right under the First Amendment, but are concerted efforts to harass and physically intimidate officers of the court, which is a crime. The tools being used include cyberstalking, gang stalking, violence, physical intimidation, death threats, and harassment.

Who is leading these systemic efforts? Are three-letter agencies involved? How deep does the propaganda and censorship go? Is this even a real concern or just another conspiracy theory? These are legitimate questions and the public deserves answers.

The American people can no longer trust that the US government behaves in a neutral fashion. Our rights to a free press and free speech are being stripped away daily. The US government, Big Tech, media, pharma, and the military are acting in a coordinated fashion to censor and create propaganda. We know that media and Big Tech are getting paid by the government to do this. We know that the media has been muzzled by the very fact that if they write anything too critical of the Biden White house, access to White House officials will be limited. During the COVIDcrisis, the HHS also paid out a billion dollars to both advertise the jab campaign and to censor critics of the "vaccine" program. This is more proof of the censorship-industrial complex.

We are pro-America and patriots. We are Constitutionalists. We believe in free speech. A strong nation. A free press. Our republic. Our democratic institutions. This is not an anti-government tirade. We are not anti-government, we are constitutional conservatives, and we are shocked and saddened by how quickly our great nation is falling into corruption, rationalized by the thesis that censorship and propaganda is necessary to "preserve democracy." That apparently only means democracy for the administrative and deep states.

# CHAPTER 24
## A State of Exception

### Government's Ability to Transcend the Rule of Law in the Name of the Public Good Is Based on the Philosophy of a State of Exception

> A state of exception is a concept introduced in the 1920s by the German philosopher and jurist Carl Schmitt, similar to a state of emergency (martial law) but based in the sovereign's ability to transcend the rule of law in the name of the public good.
>
> —Wikipedia[1]

The concept of a forever state of emergency has been refined over the twentieth century. A state of exception may be just one area of public good within a government, or it can define an entire governing structure. Modern history provides examples of both.

In his book on the concept of a state of exception, Giorgio Agamben discusses how the "state of exception" can be extended over long periods of time to control populations. His examples include how the United States detained and treated prisoners captured during the "war on terror" and how Hitler used a state of exemption to maintain control over the German government and its peoples beginning early in the 1930s.[2]

During much of his eighty-one years of life, Georgio Agamben was considered the darling of the left in Europe. His scholarly works were well received, and he was blessed with great accolades.

Then came the year 2020 and COVID-19. This is when Agamben turned his ideas about the state of exemption onto the COVIDcrisis and, with that, became the enemy of both academia and the state. He had begun writing a blog, which was "removed" by the heavy hand of authorities, so he then morphed this block of writing into the book, *Where Are We Now?: The Epidemic as Politics* published in 2021.[3]

Agamben argues that a state of exemption can be either grounded upon independent sources of law or featured as external to the set of laws governing a country. An example of an independent source of law might be a UN treaty or agreement, such as Agenda 2030 or a World Health Organization edict, for example, via the amended International Health Regulations (IHRs) that were passed illegally by "consensus" in May, 2024.[4] These could and (previously) even have absolutely come to usurp the rule of law of a constitutional republic grounded in democratic principles.

The administrative state suspending the rule of law and then making up their own rules and regulations during COVID would be an example of a state of exemption, which operated outside of the set of laws governing the country.

> The dominant powers of today have decided to pitilessly abandon the paradigm of bourgeois democracy—with its rights, its parliaments, and its constitutions—and replace it with new apparatuses whose contours we can barely glimpse.[5]
> —Agamben, Giorgio. *Where Are We Now?*

Agamben writes that, throughout the western world, the biosecurity state has become the preferred method for control of citizens and populations via imposition of a state of exception.

> We can use the term "biosecurity" to describe the government apparatus that consists of this new religion of health, conjoined with the state power and its state of exception—an apparatus that is probably the most efficient of its kind that Western history has ever known.
> Experience has in fact shown that, once a threat to health is in place, people are willing to accept limitations on their freedom

that they would never theretofore have considered enduring—not even during the two world wars, nor under totalitarian dictatorships.[6]

Agamben optimistically argues that the legitimate power derived from national sovereignty is dying. That the grasping for totalitarian control via the state of exemption ("technological-sanitation despotism") cannot be sustained. Because people eventually see through the facade.

> The dissemination of the sanitation terror needed an acquiescent and undivided media to produce a consensus, something that will prove difficult to preserve. The medical religion, like every religion, has its heretics and dissenters, and respected voices coming from many different directions have contested the actuality and gravity of the epidemic—neither of which can be sustained indefinitely through the daily diffusion of numbers that lack scientific consistency. The first to realise this were probably the dominant powers, who would never have resorted to such extreme and inhuman apparatuses had they not been scared by the reality of their own erosion.[7]

As discussed in chapter 3, psychological bioterrorism is the use of fear about a disease to manipulate individuals or populations by governments and other organizations, such as Big Pharma. Although psychological bioterrorism, including the use of a template to induce massive fear campaigns, has been developed and implemented by nation-states before, the biosecurity state's use of censorship and digitized isolationism, that is, control of the digitized public square, is a new phenomenon. New strategies, such as lockdowns, social distancing, and masking, have been used to extend the state of exemption and are also a hallmark of psychological bioterrorism. Keeping people isolated and on the sanitized net rather than talking with each other was planned to exert control and keep people compliant.

Thus, new forms of resistance will be necessary to combat these new totalitarian tactics. One such tool is using fifth-generation warfare techniques to combat the imperial state of exemption. The question is, will this soon become a non-kinetic civil war as the administrative state refuses to let go of its newfound powers? A war that must be fought to maintain our freedoms?

Agamben believes that something better will rise from the ashes of these failed states as people become aware what has been done to them.

> The powers that seek to run the world must always resort to war, whether that be a real war or a carefully constructed one. And, since in the state of peace life tends to elude any historical dimension, it should not surprise us that governments now endlessly reiterate that the war against the virus marks the start of a new historical era in which nothing will ever be the same again. And among those who willingly blindfold themselves in order not to see the unfreedom into which they have deteriorated, many accept this claim because they are convinced, not without a degree of self-aggrandisement, that they are entering into a new era after almost seventy years of peaceful (ahistorical) life. Even though, as is already more than evident, this will be an era of servitude and sacrifices in which everything that makes life worth living will have to be subjected to mortifications and restrictions, they accept subjugation with pleasure, since they foolishly believe that they have found for their lives a meaning that they had, without noticing it, lost during the peace.
>
> It is possible, however, that the war against the virus—which seemed an ideal apparatus that governments could administer and direct according to their own needs much more easily than they could a real war—will, like every other war, end up getting out of hand. And perhaps only then, if it is not too late, men will look again for that ungovernable peace that they have so rashly abandoned.[8]

During the past century, governments have learned to use the state of exemption to acclimatize people that a state of emergency is a normal condition for life. The biosecurity state has become normalized. Other epidemics, even pandemics during the twentieth century, were not declared as a state of emergency whereby entire nations, even the world, were to be locked down for extended periods of time. This is a new form of totalitarianism. And yes, locking down entire populations, vaccine passports, social distancing, mandates, masking, etc. are tools of the totalitarians.

> The Party seeks power entirely for its own sake. We are not inter-
> ested in the good of others; we are interested solely in power—
> pure power.
> Power is not a means; it is an end. One does not establish a
> dictatorship in order to safeguard a revolution; one makes the
> revolution in order to establish the dictatorship.
> —George Orwell, *1984*

We have become accustomed to living under a state of emergency, a state of exception—one in which the administrative state, via a generalized executive order, has a permanent role in controlling people and their lives. We are not a free society if we must live in a permanent state of emergency. Once the COVIDcrisis ended, the threat of a new state of emergency looms large. It is just a matter of time.

> What can you do, thought Winston, against the lunatic who is
> more intelligent than yourself; who gives your arguments a fair
> hearing and simply persists in his lunacy?
> Reality exists in the human mind and nowhere else.
> —George Orwell, *1984*

Our nation is sacrificing freedom to bureaucrats posing as false gods on an altar of scientism and security as the leviathan continues to assemble an ever more all-encompassing security state. In this case, biosecurity, energy security, environmental (climate) security, security derived from technology-centric weapons of war, and the religion of robo-transhumanism. These constantly refreshed, existential war/fear-based problem-counter problem-technological resolution loops (Hegelian dialectic) combined with the internet as an information filter and funneled are highly effective control methods. In an era in which there are such strong disincentives for kinetic warfare, the continuous "state of exception" has become a substitute. As anticipated by Orwell in his magnum opus of totalitarianism (*1984*), these loops implant and reinforce a heightened sense of constant fear into the majority of the populace. Not available to Orwell as he prophetically imagined our future, the internet has now become the perfect tool of choice for the leviathan to implant the resulting synthetic chronic fear and insecurity into the general population as a control method.

> The very word "war," therefore, has become misleading. It would probably be accurate to say that by becoming continuous war has ceased to exist. . . . War is Peace.
>
> —George Orwell, *1984*

But we the people have tools to fight back. The only way to win at fifth-generation warfare is not to play, to not fall for their lies and fearmongering. It is to do our own due-diligence and support online communities disseminating multiple viewpoints on news stories. To be a creator, share information with friends and family, write and read, is a power that still makes a difference. It may be one of our best defenses against the chronic rewriting of history and algorithmic internet revisionism which has become endemic.

> The past was erased, the erasure was forgotten, the lie became the truth.
>
> —George Orwell, *1984*

We must be ready to fight back against any new "states of exemption." We the people, must say no more.

> The masses never revolt of their own accord, and they never revolt merely because they are oppressed. Indeed, so long as they are not permitted to have standards of comparison, they never even become aware that they are oppressed.
>
> —George Orwell, *1984*

# PART V
# THE WORLD ECONOMIC FORUM

*The synchronized public health response across the UN member states allows new powers to be granted to the United Nations and its organizations at the cost of individual and national sovereignty. These universally applied regulations and multilateral agreements have given birth to an enlarged, globalized administrative state. Although this power grab has percolated for many decades, the COVIDcrisis synergized international agreements that advance the United Nations as a world government in partnership with the WEF.*

*The United Nations, through its various agreements and goals, particularly the treaty titled Agenda 2030, wants to centrally dictate the world's economy, migration, "reproductive health," monetary systems, digital IDs, environment, agriculture, wages, climate modifications, education, universal income, one world health, and other related globalist programs. The only suitable way to describe it is as a power grab.*

*The pandemic has allowed world leaders to coalesce global administrative power under the guise of public health through the UN administrative bureaucracy. Public health has been weaponized to gain control of passports, travel, banking, the environment, the international economy, and more. This is a gross violation of the individual's right to privacy, national sovereignty, and the UN charter. This has been done in partnership with the WEF.*

*Even our medicine, science, academic institutions, and academic journals have been corrupted.*

*The truth is that transnational companies want control of world governance. The Great Reset is a planned attempt to redistribute all the world's wealth and power into the hands of corporations, billionaires, banks, and, most of all, the World Economic Forum's leadership. The "Great Reset" plans to use the fourth industrial revolution to further their own ambitious plans of world dominance.*

# CHAPTER 25
# The Pandemic as a Catalyst for a New World Order

Each nation in the world has its own culture, governance structures, traditions, property, borders, and peoples. We must preserve the diversity and sovereignty of nations and cultures.

By globally synchronizing the public health response across the United Nations member states, new powers were granted to the UN and its organizations at the cost of national sovereignty. These universally applied regulations and multilateral agreements have given birth to an enlarged, globalized administrative state. Although this power grab has percolated for many decades, the COVIDcrisis acted as an accelerant to synergize international agreements that advance the UN as a world government.

The United Nations has morphed into a leviathan. Its various agreements and goals seek to centrally dictate the world's economy, migration, "reproductive health," monetary systems, digital IDs, environment, agriculture, wages, climate modifications, one world health, and other related globalist programs. To be clear, these are the goals of an organization seeking a globalized command economy, not an organization focused on world peace, ending wars, or human rights!

This UN aims to regulate every dimension of our personal and national lives. It is working to reduce and eliminate national sovereignty across the world, and thereby to decrease our diversity, our traditions, our religions, and our national identities.

The UN has partnerships and strategic agreements with member nations, as well as other globalist organizations such as the Bill & Melinda Gates Foundation, the World Bank, CEPI, The World Trade Organization, The European Union, and the World Economic Forum, known as the WEF.

## An Example of How the United Nations Operates

The WEF and the UN signed a strategic agreement and partnership in 2019. Remember that the WEF has a commitment to "stakeholder capitalism," by which private-partnerships work to control governments. The WEF developed a plan in 2020 to use the COVIDcrisis to reorganize global governance around social issues, including climate change—this plan was called the Great Reset.

The WEF is a trade organization representing the world's largest corporations. It repeatedly exploits disruptive technologies to enhance economic growth opportunities for its corporate members. The WEF is specifically designed to advance the economic power of its global elite members, otherwise known as the "billionaire class."

As the WEF feeds money into the United Nations through their 2019 strategic agreement, who is managing the conflicts of interests that come with this partnership? Where is the transparency?

The UN has fourteen specialized organizations under its leadership, all involved in global governance, including the World Health Organization or WHO.

None of these organizations is related to the scope of the original UN charter, which was focused on ending wars, promoting world peace, and protecting human rights. The UN had been quietly building power for years prior to the pandemic through various agreements and treaties.

For instance, the "2030 Agenda for Sustainable Development" is a recent example of such an agreement.[1]

Agenda 2030 has seventeen goals and 169 targets, which vary widely in scope and topic, but almost all of these goals directly affect world governance. Here are just a few examples from the Agenda 2030 treaty. Is this what the United Nations should be concerned with, or are these issues more properly addressed by the policies of sovereign nations?

We are determined to protect the planet from degradation, including through sustainable consumption and production, sustainably managing its natural resources and taking urgent action on climate change.

Achieve full and productive employment and decent work for all women and men.

Eliminate discriminatory laws, policies and practices.

Adopt policies, especially fiscal, wage and social protection policies, and progressively achieve greater equality.

Facilitate orderly, safe, regular and responsible migration and mobility of people.

By 2030, provide legal identity for all, including birth registration.

This is an Agenda of unprecedented scope and significance.

It is accepted by all countries and is applicable to all . . .

Agenda 2030 is essentially a totalitarian socialist manifesto. This United Nations Treaty contains many more forceful statements regarding the reduction of national rights. The UN has signed strategic agreements with the largest organizations, corporations, and world powers to fulfill its utopian vision for the world.

This is a new world order—with unelected officials in control. That means that we all will be ruled by a nondemocratic UN administrative bureaucracy. This is a form of inverse totalitarianism. A world order based on a command economy; one that is at its core both socialist and totalitarian.

Now, these goals and targets may be fine for any single nation to undertake, but this is a restructuring of the United Nations beyond its charter.

Early in the pandemic, the UN—through its surrogate the WHO, declared that a global vaccine passport was needed, and provided extensive guidance to member nations to standardize vaccine passports worldwide. In response, the leaders of the G20 issued a declaration in 2022 supporting development of a global standard of vaccination for international travel and the establishment of "global digital health networks" to be built on existing digital COVID-19 vaccine passports.

In June 2023, a new initiative between the EU and the WHO for strategic cooperation on global health issues was announced. This agreement seeks to "bolster a robust multilateral system with the World Health Organization at its core, powered by a strong European Union."

After failing to manage the COVIDcrisis, the WHO now seeks more money and power to control all aspects of our health and lives. They intend to amend the International Health Regulations to govern the "pandemic prevention, preparedness and response" of future outbreaks, including any public health emergencies. This includes a major role for the WHO in direct governance, as opposed to a guidance-based role.

These changes are predicated on the G20 global adoption of "vaccine passports" in 2022.[2] These passports will collect and contain private health data, and will enable surveillance, tracking, and control of individuals and populations worldwide. The passports will include not only COVID-19 vaccine data, but the status of all vaccinations. It will become a world digitized passport—including personal health information that the United Nations has no right to access.

The G20 Joint Declaration regarding vaccine passports and future pandemics is a declaration on how future pandemics will be handled.[3] It states:

> We acknowledge the importance of shared technical standards and verification methods, under the framework of the IHR (2005), to facilitate seamless international travel, interoperability, and recognising digital solutions and non-digital solutions, including proof of vaccinations.
>
> We support continued international dialogue and collaboration on the establishment of trusted global digital health networks as part of the efforts to strengthen prevention and response to future pandemics, that should capitalise and build on the success of the existing standards and digital COVID-19 certificates.

The G20 is also working with the International Monetary Fund (the UN's financial agency), the World Bank (which has a founding treaty relationship with the UN), and the Bank for International Settlements to formalize the use of central bank digital currencies in banking systems. The Bank for International Settlements specifically refers to "the disruption caused by COVID-19" as a justification for creating central bank digital currencies.

The pandemic has allowed world leaders to coalesce global administrative power under the guise of public health through the administrative bureaucracy of the UN. Public health has been weaponized to gain control of passports, travel, banking, the environment, and the international economy. This is a gross violation of the individual's right to privacy, national sovereignty, and the UN charter.

It is just a matter of time before these vaccine passports will be coupled with central bank digital currencies. Then, the passports can be used to deny the unvaccinated or other political dissenters access to travel and use of their own money.

Once international passports, central bank digital currencies, command economy aspects of the UN's Agenda 2030, and the WHO amendments to the IHRs are implemented, the groundwork for a new world order will be complete. A global administrative state, whose core power resides with the UN. The US deep state views its relationship with the UN as one where it has kept some degree of organizational control. This new world order will become a spiderweb of rules, regulations, agreements, and treaties within which individuals and nations will be trapped like flies. This new global governance will be virtually unbreakable. From there, it is only a matter of time before national sovereignty becomes obsolete. This is a reality unless we fight to stop this madness.

For this reason, the power of the United Nations must be exposed and curtailed.

Globalists seeking to advance their agendas are using the model of the European Union, whereby rules and regulations stymie national sovereignty, to build a worldwide system of control. All must fight this takeover at the local, national, and international level. We must use the courts, our legislatures, media, public protests, and the power vested in our national and state sovereignty to fight this. If all else fails, individual nations may need to withdraw from the UN's New World Order in order to remain free.

Let's work together to keep our personal and national sovereignty safe for future generations. A New World Order is not needed, is not acceptable, and we the people and our sovereign governments should unequivocally reject this globalized takeover.

# CHAPTER 26
# You Have Owners

> You have no choice.
> You have owners.
> —George Carlin

Those of us in this movement for individual sovereignty sometimes forget that for most people, the World Economic Forum (WEF) is a meeting in Davos where the rich and famous like to hang out once a year. They have no idea what the WEF truly is about and what it has accomplished over the last fifty years. Even those of us who follow the WEF often forget what their true mission is and how deeply they are involved in crafting the new world order, which was first formally laid out in the book *COVID-19: The Great Reset*.[1]

The truth is that transnational corporations want control of world governance. The Great Reset is a planned attempt to redistribute all the world's wealth and power into the hands of corporations, billionaires, banks, and, most of all, the World Economic Forum's leadership. The "Great Reset" plans to use the fourth industrial revolution to further their own ambitious plans of world dominance.

It is a world where transhumanism has become a reality. The boundaries between man and machine are blurred. This is the world of nightmares, of a dystopian future of overloads and underlings; of the "technologically augmented" and the "normies." Of Physicals, Virtuals, Machines, and Overlords.

> **The Fourth Industrial Revolution (Industry 4.0)** is a term used to refer to the next generation of technological advances; where it is anticipated that the differences between physical, digital, and biological technologies disappear. This is a world where machines and computers evolve independently, where new biological entities and evolutionary changes are being controlled by artificial intelligence, where brain waves can be manipulated. It is, quite literally, a brave new world.

What truly sets Industry 4.0 technologies apart is the novel way in which hardware, software and connectivity are being reconfigured and integrated to achieve ever-more ambitious goals, the collection and analysis of vast amounts of data, the seamless interaction between smart machines, and the blurring of the physical and virtual dimensions of production.[2]

To get an idea of how the WEF is using Industry 4.0 now, take the example of smart cities. The WEF is using of the threat of "climate change" to drive the development and state/business endorsement of smart cities. These are proposed to be run by the World Economic Forum in conjunction with the United Nations, who are leading the G20 to build a "Smart Cities Alliance on Technology Governance."[3]

The ability to track and control all peoples in a city, to control crime, carbon credits, food, vaccine status, transport, etc. is a future most do not wish to partake in. This is a future that forms the basis of the near-term dystopian Spielberg film *Minority Report*. Yet, what choice do us underlings have? Who gets to decide what is right and wrong when the infrastructure is being developed globally and implemented regionally with little or no transparency? Is this just another case of *"those with the gold make the rules"*?

Who are the globalist members of the trade organization known as the World Economic Forum (WEF) and the operatives that they have trained, why should you care, and what can you do about it? The first step to doing something about the WEF, is understanding what it is and isn't.

The membership of the WEF is divided into three general categories:

- regional partners,
- industry partner groups,
- and the most esteemed, the strategic partners.

The WEF boasts 100 "strategic partners" who are drawn from the largest corporations in the world. The list of "strategic partners" reads like a list of the 100 most woke companies and organizations, which include the Bill & Melinda Gates Foundation, Open Society Foundations, Wellcome Trust, BlackRock, Bain, Microsoft, Google—it goes on and on.[4] Their owners and managers are often referred to as "Davos Man," due to their yearly retreats held in Davos, Switzerland.

Some of the recent activities of the WEF (from their website):

- The WEF has a strategic partnership with the UN, with the focus being on financing and implementing the 2030 Agenda, climate change, health, digital cooperation, gender equality and empowerment of women, education and skills.
- World Economic Forum is leading the G20 "Smart Cities Alliance on Technology Governance."
- The WEF lists 103 Partnerships and Collaborative Arrangements with World Health Organization involvement (updated 2019).
- The World Economic Forum is partnering with businesses and governments to engage with the nascent market for blue carbon, the carbon captured and sequestered by ocean ecosystems.
- Nine new industrial clusters from Europe, United States, and Asia are joining the Transitioning Industrial Clusters toward Net Zero initiative.
- Centre for the Fourth Industrial Revolution (WEF) to anticipate, understand, and shape the trajectory of technological change for human-centered and society-serving outcomes.

## Corporatist-Style Stakeholder Capitalism

The WEF is made up of the largest transnational organizations in the world. This is their lobbying organization. It is also a guild. They have basically built a political juggernaut based on advancing corporatist "public-private partnerships" with the United States, World Health Organization, The

United Nations, The World Bank, European Union, the Five-eyes nations (UK, Canada, Australia, New Zealand, and the USA), China/CCP as well as any other country that will join in their cause (notably Russia and the WEF have decided to part ways[5]).

The political science term "fascism" has been so weaponized, abused, and overused that it has lost much of its utility to describe a category of political systems, but a strong case can be made that this form of corporatism is synonymous with the original intent of the term "fascism."

The WEF business model has been to enable its member corporations to create disruptive technologies that will drive markets and increase profits.

The goals of the WEF are not really about environmental, social, and governance (ESG), which is a set of aspects, including environmental issues, social issues, and corporate governance that can be considered in investing developed by the UN, smart cities, climate change, transgender rights, or even human rights. The WEF is about gaining governmental control via corporatism. It bears repeating that this is a trade organization of the largest transnational organizations in the world. Never forget that fact as you read their endless stream of feel-good press releases from the various WEF outlets and acolytes.

Stakeholder capitalism is nothing more than fascism tied up in a pretty package. Government and that largest corporations in the world are working together to create a reality where consumer choice is limited.

As an example, the United Nations has played right into their hands.

The United Nations (UN) and the World Economic Forum (WEF) signed a Strategic Partnership Framework in June 2019 to "deepen institutional engagement and jointly accelerate the implementation of the 2030 Agenda for Sustainable Development."[6]

This strategic partnership has led to the control of world-wide regulatory processes for new technologies and for global governance The WEF paints its injection into global politics with pretty words. But the truth is, the WEF is about profit. If they can control politicians, control governments, control the new world order, control vital industries, then they can increase the profits of their corporate members. The WEF is a monopolist's dream organization, and a quick review of the Strategic Partners list reveals many of the most successful corporate monopolists in recorded history. The WEF's "Great Reset" plans to remake the world's governance and the

UN's "Agenda 2030" (a climate change treaty signed into law by President Obama) are two sides of the same coin.[7,8] The WEF and the UN are now both strategically and tactically one organization. Their agendas are intertwined. This is what regulatory capture looks like.

## The WEF Regionally

The WEF regional organizations and members do not act alone. These regional organizations have developed various groups of globally distributed trainees and graduates. These young acolytes generally act in accordance with the detailed policies and positions developed and distributed by WEF leadership. The many training programs have been operating for over three decades, resulting in placement, distribution, and rapid advancement of thousands of WEF-trained operatives worldwide. WEF chairman Klaus Schwab has famously claimed that these operatives have been strategically inserted into key positions in various governments, as well influential positions in important industries such as media, finance, and technology.

The World Economic Forum even has a formal committee of university presidents who come together regularly to discuss and decide policy at the top universities in the world. These presidents are committed to supporting the World Economic Forum, whose main agenda is "stakeholder capitalism"—another word for corporatism. Corporatism is a general term and applies to many political structures with subtle differences. At one extreme is the authoritarian/totalitarian version championed by Mussolini and his followers, and at the other end the softer worker/team/supervisor structures often observed in socialistic western European countries. However, all forms of corporatism share common key characteristics.

A Samuel Gregg article in *The Spectator* sums up themes and critcisms shared by all versions of the WEF/Klaus Schwab style of corporatism:

> One is the necessity of limiting market competition in order to preserve social cohesion. Another is mandating cooperation between representative groups of different social and economic sectors—a process overseen and, if necessary, enforced by government officials for the sake of the common good. . . . Corporatism—including its *Schwabian* expression, isn't big on freedom. It's all about forming and then maintaining a consensus

on economic and social policies. For this reason, corporatism doesn't cope well with dissent. Indeed, it discourages any questioning of the consensus, whether the issue is tax-rates or climate change.

The language of corporatism, like that of Schwab's WEF, may be one of coordinated consultation, but the agenda is one of control. For what matters is the harmonization of views, no matter how absurd the idea and or how high the cost in liberty.

Not only does this generate groupthink. It encourages the marginalisation of those who dispute the consensus. If you have reservations about, say, open borders, don't be surprised if you are branded a xenophobe. If you decline to have your workforce unionized, you're likely be labeled a market fundamentalist who treats his employees as mere objects.

Another problem is the collusion and cronyism fostered by corporatism. Corporatist structures facilitate client-patron relations between businesses and governments. That in turn produces insiders and outsiders . . .

Lastly, corporatist-style stakeholder capitalism is decidedly ambivalent about democracy. The emphasis is upon insiders negotiating with each other, and then presenting the populace with a series of faits accomplis about anything ranging from fossil fuels to ESG.[9]

## The WEF Young Global Leaders Program
To quote the presiding leader of the WEF:

What we are very proud of, is that we penetrate the global cabinets of countries with our WEF Young Global Leaders. (YGL)
—Klaus Schwab (2017)

Who are the Young Global Leaders, the chosen few that are trained and tasked with carrying out the "Great Reset"? The Malone Institute, working together with the Pharos Media group, assembled a complete list of graduates from the three-to-five-year program. This list goes back to the founding of the Young Global Leaders program, which is at least forty years old and includes thousands of graduates from the five-year training program, whose training manuals have been kept secret to this day. The WEF Young Global Leaders list can be found at maloneinstitute.org.

The Young Global Leaders have been trained to believe in and support a globalist form of unelected government in which international business is at the center of the management and decision-making process. They have been trained to advance the interests of a global transnational government, which represents a public-private partnership in which the business interests of the WEF members take precedence over the constitution of the United States. A global transnational government that places the United Nations and global public-private partnerships politically and organizationally above sovereign nations. The WEF believes that the concept of the independent Westphalian nation-state is obsolete and must be replaced with a global government structure that controls all. The ends justify the means to these organizations.

The Westphalian nation-state refers to a system of states or international society comprising sovereign state entities possessing the monopoly of force within their mutually recognized territories. This concept is often associated with the Treaties of Westphalia in 1648, which ended the Thirty Years' War in Europe and established the modern system of sovereign states.

The Westphalian nation-state is based on several key principles:

- Sovereignty: Each state has exclusive sovereignty over its territory and is not subject to external authority.
- Territorial Integrity: States have the right to maintain their territorial integrity and are not subject to external interference.
- Equality: States are equal in the eyes of international law and are not subject to domination by other states.
- Nonintervention: States have the right to noninterference in the internal affairs of other states.
- Diplomacy: Relations between states are conducted through formal diplomatic ties between heads of state and governments.

The WEF ultimately wants globally frictionless business structured under corporatist (the modern embodiment of fascism) leadership. Frictionless business is where a company has optimized not only its operations, technology, and processes to eliminate obstacles, delays, and inefficiencies, but also for the intersection of corporate activities with government regulations. In this view, government regulatory activity represents transactional friction. Transnational corporations want regulations, laws, digital IDs, transport systems, education, and governments to be uniform across the world because this will reduce the transactional costs and complexities—*ergo* friction—of its external business activities.

Interestingly, the WEF and the UN have a strategic agreement to promote and accelerate the UN's Agenda 2030 global treaty. Agenda 2030's 17 targets and 169 goals include universal education, a universal living wage, universal healthcare, universal IDs, universal access to the internet, etc. The list goes on and on. Agenda 2030 is the treaty that codifies the principles of the "Great Reset" and "New World Order." Below are just a few sections from the Agenda 2030 treaty,[10] selected to illustrate the nature of the planned restructuring of the current Westphalian order:

- Promote a universal rules-based, open, non-discriminatory, and equitable multilateral trading system under the World Trade Organization.
- Enhance global macroeconomic stability, including through policy coordination and policy coherence.
- Ensure universal access to sexual and reproductive health and reproductive rights.
- Ensure universal health coverage, including financial risk protection.
- Ensure universal access to affordable, reliable, sustainable and modern energy services; sustainable transport systems; and quality and resilient infrastructure.
- We will adopt policies which increase productive capacities, productivity and productive employment, financial inclusion, sustainable agriculture, pastorialist and fisheries development, sustainable industrial development.
- By 2030, ensure that all girls and boys complete free, equitable, and quality primary and secondary education.

Universal governmental systems are a process whereby cultural traditions will be eliminated. This is the disassembly of the very cultural heritage that we are each born to. It champions the dissolution of national sovereignty.

Frankly, for the transnational corporation, structuring regulations to favor one customer (the government) versus 8 billion customers is another way to advance the concept of frictionless business benefits, much as we say Pfizer selling its mRNA vaccine products via contracts to individual governments, which then distributed and marketed the products. The hidden hands of communist, socialist, and fascist belief systems are at the very core of this document. This is corporatism on a scale never seen before.

The UN is fundamentally antidemocratic, and its views are both fundamentally corporatist and globalist, which is another way of saying that the UN has been transformed into a champion of a modernized form of totalitarian fascism—the fusion of the interests of business with the power of the state—on a global scale. The truth is that these "young leader" graduates may not represent the interests of the nation-state in which they reside, work, and may hold political office, but rather their allegiance appears to be to the WEF vision of a dominant single world government that exercises dominion over nations and their constitutions, which in turn is guided by Global Public-Private Partnerships.

In our opinion, trainees and WEF members in politics, particularly those who have been used to "penetrate the global cabinets of countries," should be forced to register as foreign agents within their host countries.

## Why Should You Care?

The WEF has helped mastermind the globally harmonized planning, development, and implementation of the lockdowns, mandates, authoritarian vaccine campaigns, suppression of early treatment options, global targeting of dissenting physicians, censorship, propaganda, information, and thought control programs, which we have all experienced since late 2019.[11]

For instance, the Johns Hopkins Center for Health Security in partnership with the World Economic Forum and the Bill & Melinda Gates Foundation hosted Event 201, a high-level pandemic exercise on October 18, 2019, in New York, NY. The exercise built the public/private partnerships that allowed lockdowns, travel restrictions, censorship, vaccine passports, etc. to easily become the norm. These plans have not changed; in fact more recent "war games" suggest an even heavier-handed response to the "next" public health crisis. Psychological bioterrorism is being applied to the general public to get compliance for the next faux pandemic, which very well might be "bird flu" (H5N1).

We need our politicians to fight for us. We must mobilize through protests, social media, and other means to express our displeasure in the ongoing US/WEF relationship. We must remain flexible to exist as free people in a world increasingly dominated by globalist totalitarianism.

But questions remain. How do we help save this country from falling under the control of the UN and the WEF? How do we, as a nation, survive this onslaught?

The answer can be found in a return to the decentralized nation-state system based on the time-tested structure of Westphalian national sovereignty.

# CHAPTER 27
# Top Universities and Academic Journals Are Pawns of the WEF

## The WEF's Committee of Presidents from the World's Leading Universities

One of the most unsettling events of the past three years has been the globalized, coordinated messaging of socioeconomic messages and policies throughout the world. All of us who have been so actively advocating for freedom and sovereignty often wonder: Who is controlling this? How does this happen?

We remember spending time in 2022 with a friend from South Africa. We were discussing transgender policies across the world. We were all very disturbed, not just by the policies but also by how they came about. How did the institutionalized teachings of non-binary genders in schools and the importance of youth "transitioning" spread across the world so quickly? How is it possible that South Africa would be immersed in the same battles for "trans rights," as the United States and most of Europe? Of course, it isn't possible without coordination.

Then the conversation turned not just to the pandemic policies of masking, mandates, and lockdowns, but to climate change, the elimination of gas-fueled cars, Agenda 2030, the move to eliminate private ownership of items such as autos and housing, digital IDs, digital currency, the fifteen-minute "smart" cities, taking away private land for conservation, globalized censorship, etc. All this is happening, not just in one country, but across the world. The coordinated list seems endless.

We don't remember a period in our lives where most of the world governments agreed on so much. Where did these policies originate? Who is coordinating them? How did this happen? The more we have dug into this question, the more disturbed we were by the answer.

The WEF has a mission to reeducate and co-op top education leaders. It has a formal committee of presidents from the world's best universities. These presidents come together regularly to discuss and decide policy at the top universities in the world and have committed formally to supporting the World Economic Forum and its agendas.

From the WEF Website:[1]

> The Global University Leaders Forum (GULF) community consists of the presidents of the world's leading universities who are committed to supporting the Forum's mission of improving the state of the world. Together GULF presidents identify and address matters of common interest, including trends, challenges and best practices in higher education, research and societal impact. The community is comprised of 29 members and is chaired by Suzanne Fortier, Principal and Vice-Chancellor, McGill University.
>
> In 2021, the GULF community will focus on how universities can facilitate a more equal and inclusive recovery from the COVID-19 pandemic, including through exploring the skills for the future and reskilling, social inclusion, and climate action.
>
> GULF presidents and faculty engage in multiple ways with the Forum:
>
> • Expert networks: opportunities for experts to contribute to expert communities including the Global Future Councils
> • Insight development: opportunities to contribute to new research, disseminate new insights and collaborate on enhancing Strategic Intelligence
> • Action: opportunities to shape the world through 18 platforms addressing social, environmental, technological and industry challenges

Universities such as Stanford, MIT, Princeton, Yale, Berkeley, University of Pennsylvania, and University of Chicago are members. International college president memberships include Oxford, University of Cape Town (South Africa), as well as top Chinese and European universities. There is a platform of eighteen ideologies that these presidents are asked to support and disseminate throughout their campuses and society.

These university leaders have been awarded special status within the WEF and are asked to sit on other councils, such as the "Global Future Councils."[2]

> The World Economic Forum's network of Global Future Councils is the world's foremost multi-stakeholder and interdisciplinary knowledge network dedicated to promoting innovative thinking to shape a more resilient, inclusive and sustainable future.
>
> The network convenes around 600 of the most relevant and knowledgeable thought leaders from academia, government, international organizations, business, and civil society, grouped in expertise-based thematic councils. It is an invitation-only community, and members are nominated for a two-year term.

The Global University Leaders Forum seems to us to be yet another way that the WEF has co-opted world leaders. These leaders are doing the WEF's work in ways we can only imagine.

People often remark that the WEF does not hold positions of great authority and that it is full of pomp and circumstance but no substance. Nothing could be further from the truth.

In 2022, *The International Journal of Arts of Social Science* published a paper titled: *"The World Economic Forum, The Lancet, and COVID-19 Knowledge Gatekeeping."* That paper is seminal in understanding just how corrupting the WEF as well as the WHO has become to scientific journals, scientists, universities, and media (fact-checkers). The purpose of the study was to identify any established links between the World Economic Forum and the notorious *Lancet* article titled "Statement in support of the scientists, public health professionals, and medical professionals of China combatting COVID-19."[3] The general study design consisted of a comprehensive literature review that was guided by the principles of

Gatekeeping Theory and the Political Economy of Knowledge Theory. The abstract includes the following summary of methods and conclusions:

> Relevant online pieces of literature were sampled through snow-balling technique using the Google search engine platform to elucidate on the funding and ownership of the Lancet, and the 27 authors of the said article and their affiliations with higher learning institutions vis-à-vis their connections with the World Economic Forum to highlight their implications to gatekeeping and COVID-19 knowledge production in journal publications, particularly that of The Lancet.
>
> Results revealed that the WEF has penetrated all knowledge institutions that benefit from the natural COVID-19 virus origins hypothesis and the silencing of contrarian hypotheses, including the lab leak narrative. A model of the WEF knowledge production complex against the lab leak hypothesis was presented to visually represent the influence of the WEF on scientific journal gatekeeping in the context of The Lancet.

The paper goes on to document that almost all of the twenty-seven Lancet authors and their universities have strong affiliations to the WEF. Furthermore, the study documents that virtually the entire peer-reviewed journal ecosystem has been bought or corrupted by outside entities in one way or another.

> The fact that the authors of the controversial article in The Lancet are all quite involved with high-profile organizations like the UN-FAO, WHO, and the USAID reveals much about why they decided to support the actions that led to the immediate "conspiratorialization" of other hypotheses on the virus origins, and mass immunizations they heavily promoted not long after the lockdowns were in place all over the world.
>
> Assuming that the UN-FAO, WHO, and the USAID operate within a seamless system, embodied by the One Health approach they championed years before the pandemic happened, it would

not be difficult to think that the editorial processes linked to and supported by their system will work toward their and the WEF's benefit and advantage.

The data show that the WEF is part of the micro and macro environments that shape editorial gatekeeping. There is a playing field biased toward their system and only ideas that promote their system will have a chance to be heard. That the lab leak hypothesis is silenced is what the article of the 27 authors may have likely aimed to ensure . . .

The authors' closing comments basically infer that the WEF has deeply corrupted *The Lancet*, historically, one of the top medical journals in the world, and based on this example, that the WEF has acted to corrupt virtually all-important academic institutions.

One can infer that the WEF has penetrated all the institutions that shape the minds of people, through their policies and programs. . . .

The top executive editors of The Lancet, its owners, and funding agencies aside, the WEF has undeniably positioned itself to influence future leaders, policymakers, and knowledge gatekeepers like The Lancet, especially those in prestigious schools that can only be accessed by the privileged and the wealthy. It is not difficult to think that the interest of the WEF would be top-of-mind among the students and graduates of such universities compared to the multitude who have no interest in the workings of the WEF at all.

In essence, the WEF has completely co-opted almost all of the academic journals throughout the world. The academic elite has had their holy grail, the peer-reviewed process, corrupted. The corrupting influence of corporatism has invaded the hallowed halls of academia, medicine, and science.

In 2019, the WEF and the United Nations signed a massive strategic partnership agreement. Now, the power of the WEF is backed up the power of the UN and vice-versa.

New York, USA, 13 June 2019 – The World Economic Forum and the United Nations signed today a Strategic Partnership Framework outlining areas of cooperation to deepen institutional engagement and jointly accelerate the implementation of the 2030 Agenda for Sustainable Development. The framework was drafted based on a mapping of existing collaboration between the two institutions and will enable a more strategic and coordinated approach toward delivering impact.[4]

The United Nations is no longer focused on representing nations and preventing kinetic war; it is a partner with the organization which represents the interests of the one hundred largest transnational corporations in the world: the WEF. We can only estimate the massive amount of money that now flows into the United Nations' coffers from this partnership. When the UN becomes beholden to corporations for their very existence, this becomes corporatism on a scale the world has never seen before. Corporate capture of globalized governance is not healthy for the world.

The United Nations and the World Economic Forum do not have officials who represent the people. Their leaders have not been elected to make decisions on our behalf or on our nation's behalf. The agendas of these organizations are not those of our nation and do not reflect our concepts of rights to personal or even national sovereignty. As discussed earlier, through vessels such as Agenda 2030 and the World Health Organization's (a UN umbrella organization) newly modified international health regulations (IHRs), there is the appearance that the UN wishes to supersede national law and both national and personal sovereignty.

In this country, politicians with affiliations to the UN and the WEF need to declare themselves as foreign agents through the Foreign Agents Registration Act (FARA), which imposes public disclosure obligations on persons representing foreign interests. It is an inherent conflict of interest to both represent and support the WEF, a foreign entity, and the US government. Likewise, many of the university presidents named as WEF GULF leaders are from public institutions. They have a duty, as public officials, to report this as a conflict of interest with their institution. They have become foreign agents. The WEF has intentionally, openly, and proudly "infiltrated" both our government and our leading academic institutions.

The WEF has gained much legitimacy by partnering with academic organizations as well as global organizations like the UN, as well as governments. It has become entwined and entangled in world leadership, which has allowed them to capture these globalized conduits of power. In the next part of the book, we delve into what that might mean for our future and that of our children.

# PART VI
# THE NEW WORLD ORDER—GLOBAL CONTROL

*We begin this part with an introduction to the history of the United Nations and then discus how the UN has morphed into a socialist leviathan that wishes to take the reins of world power with a little help from its transnational corporate friends.*

*The UN is using the power of the internet to censor and control what people view. They are doing this to control the narrative. By controlling the narrative, they hope to direct public opinion to support their socialist, corporatist, and globalist agenda.*

*With the appointment of the UN's Secretary-General António Guterres to a second term, whose history as a socialist is well documented, the socialist and even communist policies that are the backbone of the UN became solidified. The use of a contrived climate change agenda to shape global policies toward a command economy has become ever more obvious as data demonstrate that the models upon which this edifice has been constructed repeatedly fail in their predictions. The UN has even decided that they can control the science, including what is found in the search results on Google. One glaring example includes the UN directing Google to change the algorithms on search results regarding climate change.*

*In the end, the UN and its partner the WEF hope to use a transhumanism agenda to drive human evolution by using genetic therapy, robotics, brain implants, and the like. A new world order of Physicals, Virtuals, Machines, and Overlords is coming – unless we, the people, find a way to block it.*

*The problem is one of pattern recognition. The future is already here, unequally distributed, but we just can't seem to recognize it yet.*

# CHAPTER 28
# The United Nations' New Rules for Ruling the World

The UN has sought to be more than just an organization to promote international peace and security. The modern UN is a complex organization that has tasked itself with world governance. According to its website, this is the breakdown of how it now views its global responsibilities.

> Due to the powers vested in its Charter and its unique international character, the United Nations can take action on the issues confronting humanity in the twenty-first century, including:
> - Maintain international peace and security
> - Protect human rights
> - Deliver humanitarian aid
> - **Promote sustainable development***
> - Uphold international law
>
> The United Nations was created in 1945, following the devastation of the Second World War, with one central mission: the maintenance of international peace and security. The UN accomplishes this by working to prevent conflict, helping parties in conflict make peace, deploying peacekeepers, and creating the conditions to allow peace to hold and flourish. These activities often overlap and should reinforce one another, to be effective.
>
> The UN Security Council is primarily responsible for international peace and security. The General Assembly and the

Secretary-General play major, important, and complementary roles, along with other UN offices and bodies.

(*Note how the UN has cunningly added "Promote sustainable development" to their vision of how the charter is to be implemented in the twenty-first century).

## What Are the Seventeen "Sustainable Development" Goals of the UN?

The secretary-general of the UN is essentially the president of the UN. The Secretary-general is elected by the ambassadors of member nations for a five-year term. These ambassadors are not voted into power by the people but are appointed by "world leaders." Since the founding of the UN in 1945–1946, there have only been nine secretary-generals. Generally, secretary-generals serve multiple terms, usually without challenge.

The role of the secretary-general is that of the chief administrative officer of the UN, and is also to serve as Chair of the United Nations System Chief Executives Board for Coordination (CEB), which brings together the Executive Heads of all UN funds, programs, and specialized agencies twice a year to coordinate all of management issues facing the United Nations System. Frankly, the Secretary-General may be the most important job in the world. So why do most people not even know who occupies the post?

## Who Is António Guterres?

António Guterres was raised and educated under a dictatorship in Portugal, which has influenced his political views since. He studied physics and electrical engineering at of the University of Lisbon, where he graduated in 1971. He initially worked as an assistant professor. But when he joined the Socialist party in 1974, Guterres left academia and entered politics. After the Carnation Revolution in Portugal circa 1974, Guterres worked within the Portuguese Socialist Party and was elected as a socialist MP in 1976.

From 1992 to 2002, he was secretary-general of the Portuguese Socialist Party, a position he held until 2002. He was vice president and later served as president of the Socialist International. Guterres was elected prime minister of Portugal from 1995 to 2002 and has worked in the United Nations since then. He began his term as secretary-general in 2017. His vision of a socialist world is one that the UN seems to have fully embraced, and when he was appointed to his second term in 2022, he called for "transformation and a new era of solidarity and equality." He also stated during his acceptance that:

> Our greatest challenge—which is at the same time our greatest opportunity—is to use this crisis to turn the tide, pivot toward a world that learns lessons, promotes a just, green and sustainable recovery and shows the way via increased and effective international cooperation to address global issues.[1]
>
> —Secretary-General, António Guterres

In 2021, he presented a report titled "Common Agenda," outlining his vision for the UN for the next five years.[2]

Here are some quotes from the secretary-general's 2021 report:

> Member States agreed that our challenges are interconnected, across borders and all other divides. These challenges can only be addressed by an equally interconnected response, through **reinvigorated multilateralism and the United Nations at the centre of our efforts**.
>
> That is why Our Common Agenda is, above all, an agenda of action designed to accelerate the implementation of existing agreements, including the Sustainable Development Goals.
>
> It should also include updated governance arrangements to deliver better public goods and usher in a new era of universal social protection, health coverage, education, skills, decent work and housing, as well as universal access to the internet by 2030 **as a basic human right**.
>
> Now is the time to **end the "infodemic" plaguing our world by defending a common, empirically backed consensus around facts, science, and knowledge**. The "war on science" must end.
>
> I am calling for a global code of conduct that promotes integrity in public information.
>
> [*Ergo*, censorship?]
>
> Now is the time for a stronger, more networked and inclusive

multilateral system, anchored within the United Nations. Effective multilateralism depends on an effective United Nations, one able to adapt to global challenges while living up to the purposes and principles of its Charter. For example, I am proposing a new agenda for peace, multi-stakeholder dialogues on outer space and a Global Digital Compact, as well as a Biennial Summit between the members of the Group of 20 and of the Economic and Social Council, the Secretary-General and the heads of the international financial institutions.

Not surprisingly, under his leadership, the UN has morphed into a socialist-globalist-corporatist monster.

In the United States, 94 percent of all international agreements are *not* approved by Congress but signed by presidential executive order.

In the United States, there are two categories of agreements that are binding under international law: treaties, which require the formal consent of a two-thirds majority of the Senate, and executive agreements, which the president can be authorized to conclude on a variety of grounds. These grounds may include the consent of the Senate to a prior treaty to which the agreement is pursuant, the enactment by Congress of a statute to which the agreement is pursuant, or the president's independent constitutional authorities.

Despite popular understanding, executive agreements are a well-established means of entering international agreements and account for the overwhelming majority—94 percent—of international agreements in the United States in the modern era. They are also on par with treaties in force and weight under international law, as both can create international legal obligations for the United States.

The Authority for US Participation in the Paris Climate Agreement, entered by the United States from 1985 through Republican and Democratic administrations and congresses.

The above rationale was used for the Paris Agreement, which President Obama signed but was never reviewed by the Senate nor approved by Congress. This "agreement" affirmed Agenda 2030.

But when is an agreement not an agreement? When the agreement is a treaty. The Paris Agreement is a treaty.

From the United Nations Climate Change Office.

> The Paris Agreement is a legally binding international treaty on climate change. It was adopted by 196 Parties at the UN Climate Change Conference (COP21) in Paris, France, on 12 December 2015. It entered into force on 4 November 2016.

When the executive office, through the progressive think tank the *Center for American Progress*, made the case that the Paris Agreement could be signed by the executive office without the two-thirds approval by the Senate, they slyly forgot to mention that the UN considers the Paris Agreement a treaty. This is the "treaty" that President Trump withdrew from and President Biden rejoined.

The Paris Agreement treaty, with its closely linked Agenda 2030, gave rise to the "Inflation Reduction Act" that was signed in 2022. This law, labeled the "Climate Change Bill," implemented many of the UN's sustainability goals outlined in Agenda 2030. So, this treaty was both entered into and withdrawn without approval from Congress. Yet the United States Constitution is very clear about what is and what isn't a treaty.

The United States Constitution provides that the president *"shall have Power, by and with the Advice and Consent of the Senate, to make Treaties, provided two-thirds of the Senators present concur"* (Article II, section 2). Treaties are binding agreements between nations and become part of international law. Treaties to which the United States is a party also have the force of federal legislation, forming part of what the Constitution calls *"the supreme Law of the Land."*

The Senate does not ratify treaties. Following consideration by the Committee on Foreign Relations, the Senate either approves or rejects a resolution of ratification. If the resolution passes, then ratification takes place when the instruments of ratification are formally exchanged between the United States and the foreign power(s).

A bill introduced by Rep. Lauren Boebert: H.R.376 - Paris Agreement Constitutional Treaty Act would:

"prohibit taking any action to carry out the goals of the United Nations Framework Convention on Climate Change—commonly known as the Paris Agreement—unless the Senate first ratifies the agreement. Further, the bill prohibits the use of any funds to advance the agreement."

Unfortunately, this bill never had congressional support and never made it out of committee.

Rep. Lauren Boebert is correct in her analysis. The Paris Agreement needs to have Senate approval before it is formally accepted as a treaty by the US government. This must be one of the first issues addressed by the new president in 2025. The Paris Agreement must not be allowed to proceed as if it were a signed treaty. The rule of law must be followed.

## The Executive Office Is Not Following the Constitution

We all know about the World Health Organization's IHRs, which could potentially place the WHO globally in control of public health emergencies. They could be signed into existence by the Executive office without Congressional oversight or approval.

US Sen. Ron Johnson (R-Wis.) "introduced the No WHO Pandemic Preparedness Treaty Without Senate Approval Act" in May 2022. This legislation would have required any convention or agreement resulting from the work of the World Health Organization's (WHO) intergovernmental negotiating body to be deemed a treaty, requiring the advice and consent of a supermajority of the Senate." This bill has not received congressional support and has stalled in a committee. A similar bill in Congress has met a similar fate. However, forty-nine Republican Senators have signed a letter in 2024 begging President Biden not to sign the WHO Pandemic treaty.

The reality is that the US executive branch, the White House, and the administrative state are out of control and in breach of the US Constitution on multiple fronts, not the least of which is disrespecting Congress's role in approving treaties and constitutionally protected free speech rights.

There is a solution to executive overreach.

Congress must step in and reaffirm their right to approve or reject treaties, even those masquerading as international agreements. The easiest way to do this is by a stand-alone bill or a rider to a bill reasserting the power of Congress alone to approve or disapprove of all international agreements that meet the criteria of a treaty. Such legislation could be upheld in the courts, if vetoed by President Biden or any other US president. It is also important for the Supreme Court to reassert the proper separation of powers and to confirm the primacy of both the First and Second Amendments to the US Constitution.

Furthermore, the unconstitutional assertion that the executive branch can employ international agreements as a work-around for a treaty otherwise requiring congressional approval must be challenged and clarified by Congress.

# CHAPTER 29
# The United Nations' Global "Plan" to Eradicate Free Speech

We must all work to eradicate [hate speech] completely.
—Secretary-General António Guterres[1]

The "International Day for Countering Hate Speech" has been designated by the UN as June 18. Yes, officially, there is now a special day to promote and legitimize propaganda and censorship. During 2024, on that day, United Nations Secretary-General António Guterres released a press release outlining the new UN "plan of action" to censor speech and calling for more governmental propaganda.[2]

> The United Nations Strategy and Plan of Action on Hate Speech provides a framework to tackle both the causes and impacts of this scourge. And the United Nations is currently preparing Global Principles for Information Integrity to guide decision makers around these issues.
> —Secretary-General António Guterres

Basically, the UN will be rolling out new edicts requiring nations to censor citizens and organizations by documenting what they perceive as harms done by free-speech "this scourge."

Hate speech today targets a broad range of groups, often based on grounds of race, ethnicity, religion, belief or political affiliation.
—Secretary-General António Guterres

So, hate speech now includes speech criticizing a belief or specific political affiliation. When did the definition of hate speech change? Who knew?

Secretary-General António Guterres then states that each nation already has an obligation under international law to censor as well as propagandize; he writes:

States have an obligation under international law to prevent and combat incitement to hatred and to promote diversity, mutual understanding and solidarity. They must step up and implement these commitments, while ensuring that the measures they take preserve freedom of speech and protect minorities and other communities.
—Secretary-General António Guterres

Wait! What?

So, the UN has already passed international law to "prevent and combat incitement to hatred and to promote diversity, mutual understanding and solidarity." To which each nation has already committed to. So, according to the UN:

- There are international laws that nations must prevent and combat "incitement to hatred."
  (*What the heck is hatred and who gets to define it? Does this include saying bad things about a "belief" or "political group"? Who decides what beliefs or political groups?*)
- There are international laws that nations must promote diversity.
  (*Diversity—a code word for?*)
- There are international laws that nations must "promote mutual understanding."
  (*What the heck is "mutual understanding." When and how did the USA commit to that via international law?*)
- There are international laws that nations must promote solidarity.
  (*The term "solidarity" is a well-defined modern term for socialism*)

In this context, the solidarity movement is described as "a democratic, revolutionary socialist, feminist, anti-racist organization." Its roots are in strains of the Trotskyist tradition but have departed from many aspects of traditional Leninism and Trotskyism. It is more loosely organized than most "democratic centralist" groups, and it does not see itself as the vanguard of the working class or the nucleus of a vanguard. It was formed in 1986 from a fusion of the International Socialists, Workers Power, and Socialist Unity. The former two groups had recently been reunited in a single organization, while the last was an expelled fragment of the Socialist Workers Party (SWP). Solidarity's name was originally in part an homage to Solidarność—a US-backed labor union in Communist Poland which, in Solidarity's view, had challenged the Soviet Union from the Left.

So . . .

The self-described socialist UN Secretary-General António Guterres, who served as secretary-general of the Portuguese Socialist Party from 1992 to 2002, and his comrades have basically inserted language into various treaties to ensure that the UN's globalist agenda is built upon a backbone of socialism.

So, where is that international law, exactly? The international law(s) that state that each nation commits to propaganda and censoring free speech in the name of some ambiguous terminology, that now also includes speech that targets political affiliations and beliefs.

What are the international laws that state that each nation commits to "solidarity"?

> There is no acceptable level of hate speech; we must all work to eradicate it completely.
>
> —Secretary-General António Guterres

Who put Secretary-General António Guterres, a card-carrying socialist, in charge of the world?

Ummm . . . we did?

But beyond that, where are those international laws? Look no further than Agenda 2030.

Agenda 2030 is a UN treaty which is supposed to drive sustainable development and eradicate poverty "in all its forms and dimensions." But

Agenda 2030 does so much more than that. Agenda 2030 promotes socialism, emphasizing government intervention, a redistribution of wealth, a
universal living wage for everyone (working or not), a program of universal
education, universal healthcare, and the creation of a globalized governing
body—with a centrally controlled globalized governance system. President
Obama signed Agenda 2030 just before he left office in 2016.

If elected, President Trump must commit to removing the United States
from this executive agreement. Furthermore, the Senate must insist upon
ratifying this treaty, which would then require a two-thirds vote to pass.
President Obama had no right to sign this as an executive agreement, as it
is one of the most flawed and overreaching treaties that the UN has ever
passed. The Senate must assert its fundamental duty under the Constitution
to ratify this treaty ASAP.

In reading Secretary-General António Guterres's statement on censoring free speech, one is left to wonder how the UN intends to censor and
propagandize free speech. The only way it is possible to both censor people
from saying wrong-speak and to preserve free speech is to make "wrong
speech" separate from "free speech" in the eyes of the law. All a nation or
the UN needs is a high-profile court case or two, and some new international agreements passed (courtesy of the UN). You know, a law here, a
law there, a court case supporting those laws, and then "wrong-speech" is
not included in the definition of "free-speech." Then Bob's-your-uncle, the
issue is resolved, right?

This is exactly what the 2024 United Nations' "United Nations
Global Principles For Information Integrity Recommendations for Multi-
stakeholder Action" does.[3] The United Nations commits to limiting free
speech across the globe in this document by:

- Scale up efforts. Intensify efforts to strengthen information
  integrity, including through context-specific research, monitoring, risk assessment, community engagement and coalition building across diverse contexts and languages. Integrate
  information integrity into programmes and operations to
  enhance prevention, mitigation and response and identify
  emerging opportunities and challenges.
- Support regional and national multistakeholder action plans

and coalitions, making use of existing mechanisms, and calling on the Organization's expertise and experience in international capacity-building and coordination.

- Establish a multilingual online information integrity resource hub with shared research, guidance, and best practices applicable to diverse contexts to support initiatives at the global, regional, and national levels.
- Establish a central unit in the United Nations Secretariat to develop innovative and nuanced approaches to addressing risks to the integrity of the information ecosystem.
- Undertake advocacy. Promote and advocate for the Global Principles at the global level and across countries and communities, with particular attention to underserved contexts and groups in situations of vulnerability and marginalization. Actively contribute to social cohesion and strengthen resilience of communities to risks to information integrity, supporting efforts to realize the Sustainable Development Goals.[4]

The other relevant important point that the UN enunciates is that Big Tech must be controlled by limiting advertising opportunities for those companies that do not comply with the censors. Furthermore, the UN has been building a barrier to control the world by weaving a web of international laws meant to control sovereign nations. They write:

- The Global Principles present an occasion for individuals, public and private entities, including the United Nations system, Governments, media, civil society organizations and for-profit corporations across the technology, advertising and public relations sectors, to align with the rights and freedoms enshrined in international law and form broad coalitions for information integrity.
- The Global Principles build on the ideas proposed in Our Common Agenda and in the United Nations Secretary-General's policy brief 8: information integrity on digital platforms. In addition to being grounded in international law, including international human rights law, the Global Principles

complement the relevant United Nations Guiding Principles on Business and Human Rights, the UNESCO Guidelines for the Governance of Digital Platforms, the United Nations Plan of Action on the Safety of Journalists and the Issue of Impunity, the UNESCO Recommendation on the Ethics of Artificial Intelligence and the United Nations Strategy and Plan of Action on Hate Speech.

- The Global Principles offer a resource for United Nations Member States in their considerations toward A Pact for the Future and the Global Digital Compact. In this way, the Global Principles further reflect the unwavering commitment of the United Nations to strengthening information integrity and are intended to guide the work of the Organization into the future . . .

- Establishing a more nuanced global understanding of information environments and enhancing targeted, evidence-based actions for the promotion of information integrity will require expanding the availability, quality, and usability of data and insights. Ensuring privacy-preserving data access for a diverse range of researchers will strengthen collective efforts to fill research gaps and inequalities.

- Cooperate with independent, third-party organizations to conduct and make public ongoing human rights risk assessments related to all products and services to proactively minimize societal risks and mitigate potential harms, including in advance of and around pivotal societal moments . . .

- Cooperate with independent, third-party organizations to develop content moderation processes in line with international human rights standards and ensure that such policy is enforced consistently and non-arbitrarily across areas of operation. Allocate sufficient resources for human and automated content moderation and curation, applied consistently across all languages and contexts of operation. Take measures to address content that violates platform community standards and undermines human rights, such as limiting algorithmic amplification, labelling and demonetization. Make publicly

available disaggregated data on the implementation of content moderation policies and on resources allocated for content
moderation across languages and contexts of operation.[5]

Governments, local authorities, religious, corporate and community
leaders have a duty to invest in measures to promote tolerance, diversity and inclusivity, and to challenge hate speech in all its forms.[6]

—Secretary-General António Guterres

Reading through the UN's lengthy "Principles of Information Integrity" is
difficult, because almost every section is carefully constructed to present a
nuanced plan. Yet, words like "diversity, inclusion, human rights, potential
harms" combined with other phrases such as "limiting algorithmic amplification, labelling, content moderation policies, and demonetization" jump
out in almost every paragraph. This is a future plan to control the world,
based on the UN's woke programmatic goals.

We, as a people, as a nation must stand up and say no to this assault on
our fundamental rights as United States Citizens.

The founders of this great nation knew that the unpopular, the ugly, and
the controversial speech is precisely what needs protecting. What matters
here is our fundamental right to say whatever we want. This freedom is at
the heart of our Constitution, and to remaining a free people.

The globalists, the socialists, and the communists seem to need to control society because they distrust the free will and thought of the general
populace. Their power can only be maintained by removing our rights to
free speech, and that means *all* speech. When it becomes a crime to speak
of certain things, when the government becomes the arbitrator of "good
speech," and by extension to control thought, we are no longer free.

The UN has once again overstepped. The issue at hand is the right of
people to express themselves. Good, bad, or indifferent.

But even more importantly, the UN is not above that independent nation
known as the United States of America. In 1776, this country fought for our
freedom to be a sovereign land and won, after a long, bloody war. The right
to speak is one of the most important freedoms that we have, it is a defining
feature of this great country. Let's not lose it now in a bloodless coup to the
fascist, socialist, globalist organization known as the United Nations.

# CHAPTER 30

# "We Own the Science and the World Should Know It"

## And According to the United Nations, "Big Tech" Knows It, Too

Melissa Fleming, Under-Secretary-General for Global Communications of the United Nations, spoke on a World Economic Forum disinformation panel on September 28, 2022. A transcript of that video reads:

> We partnered with Google, for example. If you Google climate change, at the top of your search, you will get all kinds of UN resources. We started this partnership when we were shocked to see that when we'd Googled climate change, we were getting incredibly distorted information right at the top.
>
> We are becoming much more proactive. *We own the science and we think that the world should know it,* and the platforms themselves also do. But again, it's a huge, huge challenge that I think all sectors of society need to be very active.[1]

So, the United Nations claims that they "own the science." For this reason, they have partnered with the Big Tech platforms to manipulate search results, and they are pouring vast quantities of money into globalist media outlets to ensure their version of "*the science*" is the only one that we get to read.[2]

The thing is—when you listen to the full panel discussion cited above, the UN speaker Ms. Fleming is not just saying that the UN is censoring speech on climate change. She also suggests that the UN with the WEF is censoring many scientific discussions, such as on the topic of COVID-19, and the UN censors ALL misinformation that the UN deems unhelpful for a *"stable, peaceful, harmonious, and UNITED world."* This means that search algorithms in the Googleweb are being manipulated so that users only see those results that favor the UN's point of view on science-related *or* political issues. With this position, the UN basically seeks to only promote or permit internet access to information which advocates for globalist perspectives. On Google, the public can no longer easily find search results that differ from the UN's official narratives. Of course, COVID-19 is only one such science-related topic. Climate change is another topic that is actively being censored, results manipulated and of course, dissident voices shadow-banned. The risks and benefits of using "clean" energy versus petroleum products is another area where Google and world governments actually suppress dissident voices, including scientists, on the internet and in search results.

Fleming explicitly states that the UN and their WEF partners are intentionally training and creating controlled-opposition scientists, physicians, and social media influencers to assist in their global propaganda campaigns managed via partnerships with corporate media and Big Tech.

Moderating the "Tackling Disinformation" panel mentioned above was the WEF managing director Adrian Monck. Mr. Monck states that there has been a *"professionalization of disinformation,"* including *"COVID-19 state-sponsored actors engaged in that."* What does that even mean? That somehow those of us who were critical of the COVID-19 policies are *"state sponsored"* actors? Frankly, his statements during the discussion were bizarre and paranoid, but indicative of how the WEF views social media. That is, nefarious "state-sponsored" operatives are feeding the uneducated masses untruths that oppose the consensus of scientists. The truth is that science is never a consensus; it is always evolving and changing. Paradigm shifts can occur swiftly, or sometimes those shifts can take years. World governments and organizations cannot be allowed to stifle scientific debate in the public square. Censorship of ideas, even wrong ideas, is against the very nature of the scientific enterprise.

This is what is clear. The actions of the UN, acting with its strategic partner, the WEF, to stifle free speech have created a dangerous situation for our country and the world. The United Nations is clearly engaging in psyops operations—*ergo,* the UN itself is engaged in PsyWar against those who disagree with its point of view. They are performing *information control* on all of us. This is beyond anything we all could have imagined ten years ago. We all used to joke about "1984," now it just seems like a cliché. Because that future is here. In this country, this is a situation that only Congress can rectify.

UN Global Communications representative Melissa Fleming's other remarks in this discussion were astounding, here are a few examples:

> We partnered with Google. For example, if you Google "climate change," you will, at the top of your search, you will get all kinds of UN resources.
> Another really key strategy we had was to deploy influencers [. . .] and they were much more trusted than the United Nations.
> We trained scientists around the world and some doctors on TikTok, and we had TikTok working with us.

The UN, with its strategic partner the WEF, wants to own more than "The Science." They want to own and control what is published on the internet in total. They want to own "The Politics," "The World Agenda," and "The Narrative." Not only that, but they want to crush any opposition to their plans.

WEF managing director Mr. Monck also called critics of the WEF and components of its great reset agenda white supremacists and anti-Semites. It is a way to cast shade on those who are fighting for freedom of the press, national sovereignty, and the right to own property. A right written into the very structure of our republic. Mr. Monck states:

> Own nothing, be happy. You might have heard the phrase. It started life as a screenshot, culled from the internet by an anonymous anti-semitic account on the image board 4chan. "Own nothing, be happy—The Jew World Order 2030," said the post, which went viral among extremists.
> —Adrian Monck, WEF, 2022

This statement of course, is completely false. In fact, it is disinformation and black propaganda, The phrase didn't "start life as a screenshot . . . culled from the internet by an anonymous anti-semitic account on the image board 4chan" as the WEF director states. The phrase came directly from a video on the WEF's own website and social media channels in 2016. The title from the WEF website was: "'You'll own nothing. And you'll be happy'—8 Predictions for the World in 2030, WEF, 2016." This WEF video promotes a sanitized form of socialism that many global corporatists promote. The socialist ideal of a society where ownership is forbidden, has now been labeled a "circular business economy." This web page was removed from the WEF website, but the video can still be accessed.[3]

Furthermore, WEF member corporations, the largest corporations in the world, don't want the consumer to own anything. They want to maintain control of resources. In a video, Royal Philips Electronics CEO Frans Van Houten explained the concept of circular economy business models to the WEF in 2016. He states:

> "In circular economy business models, I would like products to come back to me as the original designer and manufacturer," he said, adding, "and once you get your head around that notion, why would I actually sell you the product if you are primarily interested in the benefit of the product?
>
> "Maybe I can stay the owner of the product and just sell you the benefit as a service."

"Circular economy business models" are nothing less than socialism via corporate control, wrapped up in a pretty package. Whereby all products become services to be rented out. This is what the unelected globalists are striving for. This is the meaning of "you will own nothing and be happy." They have realized that by working with the UN to influence nations—they can rent products without having to sell anything. Collecting the profit from both governments and rental agreements, which in the long-term are much more profitable than merely selling the product once. This is the economy that the UN and the WEF envision. A joint globalist agenda.

However, an ownerless future is not only against our constitution, which confers the right to own property, but it would not be a happy outcome for individuals—as the ownership of property is critical to human happiness.[4] Such a society basically makes the individual a slave to corporations. The interesting thing is that the backlash from the promotion of these videos promoting a "circular business economy," *ergo* a modified form of socialism, is that the WEF and the UN took these videos and web pages off their websites. Furthermore, fact-checkers denied the origin and meaning of these videos. This had to have been coordinated at the highest levels of these organizations.

The United States of America as a country, and the free people who are citizens of the United States, cannot let the UN and their WEF strategic partners control what we write and publish, what we get to read, our ability to buy products, and even what we think. We must elect leaders who are willing to stand up to the UN and other globalist entities. Congress must become engaged—the UN is out of control, and the current president of the United States, Joe Biden, as well as his administration, are acting like captured allies of the globalists.

So, wake up. We are being led down a very dangerous road by the hyperwealthy who have neither respect nor empathy for individuals. They want to rule the world. This is the face of evil. And that is the Dementor that is sucking at our souls. But how do we stop this madness? If you are with the forces of good, please help us, please help humanity, and please help our children. Stand up. It is time to act.

Or forever hold your peace.

# CHAPTER 31
# Physicals, Virtuals, Machines, and Overlords

The World Economic Forum, its founder and CEO Klaus Schwab, and Yuval Noah Harari (the WEF's transhuman futurist) share a dark vision of the future. This path for humanity, which they are so aggressively advancing throughout the world, is based on projections that humanity's future will consist of an anticipated "fourth industrial revolution."

What is the fourth industrial revolution?

> **The Fourth Industrial Revolution** is based on the concept that rapid changes to technology, industry, and societal norms in the 21st century will be due to increasing interconnectivity and smart automation. Technologies such as artificial intelligence, gene editing, robotics, and transhumanism will blur the lines between the physical, digital, and biological worlds.

## Who Wins and Who Loses in This Version of the Future?

Fundamental shifts are taking place in how the global production and supply network operates through ongoing automation of traditional manufacturing and industrial practices, using modern smart technology, large-scale machine-to-machine communication (M2M), and the internet of things. This integration results in increasing automation, improving communication and self-monitoring, and the use of smart machines or AI that can analyze and diagnose issues without the need for human intervention.

It also represents a social, political, and economic shift from the digital age of the late 1990s and early 2000s to an era of embedded connectivity distinguished by the omni-use and commonness of technological use throughout society (e.g., a metaverse) that changes the ways humans experience and know the world around them. It posits that we have created and are entering an augmented social reality compared to just the natural senses and industrial ability of humans alone.

WEF CEO Schwab has proclaimed that a key element of the COVIDcrisis-fueled "Great Reset" will be to advance and shape this "Fourth Industrial Revolution." And in public statements, he has explained what this means, which is the merging of man with machines. "What the fourth industrial revolution will lead to is a fusion of our physical, digital and biological identity," Schwab explained in a speech to the Chicago Council on Global Affairs.

This is not a "conspiracy theory." Schwab even wrote a book on the subject in 2016 entitled *Shaping the Future of The Fourth Industrial Revolution*.[1] In it, he explains how looming technological changes will allow governments to "intrude into the hitherto private space of our minds, reading our thoughts and influencing our behavior." The title is a tell. This vision is not inevitable, but rather will have to be shaped if it is to develop in the way that he and his WEF colleagues envision. Once again, a quote from Herr Dr. Schwab, in which this vision is presented as inevitable.

> "Fourth Industrial Revolution technologies will not stop at becoming part of the physical world around us—they will become part of us," according to the future envisioned by Schwab. "Indeed, some of us already feel that our smartphones have become an extension of ourselves. Today's external devices—from wearable computers to virtual reality headsets—will almost certainly become implantable in our bodies and brains."[2]

Among those technologies are "active implantable microchips that break the skin barrier of our bodies," Schwab explains. These "implantable devices," Schwab continued, "will likely also help to communicate thoughts normally expressed verbally through a 'built-in' smartphone, and potentially unexpressed thoughts or moods by reading brain waves and other signals."

Schwab suggests that governments would use these technologies to determine who may travel and even for "pre-crime" purposes. To quote Schwab again:

> "As capabilities in this area improve, the temptation for law enforcement agencies and courts to use techniques to determine the likelihood of criminal activity, assess guilt or even possibly retrieve memories directly from people's brains will increase," he explains, adding that authorities might require "a detailed brain scan to assess an individual's security risk."

One wonders if such a brain scan will pre-identify individuals with socio/psychopathy and/or megalomaniac tendencies? And will this be required for both commercial as well as private jet flights? Or will this be another case of "Good for thee but not for me."

This is a vision of the future which is commonly referred to as "transhumanism." The focus of Klaus Schwab and his wingman Yuval Noah Harari seem to be on bringing this vision to maturity, while convincing the members of the trade organization comprised of the largest companies in the world, that is the WEF, of how much more money, power, and monopolistic control can be had if they will only get on board with the program.

> "It is very likely, within a century or two, *Homo sapiens,* as we have known it for thousands of years, will disappear," Harari said at the Carnegie Council for Ethics in International Affairs recently. "We will use technology to upgrade ourselves—or at least some of us—into something different; something which is far more different from us than we are different from Neanderthals."[3]

What does jolly Santa Klaus and the WEF envision as the nature of their brave new world? George Jetson comes to mind. By the way, where *are* those flying cars they promised us?

Danish Parliamentarian Ida Auken's post, which has now been removed from the WEF website, clarifies the direction and goals of all this transhumanism.

> Welcome to the year 2030. . . . I don't own anything, I have no real privacy. No where I can go and not be registered. I know that, somewhere, everything I do, think and dream of is recorded.

But her biggest concern is those who refuse to participate.

> "My biggest concern is all the people who do not live in our city," Auken explains, noting that some stubborn individuals refused to merge with machines. "Those we lost on the way. Those who decided that it became too much, all this technology. Those who felt obsolete and useless when robots and AI took over big parts of our jobs. Those who got upset with the political system and turned against it."

You are not alone if you cannot shake images of the *Matrix* and *Terminator* film series out of your mind.

What does the social structure of global human society look like as we move into this envisioned Transhumanist/Fourth Industrial Revolution world?

Historically, most political and social scientists from the mid-twentieth century to the present, as well as corporate media pundits who repackage the work product coming from academe and think tanks, have relied on the conceptual structure of lower, middle, and upper classes as they try to categorize and comprehend political and social trends. In parallel, others use the Marxist terms bourgeoisie (and the related petty bourgeoisie) and proletariat.

Since a series of radio interview discussions which Robert had with Mr. Glenn Beck, we have become convinced that these twentieth-century frameworks, including the dialectic of Republican versus Democrat (US political parties) or "liberal" versus "conservative" were no longer particularly useful in trying to understand what is happening in the US (and Western world) body politic. Back then, we had become convinced that the emergent new tension was between those who were committed to a collectivist vision (let's call them Socialists, or maybe Marxists, for want of a better term, combined with fascist-corporatism) versus those committed to an independent, autonomous vision of personal sovereignty.

So much time seems to have passed since then, and we are now persuaded by an alternative construction of modern social and political reality which is emerging from the fringes of academic and other thought leader essays on Substack and online journals such as UnHerd. That being that society is now being divided into Physicals, Virtuals, Machines (I guess that includes Borg-like transhumans?), and a very small, elite group of "Davos Man" Overlords.

What could possibly go wrong?

In the classic novel *Animal Farm*, George Orwell provides a metaphorical analysis of the Stalinist version of totalitarianism, in which a small caste of Party members lived very well and the rest of the population did not. This is the caste of the Overlords. The book is a warning that ordinary people in society must not give up their power, or a caste of rulers will rise and repeat all the excesses typical of past totalitarians throughout history. Technology may change, and every totalitarian regime is different, but fundamental human behaviors never change. Orwell writes:

> The creatures outside looked from pig to man, and from man to pig, and from pig to man again; but already it was impossible to say which was which.
>
> —George Orwell, *Animal Farm*

As envisioned in Schwab's transhumanism-dominated future, the "Davos Man" monopolist Overlords will hold all assets, and control all financial transactions. This vision is at the heart of the famous WEF phrase, "You will own nothing and be happy." The business model behind this is an advanced version of modern corporate rent-seeking behaviors, in which a few companies and their owners will control all physical assets. Think BlackRock, State Street, Vanguard, and Bank of America, who are already well on their way to completing this objective. Then these resources will be allocated out on basically a rental basis "for the greatest good for the greatest number." Utilitarian/Marxism with a dash of command economy thrown in. "From each according to his abilities, to each according to his needs." At least for the lower castes.

So, now we have defined the Overlords and their machines. What about the physical and virtual castes?

The battle now being fought, while the Overlords, their databases and machine learning algorithms look on, is between those whose power and interests are grounded in the material world, and those whose wealth comes from the virtual world. The political analyst N. S. Lyons characterizes this as a class and culture war between "Physicals" and "Virtuals."

In this formulation of the new class structure, Physicals are those who work at physical labor-intensive jobs such as construction, farming, manufacturing, trucking, mining, warehouses, shipping, and delivery. Activities which are grounded in physical and material reality. In contrast, Virtual workers are at least one layer removed from the physical world labor. Examples include those employed in finance, banking, academe, bench scientific research, general education, media, information technology, and investment portfolio management.

The key difference between these two classes or castes is that they define truth and morality in very different terms and from very different perspectives. Predictably, Physicals see truth and morality as being more absolute, whereas Virtuals have a more surrealistic sense of truth and morality as fluid and elastic, and dependent on the perspective, emotions, and belief system of each individual. But in today's post-third industrial revolution world, the elite who dominate political and economic decision-making, and who benefit from the transfer of power and wealth from those performing Physical occupations to the Virtuals, it is the latter who control institutional power.

Mary Harrington (writing from the perspective of United Kingdom politics), provides advice to "Physicals" confronting this new reality:

> Mutinous Physicals may need to learn from the truckers: Trudeau eventually ended the protest by freezing protesters out of their own bank accounts. Even the most capable Physicals can't easily get by in the modern world without access to Virtual finance and tech.
>
> Another possibility is a more thoroughgoing push to turn what's left of working-class Physicals into the "useless class"

some predict will emerge if AI and automation replace human-powered jobs. This would represent the final Virtual victory: for without even the option to withdraw their labour, it's hard to see on what basis such a group could compel elites to consider their political interests. This condition of political weakness would be even more pronounced should UBI [universal basic income] replace earned wages: few adolescents, however rebellious, will do more than pull faces at their parents if they're afraid their pocket money will be stopped.[4]

And here is the rub. Virtuals are deeply invested in the belief that reality is whatever they believe it to be. Truth is relative. There is no objective truth, reality, nor ethics. In the world of online gaming and virtual reality, there is no objective ground truth, no actual physical reality to contend with. Only a sort of "truthiness," a sense of "that seems plausible." And a whole lot of fantasy. And from this perspective, many of the social divides which are tearing up the electorate and redefining politics in the United States suddenly start to make sense. Back to Mary Harrington again for more key insights:

> This class-inflected contest between the virtual and the real economies is the core of the class and culture war now being fought across the West. It also helps to make sense of how apparently unrelated issues, such as trans rights and immigration, can become bitter battlefronts in the same war.
>
> Trans rights make sense as a proxy for the Virtuals' core moral claim: that ideas matter more than the material world. When we consider what a person is in legal terms, do we prioritize the material fact of their biological sex, or their inner, abstract idea of who they are? Understandably, the Virtuals prefer the answer that places their class of work, their worldview and by extension their political interests at the top of the moral pile.
>
> High immigration, meanwhile, is a material positive to Virtuals: more people means more growth. This material upside is then moralized in terms of "openness," "culture," "freedom" and so on. For working-class Physicals, though, high immigration means stiffer competition for jobs.

Fortunately or unfortunately, what neither Mary Harrington nor the Virtuals seem to appreciate is that from the perspective of the Overlords, Virtuals are even more expendable than the Physicals are. Someone needs to run the farms, milk the cows (or at least maintain the robotic milking machines), collect the trash, and treat the ill. The Virtuals are the ones at greatest risk of replacement by computational algorithms and are already finding themselves being made "redundant" by artificial intelligence-based algorithms at a surprisingly fast rate. They may be the first to be forced into universal basic income slavery allocated via central bank digital currency with a social credit score topping just to make sure that they do not get uppity.

In closing, we hope that readers who have not previously encountered these new ideas of Transhumanism, the Fourth Industrial Revolution, and the new caste structure of Physicals, Virtuals, Machines, and Overlords can now appreciate that there are fundamental shifts in the structure of modern society, which are being actively promoted and imposed upon us by a variety of political and economic actors.

In his book *The Revolt of the Elites*, Christopher Lasch summarizes the situation nicely.

> The thinking classes are fatally removed from the physical side of life . . . Their only relation to productive labor is that of consumers. They have no experience of making anything substantial or enduring. They live in a world of abstractions and images, a simulated world that consists of computerized models of reality—"hyperreality," as it's been called—as distinguished from the palatable, immediate, physical reality inhabited by ordinary men and women. Their belief in "social construction of reality"—the central dogma of postmodernist thought—reflects the experience of living in an artificial environment from which everything that resists human control (unavoidably, everything familiar and reassuring as well) has been rigorously excluded. Control has become their obsession. In their drive to insulate themselves against risk and contingency—against the unpredictable hazards that afflict human life—the thinking classes have seceded not just from the common world around them but from reality itself.[5]

Which are you? Physical, Virtual, Transhuman machine, or Overlord? Which world do you want to live in? The sterilized, depopulated, and highly managed city of Danish Parliamentarian Ida Auken's fantasies, or the physical world for which she has such distain?

And more importantly, what is the world that you wish to have your children inherit?

We have made our choice. We prefer to join Candide and go work in the garden.

What we would like people to think about is what are positive alternative visions of the future? Whether Physical, Virtual, or a blend of the two, if we want to beat the Overlords (and their transhuman machines), we need to create our own great narrative. One that evokes *Morning in America* rather than *The Matrix* and the *Borg* as the future of humankind.

And most importantly, what we want to know, is *"are you kind?"*

# CHAPTER 32
# Global Public-Private Partnerships and the United Nations

Basically, the government leaders are bribed by business leaders to co-sign and fund imaginary threats that create policies that benefit connected businesses. Essentially, monopolies or oligopolies are formed where economic rents are extracted from unsuspecting populations. The connected business leaders gain access to insider knowledge on the policies coming and plan accordingly with government contracts coming their way first; then, they roll out their revenue schemes to the public. It's fraud, the likes of which we have never seen. None of this would be possible without debt-based fiat money from central banks. I also suspect the intelligence agencies run enforcement for this group and blackmail those government employees without a conscience. They are either rewarded with plum jobs when they go to the private sector or with outright bribes.

—Edward Dowd, former BlackRock investment fund manager

In our many travels and interviews, one of the most frequent questions involves some variation of "who are the puppet masters?" behind the harmonized propaganda, censorship, PsyWar, and COVIDcrisis mismanagement that has now emerged from the shadows into full view of anyone who will not avert their gaze.

How is it that so many demonstrably false and counterproductive narratives are not only globally promoted but, once they emerge, are rapidly transformed into globally accepted public policies without significant debate or scrutiny? Repeated global harmonization of bad policy decisions not only implies but requires centralization. Globally centralized decision-making indicates the existence of some cabal, organization, or group with sufficient power, wealth, and influence to unilaterally deploy not only a globally harmonized PsyWar campaign but to promptly propagate governance decisions across a wide range of what were previously believed to be independent, sovereign nation-states. Based on this repeated pattern of harmonized priorities, cited justifications, actions, and messaging, it appears that centralized, transnational world (or regional) governments already exist in a functional, operational sense. Under the Westphalian system of autonomous nation-states that guides current governance and international relations, how can that be?

To recap what was discussed in a previous chapter, the Westphalian system is named after the Peace of Westphalia, which was signed in 1648 and ended the Thirty Years' War in Europe. This system enshrines the principle that each state has exclusive sovereignty over its territory and domestic affairs, excluding all external powers, and is a fundamental tenet of international law.

Key Principles of the Westphalian system:

- Sovereignty: Each state has sovereignty over its territory and domestic affairs, meaning no external power can intervene in its internal affairs.
- Territorial Integrity: States respect each other's territorial integrity, meaning that no state can annex or occupy another state's territory without its consent.
- Noninterference: States do not intervene in each other's internal affairs, allowing each state to manage its own domestic issues independently.
- Equality: All states, regardless of size, power, or wealth, are equal and have the same rights and responsibilities.

Obviously, many of these principles are functionally aspirational, and a wide variety of military and diplomatic "work-arounds" have been devised since 1648. These work-arounds enable nation-states or groups of aligned nation-states with more size, power, and wealth to exert influence or control over those with less. Various terms of political science have been devised to describe these work-arounds. Such terms include colonialism, imperialism, alliances, soft power, and hegemony, among many others. However, all are based on the assumption that the autonomous nation-state represents the highest-ranking governing political structure. Functionally, this assumption is no longer valid.

Despite the partial success of these predictable efforts to circumvent the core principles, the Westphalian system has guided the structure of international relations and international law for centuries, as it established the concept of state sovereignty and the principle of noninterference in domestic affairs. This system has been the foundation of the modern international system of sovereign states and has shaped how states interact. While the system has clearly been influential, it is also criticized as deeply flawed— arguably the worst system except for all others that came before. One criticism is that it has led to a system of anarchy, where states are left to fend for themselves and may resort to violence to achieve their goals. Austrian school economists such as Murray Rothbard argue that the modern anatomy of the nation-state is fundamentally flawed and should be replaced with an even more anarchic free-market system. Others observe that the rise of global governance, transnational corporations, "investment funds," corporatist-aligned trade unions, self-appointed global governance organizations, and international institutions have challenged the Westphalian system, eroding state sovereignty.

Since World War II and accelerating during the latter decades of the twentieth century, a trend toward the emergence of financially powerful transnational organizations that are functionally independent of nation-states developed. Examples include quasi-governmental global organizations such as the United Nations (UN), World Health Organization (WHO), International Monetary Foundation (IMF), Intergovernmental Panel on Climate Change (IPCC), and World Trade Organization (WTO); nongovernmental "philanthropic" organizations such as the Gates Foundation and Wellcome Trust; "national" banks tied together into a functional cooperative by the Bank of International Settlements; massive global "investment funds" which dwarf the financial resources of most nation-states including

BlackRock, State Street, Vanguard, Bank of America and their kin; and a variety of globalist-oriented cabals and corporatist trade organizations such as the Club of Rome, the Atlantic Council, the Bilderberg Meeting group, the Council on Foreign Relations, the Aspen Institute for Humanistic Studies, and of course, the World Economic Forum.

Fueled by a variety of global twenty-first-century financial, political, geophysical, and medical "crises," these transnational think tanks and organizations, together with a handful of major globalized corporations that sponsor much of their activities, have formed alliances that exceed the power, influence, and financial resources of most if not all nation-states. Any economics or political science student can attest that such a power imbalance cannot be sustained. We argue that the wide range of current efforts to advance and structure global governance organizations is the logical consequence of these imbalances. Since the most economically dominant of these various transnational entities are intrinsically corporatist, it is self-evident that the emerging global governance organizations are corporatist.

The repeated history of the various forms of corporatism, often labeled "fascism" during the early to mid-twentieth century, has been the development of totalitarian political governance structures. In the twenty-first century, these corporatist political structures have come to rely on computational modeling and artificial intelligence algorithms informed by massive databases to guide decision-making. Databases that seek to identify and characterize the activities and biases of virtually all human beings and all available data concerning the nature of the world—geophysics, climate, resources, "one health," energy, and any other useful predictive parameters. All combined within computational modeling algorithms, which are now accepted as an object of faith and have become a surrogate for measurable truths.

All of this has given rise to centralized, globalized, arbitrary, and capricious decision-making on a scale never before possible. Once the models have been run and the centralized decision-making has been performed, then the propaganda, censorship, and modern PsyWar technologies are deployed by various means, including captured "intelligence agencies" and the corporate media (which is owned and controlled by the same transnational organizations) to enforce these decisions.

This is the structure of modern techno-totalitarianism: an interwoven corporatist web that unilaterally controls and implements globalized policies, is answerable to no one, and recognizes no law other than its own interests and privilege. At the center of this web lies global public-private partnerships, or G3P. Caught like flies in this global financial and political web, politicians, political parties, indebted nation-states, and even multinational treaty and alliance organizations such as NATO and the European Union must dance to the tunes called by the G3P.

Global Public-Private Partnerships (G3P) are structured collaborations between international intergovernmental organizations, such as the United Nations, the World Health Organization, the World Economic Forum, and private companies to achieve shared goals and objectives. The asserted benefits used to justify G3P include:

- Increased efficiency: G3P can leverage the strengths of both the public and private sectors to achieve common goals more efficiently.
- Innovative solutions: G3P can efficiently foster innovation and the development of new solutions to address global challenges.
- Shared risk and resources: G3P can share the risks and resources between the public and private sectors, reducing the financial burden on governments and increasing project effectiveness.
- Global impact: G3P can significantly impact global development and public health, addressing challenges that transcend national borders.

Both the United Nations and the World Health Organization have established various agreements and treaties with transnational organizations, such as the World Economic Forum, and typically do not disclose governance details, funding, terms, and conditions of G3Ps to the general public.

These G3Ps form a worldwide network of stakeholder capitalists and their partners.[1] This association of stakeholders (the capitalists and their partners) comprises global corporations (including central banks), philanthropic foundations (multibillionaire philanthropists), policy think tanks, governments (and their agencies), nongovernmental organizations, selected academic and scientific institutions, global charities, labor unions and other chosen "thought leaders," including the various networks funded, trained, and placed into influential positions by the World Economic Forum "Young Leader" and "Young Influencers" programs.

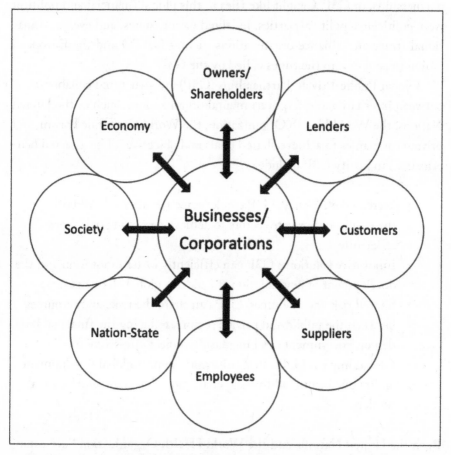

**Figure 1:** Original Flower Petal Diagram, "Stakeholder Capitalism" after 1971 "Modern Company Management in Mechanical Engineering."

*Dr. Klaus Schwab defines "stakeholder capitalism" as a form of capitalism in which companies seek long-term value creation by taking into account the needs of all their stakeholders, and society at large. Dr. Schwab asserts that this approach was common in the post-war decades in the West when it became clear that one person or entity could only do well if the whole community and economy functions well. There was a strong linkage between companies and their community. In Germany, for example, it led to the representation of employees on the board. As sourcing, production, and selling took place mostly locally or at least regionally, there was a connection with suppliers and clients as well. As described by Schwab, this fostered a strong sense that local companies were embedded in their surroundings, and mutual respect grew between companies and local institutions such as government, schools, and health organizations. It led to a constellation of stakeholders as diagrammed above and envisioned by Dr. Schwab in his 1971 book* Modern Company Management in Mechanical Engineering.

When placed into context with the "flower petal" or "satellite" model of stakeholder capitalism promoted by Dr. Klaus Schwab in his 1971 book *Modern Company Management in Mechanical Engineering,*[2] G3P operate as satellites closely tied to corporations, in partnership with global governance (United Nations), and above state and society. Under our current model of Westphalian national sovereignty, the government of one nation cannot make legislation or law in another. However, through global governance, the G3P creates policy initiatives at the global level, which then cascade down to people in every nation. This typically occurs via an intermediary policy distributor, such as the IMF or IPCC, and the national government then enacts the recommended policies.

The policy trajectory is set internationally by the authorized definition of problems and their prescribed solutions. Once the G3P enforces the consensus internationally, the policy framework is set. The G3P stakeholder partners then collaborate to develop, implement, and enforce the desired policies. This is the essence of the "international rules-based system."

In this way, G3P are able to control many nations at once without having to resort to legislation. This has the added advantage of making any legal challenge to the decisions made by the most senior partners in G3P (which typically have authoritarian hierarchies) extremely difficult.

The organizational predicate for the planned global governance is the European Union (EU). The EU has pioneered a system wherein nation-states and their elected governing bodies are subsidiaries of a centralized super-governmental organization located in Brussels. That organization includes an elected representative parliament, but any recommendations developed or "approved" at the European Parliament level can be overturned by the unelected, appointed European Council acting in coordination with a president who is formally appointed by national leaders, which appointment is then "confirmed" by the European Parliament. The citizens of the EU directly elect neither the European Council nor the president of the European Union, and the authorities of both the council and president are above those of individual national governments. Both the council and president can unilaterally enter into agreements with corporations and other supranational organizations such as G3P, such as the contract agreement struck between the EU Council, president, and Pfizer for COVID mRNA vaccine acquisition. By analogy, the United Nations, which explicitly seeks to become the governing body of global government, does not and will not be directly elected by, nor will it be accountable to, the citizens of UN member states. However, it will be able to be held accountable by the G3P.

G3P have traditionally been referenced in the context of public health—specifically in United Nations documents, including documents from UN agencies such as the World Health Organization (WHO). The WHO's 2005 document "Connecting For Health," in noting what the Millennium Development Goals meant for global health, revealed the emerging role of G3P:

> These changes occurred in a world of revised expectations about the role of government: that the public sector has neither the financial nor the institutional resources to meet their challenges, and that a mix of public and private resources is required. [. . .] Building a global culture of security and cooperation is vital. . . . The beginnings of a global health infrastructure are already in place. Information and communication technologies have opened opportunities for change in health, with or without policymakers leading the way. [. . .] Governments can create an enabling environment, and invest in equity, access and innovation.

This statement again reveals the United Nations' core belief that the Westphalian system of sovereign nation-state primacy is obsolete. In the envisioned new world order, nation-states are relegated to a secondary enabling role, and rather than setting foreign policy are to focus exclusively on resolving internal social justice issues and technical advancements. The revised role of sovereign nation-states implies they will no longer lead the way forward. Traditional policymakers will not be making policy anymore; rather, the United Nations, in cooperation with G3P partners, will set global agendas and policies.

Under this system, national governments must be relegated to creating the UN and G3P's enabling environment by taxing the public and increasing government borrowing debt. This debt is owed to the senior partners in the G3P. They are not only creditors; these same partners are also the beneficiaries of the loans. They use the circular logic of the propagandized term "public investment" to create markets for themselves and for the wider G3P stakeholders.

"Public Health" has served as the Trojan horse for the development of the G3P ecosystem. This was described and briefly analyzed in an editorial published in the academic journal "Tropical Medicine and International Health" titled "Editorial: Partnership and fragmentation in international health: threat or opportunity?," authored by Kent Buse and Gill Walt of the George Institute for Global Health. The editorial suggests that the G3P structure was a response to growing disillusionment in the UN project as a whole, combined with an emerging realization that global corporations were increasingly key to policy implementation. This correlates to the development of the stakeholder capitalism concept, popularized by Klaus Schwab beginning in the 1970s.

Buse and Walt describe how G3Ps are designed to facilitate the participation of a new breed of corporation. In theory, these new entities recognize the folly of previously destructive business practices and instead commit to the logic of the stakeholder capitalism concept, emphasizing socialist objectives such as promoting diversity, equity, and inclusion rather than a primary focus on profit and return on investment. This new breed of globally conscious corporations would achieve these objectives by partnering with governmental bureaucracies and established political elite to solve global problems, typically framed as existential threats to the global environment. Examples include "one health" infectious disease risks and climate change. Such threats are defined by the G3P and by the scientists, academics, and economists that the relevant G3P have selected and funded.

The two researchers identified a key Davos address, delivered by the UN's then-Secretary-General Kofi Annan to the WEF in 1998, as marking the transition to a G3P-based global governance model:

> The United Nations has been transformed since we last met here
> in Davos. The Organization has undergone a complete overhaul

that I have described as a "quiet revolution." [. . .] A fundamental shift has occurred. The United Nations once dealt only with
governments. By now we know that peace and prosperity cannot
be achieved without partnerships involving governments, international organizations, the business community and civil society.
. . . The business of the United Nations involves the businesses
of the world.

Buse and Walt claimed that this shift signified the arrival of a new type of
responsible global capitalism. However, that is not how many corporations
view this arrangement. Buse and Walt acknowledged why the G3P was
such an enticing prospect for the global giants of banking, industry, finance,
and commerce:

Shifting ideologies and trends in globalization have highlighted
the need for closer global governance, an issue for both private
and public sectors. We suggest that at least some of the support
for G3Ps stems from this recognition and a desire on the part of
the private sector to be part of global regulatory decision-making
processes.

The conflict of interest is obvious. We are simply expected to accept, without question, that global corporations are committed to putting humanitar-
ian and environmental causes before profit. Supposedly, a G3P-led system
of global governance is somehow beneficial for us.

Believing this requires a considerable degree of naivete. Many of the
G3P-associated stakeholder corporations have been convicted or publicly
held accountable for corruption and crimes, including war crimes. The
apparently passive agreement of the credulous political class (*ergo*, "deep
state") is that these "partners" should effectively set global policy, regulations, and spending priorities. It may seem naive, but it is actually a consequence of widespread corruption.

This naivete is a charade. As many academics, economists, historians,
and researchers have pointed out, corporate influence, even dominance of
the political system, has been increasing for generations. Elected politicians
have long been the junior partners in this arrangement.

With the arrival of G3Ps, we witnessed the birth of the process that formalized this relationship—creating a cohesive new world order. The politicians didn't write the script; it is delivered to them in various forms, including the WEF "young leader" training program, and they then operationalize these plans within their respective nation-states.

Understanding the difference between "government" and "governance" in the global context is important. Based on the concept of a social contract validated through quasi-democratic mandates, governments claim the right to set policy and decree legislation (law).

Western representative "democracies," which are technically not even democracies at all, practice a model of the national government in which elected representatives form the executive branch, which presents and ultimately enacts generally worded legislation. This is then operationally managed by a permanent unelected bureaucracy (the administrative state) which is given considerable latitude to interpret legislative intent, and to which the judicial system (courts) defer as the definitive experts (in the United States, this is referred to as "Chevron deference" consequent to a Supreme Court precedent). As observed by Murray Rothbard in *Anatomy of the State*, the judicial systems of these "democracies" (*ergo*, the courts) act to legitimize and defend the state, rather than serving to guarantee the rights and interests of the citizenry.

Perhaps the closest thing to this form of national government on an international scale is the United Nations General Assembly. It has a tenuous claim to democratic accountability and can pass resolutions which, while they don't bind member states, can create "new principles" that may become international law when later applied by the International Court of Justice.

However, this isn't really world "government." The UN lacks the authority to decree legislation and formulate law. Its "principles" can only become law via judicial ruling. The nonjudicial power to create law is reserved for governments, whose legislative reach only extends to their national borders.

Due to the often fraught relationships between national governments, a world government is starting to become impractical. Given the non-binding nature of UN resolutions and the international jockeying for geopolitical and economic advantage, there isn't currently anything we could call a world government.

National and cultural identity are also a consideration. Most populations aren't ready for a distant, unelected world government. People generally want their nations to be sovereign. They want their federal representatives to have more democratic accountability to constituents, not less.

The G3P would certainly like to run a world government, but imposing such a system by overt force is beyond their capability. Therefore, they have employed other means, such as deception and propaganda, to promote the notion of global governance.

Former Carter administration advisor and Trilateral Commission founder Zbigniew Brzezinski recognized how to make this approach easier to implement. In his 1970 book *Between Two Ages: America's Role in the Technetronic Era*, he wrote:

> Though the objective of shaping a community of the developed nations is less ambitious than the goal of world government, it is more attainable.

Numerous G3Ps have formed over the last thirty years as the concept of global governance has evolved. A major turning point was the WEF's perspective on multistakeholder governance. With its 2010 publication of "Everybody's Business: Strengthening International Cooperation in a More Interdependent World," the WEF outlined the elements of G3P stakeholders' form of global governance.

Global Agenda Councils were established to deliberate and suggest policy covering practically every aspect of our existence. The WEF created a corresponding global governance body for every aspect of society. Nothing was left untouched: values, security, public health, welfare, consumption of goods and services, access to water, food security, crime, rights, sustainable development, and global economic, financial, and monetary systems.

WEF Executive Chairman Klaus Schwab spelled out the objective of global governance:

> Our purpose has been to stimulate a strategic thought process among all stakeholders about ways in which international institutions and arrangements should be adapted to contemporary challenges. . . . The world's leading authorities have been working in

interdisciplinary, multi-stakeholder Global Agenda Councils to identify gaps and deficiencies in international cooperation and to formulate specific proposals for improvement. . . . These discussions have run through the Forum's Regional Summits during 2009 as well as the Forum's recent Annual Meeting 2010 in Davos-Klosters, where many of the emerging proposals were tested with ministers, CEOs, heads of NGOs and trade unions, leading academics and other members of the Davos community. . . . The Global Redesign process has provided an informal working laboratory or marketplace for a number of good policy ideas and partnership opportunities. . . . We have sought to expand international governance discussions . . . to take more pre-emptive and coordinated action on the full range of risks that have been accumulating in the international system.

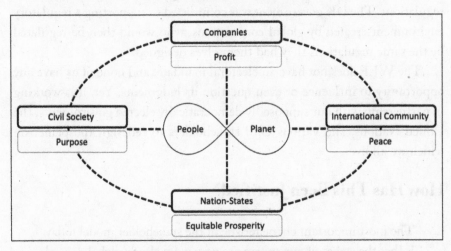

**Figure 2:** Updated World Economic Forum "Global Stakeholder Model" for "Stakeholder Capitalism."

*The World Economic Forum currently advocates an updated stakeholder capitalism model. In this model, the WEF asserts that this will facilitate governments focusing on creating the greatest possible prosperity for the greatest number of people (Socialist Utilitarianism). The WEF believes that civil society exists to advance the interests of its constituents and to give meaning or purpose to its members. Companies aim to generate an economic surplus, measurable in profits in the short run, and long-term value creation in the long run, and the overarching goal for the international community is to preserve peace. The WEF posits that, under this model, when the well-being of people and planet are at the center of business, the four remaining key groups of stakeholders will contribute to their betterment, as all of these groups and their goals are interconnected.*

The logic of stakeholder capitalism places business at the center of global governance. It is an updated, modernized form of Fascism cloaked in socialist/Marxist ideology and language.

By 2010, the WEF had begun what it called a "Global Redesign" process, which defined the international challenges and proposed solutions. Fortunately for the G3P, these proposals meant more control and partnership opportunities. The WEF sought to spearhead the expansion of this international governance.

Here is one example: In 2019, the UK Government announced its partnership with the WEF to develop future business, economic, and industrial regulations. The UK government was committed to supporting a regulatory environment created by global corporations, who would then be regulated by the same regulations they had themselves designed.

The WEF does not have an electoral mandate, and none of us have any opportunity to influence or even question its judgments. Yet, it is working in partnership with our supposedly democratically elected governments, the United Nations, and various G3P stakeholders to redesign the planet on which we all live.

## How Has This Been Justified?

The most important characteristic of the stakeholder model today is that the stakes of our system are now more clearly global. [ . . . ] What was once seen as externalities in national economic policy making and individual corporate decision making will now need to be incorporated or internalized in the operations of every government, company, community, and individual. The planet is [ . . . ] the center of the global economic system, and its health should be optimized in the decisions made by all other stakeholders.

—Klaus Schwab, founder and executive chairman, World Economic Forum; Peter Vanham, head of communications, chairman's office, World Economic Forum[3]

The rise of the G3P as the new masters of the universe has been actively promoted and enabled by the World Economic Forum, which is basically a trade union representing the thousand largest corporations in the world. Under the globalist WEF model, G3P will provide guidance and oversight of all aspects of the entire earth as an ecosystem, because at the heart of the current WEF stakeholder capitalism model lies the belief that the current network of Westphalian governments has failed to prevent the development of the tragedy of the commons,[4] and business must assume responsibility for the entire ecosphere.

The G3P oversight model usurps democratic government (or indeed government of any kind) by placing global corporations at the center of decision-making. Despite deriving authority only from the corporatist organizations that appointed them, the leaders of the G3P assume their own modern interpretation of the "divine right of kings," and exert unilateral and unrestricted authority by virtue of their appointment to leadership positions by major transnational corporations. The logic of deriving authority from a social contract based on a democratic process is now generally considered obsolete and counterproductive by virtually all globalists. This position is familiar to students of other organizations which position themselves as key components of a new world government; for example, similar logic is seen in the unilateral decision-making power vested in the appointed leaders of the United Nations and the World Health Organization.

The tragedy of the commons refers to the concept that, should many people enjoy unfettered access to a finite, valuable resource such as a pasture, they will tend to overuse it and may end up destroying its value altogether. Even if some users exercised voluntary restraint, the other users would merely supplant them, and the predictable result would become a tragedy for all. Originally developed and promoted by American ecologist and microbiologist Garrett James Hardin, the concept is considered a Neo-Malthusian approach to the perceived risks of human overpopulation. An advocate for depopulation, Hardin blamed the welfare state for allowing the tragedy of the commons; he claimed that where the state provides for children and supports large families as a fundamental human right, Malthusian catastrophe is inevitable. Hardin stated in his analysis of the tragedy of the commons that "Freedom in a commons brings ruin to all." This logic is central to both modeling biases and many of the policies and positions advocated by the WEF, the UN, and their various G3P partner organizations.

Current globalist theory holds that the G3P will oversee everything as extensions of the major transnational corporations committed to stakeholder capitalism, in partnership with the UN and its affiliate organizations. That includes every government, all business, our so-called communities, and each of us as individuals. Once this is understood, then the insatiable need for digital identification of all human beings and livestock, coupled to central bank digital currency and social credit scores makes more sense. Human beings are not the priority. The priority is the planet. Or so the WEF claims. Centralised control of the entire planet—all its resources and everyone who lives on it—is the core ethos of the G3P. There is no need to interpret G3P intentions. We don't have to read between the lines. It is stated plainly in the introduction to the WEF's Great Reset initiative:

> To improve the state of the world, the World Economic Forum is starting The Great Reset initiative. . . . The Covid-19 crisis . . . is fundamentally changing the traditional context for decision-making. The inconsistencies, inadequacies and contradictions of multiple systems—from health and financial to energy and education—are more exposed than ever. . . . Leaders find themselves at a historic crossroads. . . . As we enter a unique window of opportunity to shape the recovery, this initiative will offer insights to help inform all those determining the future state of global relations, the direction of national economies, the priorities of societies, the nature of business models and the management of a global commons.[5]

Contrary to the hopes of researchers Buse and Walt, we see an emergent global, corporate totalitarian society that posits that the global deployment of propaganda, censorship, and PsyWar is justified in the name of necessary planetary stewardship consequent to the failure of the Westphalian nation-state model when confronted by global challenges and existential crises. Under this socialist totalitarian model, G3P in partnership with the UN and transnational corporations will determine the future state of global relations, the direction of national economies, the priorities of societies, the nature of business models, and the management of the global commons. There is no opportunity or reason for either sovereign nation-states or individuals to participate in either their planning or the subsequent formation of policy.

## G3P and Globalist Think Tank Over-Reliance on Computational Modeling for Policy Development

Although governments technically do not have to implement G3P policy, in reality they do. Global policies have been an increasing facet of our lives in the post-World War II era. The mechanism of translating G3P policy initiatives, first into national and then regional and eventually local policy, can be clearly identified by looking at sustainable development.

In 1972, the privately funded independent policy think tank Club of Rome (CoR) published *The Limits to Growth*. As was done in the early phases of the COVIDcrisis, when grossly flawed computational modeling-based mortality projections were used to justify totalitarian policies, the CoR used computer models to predict what it decreed were the complex problems faced by the entire planet: the "world problematique."

The opinions offered by the CoR derived from the commissioned work of the Massachusetts Institute of Technology's (MIT's) system dynamic "World3 model." The MIT World3 model is a system dynamics model developed by the Massachusetts Institute of Technology (MIT) in the 1970s. It is a computer simulation of interactions between population, industrial growth, food production, and limits in the ecosystems of the earth. The model was originally created as part of a Club of Rome study and published in the book, *The Limits to Growth* in 1972.

The World3 model has five main sectors:

- Population: The population sector models the growth and decline of the world population, taking into account factors such as birth rates, death rates, and maturation processes.
- Agriculture: The agriculture sector models the production of food, considering factors such as crop yields, land use, and resource availability.
- Industry: The industry sector models the growth and decline of

> industrial production, considering factors such as technological innovation, resource availability, and pollution.
> - Resources: The resources sector models the availability and depletion of nonrenewable resources, such as fossil fuels and minerals.
> - Pollution: The pollution sector models the release and accumulation of pollutants in the environment, considering factors such as industrial waste, population growth, and technological innovation.

This model assumes that the global population would deplete natural resources and pollute the environment to the point where "overshoot and collapse" would inevitably occur. The tragic Neo-Malthusian scenario predicted by Hardin is now widely discounted by his academic peers. The World3 model is not a scientific "fact" but rather summarizes a series of predicted scenarios. So far, none of the predictions made by the World3 model have come to pass, although the model continues to be defended as widely recognized and influential in the field of system dynamics and sustainability, providing insights into the complex interactions between population, industry, and the environment.

The scientific and statistical debate over the claims in *The Limits to Growth* has been prolific. However, ignoring all doubts, the World3 model has been firmly planted at the center of the sustainable development policy environment.

In 1983, the Brundtland Commission was convened by former Norwegian Prime Minister Gro Harland Brundlandt and then-Secretary-General of the UN Javier Pérez de Cuéllar. Brundtland was a member of the Club of Madrid think tank and Pérez de Cuéllar was a Club of Rome member. Based upon the highly questionable assumptions in the World3 model, they set about uniting governments from around the world to pursue sustainable development policies.

In 1987, the Commission published the Brundtland Report, also known as Our Common Future. Central to the idea of sustainable development, as outlined in the report, was population control (reduction). This policy decision to get rid of people won international acclaim and awards for the authors.

The underlying assumptions for these policy proposals weren't publicly challenged at all in corporate (mainstream) media. Although an academic and scientific debate raged, it remained almost completely unreported. As far as the public knew, what were no more than unscientific assumptions and speculations were proven facts. It is now impossible for any to question these unproven assumptions and obviously inaccurate models without being accused of "climate denial" and being subjected to the now familiar spectrum of PsyWar strategies and tactics.

From the Brundtland Report emerged the Millennium Development Goals, which in 2015 gave way to the United Nations' full adoption of Sustainable Development Goals (SDGs). Since then, these SDGs have been translated into government policy in country after country. For example, in 2019 the UK government proudly announced its Net Zero policy commitment to sustainable development goals. SDGs had already been making an impact at the regional and local levels in counties, cities, towns, and boroughs across the UK. Now nearly every council across the country has a "sustainable development plan."

Regardless of what you think about the global threats we may or may not face, the origin and the distribution pathway of the resultant policy is clear. A privately funded, globalist think tank was the driver of a policy agenda which led to the creation of a global policy framework, which has been adopted by governments the world over, and which has impacted communities in nearly every corner of the Earth.

SDGs are just one among numerous examples of G3P global governance in action. Elected politicians' role in this process is negligible. They merely serve to implement and sell the policy to the public.

Under the current WEF "stakeholder capitalism" model, approved policy positions are developed at a global level, not at the level of an individual nation-state, which is relegated to second-tier status and only tasked with focusing "on creating the greatest possible prosperity for the greatest number of people," a rephrased version of the central tenet of utilitarianism.

The source phrase "the greatest good for the greatest number" is attributed to Jeremy Bentham, an English philosopher and social reformer of the late 1700s. It is a central concept in his philosophy of utilitarianism, which emphasizes the idea that moral actions should aim to maximize overall happiness or well-being. This is the singular role and responsibility assigned to the nation-state under the WEF "stakeholder capitalism" model.

This naive and flawed model is built on a foundation forged from fusing outdated socialist/Marxist, utilitarian, fascist/corporatist, and neo-Malthusian philosophies. This should come as no surprise, as "stakeholder capitalism" has been primarily crafted by corporatist octogenarians whose philosophical positions were formed during the early to mid-twentieth century and promoted by various interests and organizations that stand to benefit from the imposition of this "New World Order."

As things currently stand, who you elect doesn't matter; the policy trajectory is set at the global governance level, not at the national level. This is the totalitarian nature of modern G3P, which act in close cooperation with globalist transnational corporations and the United Nations. Nothing could be less democratic.

It is up to all of us to change this. We desperately need a new paradigm that addresses current reality, not some antiquated amalgam of old political philosophies born of twentieth-century conflicts, which are being unilaterally applied and enforced on the human community using PsyWar methods to achieve global compliance with arbitrary policies justified by naive, biased computational modeling.

\* Footnote: This chapter has incorporated some analysis and edited text from Iain Davis's open-source/Creative Commons blog post titled "What Is the Global Public-Private Partnership."

# PART VII
# RESILIENCY AND DECENTRALIZATION

A journey of a thousand miles begins with a single step.
—Lao Tzu

*We think that time is now at hand, a time for the emergence of an alternative to the dark "fourth industrial revolution," which is essentially a centralized and corporatized monopolist/totalitarianism vision. This version of a global future is being aggressively "shaped" and promoted by the World Economic Forum (WEF) and the affiliated organizations of the World Health Organization (WHO), World Trade Organization (WTO), United Nations (UN), governments, and many global elitist organizations who presume to know what is best for the rest of us. Their naive vision of a socialist/Marxist "New World Order" reflects the confluence of flawed computational modeling, narcissistic self-interest, and outdated political, environmental, and economic philosophies. To no one's surprise, they repeatedly fail real-world tests and data.*

*There is a sense of an emerging organically developing awareness that humanity may self-assemble under some form of a decentralized networked model that is different from what currently exists. But how can we create something that has never existed before? Globally decentralized alternatives to the dark visions that are being embedded into our very brains by mainstream media and entertainment will require a decentralized process. And yet, this decentralization vision must somehow be conceived and implemented on a global level. The way forward is for individuals to interact and develop a new way of organizing and interacting with each other, in ways that do not involve the globalized services and ownership of an elite oligarchy.*

*One such way to begin to break the stranglehold of the globalized, fascist state is through citizen journalism. This is why alternate media is so threatening to the administrative state and globalist narrative control; it is almost completely decentralized. We argue that modern, internet-based citizen journalism is the most disruptive information technology in modern history. And this is why it has become necessary for those who wish to maintain the ability to control national and global narratives to invest in the censorship-industrial complex and the mercenary army organizations available for hire to eliminate this decentralized information threat.*

*However, above and beyond the relatively straightforward task of cataloging the harms and informing people of what is being done to them on a routine basis through the use of alternative social media channels, what may be even more effective is to enable the development of next-generation tools and capabilities designed to support and empower the global explosion of citizen journalism. In this new PsyWar-fueled surrealistic reality where feelings and beliefs can substitute for actual data, we believe that information actually does yearn to be free, and that decentralized citizen journalism can save us from the threat of a globalist central command economy designed to serve an elite oligarchy. The hope is that eventually, some sort of WEB 2.0 will emerge, evolving from the now cludgy but effective blockchain technologies.*

*If people can learn to recognize advanced propaganda and mass-scale mind control PsyWar technology as it is deployed, then people will both be able to see through and consequently become much more resistant to these methods and technologies.*

*For those who reject a global public-private partnership(G3P)/United Nations–led, World Economic Forum–managed technofascist, totalitarian, global state and are committed to the fundamental principles defined in the US Constitution and Bill of Rights, the challenge is to define the alternative future that we wish for our children.*

*The journey starts with our personal lives. We build business and trading networks with people and organizations who have integrity and are, in this way, worthy of our business. This is what most of us want in both our business transactions and our personal lives.*

*The power to shape the future that our children and children's children will inhabit is in our hands. It is time to begin building anew. A journey of a thousand miles begins with a single step. First one step, then another, then another, and soon the journey to a better future will be well along.*

# CHAPTER 33
# Enabling a Decentralized World

How can we create something that has never existed before?

There is something in the wind, a subtle global emerging realization that there needs to be a different organizational model for world affairs. In our experience, when the time is right for a new idea or technology, it will often arise independently in many places all over the world. We sense an organically developing awareness that humanity should self-assemble under some form of a decentralized, networked model, which is different from what currently exists.

We think that time is at hand now, a time for emergence of an alternative to the dark "fourth industrial revolution," which is based on a centralized monopolist/totalitarianism vision. This future is being aggressively "shaped" and promoted by the World Economic Forum (WEF) and the affiliated organizations of the World Health Organization (WHO), World Trade Organization (WTO), United Nations (UN), and the great many global elitist organizations (such as the Club of Rome and so many others) who presume to know what is best for the rest of us.

Why do so many of us have a visceral response to this vision? What is really wrong with a centralized monopolist/totalitarianism command economy-based model, such as the WEF and its allies so actively promote?

After all, the big money seems to think that the China/CCP model works quite well. It is easy to pick at issues of censorship, propaganda, thought control, all of the known issues with centralized command economies, and the grinding dehumanization which seems to be a hallmark of every totalitarian regime in the written history of the world. The core problem with relying on "big money" to envision the future and make decisions for all of us is the inherent financial and political conflict of interest that comes with this dependency.

The WEF, with its allied organizations and trained acolytes, seem to believe that all of those limitations can be overcome if they just had more complete data and better technology. You can be made happy in a world in which you are freed from the burden and responsibilities of ownership, if you will just concede free will to the anointed central managers and allow them to gather comprehensive data about you. So that you can be predictively modeled as an "agent" in a massive computational matrix. All you need to do is just let Big Brother have his way with you.

It is often said that only 10 percent of any given population of humans truly wants to be free, and will accept the burdens of personal responsibility which come with that position. The rest mostly just want to be told what to do. So why should the needs of the few (the 10 percent) outweigh the needs of the many (those who just want to be told what to do)? The problem being that free will has been obliterated through the use of PsyWar techniques. When the large majority of people aren't thinking for themselves, who is actually the puppet master?

As we ponder these issues, for us it comes down to the consequences of allowing and empowering monopolies. In addition to the proven soul-destroying aspects of monopolistic totalitarianism, the price paid is the death of innovation.

During the COVIDcrisis, we have seen the cost of monopolistic global capture of "World Health" policies by an elite cabal of media, tech, large pharma, centralized finance, nongovernmental "pathophilanthropic," and transnational corporations. From our point of view, what we have seen is gross mismanagement by these centralized globalist organizations leading to huge and avoidable economic, educational, physical and psychological health and excess mortality adverse impacts.

And based on this atrocious record, these same organizations are now attempting to justify even more power, capital, and control for themselves. No surprise there. Monopolists are as monopolists do. Monopolists will monopolize.

The truth which is not allowed to be spoken is that this complex, interlaced global tragedy that we have labeled the COVIDcrisis, could have been easily avoided if time-tested solutions were cultivated instead of suppressed. Just to provide one notable example to illustrate the general point. "The Great Barrington Declaration" was an alternate public health plan for dealing with the COVID-19 pandemic that was not in any way radical; it was an expression of sensible, time-tested public health norms for respiratory disease. That is to allow the general population to build immunity, while focusing protection on the most vulnerable. That lock-downs and keeping children out of schools would do nothing to mitigate the risk of catching the disease. The principal authors of the Great Barrington Declaration were gobsmacked by the coordinated pushback, because what they were advising was basically "standard of care" public health wisdom developed and validated over decades. But those who set national and global policy were actually not well qualified to do so. When they encountered an alternative representing accumulated wisdom, instead of the faddish, ad-hoc "China Model" which they had advocated, the deep state who had concocted the globalist position taken by the US government responded harshly. We now know that this response was coordinated by Dr. Fauci, head of NIAID and Dr. Collins, head of NIH as well as Dr. Bob Kadlec, assistant secretary for preparedness and response (ASPR).[1]

Seeking to look at this in the "big picture" sense, monopolistic or totalitarian practices create revolutions. Basically, under monopolies (corporate or political), there are strong incentives to eliminate competition in order to ensure continuity—continuity of profit (cash cow), or continuity of concentrated political power (totalitarianism). The consequence is that, over time, the gap between the current solution (to whatever the core problem in question is) and the theoretical optimal solution (*ergo*, the unmet need) grows larger and larger.

In an open, decentralized organizational structure, typically multiple solutions are continually being brought forth and tested, and so the tension of that gap tends to get resolved before the gap gets too large. This creates an environment where the "disruptive events" or discontinuities get resolved more as a series of "evolutionary" bumps in the road rather than as revolutions. But if the forces of monopolistic or totalitarian controls are allowed free rein, then these discontinuities between current and optimal solutions grow larger and larger over time, and at some point, the tension between the current solution and the unmet need get resolved abruptly, to which resolution (if the gap was large enough) we apply the term "revolution." Technological revolution, business revolution, social revolution, or political revolution.

In a sense, the Bronze Age collapse of approximately 1177 BC appears to have been the consequence of a catastrophic propagating failure of a global totalitarian political system. Centralized totalitarian systems eventually fail. And when they fail, they do so catastrophically.

We can learn a lot from this history, and in particular we can learn from what came afterwards. Basically, after a fairly brief "dark age," history records the rise of the Greek city-state organization exemplified by the pinnacle of Athens and the Athenian political system, which is often considered the birthplace of much of what we define as "democracy." We suggest that what the Athenian system of yore really represented was a locally decentralized solution to political organization and management. Out of the destruction of civilization wrought by the catastrophic failure of global centralized totalitarian political governance systems emerged the decentralized, self-assembling system of the Athenian city-state.

Acknowledging the selection bias of whom we talk to while constantly traveling or broadcasting to medical freedom-related meetings these days, what we hear from every quarter and from all over the world is an emerging sense of a need to find a different way of organizing ourselves as a species. A sense that the management and political structures that currently exist are outdated and inadequate for the current interconnected and interdependent global community. That these current models select for narcissistic, sociopathic, and psychopathic leaders who, by their very nature, are biased toward hierarchical, monopolistic, and totalitarian organizational structures. The same organizational bias that became dominant during the Bronze Age and which yielded a cascading catastrophic failure of the entirety of Western civilization.

What we hear, again and again, is an emerging sense of mistrust of centralized political and economic structures, and a desire to find some way to organize communities under a decentralized method of self-determination. Political and other organizational structures grounded in principles of commitment to integrity, autonomy, sovereignty, respect for human dignity, and a commitment to community.

To provide one example of many, the idea of the semiautonomous states comprising the "United States," under the structure envisioned and embodied in the documents called the US Constitution and Bill of Rights, was originally intended to enable each state to function as a sort of semiautonomous "laboratory of democracy." In contrast to the decentralized competition of Greek or Roman city-states, the states which comprised the "United States" all agreed to a charter that bound them together to enable shared objectives (notably commerce and defense) while also protecting individual autonomy within each (more localized) political structure. Over time, this system has become perverted by the growth of a centralized overarching and domineering political structure which is often referred to as the "administrative state," but this was not the original intent and charter. The original intent was to bind the semiautonomous states (metaphorically akin to the Greek city-state) into what was essentially a shared alliance structure with well-defined rules of engagement and self-governance. Fundamentally, a win-win governance solution designed to protect collective autonomy and local decentralized sovereignty. As far as we are concerned, when viewed through the lens of long-term historic political trends, this structure represented an evolutionary (not revolutionary) step forward in human political and economic organization. Evolutionary in that it built upon the wisdom and experience of millennia, rather than purporting to advance an entirely novel political organizational structure (contrast being socialist-Marxism, for example).

So, how do we move beyond a vague sense that a different, decentralized global and local organizational structure and ethic is needed, to something that is more operational and practical? How can a global community develop a different way forward from that which exists presently, or which has ever existed? How can people develop a new way forward without falling into the same traps which have given rise to the totalitarian Marxist-corporatist (fascist) globalist vision being promoted and "shaped" by the WEF and its affiliates?

There is considerable benefit to the gift of having a "worthy opponent," and Schwab, Harari, and their future vision of the WEF appear to be a bespoke fit for that purpose. But is their vision likely to prevent or accelerate the boundary/singularity of a cascading collapse of global organization such as occurred at the end of the Bronze Age? We suggest that our true opponent is the singularity event, which would yield a postapocalyptic world that is so well explored in dystopian near-term literature and film (for example, the *Mad Max* series and so many others).

When we discuss this with others who are trying to build "intentional communities" in response to the threat to freedom, autonomy, innovation, and sovereignty posed by the globalist visions of the WEF et al., what we encounter is that our thinking tends to fall back into the same logic traps which have resulted in the current system. The logic often falls back to the need for some centralized political structure or committee (United Nations, for one example) to serve some sort of enforcement or policing function. The need for some sort of structure to ensure that certain prohibited ideas and communications are disallowed. To take an extreme example, we think we can all agree that child snuff film porn should not be allowed. There are no "cultural relativism" arguments to be made in favor of snuff porn. And from there, it is a slippery slope that quickly leads to justifying a wide range of censorship practices.

Personally, we believe that diversity is not only good, but it is essential for the advancement of humanity as a species. We believe that the belief that humankind should be homogenized, which is at the core of much of the WEF belief system, is critically wrong. But why do the WEF and the UN believe in a "one ring to rule them all" style of government? To recap, we think it all comes down to transactional friction. In business, "friction" has a different meaning from the common one. Friction is the idea that the matrix of independent, sovereign government regulations, borders, cultural differences, and heterogeneous business practices create undue burdens on the corporation. That the way to reduce that burden is to remove this friction by creating uniform laws, borders, cultures, business practices. Because the WEF is the largest trade organization in the world and directly influences global governance through its partnership with the UN, it makes sense that the UN and the WEF are working together to remove friction. The Agenda 2030, with its sixteen goals and 169 targets, is nothing more than a procedural manual for removing friction while creating new business opportunities for WEF allied transnational corporations.

The reduction of friction, while creating still stronger guilds through WEF and UN partnerships, will stifle innovation. Which will inevitably lead the discontinuity between current "approved" solutions and the unmet need as discussed above. Which will eventually lead to global catastrophic failures. This is essentially what we have all experienced with the COVIDcrisis and the climate change agenda, which continues to this day. This is what is happening with the new H5N1 bird flu pandemic, which is being used to gin up more money to put into the coffers of Big Pharma and biotech. The combination of the global, harmonized failure of commitment to integrity and intolerance toward innovation has resulted in one of the most profound leadership and policy failures of human history. So, in our opinion, we need to enable a global interconnectedness that is firmly grounded in a shared commitment to integrity as well as to the diversity of nations, cultures, religions, and people. But once again, there are traps within such a structure. Cultural relativism being one example.

How can we proceed, acknowledging that everything that we can envision will be biased by the solutions (and errors) of the past?

We suggest that we can only do so by enabling an evolutionary, decentralized approach. We cannot rely on some small group of "sages," some single think tank structure, to come up with a vision and structure which can guide humanity toward a better way to enable the species to fulfill its potential without destroying our souls, our families, our highly evolved shared sense of ethics, and of what is right and proper, including for our environment.

In short, here is our modest proposal, with explicit and humble reference to the brilliant 1729 monograph of Thomas Swift.

A wide variety of "intentional communities" are self-assembling all across the globe. Each of these are emerging to address different needs, and each represents a different point of view. We suggest that some sort of congress, physical or virtual, is convened with representatives from these diverse communities. The purpose of such a congress would not be to develop solutions, but rather to define the problems which will benefit from a new political structure. One that is forward-looking, designed to enable global connectivity and cooperation while maintaining diversity, autonomy, and individual, group, or national sovereignty. Such a structure must enable rather than stifle innovation. Such a structure must be based on a shared commitment to integrity and transparency, which is the foundation upon which trust is built.

In short, the charter of such a congress would be to define global needs, not to formulate the solutions. That would be enough. That alone would be a major achievement.

Once the problem set is defined, then move into development of multiple, independently derived proposed solutions. The series of case studies described by Irving L. Janis in his masterwork *Groupthink: Psychological Studies of Policy Decisions and Fiascoes* provides a road map for this phase of cooperative envisioning of an alternative future.[2] Basically, establish a cluster of fully independent working groups and task each with developing proposed solutions to the defined problem set, the unmet global needs. Deadlines will be required, both to expedite and to focus the efforts of each group. Upon independent completion of this tasks, proposed solutions would be presented, discussed, studied, and then an initial non-binding charter (grounded in the benefits of independent decentralization) developed based on the outcome. A key challenge will be how to adjudicate what are the optimal compromise or compromises. One of very many challenges which would have to be negotiated. From this a charter, a constitution would be developed, much as occurred in the founding of the United States. This would then be submitted to the autonomous "intentional communities" for discussion, negotiation, and eventual endorsement. Of course, as this is a decentralized plan, most likely there will be many autonomous endeavors—all working toward similar goals, with different outcomes, and that is okay. Basically, facilitated, decentralized trial and error. Which has always been the way of the Westphalian nation-state system. Let different sovereign nation-states develop their own solutions, and take a free market approach to identifying the most optimal solutions.

That is our modest proposal. In our opinion, global decentralized alternatives to the dark visions of the WEF and its controlling organizations will require a global decentralized process. Furthermore, engaging both regional and global communities in development of such a solution will help promote buy in from those involved.

In conclusion, we suggest that the way forward cannot be arrived at without finding some way for groups representing autonomous individuals and organizations to interact and develop new ways of organizing and interacting with each other. For mutual defense and not only economic but also spiritual growth. While sharing a commitment to integrity, human dignity, and community.

Please consider the comments above not as an end point, but rather as a starting point. Unlike Drs. Schwab and Harari, we do not presume to know the answers. Rather, we seek to provide some guideposts to facilitate discussion and collective problem-solving.

We do not presume to know what an optimal decentralized future for humanity looks like. And we are wary of any others who presume to have the answers. Instead, we place our faith in the potential for humankind to evolve a way forward to a brighter future, step by step, via trial and error, over centuries and millennia. What we seek with this chapter is to provide an initial road map that could help us to pass the fork in the road, the singularity event, and to choose a path that leads to empowerment, autonomy, freedom, and innovation.

How do we escape these dark dreams and darker times? How do we remain positive? How do we convince the next generations that the "fourth industrial revolution" of transhumanism and thought control is not inevitable and that there can be a better future for humanity? A future of belief and striving for an ethical future that respects the individual, the community and the environment, and is grounded in a time-tested commitment to families, health, and longevity in a balanced world. That these more "traditional values" which have stood the test of time across millennia and many civilizations are worth fighting for. Having the willpower to exercise and eat right, invest time in family and friends, be a part of a community, and develop a long-term, loving, monogamous relationship are the not-so-secret, time-tested keys to a long and happy life. That living as a free human is a right that cannot be denied.

We can only convince the next generation to continue to believe in humanity by providing role models, by creating positive visions with the use of the modern tools available to us. Fifth-gen warfare techniques and tools, the very same PsyWar strategies that they deploy on us, can be turned around and used against the globalist machine. The "fourth industrial revolution" is not a vision of a better future, but a vision of a decentralized, culturally diverse world where we don't all share the same education, wages, living conditions, goals, standard of living, and religion, is a world rich in traditions. Where food is diverse, as are the ways to live and be healthy. Such positive visions are, in the end, what will be the savior of future generations.

# CHAPTER 34
## Choosing Life and Waking up
## Future Generations

For the uninitiated, those who are not consumers and fans of the literary genre, cyberpunk is a subgenre of science fiction set in the not-too-distant future. The common theme in this literary tradition is how individuals (the punks) living in a dystopian high-tech world fight the mega-corporations that control everything.

As young adults, we both read the early works of cyberpunk. We knew the visions of William Gibson as he released *Neuromancer* in 1984 while Robert was still in medical school. That book was transformational, so different from any science fiction that we had read in the past that we knew this was something special. Soon after, Bruce Sterling and others exploded onto the scene.

Born as the internet first began to change the world, this genre imagined new realities where hacker culture combines with augmented humans, where everyone is "plugged in," and where hardcore antiheroes live in a high-tech, corporatist world. What could possibly go wrong?

As time passed, indulging our passion for science fiction became an unaffordable luxury, as our reality became a college education, a young family, science and an academic career, with little time for recreational reading. Surrounded by our own personal reality bubble, we were unaware of how this subgenre of our youth developed and came into its own in a big way. Later on, when we rediscovered this (now mature) subgenre via our boys' own reading passions, it was like running into a childhood friend. What had been the dark, near-term sci-fi alt-vision of reality developed by those revolutionary writers of the 1980s and 1990s had foreshadowed much of the internet culture that now surrounds us.

The future is already here—it's just not evenly distributed.
—William Gibson, *The Economist*, December 4, 2003

Cyberpunk ideas of a near-term dystopian future, with little hope for a "normal" (traditional) life, became accepted as a normalized, hip, and predictable future for mankind—an emerging consensus narrative—and then morphed into comic books, video games, virtual reality, social media platforms, and Reddit threads to emerge as a dominant "new normal" paradigm for many people under forty.

Then came the graphic novels and shortly thereafter, the amazing ascendency of Marvel Cinematic Universe. Instead of the classics, young minds were filled with a series of dystopian comic-book heroes and futures where what really mattered was surviving, not thriving, and reality was whatever one imagined it to be. These visions which once became alive only through the pages of paperback novels entered the era of hyperrealistic three-dimensional movies, computer games, and virtual reality. No longer just words on a page but a whole universe of dark, extremely dystopian, and violent visions to grow up in.

These visions of a dark urban future for mankind are seductively realistic. They have also been very accurate in predicting new technologies and political realities. Writers of science fiction have a way of visualizing fantasies of the future which then become reality.

We believe that it is important to offer a counterbalance to this dark future.

Subjected to the intensity of the academic crucible of our own choice, over time we matured as individuals and as a couple. Influenced in part by the writing of Ayn Rand and our own small orchard-farming past, in our late forties we intentionally turned our backs on both the soul-destroying reality of academic life, as well as the developing urban dystopia envisioned in the cyberpunk genre and all of its offspring, and elected to build our family, our careers, our lives together by creating our own personal rural paradise.

But not everyone who is hunkered down in their condo or apartment, bombarded by industrial-grade fearporn, can see through the dark foreboding smog of the present toward a brighter future. Which is why it is not enough to reject the new world order and these visions of an apocalyptic crumbling of Western culture. Providing leadership requires that we must also offer a positive alternative.

## The Future Is Now

Fast-forward twenty or thirty years, and 1980s cyberpunk no longer seems like a dystopian future; a cautionary example of one of many futures that may or may not happen. Our present and near-term future seems to have morphed into an eerily familiar landscape as science, technology, and cults of scientism fuse with globalized corporatism, banking, and finance—all of which seems to be leading mankind to a very dark place.

Of course, there is a difference between science fiction's murky dreams and visions, including cyberpunk, and informed speculation. But technology development is guided by the dreams of the young. In turn, the young are influenced by what they see happening in the world, where civilization is being driven to, and the visions of those who came before. The dreams of the best and the brightest of their elders have all too often been transformed into dark futuristic nightmares.

Throughout our lives, threats of a ruined planet, plagues, synths, robots, AI, overpopulation, corruption, avarice, increasing governmental control, corporatism, censorship and narrative manipulation, global totalitarianism, and world domination by transnational corporations have directed the Overton window of allowable discourse, of allowable futures, toward a selected subset of dark "transhumanist" realities that nobody (besides Yuval Harari and his ilk) really wants to acknowledge. Yet here we are. On the threshold of passively accepting a profoundly dystopian future of a "Fourth Industrial Revolution," "Great Reset," and fifteen-minute segregated ghettos imposed by globalist totalitarians.

> History began when humans invented gods, and will end when humans become gods.
>
> —Yuval Harari

Is it any wonder that these dystopian visions, which now fill the heads of the young, are what has been and are being actively and globally promoted by a cabal of the hyper-wealthy, their corporations, their globalist guilds, their "nongovernmental organizations," and their "global public-private partnerships"?

How do we escape these dark dreams and darker times? How do we remain positive? How do we convince the next generations that the "fourth industrial revolution" of transhumanism and thought control is not inevitable, and that there can be a better future? A future of belief and striving for an ethical framework that respects the individual as well as the community, and is grounded in a time-tested commitment to families, health, and longevity in a balanced world. That these more "traditional values" which have stood the test of time across millennia and many civilizations are worth fighting for. That having the willpower to exercise and eat right, invest time in family and friends, be a part of a community, and develop a long-term, loving monogamous relationship are the not-so-secret, time-tested keys to a long and happy life. Living as a free human is a right that cannot be denied.

We can only convince the next generation by providing role models, by creating positive visions with the use of the modern tools available to us. The fourth industrial revolution is not a vision of a better future. In contrast, a vision of a decentralized, culturally diverse world where we aren't all forced to share the same education, wages, living conditions, goals, standard of living, and religion, is an achievable positive vision. A world rich in traditions. Where culture and food are diverse, as are the ways to live and be healthy. Such positive visions are, in the end, what will be the savior of future generations.

# CHAPTER 35
# PsyWar and Government: How It Ends

## Lack of Market Force Corrections Combined with PsyWar Propaganda Yields Unstoppable Governmental Parasitic Growth

Just in case you didn't notice, since the 1980s, the United States has developed a big problem which is growing exponentially. The US national debt has become unsustainable. To a significant extent, this debt is enabled by irresponsible printing and injection of fiat currency into the overall US economy by an unaccountable private "Federal Reserve" Bank. Today's Federal Reserve routinely acts as a willing enabler rather than a check on administrative and deep state spending. The management of the Federal Reserve has become integrated into the interests and culture of the permanent bureaucracy. But that is merely one of many symptoms of a deeper problem.

Many factors drive this explosion of debt, but near the top of the causation list is that the executive branch and its permanent bureaucracy (administrative state + deep state) just do not care. They have no pressing reasons to care. They have developed a whole special economic logic to justify and rationalize not caring, called modern monetary theory (MMT).

Functionally, unlike either industry (market forces) or the military (failed wars), there are no external forces currently limiting the expansion of the dysfunctional, counterproductive and (frankly) parasitic behavior of today's Executive branch. Legislative branch oversight has been emasculated by consent with lobbyists collectively clamping down the Burdizzo, and in 1984 the Judicial branch conceded its authority to serve as a functional check on executive/administrative branch arrogance via the Supreme Court Chevron Deference decision. And like the Federal Reserve, the informal "fourth estate" (corporate media), which historically provided a separate and semiautonomous oversight function, has also been captured by this permanent bureaucracy. The recent Supreme Court decision rejecting the Chevron Deference precedent may usher in a new era where the explosive growth of the administrative state is checked by the courts—even if Congress continues to not do its job.

The administrative and deep state have been so successful in capturing and manipulating media and related communication (largely via CIA, FBI, CISA and intelligence community infiltration) that they are able to seamlessly deploy advanced modern propaganda, PsyWar technologies, and financial giveaways to control all narratives and information which might otherwise cause the majority of the electorate (and their congressional representatives) to check their actions. And in this way, they completely avoid accountability. Hence, the CIA, FBI, and DHS-CISA, as well as the intelligence community at large, have become enablers of administrative and deep state excesses and overreach. With this corrupted information ecosystem, there cannot be any accountability of the administrative and deep state. In cooperation with a variety of corporate and NGO partners via "public-private partnerships," the executive branch has completely captured and co-opted all oversight mechanisms that could enable or enforce checks and balances. The "ballot box" is well on its way to becoming a mere inconvenience because, for the majority of voters, the synthetic false reality projected by captured media is the only political "reality" they encounter.

Modern nation-states fail by suffocating under the weight of bloated unaccountable bureaucracies whose primary objectives are to serve and sustain themselves rather than to promote and defend the general welfare and security of the citizenry. The social contract is stomped into dust by the boot of an uncontrollably arrogant, authoritarian, self-serving bureaucracy.

> To what purpose are powers limited, and to what purpose is that
> limitation committed to writing, if these limits may, at any time,
> be passed by those intended to be restrained?
> —John Marshall, chief justice of the United States
> from 1801 to 1835

In discussing the current state of US federal government, the terms "administrative state" and "deep state" are often tossed about as if they are one and the same, but that is most definitely not the case. As described by Kash Patel, the deep state is a type of shadow governance made up of informal, extra-constitutional, secret, and unauthorized networks of power operating independently of a nation-state's duly elected political leadership, acting in pursuit of agendas and goals that are separate from the interests of the citizenry. Jeffrey Sachs describes the deep state as being the security state, made up of a small number of individuals, mostly from the alphabet agencies.

"Administrative state" is a term used to describe the phenomenon of executive branch administrative agencies that exercise bureaucratic power to create, adjudicate, and enforce their own rules. The administrative state abuses congressional non-delegation, judicial deference, executive control of agencies, procedural rights, and agency dynamics to assert control over and above both republic and constitutional principles.

Another related term often used to describe the modern American bureaucratic state is "Leviathan," a word with biblical origins repurposed as the title of Thomas Hobbes's monarchist 1651 book which advocates a strong centralized government. Hobbes argues that civil peace and social unity can be best achieved through the establishment of a commonwealth via a social contract. Hobbes's ideal commonwealth is ruled by a singular sovereign power responsible for protecting the security of the commonwealth, while being granted absolute authority to ensure the common defense.

In many ways the modern American administrative and deep state, with its "public-private partnerships," has come to resemble the seventeenth- through nineteenth-century British monarchy, with an entrenched bureaucracy (the permanent administrative state) functionally managed by a largely hereditary elite, surrounded by the concentric status rings of courtiers which comprise the deep state (in the current embodiment), all allied with a massive global corporatist organization (the East India Company). Within the growing hereditary ruling American oligarchy there is some degree of turnover and palace intrigue, as the fortunes of some wane while others rise. As with the rise of the British bourgeoisie and mixing of gentry with financially successful upper middle castes, this often reflects broader financial and technological trends within the overall geopolitical and geo-economic context in which a globalized oligarchy competes.

The obvious irony is that this type of system was precisely what the American Revolution was intended to overturn and precisely what the US Constitution was written to prevent.

And above all of this, we have now added a transcendently powerful new capability to the Leviathan of old. The rise of the CIA and its "Mockingbird/Mighty Wurlitzer" infiltration of both media and academia, the FBI and its politically weaponized COINTELPRO-type surveillance, infiltration and disruption capabilities, the DoD and its psyops/PsyWar capabilities designed for offshore conflicts but turned against domestic citizenry to support executive branch-defined "crisis" management, together with the explosive growth of a new censorship-industrial complex has yielded a "Leviathan" with reality-bending information control capabilities the likes of which the historic British monarchy could only dream of. Propaganda has come a long way from the days of Edward Bernays's seminal 1928 book by the same name.

## The State Department Is Also Censoring and Limiting the Circulation of Disfavored Press Outlets

According to a lawsuit filed in December on behalf of two media organizations, those being The Daily Wire and The Federalist, as well as the State of Texas and AG Ken Paxton versus the US Department of State (the State Department) through its Global Engagement Center (GEC) and various US government officials, it is alleged that the defendants are actively intervening in the news-media market to both censor and limit the circulation of disfavored press outlets.[1] These illegal activities are being done covertly to suppress the speech of the American press and are a direct violation of the First Amendment of the US Constitution. Furthermore, as the State Department is only authorized to spend taxpayer dollars for the administration of foreign affairs, this program also violates its congressional mandate.

The lawsuit states:

> The Daily Wire, LLC ("The Daily Wire"), FDRLST Media, LLC ("The Federalist"), (jointly "Media Plaintiffs"), and the State of Texas bring this civil action to halt one of the most egregious government operations to censor the American press in the history of the nation against the above-named Defendants for

declaratory and injunctive relief, and other appropriate relief, and allege as follows:

1. The U.S. Department of State ("State Department"), through its Global Engagement Center ("GEC"), is actively intervening in the news-media market to render disfavored press outlets unprofitable by funding the infrastructure, development, and marketing and promotion of censorship technology and private censorship enterprises to covertly suppress speech of a segment of the American press.

2. Defendants have been granted no statutory authority to fund or promote censorship technology or censorship enterprises that target the American press, tarring disfavored domestic news organizations as purveyors of "disinformation." There is no enumerated general power to censor speech or the press found in the United States Constitution, and the First Amendment expressly forbids it, providing: "Congress shall make no law . . . abridging the freedom of speech or of the press." U.S. CONST. amend. I.

3. The full breadth of Defendant GEC's censorship scheme is currently unknown. At a minimum, Defendant GEC has funded, promoted, and/or marketed two American censorship enterprises: the Disinformation Index Inc., operating under the name Global Disinformation Index ("GDI"), and NewsGuard Technologies, Inc. ("NewsGuard"). These entities generate blacklists of ostensibly risky or unreliable American news outlets for the purpose of discrediting and demonetizing the disfavored press and redirecting money and audiences to news organizations that publish favored viewpoints.

4. Media Plaintiffs are branded "unreliable" or "risky" by the government-funded and government-promoted censorship enterprises of GDI and NewsGuard, injuring Media Plaintiffs by starving them of advertising revenue and reducing the circulation of their reporting and speech—all as a direct result of Defendants' unlawful censorship scheme . . .

Yet, without authority and in direct violation of Congress statutory appropriation, Defendants have converted State Department resources and tools of warfare—information warfare—which were developed in the context of national security, foreign relations, and to combat American adversaries abroad, to use at home against domestic political opponents and members of the American press with viewpoints conflicting with federal officials holding the reins of this unlawful administrative power . . .

This lawsuit seeks injunctive relief to halt the unconstitutional and ultra vires actions of the State Department and put an end to one of the most audacious, manipulative, secretive, and gravest abuses of power and infringements of First Amendment rights by the federal government in American history.

On February 6, 2024, the plaintiffs (Daily Wire, The Federalist, and the State of Texas) filed a Motion for Preliminary Injunction to stop:

The Department of State, the Global Engagement Center, Antony Blinken, Leah Bray, James P. Rubin, Daniel Kimmage, Alexis Frisbie, and Patricia Watts, who are sued in their official capacities, from continuing to research, assess, fund, test, market, promote, host on its government platform, and/or otherwise assist with or encourage the development or use of technology that targets in whole, or in part, Americans' speech or the American press.

The lawsuit itself is a fascinating read. It is a detailed, accurate, but only partial history of the PsyWar (information warfare) that the US government has unleashed upon its own citizens.

The amount of money, resources and talent being frittered away on spying, censoring, creating propaganda and eliminating free speech and reach is vast. The Washington DC-based administrative/deep state has emerged as a separate entity unto itself, with its own culture, purpose, privileges, and prerogatives. A key characteristic of this separate cultural phenomenon and mindset—often geographically referred to as the "inside the beltway" set (referring to the I-495 freeway loop encircling DC), is a focus on self-preservation and personal advancement, rather than on achieving a mission, producing a deliverable, or serving the needs of outside-the-beltway flyover state serfdom.

Imperial DC beltway denizens form an incestuous culture, much like any historic imperial court. Passive-aggressive "slow walking" of initiatives has been refined to a fine art. Sexual favors are routinely exchanged to seal short-term alliances, both within agencies and between contractors and "Govies." Nuances of administrative regulations are weaponized to enable petty counterproductive one-upmanship. "Beltway bandit" corporations, lobbyists (registered and unregistered), and "think tanks" cultivate, collect, and support deep state "swamp monsters" when the political wing they are allied with is out of power for a period, anticipating that these courtiers will be rotated back in with the next political shift or executive branch "change" in leadership. And all are tied together in a revolving maypole dance. Together, they collectively weave a Uniparty in which the commonalities of shared commitment to advancing the interests of the administrative/ deep state court are far more important and lasting than any inconvenient superficial narrative about serving the interests of the general electorate and citizenry. In this beltway culture, actually solving national problems takes a back bench to the pageantry and Machiavellian machinations of the elite courtiers and their allies.

No wonder the general populace often feels that their votes for elected federal officials are irrelevant. Because they are, in fact, increasingly irrelevant. And as if that were not bad enough, the permanent administrative state considers elected and politically appointed officials to be "temporary employees." The shadowy members of the unaccountable Senior Executive Service (SES) are the ones that actually administer the government.

But with the advance of PsyWar capabilities, bolstered by advances in modern psychology, and combined with algorithmic control, censorship, and manipulation of all information, deep state beltway denizens have been able to achieve a propaganda capability which rivals the atomic bomb in its political implications.

These actors are now able to decouple their activities from objective truth. There can never be any accountability or consequences for mismanagement or misdeeds when they are able to effectively control all information and communication. Objective reality has become a theoretical post-modernist, surrealist construct, able to be contorted, molded, and enforced to comport with any synthetic version of reality which best supports administrative state, SES, and deep state objectives. Corporate and social media lapdogs (rapidly becoming dominant via alliances with globalized investment funds) are bolstered and legitimized by co-opted academia. Together they often act under the strong influence of administrative state "intelligence" agencies and deep state actors, and stand ever ready to create, control, propagate, and reinforce whatever narrative is needed.

Desire to achieve this sort of reality-bending groupthink or mass psychosis has been a common feature of bureaucracies, aristocracies, monarchies, and oligarchies for as long as historical records have been kept. But what is different now is the power and penetration of modern digital algorithmic control mechanisms. We now witness the creation of a lobotomized servant caste which enables an administrative bureaucracy nirvana of complete lack of accountability is now within reach. What could possibly go wrong?

We believe that a short answer is "paradigm shift." This type of cognitive landscape, in which a synthetic reality is preserved and maintained despite increasing divergence from objective reality, is a setup for abrupt introduction of more adaptive alternatives. Examples of synthesized false realities include an unsustainable federal debt, a collapsing "safe and effective" COVID vaccine narrative, and the intrinsic contradictions of human activity-driven carbon dioxide levels representing a global existential crisis. Actively fabricated false realities create a situation where current governmental solutions drift further and further from optimal.

At some point, an abrupt disruption in perception, power, global finance or available technology will occur—a paradigm shift. And when a system, technical or political, has been prevented by externals from adapting to changing conditions (such as happens with propaganda), then a crisis can trigger catastrophic realignment of divergent synthetic and objective reality. In politics, these "earthquake" moments reflect abrupt resolution of shifting internal forces which have built up tension along a fault line, and often result in either revolutions or catastrophic failures of economies and civilizations.

Functionally, the US government is now managed by disconnected Senior Executive Service (SES) "leadership," also known as part of the administrative state as well as the deep state castes, massive transnational financial institutions, public-private partnerships, corporate lobbyists, and globalist nongovernmental organizations such as the UN, WHO, WEF and Gates Foundation. This supra-constitutional alignment has enabled permanent administrative and deep state "management" of an out-of-control federal budget which supports a grotesque obsession with their maypole dance, court drama, one-upmanship, and Machiavellian machinations. And all who object are censored, subjected to character assassination and labeled fringe outliers by captured media.

Rather than solving the missions and problems which plague the electorate that they currently parasitize, these erstwhile public servants have removed any ability of citizenry and electorate to provide the oversight, control and correction function originally designed into the US Constitution by those with lifelong experience in dealing with an earlier Leviathan. One that was also characterized by arbitrary and capricious administrative authoritarianism. And in the current embodiment we now have amazingly powerful psychological tools placed in the hands of venal, self-serving, immature and all too often sociopathic individuals seeking self-gratification.

## Indeed, What Can Possibly Go Wrong? Abrupt, Catastrophic Economic and/or Military Collapse, That's What

How many wars has the United States lost since World War II? And now this amazingly expensive and corrupt Ukrainian foreign adventure is deconstructing itself. Which (mis) adventure seems to have mostly worked to strengthen and hone Russian military might while depleting and fracturing NATO unity and capabilities. Biden sought to drain and exhaust Putin, thereby yielding Russian regime change. In an amazing feat of geopolitical jiujitsu, the precise opposite may well come to pass.

And then we have the obscenely bungled public health and financial responses to the COVIDcrisis. And growing awareness that the "climate crisis" has been synthesized and weaponized to advance a variety of geopolitical power, control, and financial objectives.

This level of massive administrative and deep state mismanagement is not sustainable, even with US economic and natural resource muscle.

History and archaeology are littered with the bones of civilizations and bureaucracies that became inwardly focused and lost track of their function and purpose. We would love to believe in a fairy tale world in which modest modifications in administrative agency guidelines and practices could result in a more functional ruling bureaucracy. But we are too old for fairy tales, and have spent too many years in the bowels of the federal administrative state.

We fear that the dysfunctional and fundamentally corrupt DC beltway culture will not change until we have a massive paradigm shift of some sort or another. Resolving these structural problems will require a major correction. It could occur at the ballot box, but the power of the intelligence community/censorship-industrial complex to distort reality to protect itself may have already reached a stage where this cannot happen. However, the debt, the massive unsustainable debt, combined with the insatiable hunger of the administrative and deep state working cooperatively with the industrial masters of forever war and "biodefense" may soon trigger a global paradigm shift in power and finance.

And if that happens, we can only hope that we have enough guns, ammo, farm infrastructure, and a well-developed network of like-minded friends to ride out the following storm.

But in such a brave new world, getting diesel for trucks and tractors will definitely be a problem. Probably time to dust off our equine teamster skills and train some horses to pull.

# CHAPTER 36

## Integrity, Like Paradise, Once Lost Can Never Be Recovered

> For what shall it profit a man, if he shall gain the whole world, and lose his own soul?
>
> —Mark 8:36

> I am sure that in estimating every man's value either in private or public life, a pure integrity is the quality we take first into calculation, and that learning and talents are only the second.
>
> —Thomas Jefferson[1]

Integrity, dignity, and community are three key guideposts on the road out of pandemic crisis and PsyWar hell.

Integrity is a curious word. Triple meanings which buttress one to the other.

Integrity:

1. Steadfast adherence to a strict moral or ethical code.
2. The state of being unimpaired; soundness.
3. The quality or condition of being whole or undivided; completeness.
   —*American Heritage Dictionary*, 5th Edition

Human beings can be characterized by exhibiting integrity or its opposites, hypocrisy and deceit. Buildings can have structural integrity or they can be unsound, a danger to inhabitants. Organizations can have integrity or can be corrupt. And a nation can have integrity, or be divided against itself.

One needs to look no further than the latest headlines. Election integrity has become one of the most trending of hashtags (in United States, Brazil, and so many other places). Nord Stream (NS) and Nord Stream 2 (NS2) have been sabotaged, most certainly not by either Russia or Germany, but fearing retaliation no one dares even whisper the name of the culprit all know to be responsible. The deep corruption associated with the Biden family and the role of corporate media in trying to keep it from impacting elections continues to be exposed. The omniscient Anthony Fauci has followed in the footsteps of Hillary Clinton and so many others in deploying the "I cannot remember" defense, but with a new wrinkle of belligerent defiance; recently testifying that "I have a very busy day job running a $6 billion institute. I don't have time to worry about things like the Great Barrington Declaration." Clear and compelling evidence released to Blaze Media under FOIA request document otherwise. During the COVIDcrisis, both CDC director Rochelle Walensky and Deborah Birx resorted to substituting "hope" for data in making major public health decisions, and then enforcing these decisions via deployment of highly refined psychological operations techniques against objecting United States Citizens. Just to highlight some of the most recent examples.

We argue that the imperial administrative state, which the United States federal government has been transformed into, has clearly lost any semblance of integrity.

Recently the entire corporate world came to a standstill, due to a small coding error in an update from Crowdstrike, a globalized, internet security firm. The ramifications of this disaster, which caused airline and railroad travel to come to a stop, and financial institutions to screech to a halt for days, shows just how dangerous centralization is. The largest internet crash was so large, that days later, the "blue screen of death" shuttered computers around the world, long after the initial coding error had been resolved.[2] This traumatic event is a wake-up call that we need decentralized systems. Civilization needs a monetary system that is not digitized. Trains, planes, and automobiles must be able to function without the internet. Supply chains must have a plan B and even a plan C.

We are often asked, "What can we do to fix the [fill in the blank] federal agency?" And all we can say is that the picture is grim, because agency after agency has been thoroughly corrupted. There is little or no structural integrity left. If these agencies were buildings, the only option an inspector would have would be to condemn them. They are teardowns. They must be rebuilt on solid ground, beginning with new footings. And if the legal citizens of the United States will not do this, then others will do it for us. As any who have studied the infiltration of the Chinese CCP will attest, that corrupt and unethical expansionist organization is well on the way to doing it for us.

Like paradise, once integrity has been lost, it cannot be regained.

For what shall it profit a nation, if it shall gain the whole world, and lose its own soul?

Each of us now faces a series of binary decisions. Either this or that. Assuming that you are committed to personal sovereignty and guiding your own future, making your own decisions. To be blunt, not everyone wants to be free. Many just want to be told what to do. Which type of person do you choose to be? Sovereign and free, or dependent on the arbitrary and capricious favor of a monopolist cabal?

Are you willing to cast your lot with the Overlords and their Machines, and for you and your children to become post-modern indentured servants (with no escape other than death) living in a fourth industrial revolution hellscape under a centralized corporatist (*ergo,* technofascist) totalitarian world government run by technocrats and economist/bankers on behalf of global oligarchs?

If the future which King Charles III, Klaus Schwab, and the infamous Silicon Valley darling Harari (the very title of whose most recent published ramblings proclaim that man is God) is not for you, and you do not like the idea of owning nothing and being happy living within a globalized fascist state, then what are your options?

At this point, the most viable alternative seems to be to get working on building a parallel social structure that can exist alongside or even tunneled within the fascist imperial state and might eventually replace it. How could such an organization be structured?

Well, once upon a time, a group of merchants, landholders, and farmers faced the same problem when confronting another mad British king, George III. It was a period of intense intellectual ferment and yielded the amazing legal policy consensus documents and treaty agreements known as the US Constitution and the Bill of Rights, which remain the definitive treatise on how to structure a limited representative government.

Strangely, both corporate media and the US "Democrat" political party have labeled those who remain committed to practicing the principles and defending the substance of these documents as "far right," and apply the terms radical, far-far right, and even fascist when seeking to define and demonize what is a fundamentally conservative political (and economic) position. These terms are applied to members of the current populist movement who seek to return to a limited federal government and who share an abiding commitment to an autonomous nation which operates under those principles. A commitment to rekindling American greatness. Simply stated, to making America great again.

For those who reject a United Nations-led, World Economic Forum-managed fascist totalitarian, global state and are committed to the fundamental principles defined in the US Constitution and Bill of Rights, the challenge is to define the alternative future that we wish for our children.

The anarchy of local warlords and *Mad Max* political landscapes await future generations if we do not seize the opportunity to present an alternative positive vision which the persuadable middle views as a preferred option. Does any sane person imagine that the "shaped" future envisioned by Charles, Klaus, Harari, and their financial partners can be sustained? This is a last-gasp grab for power by the imperium. They have overreached, and the current system is already careening from crisis to crisis, teetering on the brink of collapse.

We need a process for enabling a decentralized human network of communities as an alternative to the centralized technofascist dystopia that the WEF seeks to shape and force on us. But what processes, terms, and conditions of engagement can we use to shape such a network of intentional communities? The starting point needs to be a clear understanding of shared guiding principles, and a realistic, enforceable commitment to those ideals. We believe that personal, institutional, and political commitment to integrity, human dignity, and community would be a good start.

The WEF and its sponsors BlackRock, Vanguard, State Street, and Bank of America have deployed the social credit scheme-like ESG (environmental, social, governance) scoring system in a remarkably short time, including "independent" ESG auditor organizations. We suggest that deployment and validation of integrity standards would be both trivial and remarkably straightforward in comparison.

Once such a system is implemented, one can start to choose to only do business with others who are committed to acting with integrity. One can build business and trading networks with people and organizations who strive to demonstrate that they have integrity and are, in this way, worthy of your trust. This is what most of us want in both our business transactions and in our personal lives.

The power to shape the future which your children will inhabit is in your hands.

It is time to begin building anew. First one step, then another, then another, and soon the journey will be well along.

# CHAPTER 37
# The Battle of Evermore

> Anyone who has the power to make you believe absurdities has the
> power to make you commit injustices.
>
> —Voltaire[1]

We all sense an impending battle. But do we know who is friend and who
is foe?

Do we actually understand who our allies and our opponents are? Who
is right, and who is wrong? What is true and what is propaganda?

Simple stereotypes will not lead to victory.

Both sides on these battle lines think they represent the future. Both
sides think they are working to save the world.

All passionately believe that they fight for the common good.

On one side, with a sense of noblesse oblige, a transnational elite works
to advance a unified, globalized, centralized political and economic world
order. A world order based on a command economy rooted in massive databases, computational modeling, predictive artificial intelligence-driven
decision-making, and the merging of man and machine to create a new
species.

Fulfilling this objective is believed to require universal surveillance,
propaganda powered by modern psychology, algorithmic censorship, cultural homogenization, and centralized automated economic controls and
resource allocation.

We believe that this will be a digital, technocratic, and bureaucratic
hell.

We believe that Yeats's rough beast, its hour come round at last, now slouches toward Geneva to be born.

We believe in humanity. And we believe in the divine.

We believe in the pragmatic benefits of the Principle of Subsidiarity; decision-making authority should be decentralized to the lowest level possible, where it can be exercised most effectively.

Local authorities should be responsible for matters that can be handled at that level, rather than relying on higher authorities. Decisions should be made as close to the affected individuals or communities as possible.

We believe in decentralization, nationalism, unique cultural identities, individual and national sovereignty, and the power of human innovation.

Globally centralized planning and control will destroy the ability of individuals, cultures, and nations to innovate. Globalized, centralized planning and control will kill the motivation and ability of the human race to adapt to changing conditions. Do we really need another example before we can learn this lesson? Or does each era need to recycle history?

Elevating a new global centralized nobility will not lead to prosperity, innovation, and effective adaptation; it will destroy these things. We have seen the failure of this approach over the last few years of the COVIDcrisis, and throughout recorded history. How many more examples do we need?

We believe in the power of diversified independent human thought, decentralized interconnectedness, cultural heritage, and freedom.

In this coming battle, we do not know which vision will prevail.

What we do know is that old imperialistic models are outdated, and old empires and old ways of geopolitical thinking face imminent collapse. But they will not go quietly into the night.

And what we are absolutely sure of is that censorship will not save the current versions of imperialism which hide behind a propagandized definition of "Democracy."

And that the weaponization of fear of infectious disease to control human behavior is ethically evil, and that those who deploy these unethical practices to advance their objectives of political power, profit, and control should be shamed and condemned.

The use of psychological bioterrorism is wrong, and it must stop.

For the sake of our children, we must oppose both transhumanism and weaponized fear.

And we must insist on freedom, Dammit.

> We know that they are lying, they know that they are lying, they even know that we know they are lying, we also know that they know we know they are lying too, they of course know that we certainly know they know we know they are lying too as well, but they are still lying. In our country, the lie has become not just a moral category, but the pillar industry of this country.
>
> —(attributed to) Aleksandr Solzhenitsyn

# A PsyWar Glossary

**Administrative state** is a term used to describe the phenomenon of executive branch administrative agencies exercising the power to create, adjudicate, and enforce their own rules. The administrative state uses nondelegation, judicial deference, executive control of agencies, procedural rights, and agency dynamics to assert control above the republic and democratic principles.

**Advocacy journalism** is a subset of journalism that adopts a nonobjective viewpoint, usually for some social or political purpose.

**Algorithms** on social media and in search engines are computational processes. Online platforms such as Google, Facebook, Instagram, TikTok, and X use algorithms to predict what users are interested in seeing, isolate users who break "community standards" or government censorship rules, and maximize revenues. Algorithms filter and prioritize the content that the user receives, based on their individual user history. Algorithms can isolate different user groups into echo chambers and away from other others or bring users together.

**Artificial intelligence (AI)** is a branch of computer science that focuses on creating machines that can perform tasks that typically require human intelligence. A key characteristic of AI is that it can learn from data and improve performance over time. AI systems learn from experience, understand natural language, recognize patterns, solve problems, and make decisions.

**Astroturfing** (*ergo*, fake grass roots) is the practice of masking the sponsors of a message or organization to make it appear as though it originates from and is supported by grassroots participants. Astroturfing gives organizations credibility by hiding information about the source's financial or governmental connections. An Astroturf organization is an organization that is hiding its real origins in order to deceive the public about its true intentions.

**Asymmetric warfare** is a type of war between opponents whose relative military power, strategy, or tactics differ significantly. It often involves insurgents or a resistance movement against a standing army or a more traditional force.

**Advocacy journalism** is journalism that advocates a cause or expresses a viewpoint with a specific agenda. It is often designed to increase or decrease the Overton window. It is a form of propaganda.

**Bad-jacketing.** Rumors and gossip meant to disenfranchise and destroy a movement or quell enthusiasm.

**Black ops** is an abbreviation for "black operations," which are covert or clandestine activities that cannot be linked to the organization that undertakes them.

**Black propaganda** falsely claims a message, image, or video was created by the opposition in order to discredit them.

**Bot** is an automated account programmed to interact like a user on social media. Bots are used to push narratives, amplify misleading messaging, and distort online discourse. The name "bot" came from a shortened version of the name robot.

**Botnet** is a network of devices infected with malware, controlled by an attacker to launch distributed denial-of-service (DDoS) attacks or spread malware.

**Chaos agents** are a person or people that purposefully causes chaos or mischief within a group, for their own personal entertainment or as a tool to cause organizational fragmentation. It is a tool often used by intelligence agencies.

**Community technology** is the practice of synergizing the efforts of individuals, community technology centers, and national organizations with federal policy initiatives around broadband, information access, education, and economic development. (Wikipedia)

**Computational propaganda** is an "emergent form of political manipulation that occurs over the internet" (Woolley and Howard, 2018, p. 3). This type of propaganda is often executed through data mining and algorithmic bots, which are usually created and controlled by advanced technologies such as AI and machine learning.

**Computational propaganda (EU Parliament definition)**: "the use of algorithms, automation, and human curation to purposefully distribute **misleading information** over social media networks." These activities can feed into influence campaigns: coordinated, illegitimate efforts of a third state or non-state agent to affect democratic processes and political decision-making, including (but not limited to) election interference. It is asserted that disinformation (deliberately deceptive information) turns one of democracy's greatest assets—free and open debate—into a vulnerability. The use of algorithms, automation, and artificial intelligence is boosting the scope and the efficiency of disinformation campaigns and related cyber-activities.

**Computer algorithms**—to control access or speech. Example: Algorithms to enable X's policy of "Freedom of speech, not reach"

**Controlled opposition, disruptors, and chaos agents**. Historically, these tactics involve a protest movement that is actually being led by government agents. Nearly all governments in history have employed this technique to trick and subdue their adversaries. However, in fifth-gen warfare, controlled opposition often may come in the form of disruptors and chaos agents. Either "real" people or bots that generate outrageous claims that delegitimize a movement (examples currently may or may not be); "snake venom in the water" or "everyone is going to die who took the vaccine within two years." Another tactic is placing agents of chaos whose job is to basically disrupt organizations and events. This may also come in the form of "reporters" who assert fake or highly exaggerated news stories, and who most likely are funded by the opposition. "Undermine the order from the shadows" is the tactic here.

**Cryptographic backdoors** are methods that allows an entity to bypass encryption and gain access to a system.

**Cyberattack** is an attempt by an individual or organization to hack into another individual or organization's information system. The attacker seeks to disrupt, damage, or destroy the system, often for personal gain, political motives, or harm. Cyberattacks can include the use of botnet, denial-of-service, DNS tunneling, malware, man-in-the-middle attacks, phishing, ransomware, SQL injection, and zero-day exploitation.

**Cyberstalking** involves the use of technology (most often, the internet!) to make someone else afraid or concerned about their safety. Generally speaking, this conduct is threatening or otherwise fear-inducing, involves an invasion of a person's relative right to privacy, and manifests in repeated actions over time. Most of the time, those who cyberstalk use social media, internet databases, search engines, and other online resources to intimidate, follow, and cause anxiety or terror to others.

**Data mining** is the software-driven analysis of large batches of data in order to identify meaningful patterns.

**Decentralized** and highly non-attributable psychological warfare (memes, fake news).

**Deepfakes** are synthetic media that have been digitally manipulated to replace one person's likeness or voice convincingly with that of another. Deepfake techniques include using a type of artificial intelligence called deep learning to create convincing images, audio, and video hoaxes.

**Deep state** is a type of governance made up of potentially secret and unauthorized networks of power operating independently of a state's political leadership in pursuit of their own agenda and goals.

**Denial-of-service (DoS)** attack involves overwhelming a system with traffic to exhaust resources and bandwidth.

**Distributed denial-of-service (DDoS) attack** is a malicious attempt to disrupt normal traffic to a web property.

**DNS Tunneling** is the use of a domain name system (DNS) protocol to communicate non-DNS traffic, often for malicious purposes.

**DoD Military Deception Missions** are attempts to deliberately deceive by using psychological warfare to deliberately mislead enemy forces during a combat situation.

**DoD Military Information Support Operations (MISO) Missions**: Military Information Support Operations (MISO) missions involve sharing specific information to foreign audiences to influence the emotions, motives, reasoning, and behavior of foreign governments and citizens. This can include cyber warfare and advanced communication techniques across all forms of media. In the case of a domestic emergency, MISOs can be used on domestic populations.

**DoD Interagency and Government Support Missions** shape and influence foreign decision-making and behaviors in support of US objectives by advising foreign governments.

**Electronics intelligence (also called ELINT)** is technical and intelligence information obtained from foreign electromagnetic emissions that are not radiated by communications equipment or by nuclear detonations and radioactive sources.

**Electronic warfare (EW)** is warfare that uses the electromagnetic spectrum, such as radio, infrared, or radar, to sense, protect, and communicate. At the same time, EW can disrupt, deny, and degrade the adversaries' ability to use these signals.

**Emotional appeal** is a persuasive technique that relies on descriptive language and imagery to evoke an emotional response and convince the recipient of a particular point of view. An emotional appeal manipulates the audience's emotions, especially when there is a lack of factual evidence.

**Fearporn** is any type of media or narrative designed to use fear to provoke strong emotional reactions, with the purpose of nudging the audience to react to a situation based on fear. Fearporn many also be used to increase audience size or participation.

**Fifth generation (fifth-gen) warfare** is using non-kinetic military tactics against an opponent. This would include strategies such as manipulating social media through social engineering, misinformation, censorship cyberattacks, and artificial intelligence. It has also been described as a war of "information and perception." Although the concept has been rejected by some scholars, it is seen as a new frontier of cyberspace and the concepts behind fifth-generation warfare are evolving, even within the field of military theory and strategy. Fifth-gen warfare is used by non-state actors as well as state actors.

**Flooding** is a tactic that manipulates search engine or hashtag results by coordinating large volumes of inauthentic posts. Flooding may also be referred to as "firehosing."

**Fourth industrial revolution, 4IR, or Industry 4.0**, conceptualizes rapid change to technology, industries, and societal norms in the twenty-first century due to increasing interconnectivity and smart automation. This is being led by the joining of technologies such as artificial intelligence, gene editing, advanced robotics, and transhumanism, which will blur the lines between the physical, digital, and biological worlds.

**Gang stalking (cyber)** is a form of cyberstalking or cyberbullying, in which a group of people target an individual online to harass them through repeated threats, fear-inducing behavior, bullying, teasing, intimidation, gossip, and bad-jacketing.

**GARM** was the Global Alliance for Responsible Media, a cross-industry initiative established by the World Federation of Advertisers and the WEF to address the challenge of "harmful" content on digital media platforms and its monetization via advertising. This is done by rating social media platforms and websites. If an entity had a low score, advertisers, including aggregator sites, such as Google, are not allowed to advertise on those platforms. This is a de-monetization strategy. That has been used by governments to censor news stories that they find inconvenient, such as the existence of Hunter Biden's laptop, the safety and efficacy of the mRNA jab, and the origins of COVID-19. Both the participants and the terms of the GARM agreement are nontransparent. In a press release on August 9, 2024, GARM announced that it was discontinuing its activities.

GARM was launched at Cannes in the summer of 2019 and stated that it had worked hard to highlight the changes needed for advertisers to feel more confident about advertising on social media. As of November 2019, GARM was the flagship project of the World Economic Forum Platform for Shaping the Future of Media, Entertainment and Culture.

**Gatekeeping** is a process and propaganda technique of selecting content and blocking information to sway a specific outcome. It is often used in news production to manipulate the people by manipulating the writing, editing, positioning, scheduling, and repeating of news stories.

**Generative AI** means the class of AI models that emulate the structure and characteristics of input data in order to generate derived synthetic content. This can include images, videos, audio, text, and other digital content.

**Gray and dark market data sets**. A gray market or dark market data set is the trading of information through distribution channels that are not authorized by the original manufacturer or trademark proprietor.

**Gray propaganda** is communication of a false narrative or story from an unattributed or hidden source. The messenger may be known, but the true source of the message is not. By avoiding source attribution, the viewer becomes unable to determine the creator or motives behind the message. This is common practice in modern corporate media, in which unattributed sources are often cited.

**The Great Reset** is the name of an initiative launched by the World Economic Forum (WEF) and its founder, Klaus Schwab in June 2020. They are using the cover of anti-COVID measures and an overstated public health crisis, as well as emergencies such as "climate change" to push an agenda to remake the world using stake-holder capitalism (a form of socialism).

**Honeypots** (not the sexual entrapment kind). In computer terminology, a honeypot is a computer security mechanism set to detect, deflect, or, in some manner, counteract attempts at unauthorized use of information systems.

**Hypnosis** is a procedure that guides one into a deep state of relaxation (sometimes described as a trancelike state) designed to characterized by heightened suggestibility and receptivity to direction. Hypnosis can be implemented it in digital media, movies, advertising and propaganda. Trance-like experiences aren't all that uncommon. If you've ever zoned out while watching a movie or daydreaming, you've been in a similar trance-like state.

**Hypnotic language patterns** are used to influence and persuade by employing techniques such as lulling linguistic patterns, metaphor, and emotionally appealing words and phrases. Hypnotic language patterns and propaganda are connected through the use of persuasive and manipulative techniques to influence public opinion and highlights the powerful impact of language on shaping public perception and behavior.

**Industry 4.0:** The fourth industrial revolution (4IR) is a term used to refer to the next generation of technological advances, where it is anticipated that the differences between physical, digital, and biological technologies disappear. This is a world where machines and computers evolve independently, where new biological entities and evolutionary changes are being controlled by artificial intelligence, where brain waves can be manipulated. It is, quite literally, a brave new world.

**Infodemic** is the rapid and far-reaching spread of information, both accurate and inaccurate, about a specific issue. The word is a conjoining of "information" and "epidemic." It is used to describe how misinformation and disinformation can spread like a virus from person to person and affect people like a disease. This use of this technique can be deliberate and intentional.

**Inverted totalitarianism** is a managed democracy, where economic and state powers are conjoined and virtually unbridled. Regulatory control is superimposed upon the administrative state, and a nontransparent group of managers and elites run the country from within.

**Limited hangout** is a propaganda technique of displaying a subset of the available information. It involves deliberately revealing some information to try to confuse and/or prevent discovery of other information.

A modified limited hangout goes further by slightly changing the information disclosed. Commercially controlled media is often a form of limited hangout, although it often also modifies information and so can represent a modified limited hangout.

**Low-cost radios (ham, AM, local)** Throughout less-developed technologically areas in the world, these technologies are the backbone of communications.

**Mal-information** is any speech that can cause mistrust of the government, even if the information is true.

**Malware** is malicious software that breaches a network through a vulnerability, typically when a user clicks a dangerous link or email attachment.

**Man-in-the-middle (MitM)** is an attack that interferes with a two-party transaction to steal data or inject malware.

**Mass formation** is, in essence, a kind of group hypnosis that destroys individuals' ethical self-awareness and robs them of their ability to think critically. Mass formation within a population can happen suddenly.

**Mass formation psychosis** describes the individual under the spell of mass formation. Although this term is not found in the *Diagnostic and Statistical Manual of Mental Disorders* (*DSM-5*), it is our opinion that it is just a matter of time before this amendment will be included.

**Mass surveillance** is the surveillance of a population or fraction of a population. This surveillance is often carried out by local and federal governments or governmental organizations, but it may also be carried out by corporations. Often specific political groups are targeted for their beliefs and influence.

**Modified limited hangout** is a propaganda technique that displays only a subset of the available information, that has also been modified by changing some or all of the information disclosed (such as exaggeration or making things up). It is meant to confuse and/or prevent discovery of other information.

**Moral outbidding** (see purity spiral)

**NBIC** is hyper-personalized targeting that integrates and exploits "neuroscience, bio-technology, information, and cognitive" (NBIC) techniques by using social media and digital networks for neuro-profiling and targeting individuals.

**Neurolinguistic programming (NLP)** is a set of techniques that are used to improve communication, interpersonal relationships, and personal development. It is based on the idea that our thoughts, language, and behaviors are all connected. By changing one of these elements, the other elements will be altered. Hypnosis and meditation, including the use of repetitive messaging are core NLP Techniques. Other techniques including visualization, image switching, modeling of other successful people, mirroring (using body language to mirror others that you wish to gain approval of), and the use of incantations to reprogram the mind.

**Nudging** is any attempt at influencing people's judgment, choice or behavior in a predictable way that is motivated because of cognitive boundaries, biases, routines, and habits in individual and social decision-making posing barriers for people to perform rationally in their own self-declared interests, and which works by making use of those boundaries, biases, routines, and habits as integral parts of such attempts. In fifth-gen warfare, nudging can take the form of images, videos, or online messages.

**Open-source intelligence (OSINT)** is the collection and analysis of data gathered from open sources (covert and publicly available sources) to produce actionable intelligence.

**Operation Mockingbird** was organized by Allen Dulles and Cord Meyer in 1950. The CIA spent about of one billion dollars a year in today's dollars, hiring journalists from corporate media, including CBS, the *New York Times*, ABC, NBC, *Newsweek*, Associated Press, and others, to promote their point of view. The original operation reportedly involved some three thousand CIA operatives and hired over four hundred journalists. In 1976, the domestic operation supposedly closed, but less than half of the media operatives were let go. Furthermore, documentary evidence shows that much of Operation Mockingbird was then offshored to escape detection. It is rumored that British intelligence picked up many of the duties of Operation Mockingbird on behalf of the US intelligence community (see the Trusted News Initiative).

**Othering** is a phenomenon where individuals or groups are defined, labeled and targeted as not fitting in within the norms of a social group. This is a tactic used by the deep state, politicians, and the media. Chaos agents as well as propaganda are used to create a sense of divide. This influences how people perceive and treat those who are viewed as being part of the in-group versus those who are seen as being part of the out-group. This can happen on both a small and very large scale.

**Outrage porn,** also known as outrage journalism, is a form of media or storytelling that aims to elicit strong emotional reactions to expand audiences or boost engagement.

**Phishing** is the practice of sending fraudulent communications that appear to come from a reputable source, aimed at stealing sensitive data or installing malware.

**Propaganda** is a form of manipulation of public opinion by creating a specific narrative that aligns with a political agenda. It uses techniques like repetition, emotional appeals, selective information, and hypnotic language patterns to influence the subconscious mind, bypassing critical thinking and shaping beliefs and values. Propaganda can use a form of hypnosis, whereby putting people into a receptive state where they are more prone to accepting messages.

**Psychological Bioterrorism** is the use of fear about a disease to manipulate individuals or populations by governments and other organizations, such as Big Pharma. Although the fear of infectious disease is an obvious example, it is not the only way psychological bioterrorism is used. Other examples include propaganda regarding environmental toxins, unsafe drinking water, soil contamination, and climate change risks. Another name for psychological bioterrorism is information bioterrorism.

**Psychological warfare** involves the planned use of propaganda and other psychological operations to influence the opinions, emotions, attitudes, and behavior of opposition groups.

**PsyWar** is when psyops is used by governments against a foreign population or even against the citizens of a government (domestically) in a coordinated fashion.

**Publicly available raw data and surveys** used to sway public opinion by use of memes, essays, and social media posts.

**Purity spiral** is a form of groupthink where it becomes more beneficial to hold certain views than to not hold them, and more extreme views are rewarded while expressing doubt, nuance, or moderation is punished (a process sometimes called "moral outbidding"). Moral outbidding makes it beneficial to hold specific beliefs than to not hold them. Although a purity spiral often concerns morality, it is about purity.

**Ransomware** is a type of malware that encrypts a victim's files and demands payment in exchange for the decryption key.

**Realpolitik** is political philosophy (or politics) based on practical objectives rather than on ideals. The word does not mean "real" in the English sense but rather connotes "things"—hence a politics of adaptation to things as they are. Realpolitik thus suggests a pragmatic, no-nonsense view and a disregard for ethical considerations. In diplomacy it is often associated with relentless, though realistic, pursuit of the national interest.

**Repetitive messaging** is a propaganda technique whereby a large number of messages are broadcast rapidly, repetitively, and continuously throughout media without regard for truth or consistency.

**Sealioning** is a trolling or harassment tactic in online discussions and blogs. It involves the attacker asking relentless and insincere questions or requests for evidence under the guise of civility and a desire for genuine debate. These requests are often tangential or previously addressed and the attacker maintains a pretense of civility and sincerity, while feigning ignorance of the subject matter. Sealioning is aimed at exhausting the patience and goodwill of the target, making them appear unreasonable.

**Shadow banning** (also known as stealth banning, hell-banning, ghost banning, and comment ghosting) is the practice of blocking or partially blocking a user or the user's content from some or all areas of an online community. This is done in such a way that the ban is not readily apparent to the user, regardless of whether the action is taken by an individual or an algorithm.

**Social credit systems:** China's social credit system is a combination of government and business surveillance that gives citizens a "score" that can restrict the ability of individuals or corporations to function in the modern world by limiting purchases, acquiring property or taking loans based on past behaviors. Of course, how one uses the internet directly impacts the social credit score. This is the origin of the social credit system that appears to be evolving in the United States. Environmental, social, and governance (ESG) metrics are a kind of social credit system designed to coerce businesses—and, by extension, individuals and all of society—to transform their practices, behaviors and thinking.

**Social engineering** is any manipulation technique that exploits human behavior and error in order to gain access to sensitive or confidential information. Where some scammers would steal someone's personal information, social engineers convince their victims to willingly hand over the requested information like usernames and passwords. "Nudge" technology is actually applied social engineering.

**Social media algorithms** are a set of rules and calculations used by social media platforms to prioritize the content that users see in their feeds based on their past behavior, content relevance, and the popularity of post. Social media algorithms are also used to determine which posts will or won't get seen by other uses. "Free speech but not reach," first coined by Elon Musk describes the use of social media algorithms on "X" and other such platforms.

**Social media analytics (commercially available)** it is the process of gaining and evaluating data from social media networks (such as Twitter, Google, Brave, or Facebook). This process helps to determine if a social media campaign's performance was effective and make future decisions on the basis of this analysis.

**Social media manipulation (data driven)** involves a series of computational techniques that abuse social media algorithms and automation to manipulate public opinion.

**Sophistry** is the use of fallacious arguments, especially with the intention of deceiving. It is a technique often used by the media and fact-checkers.

**SQL Injection** is a code injection technique used to attack data-driven applications whereby malicious SQL statements (code) are inserted into an entry field for execution.

**Stovepiping** is a term used in intelligence analysis, which prevents proper analysis by preventing objective analysts from drawing conclusions based on all relevant data by only providing some of the raw data without context.

**Surveillance capitalism** is a business model based on the unilateral claim of human private experiences as free raw material for translation into behavioral data. These personal data are then extracted, processed, and traded to predict and influence human behavior. Specific data concerning individuals is the commodity. In this version of capitalism, the prediction and influencing of behavior (political and economic) rather than production of goods and services is the primary product. The economic success of this business model is a major contributor to the profitability of Google, Facebook, TikTok and many other social media companies. The data and tools of surveillance capitalism has been exploited for political purposes by Cambridge Analytica. In many cases the surveillance state and globalist governmental organizations have fused with surveillance capitalism to yield a new form of fascism commonly known as techno-totalitarianism.

**Switchboarding** describes the federal government's practice of referring requests for the removal of content on social media from state and local election officials to the relevant social media platforms for removal.

**Synergistic use of mixed media** to build excitement or to create outrage.

**Synthetic media** is a term used for the artificial production, manipulation, and modification of data and media, through the use of generative AI and artificial intelligence algorithms for the purpose of misleading people or changing an original meaning. Often referred to as deepfakes.

**Technocracy** is a form of government in which the decision-makers are selected on the basis of their expertise in a given area of responsibility. This system explicitly contrasts with representative democracy. Decision-makers are selected on the basis of specialized knowledge and performance, rather than political affiliations, parliamentary skills, or popularity.

**Tracking surveillance software** (such as COVID trackers, GPS and cell phone keyword searches).

**Traditional protest tools** can be combined with fifth-gen warfare. An example would be a large rally combined with social media tools to create synergy or opposition for a movement.

**Trolls** are human online agents, sometimes sponsored to harass other users or post divisive content to spark controversies as well as dis-enfranchise individuals or group members through bad-jacketing and gossip.

**The Trusted News Initiative (TNI)** is a British Broadcasting Corporation (BBC)–led organization which has been actively censoring eminent doctors, academics, and those with dissenting voices that contravene the official COVID-19 narrative as well as other narratives, such as voter fraud, elections, and current news not sanctioned by government. Partners in this endeavor include the major mainstream media organizations, Big Tech (such as Google and social media), governments, and nongovernmental organizations. Anything contrary to the government narrative is considered disinformation or misinformation and will be deleted, suppressed, or deplatformed.

**Ultra vires** ("beyond the powers") is a Latin phrase used in law to describe an act that requires legal authority but is done without it. Its opposite, an act done under proper authority, is **intra vires** ("within the powers").

**Virtue signaling** is sharing one's point of view on a social or political issue, often on social media or through specific dress or actions, to garner praise or acknowledgment of one's righteousness from others who share that point of view or to rebuke those who do not.

**Web crawler**, also known as a spiderbot, is an automated Internet program that systematically browses the World Wide Web for specific types of information.

**White propaganda** is a type of propaganda where the producer of the material is marked and indicated, and the purpose of the information is transparent. White propaganda is commonly used in marketing and public relations. White propaganda involves communicating a message from a known source to a recipient (typically the public or some targeted sub-audience). White propaganda is mainly based on facts, although often, the whole truth is not told.

**World Economic Forum (WEF)** is one of the key think tanks and meeting places for managing global capitalism and is arguably coherent enough to qualify as the leading global "deep state" organization. Under the leadership of Professor Klaus Schwab, it has played an increasingly important role in coordinating the globalized hegemony of large pools of transnational capital and associated large corporations over Western democracies during the last three decades.

**Wrap-up smear** is a deflection tactic in which a smear is made up and leaked to the press. The press then amplifies the smear and gives it legitimacy.

Then, an author can use the press coverage of the smear as validation to write a summary story, which is the wrap-up smear.

**Yellow journalism** is newspaper reporting that emphasizes sensationalism over facts. Advocacy journalists who support government narratives often use it to sway public opinion.

**Zero-day exploit** is a technique targeting a newly discovered vulnerability before a patch is available.

# Acknowledgments

Every day, the horses, dogs, peafowl, guinea fowl, chickens, emu, and goose need tending to on our farm. Trees need care. Plants need water. Every plot of earth needs weeding, mowing, and brush hogging. We all must tend the garden. For our farm, we are extraordinarily blessed to have Olivia Myers help tend our garden and take care of all our critters. This job requires work ethic, skill, strategy, patience, and brinkmanship. Olivia exudes all these beautiful traits and more. Without her, I don't know if we would finish any writing. Thank you.

Anita Snogles-Hasbury has been an enormous help in keeping our websites tended to and helping with various research projects. Her commitment and steadfast work ethic are inspiring.

Then there are so many colleagues and friends who have advised and inspired us to try to do better, including Steve Bannon, Irina Boutourline, Gavin De Becker, Del Bigtree, Andrew Bridgen, Tucker Carlson, Lilly Defina, Dr. Mattias Desmet, Ed Dowd, Dr. George Fareed, Nigel Farage, Frank Gaffney Jr., Jeff Hansen, Dr. Lynn Howard, Justine Isernhinke, Jan Jekielek, Jason Jones, Robert F. Kennedy Jr., Charlie Kirk, Dr. Pierre Kory, Philipp Kruse, Dr. Kat Lindley, James Lindsay, Reggie Littlejohn, Dr. John Littell, Anthony Lyons, Dr. Assem Malhotra, John Mappin, David Martin, Dr. Paul Marik, Dr. Peter Navarro, Neal Oliver, Mauro Rango, Dr. Jessica Rose, Laura Sextro, Chrisanna Shackelford, Robert Steiner, Jeffrey Tucker, Dr. Mark Trozzi, Dr. Brian Tyson, Dr. Bret Weinstein, and Mikki Willis, to name a few.

Of course, then there are our friends in the "quarantine club," that rebel group of conservative compadres who have supported each other through thick and thin. Included in this group are Nina and Colby May, Dr. Brooke and Ann Miller, Rep. Bob and Liz McEwin, Alyse Best Muldoon and her husband, the late great Tony La Bianco, Mercy and Matt Schlapp, Rep. Dick and Nancy Schulze, and Bill and Sarah Walton.

We also wish to thank our dear friends Kelly and Tad Coffin (also members of the quarantine club), who have helped us maintain insight and humor over the years.

Of course, we love and are so grateful to Megan and Zach Malone and their kids for their unwavering love. It saddens us that we seem to have so little time together.

Our many Substack subscribers and commenters bring us much light, insightful criticism, and valuable support. We rely on them daily to keep us in check and on the right track.

A zillion people in our lives, new and old, make such a difference with their caring. Love from all over the world, embracing us like a bubble, keeps the promoted darkness and hate that we are constantly bombarded with from corrupting our souls. Please know that we are eternally grateful even if we don't mention you by name. You are in our hearts and our minds.

# Endnotes

## Introduction

1   Shaw, G.B., *The Collected Works of George Bernard Shaw: Plays, Novels, Articles, Letters and Essays: Pygmalion, Mrs. Warren's Profession, Candida, Arms and The Man, . . . on War, Memories of Oscar Wilde and more.* 2015, Kindle, online: e-artnow. 6037.

2   Bernstein, B., "Judge Finds Former Fox News Journalist Catherine Herridge in Contempt for Refusal to Give Up Source." *National Review*, 2024.

3   Kraemer, B., "Another NC journalist who covered January 6 Capitol breach faces prosecution." *Carolina Journal*, 2024.

## Chapter 1

1   Logan, L. "Media censorship and the First Amendment, the importance of free speech. in What are Federal Health Agencies and the COVID Cartel Hiding? 2024." U.S. Senate.

2   Giles, M., "The Cambridge Analytica affair reveals Facebook's 'Transparency Paradox'." *MIT Technology Review*, 2018.

3   Epstein, R., Robertson, R.E., "The search engine manipulation effect (SEME) and its possible impact on the outcomes of elections." Proc Natl Acad Sci U S A, 2015. 112(33): p. E4512–21.

4   Desmet, M., *The Psychology of Totalitarianism.* 2022, White River Junction, Vermont: Chelsea Green Publishing. 231 pages.

5   Verity, R., et al., "Estimates of the severity of coronavirus disease 2019: a model-based analysis." *Lancet Infect Dis*, 2020. 20(6): p. 669–677.

6   Lovelace, B., Higgins-Dunn, N., "WHO says coronavirus death rate is 3.4% globally, higher than previously thought." CNBC, 2020.

7   Mantik, D.W., Corsi, J.R., *The Assassination of President John F. Kennedy: The Final Analysis: Forensic Analysis of the JFK Autopsy X-Rays Proves Two Headshots from the Right Front and One from the Rear.* 2024: Post Hill Press. 564.

8   Davis, M., *The JFK Assassination Evidence Handbook: Issues, Evidence & Answers* 2018. 248.

9    Prouty, L.F., *JFK: The CIA, Vietnam, and the Plot to Assassinate John F. Kennedy.* 2011. 377.

10   Landler, M., Brain Stelter, B., "D.C. diplomat finds a powerful new tool in Twitter." *The Seattle Times*, 2009.

11   Galeotti, M., "Will the populist wave wash away NATO and the European Union?" *NATO Review*, 2017.

12   Congress, S., Smith-Mundt Act: U.S. Information and Educational Exchange Act of 1948, C. law, Editor. 1948, USG: Washington DC.

**Chapter 2**

1    U.S. Army, Counterinsurgency Operations, U. Army, Editor. 2004, U.S. Gov: Washington DC. p. 240.

2    Bernays, E.L., *Propaganda*. 1928, New York: H. Liveright. p. 159.

3    DHS, S., "Summary of Terrorism Threat to the U.S. Homeland: National Terrorism Advisory System Bulletin," DHS, Editor. 2022, USG: Washington, DC.

4    Ibid.

5    Woolley, S., Howard, P., *Computational Propaganda. Political Parties, Politicians, and Political Manipulation on Social Media*. Vol. Kindle reprint. 2018, Oxford, UK: Oxford University Press.

6    Woolley, S., Howard, P., *0*. Vol. Kindle reprint. 2018, Oxford, UK: Oxford University Press.

7    Bernstein, C., "The CIA and the Media. How America's Most Powerful News Media Worked Hand in Glove with the Central Intelligence Agency and Why the Church Committee Covered It Up." *Rolling Stone*, 1977.

8    Ibid.

9    GCHQ, "A Brief History of the UKUSA agreement 1946–2021, U. Government Communications Headquarters (GCHQ)," Editor. 2021: UK.

10   Bilal, A., "Hybrid Warfare – New Threats, Complexity, and 'Trust' as the Antidote." *NATO Review*, 2021.

11   Miller, C., "Inside the British Army's secret information warfare machine." *Wired*, 2018.

12   Davis, I., "Swarmed by Mutton, The Mutton Crew's Hybrid Warfare Operation." Iain Davis "The Disillusioned Blogger" Substack, 2024.

13   Bridgen, A., "Eyes Needed." Twitter (X), 2024.

14   Wikispooks, E. Swaledale Mutton. May 18, 2024 [Available from: https://wikispooks.com/wiki/Swaledale_Mutton.]

15   Sweeny, H.M., "Twenty-Five Ways To Suppress Truth: The Rules of Disinformation, in Propaganda ~ Logical Fallacies," D. Paret, Editor. 2005: Online.

16   Webb, W., "U.S.—U.K. Intel Agencies Declare Cyber War on Independent Media." Unlimited Hangout, 2020.

17   Pogrund, G., Ripley, T., "Army spies to take on antivax militants." *The Sunday Times*, 2020.

18   Scully, E., "British Army's Information Warfare Unit will be deployed to tackle anti-vaccine propaganda ahead of jab rollout." *Daily Mail*, 2020.

19   Schulte, P., "Mitigating the Coming Infodemics and The Impacts of Information Disorder on the British Body Politic." Written Testimony submitted to the UK Parliament, 2020.

20   Kirk Sell, T., et.al., "National Priorities to Combat Misinformation and Disinformation for COVID-19 and Future Public Health Threats: A Call for a National Strategy." 2021, Johns Hopkins U.: Johns Hopkins University, Bloomberg School of Public Health, Center for Health Security. p. 1–29.

21   Congress, S., Smith-Mundt Act: U.S. Information and Educational Exchange Act of 1948, C. law, Editor. 1948, USG: Washington DC.

22   Harper, C.A., et al., "Functional Fear Predicts Public Health Compliance in the COVID-19 Pandemic." *Int J Ment Health Addict*, 2021. 19(5): p. 1875–1888.

23   U.S. Army, "Pyschological Operations," U.S. Army, Editor. 2010, U.S. Government: Washington DC.

24   U.S. Army. "Become a Master of Influence, Psychological Operations." 2023; Available from: https://www.goarmy.com/careers-and-jobs/specialty-careers/special-ops/psychological-operations.

25   See https://behavioralpolicy.org/what-is-nudging/.

26   Fagan, P., "Clicks and tricks: The dark art of online persuasion." Curr Opin Psychol, 2024. 58: p. 101844.

27   Junger, N. and O. Hirsch, "Ethics of Nudging in the COVID-19 Crisis and the Necessary Return to the Principles of Shared Decision Making: A Critical Review." Cureus, 2024. 16(4): p. e57960.

28   Mehra, M.R., F. Ruschitzka, and A.N. Patel, "Retraction-Hydroxychloroquine or chloroquine with or without a macrolide for treatment of COVID-19: a multinational registry analysis." *Lancet*, 2020. 395(10240): p. 1820.

29   Joseph, A., "Lancet, New England Journal retract Covid-19 studies, including one that raised safety concerns about malaria drugs." Stat News, 2020.

30   Wenstrup, B., "Wenstrup Invites Top Scientific Journals to Testify on Possible Inappropriate Relationship with Federal Government, in House Select Subcommittee: Coronavirus Pandemic 2024."

31   St. Aubin, C., Liedke, J., "Most Americans favor restrictions on false information, violent content online," Pew Research Center. 2023.

32   Expose, S., The Trusted News Initiative, "A BBC led organisation censoring Public Health experts who oppose the official narrative on Covid-19." The Expose, 2021.

33   Ekstra Bladet, S., "We Failed," Ekstra Bladet. 2022.

## Chapter 3

1   Kouzminov, A., "Information bioterrorism - a new form of global manipulation." *Current Concerns*, 2017.

## Chapter 4

1   Britannica, E., "religion," in Britannica. 2024, Britannica: Online.

2   Peters, E.H., B., "Inquisition, Roman Catholicism." Britannica, 2007 Online.

3   Feyerabend, P., *Against method: Outline of an Anarchistic Theory of Knowledge.* 1975, London: NLB ; Humanities Press. 339.

4    "The Anti-Religious Campaign in the Soviet Union. History on the Net," Salem Media, 2000–2003.
5    Lewis, C.S., "Willing Slaves of the Welfare State." *The Observer*, 1958.

## Chapter 5

1    Congress, S., "New Report Details How the Federal Government Partnered with Universities to Censor Americans' Speech." 2023, House Judiciary committee, USG: DC.
2    Congress, S., "The Weaponization of 'Disinformation' Pseudo-experts and Bureaucrats: How the Federal Government Partnered with Universities to Censor Americans' Free Speech." Congress, Editor. 2023, USG: DC.
3    DHS, S., "Summary of Terrorism Threat to the U.S. Homeland: National Terrorism Advisory System Bulletin," DHS, Editor. 2022, USG: Washington, DC.
4    Patel, K.P., *Government Gangsters: The Deep State, the Truth, and the Battle for Our Democracy*. 1st ed. 2023: Post Hill Press.
5    Congress, S., "GARM'S Harm: How the World's Biggest Brands Seek to Control Online Speech," Congress, Editor. 2024, USG: DC.
6    Fagan, P., "Clicks and tricks: The dark art of online persuasion." Curr Opin Psychol, 2024. 58: p. 101844.
7    DHS, S., "Summary of Terrorism Threat to the U.S. Homeland: National Terrorism Advisory System Bulletin, "DHS, Editor. 2022, USG: Washington, DC.
8    Saul, D., "'Freedom of Speech, But Not Freedom Of Reach': Musk Reinstates Kathy Griffin And Jordan Peterson Amid New Policy — But Not Trump Yet." *Forbes*, 2022.

## Chapter 6

1    Clarke, A.C., *Profiles of the Future: An Inquiry into the Limits of the Possible*. 1973: Henry Holt & Co.

## Chapter 7

1    Abbott, D.H., *The Handbook of 5GW: A Fifth Generation of War?* 2010: Nimble Books.
2    Kramer, F.D., "The sixth domain: The role of the private sector in warfare." Atlantic Council, 2023 (Report).
3    CISA, S., "Tactics of Disinformation," CISA, Editor. 2024, CISA USG: Internet.
4    Ibid.
5    van der Klaauw, C., "Cognitive Warfare." *The Three Swords*, 2023. 39: p. 97–101.
6    U.S .Army, "Pyschological Operations," U.S. Army, Editor. 2010, U.S. Government: Washington DC.
7    Malone, R.W., "How a 'Cybersecurity' Agency Colluded with Big Tech and 'Disinformation' Partners to Censor Americans: The Weaponization of CISA" - Interim staff report for the Committee on the Judiciary and the Select Subcommittee. "Who is Robert Malone" Substack, 2023(July 1, 2023).

8    Scully, E., "British Army's Information Warfare Unit will be deployed to tackle anti-vaccine propaganda ahead of jab rollout." *Daily Mail*, 2020.

9    Sperry, B., "What Does *Murthy v. Missouri* Mean for Online Speech?" Truth on the Market, 2024.

10   Kouzminov, A., "Information bioterrorism - a new form of global manipulation." *Current Concerns*, 2017.

11   Claverie, B., Prebot, B. Buchler, N. DuCluzel, F., "Proceedings of the first NATO scientific meeting on Cognitive Warfare" (France) 21 June 2021. NATO 2021.

12   van der Klaauw, C., "Cognitive Warfare." *The Three Swords*, 2023. 39: p. 97–101.

13   Ibid.

14   Ibid.

## Chapter 8

1    Dangerfield, M.B., "Power to the People: The rise and rise of Citizen Journalism." Tate, 2024.

2    Kuhn, T.S., *The Structure of Scientific Revolutions*. 3rd ed. 1996, Chicago, IL: University of Chicago Press. xiv, 212 p.

## Chapter 10

1    Spence, K., "CDC Partners With 'Social and Behavior Change' Initiative to Silence Vaccine Hesitancy," *The Epoch Times*. 2023, The Epoch Times: NY.

2    DHS, S., "Summary of Terrorism Threat to the U.S. Homeland: National Terrorism Advisory System Bulletin," DHS, Editor. 2022, USG: Washington, DC.

3    Extremism, C.O., "Antisemitism, False Information and Hate Speech Find a Home on Substack." Anti Defamation League, 2023.

4    Patel, K.P., *Government Gangsters: The Deep State, the Truth, and the Battle for Our Democracy*. 1st ed. 2023: Post Hill Press.

## Chapter 11

1    Bernays, E.L., *Propaganda*. 1928, New York: H. Liveright. p.159.

2    Patel, K.P., *Government Gangsters: The Deep State, the Truth, and the Battle for Our Democracy*. 1st ed. 2023: Post Hill Press.

3    Devine, M., "FBI put the Hunter Biden story right in Facebook's lap." *New York Post*, 2022.

4    Morris, E., Fonrouge, G., "Smoking-gun email reveals how Hunter Biden introduced Ukrainian businessman to VP dad." *New York Post*, 2020.

5    Haworth, I., "How the Censorship of Hunter Biden's Laptop Story Helped Joe Biden Win." *Daily Wire*, 2022.

6    Smith, K., "How Dem officials, the media and Big Tech worked in concert to bury the Hunter Biden story." *New York Post*, 2022.

7    Wilson, J.M., et al., "Non-traditional immersive seminar enhances learning by promoting greater physiological and psychological engagement compared to a traditional lecture format." Physiol Behav, 2021. 238: p. 113461.

8    Walter, J. and A. Bayat, "Neurolinguistic programming: the keys to success." *BMJ*, 2003. 326(7398): p. S165–6.

9    Walter, J. and A. Bayat, "Neurolinguistic programming: temperament and character types." *BMJ*, 2003. 326(7394): p. S133.

10   Ibid., 326(7389): p. S83.

11   Lindorff, D., "Covering (Up) Antiwar Protest in U.S. Media: March 18 DC peace march almost completely blacked out in U.S. corporate media." Fairness & Accuracy in Reporting (FAIR), 2023.

12   Andrighetto, G. and E. Vriens, "A research agenda for the study of social norm change." Philos Trans A Math Phys Eng Sci, 2022. 380(2227): p. 20200411.

13   Dobson, G.P., "Wired to Doubt: Why People Fear Vaccines and Climate Change and Mistrust Science." Front Med (Lausanne), 2021. 8: p. 809395.

14   Paterson, P. and R.M. Clarke, "Climate change risk communication: a vaccine hesitancy perspective." *Lancet Planet Health*, 2021. 5(4): p. e179-e180.

15   Malone, R.W., "Monkey Pox: Truth versus Fearporn." Who is Robert Malone, Substack, 2022.

16   Hersh, S., "How America Took Out The Nord Stream Pipeline." Seymour Hersh, Substack, 2023.

17   Staff, P., "Tracking Federal Purchases to Fight the Coronavirus: Advertising Services." Propublica, 2023.

## Chapter 13

1    MindOverMedia, S., "What is Propaganda?" Mind over Media: Analyzing Contemporary Propaganda, 2015.

2    Smith, B.L., H.D. Lasswell, and R.D. Casey, *Propaganda, Communication, and Public Opinion; a Comprehensive Reference Guide.* 1946, Princeton: Princeton University Press. vii, 1 p., 1 l., 435 p.

3    Ellul, J., *Propaganda; the formation of men's attitudes.* 1st American ed. 1965, New York,: Knopf. xxii, 320, vii p.

4    Jowett, G. and V. O'Donnell, *Propaganda & Persuasion.* Seventh edition. ed. 2019, Los Angeles: SAGE. xv, 400 pages.

5    Postman, N., *Technopoly: The Surrender of Culture to Technology.* 1st ed. 1992, New York: Knopf. xii, 222 pages.

6    Nelson, R.A., *A chronology and glossary of propaganda in the United States.* 1996, Westport, Conn.: Greenwood Press. xvi, 340 p.

7    Cunningham, S.B., *The Idea of Propaganda: A Reconstruction.* 2002, Westport, Conn.: Praeger. x, 231 p.

8    Wikipedia, entry on propaganda, 2008.

9    Bachrach, S.D., et al., *State of Deception: The Power of Nazi Propaganda.* 2009, D.C. New York: United States Holocaust Memorial Museum; Distributed by W.W. Norton. xi, 194 p.

## Chapter 14

1 Albertini, M.C., Sestili, P., Malone, R.W., Haimes, H., "Resignation in Protest," Frontiers in Pharmacology Topic Editors, "Treating COVID-19 With Currently Available Drugs". Letter to Frontiers in Pharmacology, 2021.

2 Ibid.

## Chapter 15

1 Malone, R.W., "WHO International Health Regulations: In a frantic last-minute rush, modified IHR were illegally approved by the most recent World Health Assembly." Who is Robert Malone, Substack, 2024.

2 Rubio-Casillas, A., et al., "Review: N1-methyl-pseudouridine (m1Psi): Friend or foe of cancer?" *Int J Biol Macromol*, 2024. 267(Pt 1): p. 131427.

3 Spence, K., "CDC Partners With 'Social and Behavior Change' Initiative to Silence Vaccine Hesitancy," *The Epoch Times*. 2023, The Epoch Times: NY.

## Chapter 16

1 Kennedy, R.F., *The Real Anthony Fauci: Bill Gates, Big Pharma, and the Global War on Democracy and Public Health*. Children's health defense. 2021, New York, NY: Skyhorse Publishing. xxvii, 449 pages.

## Chapter 17

1 Sackett, D. L., "Evidence-based medicine." Semin Perinatol, 1997. 21(1): p. 3–5.

2 Jureidini, J. and L.B. McHenry, "The illusion of evidence based medicine." *BMJ*, 2022. 376: p. o702.

3 Ibid.

4 Ibid.

5 Mehra, M. R., F. Ruschitzka, and A.N. Patel, "Retraction-Hydroxychloroquine or chloroquine with or without a macrolide for treatment of COVID-19: a multinational registry analysis." *Lancet*, 2020. 395(10240): p. 1820.

6 Jureidini, J. and L.B. McHenry, The illusion of evidence based medicine." *BMJ*, 2022. 376: p. o702.

7 Ibid.

## Chapter 18

1 Dunleavy, J., "Feinstein's former staffer helped funnel millions to Steele and Fusion GPS after 2016." *Washington Examiner*, 2021.

2 Petruk, G., et al., "SARS-CoV-2 spike protein binds to bacterial lipopolysaccharide and boosts proinflammatory activity." *J Mol Cell Biol*, 2020. 12(12): p. 916–932.

3 Moghaddar, M., R. Radman, and I. Macreadie, "Severity, Pathogenicity and Transmissibility of Delta and Lambda Variants of SARS-CoV-2, Toxicity of Spike Protein and Possibilities for Future Prevention of COVID-19." *Microorganisms*, 2021. 9(10).

## Chapter 19

1  Giordano, A., "Former Principal Loses Superintendent Job for Calling Women 'Ladies'." *The Epoch Times*, 2023.

2  Reyes, R., "Riley Gaines slams SF State for praising 'peaceful' protest where swimmer claims she was assaulted by trans-rights activists." *New York Post*, 2023.

## Chapter 20

1  Desmet, M., *The Psychology of Totalitarianism*. 2022, White River Junction, Vermont: Chelsea Green Publishing. 231 pages.

2  Ibid.

3  Ibid.

4  Alfano, V., L. Cicatiello, and S. Ercolano, "Assessing the effectiveness of mandatory outdoor mask policy: The natural experiment of Campania." *Econ Hum Biol*, 2023. 50: p. 101265.

5  Santarsiero, A., et al., "Effectiveness of face masks for the population." Ann Ig, 2021. 33(4): p. 347–359.

6  Miyazaki, Y., et al., "Effects of wearing an opaque or transparent face mask on the perception of facial expressions: A comparative study between Japanese school-aged children and adults." *Perception*, 2023: p. 3010066231200693.

7  Kisielinski, K., et al., "Possible toxicity of chronic carbon dioxide exposure associated with face mask use, particularly in pregnant women, children and adolescents - A scoping review." *Heliyon*, 2023. 9(4): p. e14117.

8  Akhondi, H., et al., "CO(2) Levels Behind and in Front of Different Protective Mask Types. HCA Healthc" *J Med*, 2022. 3(4): p. 231–237.

9  Tornero-Aguilera, J.F. and V.J. Clemente-Suarez, "Cognitive and psychophysiological impact of surgical mask use during university lessons." *Physiol Behav*, 2021. 234: p. 113342.

10 Desmet, M., *The Psychology of Totalitarianism*. 2022, White River Junction, Vermont: Chelsea Green Publishing. 231 pages.

11 Jowett, G. and V. O'Donnell, *Propaganda & Persuasion*. Seventh edition. ed. 2019, Los Angeles: SAGE. xv, 400 pages.

12 Bernstein, C., "The CIA and the Media. How America's Most Powerful News Media Worked Hand in Glove with the Central Intelligence Agency and Why the Church Committee Covered It Up." *Rolling Stone*, 1977.

13 Cecil, J., "Fighting Disinfomation Fast When it Matters Most." BBC, 2020.

14 McPherrin, J., "Environmental, Social, and Governance (ESG) Scores. A Threat to Individual Liberty, Free Markets, and the U.S. Economy." Heartland Institute, 2022.

15 Raynor, G., "Use of fear to control behaviour in Covid crisis was 'totalitarian', admit scientists Members of Scientific Pandemic Influenza Group on Behaviour express regret about 'unethical' methods." *Telegraph*, 2021.

## Chapter 21

1  House, S., "The Censorship-Industrial Complex: How Top Biden White House Officials Coerced Big Tech to Censor Americans, True Information,

and Critics of the Biden Administration." Final interim staff report for the Committee on the Judiciary and the Select Subcommittee., Government, Editor. 2024, USG: Washington, D.C.

2   Bloomberg, "Amazon, Alphabet among tech firms meeting with White House on coronavirus response." *LA Times*, 2020.

3   Morrison, R., "World Health Organization holds secretive talks with tech giants Google, Facebook, and Amazon to tackle the spread of misinformation on coronavirus." *Daily Mail*. February 17, 2020. Daily Mail, 2020.

4   Romm, T., "White House asks Silicon Valley for help to combat coronavirus, track its spread and stop misinformation." *Washington Post*, 2020.

5   House, S., "The Censorship-Industrial Complex: How Top Biden White House Officials Coerced Big Tech to Censor Americans, True Information, and Critics of the Biden Administration." Final interim staff report for the Committee on the Judiciary and the Select Subcommittee., Government, Editor. 2024, USG: Washington, D.C.

6   Ibid.

7   House, S., "The Weaponization of CISA: How A 'Cybersecurity' Agency Colluded with Big Tech and "Disinformation" Partners to Censor Americans," Interim Staff Report. Government, Editor. 2023, USG: Washington, D.C.

8   Tracy, R., "Mark Zuckerberg Could Be Held in Contempt of Congress: House Republicans threaten to cite Meta CEO for what they say is failure to provide adequate documents in response to subpoena." *WSJ*, 2023.

9   House, S., "The Censorship-Industrial Complex: How Top Biden White House Officials Coerced Big Tech to Censor Americans, True Information, and Critics of the Biden Administration." Final interim staff report for the Committee on the Judiciary and the Select Subcommittee., Government, Editor. 2024, USG: Washington, D.C.

10  Ibid.

## Chapter 22

1   Malone, R.W., "How a 'Cybersecurity' Agency Colluded with Big Tech and 'Disinformation' Partners to Censor Americans: The Weaponization of CISA"—Interim staff report for the Committee on the Judiciary and the Select Subcommittee. "Who is Robert Malone" Substack, 2023(July 1, 2023).

2   Nelson, S., "White House 'flagging' posts for Facebook to censor over COVID 'misinformation.'" *New York Post*, 2021.

3   Malone, R.W., "How a 'Cybersecurity' Agency Colluded with Big Tech and 'Disinformation' Partners to Censor Americans: The Weaponization of CISA"—Interim staff report for the Committee on the Judiciary and the Select Subcommittee. "Who is Robert Malone" Substack, 2023(July 1, 2023).

4   Snowden, E., Tweet @Snowden. Twitter, 2022.

5   Smith, D., "Declassified documents reveal CIA has been sweeping up information on Americans." *The Guardian*, 2022.

6   Press release, Ron Wyden Senate Office, February 10, 2022. https://www.wyden.senate.gov/news/press-releases/wyden-and-heinrich-newly -declassified-documents-reveal-previously-secret-cia-bulk-collection -problems-with-cia-handling-of-americans-information.

7   DHS, S., "Summary of Terrorism Threat to the U.S. Homeland: National Terrorism Advisory System Bulletin," DHS, Editor. 2022, USG: Washington, DC.

8   Brown, S., Tomaschek, A., "Prevent Your Google Nest from Spying on You with These Privacy Tips." CNET, 2023.

## Chapter 23

1   Jefferson, T., "I believe in dangerous freedom over peaceful slavery." 1787: Letter to James Madison.

2   Taranto, J., Rivkin, D.B., "Justice Samuel Alito: 'This Made Us Targets of Assassination.'" *Wall Street Journal*, 2023.

3   Epstein, R., Robertson, R.E., "The search engine manipulation effect (SEME) and its possible impact on the outcomes of elections." *Proc Natl Acad Sci USA*, 2015. 112(33): p. E4512–21.

4   Epstein, R., "Why Google Poses a Serious Threat to Democracy, and How to End That Threat," U.S.S.J.S.o.t. Constitution, Editor. 2019, U.S. Gov.: Washington DC.

5   Duggan, L., "Global Disinformation Index removes funders from website." UnHerd, 2024.

6   Sayers, F., "Inside the disinformation industry: A government-sponsored agency is censoring journalism." UnHerd, 2024.

7   Duggan, L., "Global Disinformation Index removes funders from website." UnHerd, 2024.

8   Sayers, F., "Inside the disinformation industry: A government-sponsored agency is censoring journalism." UnHerd, 2024.

9   Malone, R.W., "How a 'Cybersecurity' Agency Colluded with Big Tech and 'Disinformation' Partners to Censor Americans: The Weaponization of CISA"—Interim staff report for the Committee on the Judiciary and the Select Subcommittee. "Who is Robert Malone" Substack, 2023(July 1, 2023).

10   Spence, K., "CDC Partners With 'Social and Behavior Change' Initiative to Silence Vaccine Hesitancy," *The Epoch Times*. 2023, The Epoch Times: NY.

11   Felgner, P., Wolff, J.A., Rhodes, G.H., Malone, R., Carson, D., "Lipid-mediated polynucleotide administration to deliver a biologically active peptide and to induce a cellular immune response (includes mRNA)." in USPTO, USPTO, Editor. 1989, Vical: USA.

12   Felgner, P., Wolff, J.A., Rhodes, G.H., Malone, R., Carson, D., "Lipid-mediated polynucleotide administration to reduce likelihood of subject's becoming infected (includes mRNA)." in USPTO, USPTO, Editor. 1989, Vical: USA.

13   Felgner, P., Wolff, J.A., Rhodes, G.H., Malone, R., Carson, D., "Generation of an immune response to a pathogen (includes mRNA)." P Felgner, JA Wolff, GH Rhodes, Robert W Malone, D Carson. Assigned to Vical, Inc and licensed to Merck. U.S. Pat. Ser. No. 6,710,035. Date of issue: 3/23/04. Citations: 39 articles. Priority Date: 3/21/1989., in USPTO, USPTO, Editor. 1989: USA.

14 Felgner, P., Wolff, J.A., Rhodes, G.H., Malone, R., Carson, D., "Expression of exogenous polynucleotide sequences in a vertebrate, mammal, fish, bird or human (includes mRNA)." in USPTO, USPTO, Editor. 1989, Vical: USA.

15 Felgner, P., Wolff, J.A., Rhodes, G.H., Malone, R., Carson, D., "Methods of delivering a physiologically active polypeptide to a mammal (includes mRNA)." in USPTO, USPTO, Editor. 1989, Vical: USA.

16 Felgner, P., Wolff, J.A., Rhodes, G.H., Malone, R., Carson, D., "Induction of a protective immune response in a mammal by injecting a DNA sequence (includes mRNA)." in USPTO, USPTO, Editor. 1989, Vical: USA.

17 Felgner, P., Wolff, J.A., Rhodes, G.H., Malone, R., Carson, D., "Induction of a protective immune response in a mammal by injecting a DNA sequence (includes mRNA)." P Felgner, JA Wolff, GH Rhodes, Robert W Malone, D Carson. Assigned to Vical, Inc, licensed to Merck. U.S. Pat. Ser. No. 5,589,466. Date of issue: 12/31/96. Cited in 899 articles. Priority Date: 3/21/1989., in USPTO, USPTO, Editor. 1989, Vical: USA.

18 Felgner, P., Wolff, J.A., Rhodes, G.H., Malone, R., Carson, D., "Delivery of exogenous DNA sequences in a mammal (includes mRNA). "Assigned to Vical, Inc, licensed to Merck. P Felgner, JA Wolff, GH Rhodes, Robert W Malone, D Carson. U.S. Pat. Ser. No. 5,580,859. Date of issue: 12/3/96. Cited in 1244 articles. Priority Date: 3/21/1989., in USPTO, USPTO, Editor. 1989, Vical: USA.

19 Felgner, P., Wolff, J.A., Rhodes, G.H., Malone, R., Carson, D., "Generation of antibodies through lipid mediated DNA delivery (includes mRNA)." in USPTO, USPTO, Editor. 1989, Vical: USA.

20 Devine, M., "How Google manipulates search to favor liberals and tip elections." *New York Post*, 2023.

21 Wenstup, B., "Wenstrup Releases Statement Following Day 1 of Dr. Fauci's Testimony," S.S.C. Pandemic, Editor. January 8, 2024, USG: Washington DC.

22 Congress, S., E&C "Republicans Release Interim Staff Report on NIH Misconduct and Inadequate Oversight Involving Taxpayer-Funded Risky MPXV Research that Jeopardizes Public Health Security," H.E.a.C. Committee, Editor. 2024, USG: Washington DC.

23 Spence, K., "CDC Partners With 'Social and Behavior Change' Initiative to Silence Vaccine Hesitancy," *The Epoch Times*. 2023, The Epoch Times: NY.

24 Christenson, J., "NIH adviser David Morens can't recall if he deleted COVID records, laughs off Fauci FOIA evasion." *New York Post*, 2024.

25 Taranto, J., "Justice Samuel Alito: 'This Made Us Targets of Assassination.'" *Wall Streat Journal*, 2023.

26 Cooke, C.W.C., "Jamie Raskin's Absurd Theory of Forced Judicial Recusal." *National Review*, 2024.

## Chapter 24

1 Wiki, E., State of exception. Wikipedia, 2024.

2 Agamben, G., *State of Exception*. 2005, Chicago: University of Chicago Press. 95 p.

3 Agamben, G. and V. Dani, *Where Are We Now? The Epidemic as Politics*. 2021, Rowman & Littlefield,: Lanham. p. 1 online resource.

4   Malone, R.W., "WHO International Health Regulations: In a frantic last-minute rush, modified IHR were illegally approved by the most recent World Health Assembly." Who is Robert Malone, Substack, 2024.

5   Agamben, G. and V. Dani, *Where Are We Now? The Epidemic as Politics*. 2021, Rowman & Littlefield,: Lanham. p. 1 online resource.

6   Ibid.

7   Ibid.

8   Ibid.

## Chapter 25

1   UN, S., "The Sustainable Development Agenda Treaty," Editor. 2016, The United Nations: Geneva, SW.

2   Ministry of Health, I., "Initiating a Globally-Recognized Vaccine Passport, Indonesia's G20 HWG Meeting Series Welcome More International Visitors." PR Newswire, 2022.

3   Ibid.

## Chapter 26

1   Schwab, K., Malleret, T., *COVID-19: The Great Reset*. 2020, Amazon.

2   Lavopa, A., Delera, M., "What is the 4th Industrial Revolution?" Industry Analytics Platform, 2021.

3   Russo, A., "World Economic Forum to Lead G20 Smart Cities Alliance on Technology Governance." World Economic Forum Website, 2019.

4   WEF, S. "WEF Strategic Partners." 2024 [cited 2024 Feb 10, 2024]; Available from: https://www.weforum.org/communities/strategic-partnership-b5337725-fac7-4f8a-9a4f-c89072b96a0d/.

5   Heath, R., "Davos freezes out Putin and Russian oligarchs." Politico, 2022.

6   WEF, S., "World Economic Forum and UN Sign Strategic Partnership Framework," WEF, Editor. 2019, WEF: WEF.

7   UN, S., "The Sustainable Development Agenda Treaty," Editor. 2016, The United Nations: Geneva, SW.

8   Schwab, K., Malleret, T., *COVID-19: The Great Reset*. 2020, Amazon.

9   Gregg, S., "Why it isn't mad to oppose the World Economic Forum." *The Spectator*, 2022.

10  UN, S., "The Sustainable Development Agenda Treaty," Editor. 2016, The United Nations: Geneva, SW.

11  Schwab, K., Malleret, T., *COVID-19: The Great Reset. 2020*, Amazon.

## Chapter 27

1   WEF, S., "Global Unitersity Leaders Forum." WE Forum, 2023 (Accessed).

2   Ibid.

3   Calisher, C., et al., "Statement in support of the scientists, public health professionals, and medical professionals of China combatting COVID-19." *Lancet*, 2020. 395(10226): p. e42-e43.

4   WEF, S., "World Economic Forum and UN Sign Strategic Partnership Framework." WE Forum, 2019.

## Chapter 28

1　UN, S., "António Guterres secures second term as UN Secretary-General, calls for new era of 'solidarity and equality,'" UN, Editor. 2022, UN: Geneva.
2　UN, S., "Summary of Secretary-General's Report 'Our Common Agenda,'" UN, Editor. 2021, UN: Geneva.

## Chapter 29

1　António Guterres, A., "States Must Step Up Commitments to Combat Hatred, Promote Diversity, Says Secretary-General, Marking Day for Countering Hate Speech," U. Nations, Editor. 2024, UN: Geneva.
2　Ibid.
3　UN, S., "United Nations Global Principles for Information Integrity Recommendations for Multi-stakeholder Action." United Nations, 2024.
4　Ibid.
5　Ibid.
6　UN, S., "Summary of Secretary-General's Report 'Our Common Agenda,'" UN, Editor. 2021, UN: Geneva.

## Chapter 30

1　Fleming, M. "Tackling disinformation - how can we combat the lies that go viral?" (Transcript). in WEF: Sustainable Development Impact Meetings 2022. 2022. Geneva: WEF.
2　Ibid.
3　WEF, S., "World Economic Forum's '8 Predictions for the World in 2030'" - Now Deleted Video. WEF, 2016.
4　Stewart, R., Charles, M.B., Page, J. , "A future with no individual ownership is not a happy one: Property theory shows why." 2023. 152.

## Chapter 31

1　Schwab, K. and N. Davis, *Shaping the Future of the Fourth Industrial Revolution: A Guide to Building a Better World*. First American edition. ed. 2018, New York: Currency. xi, 274 pages.
2　Ibid.
3　Falk, D., "Godlike 'Homo Deus' Could Replace Humans as Tech Evolves." NBC News, 2017.
4　Harrington, M., "Can Sunak end the new class war? A deep divide exists between Virtuals and Physicals." UnHerd, 2022.
5　Lasch, C., *The Revolt of the Elites: And the Betrayal of Democracy*. 1st ed. 1995, New York: W.W. Norton. x, 276 p.

## Chapter 32

1　Schwab, K., Vanham, P., "What is stakeholder capitalism?" Davos Agenda 2021. 22 Jan 2021. By: Klaus Schwab Founder and Executive Chairman, World Economic Forum and Peter Vanham Head of Communications, Chairman's Office, World Economic Forum. 2021.

2    Schwab, K., Kroos, H., "Modern Company Management in Mechanical Engineering." Verein Deutscher Maschinenbau-Anstalten e.V. (VDMA), 1971.

3    Schwab, K.V., P., "What is stakeholder capitalism?" Davos Agenda 2021. WEF Website, 2021.

4    Hardin, G., "The tragedy of the commons. The population problem has no technical solution; it requires a fundamental extension in morality." *Science*, 1968. 162(3859): p. 1243–8.

5    Schwab, K.V., P., "What is stakeholder capitalism?" Davos Agenda 2021. WEF Website, 2021.

## Chapter 33

1    Malone, R.W., "Limited Hangout: Robert Kadlec Forced to Cover for Fauci?" Who is Robert Malone, Substack, 2023.

2    Janis, I.L., Groupthink: *Psychological Studies of Policy Decisions and Fiascoes.* 2nd ed. 1983, Boston: Houghton Mifflin. xii, 351 p.

## Chapter 35

1    Little, M.A., Cleveland, M.J., Norman, C., Paxton, K., Webster, B., Dorfman, G., Molina, R., Walters, R.D., Dokupil, S., Hilton, A.S. Stone, J., "Complaint for Declaratory and Injunctive Relief L. Attorneys," Editor. 2023, Texas State Gov: Texas State Gov. p. 69.

## Chapter 36

1    Jefferson, T., Letter to John Garland 1792.

2    McCarthy, C., et. al., "'Blue screen of death' hits NYC gov computers; jail cameras, arrest software down in 'unprecedented' global tech outage." *New York Post*, 2024.

## Chapter 37

1    Voltaire, *Collection des Lettres sur les Miracles.* 1767.